Latin America

America

History and Culture

An Encyclopedia
for Students

Barbara A. Tenenbaum, *Editor in Chief*

Volume 2

CHARLES SCRIBNER'S SONS
Macmillan Library Reference USA
New York

Library of Congress Cataloging-in-Publication Data

Tenenbaum, Barbara A.
    Latin America, history and culture : an encyclopedia for students /
    Barbara A. Tenenbaum, editor in chief.
       p.   cm.
    Includes bibliographical references (v. 4, p.   ) and indexes.
    Contents: v. 1. Acapulco — Climate and vegetation. Index — v. 2. Clothing —
Immigration and emigration. Index—v. 3. Imperialism—Platt Amendment. Index —
v. 4. Political parties — Zimmerman telegram. Bibliography. Index.
    ISBN 0-684-80576-6 (set : alk. paper). — ISBN 0-684-80572-3 (v. 1 : alk. paper). — ISBN
0-684-80573-1 (v. 2 : alk. paper) — ISBN 0-684-80574-X (v. 3 : alk. paper) —
ISBN 0-684-80575-8 (v. 4 : alk. paper)
    1. Latin America Encyclopedias.   I. Title.
F1406.T46   1999
980´.003 — dc21
                                            99-23057
                                              CIP

A Time Line of Latin America

ca. 9000 B.C.	*Humans establish settlements in Latin America.*
ca. 4000 B.C.	*Agricultural settlements develop in Amazon region.*
ca. 3500 B.C.	*Llamas are domesticated in Peru.*
1400–400 B.C.	*Chavin culture develops in South America.*
ca. 1000 B.C.	*Olmec culture flourishes in Mexico.*
ca. A.D. 100–900	*Moche, Tiwanaku, and Huari cultures develop in South America.*
	Teotihuacán and Maya cities develop in Mexico.
ca. 950	*Toltec civilization emerges in Mexico.*
ca. 1100–1474	*Chimu kingdom develops in northern Peru.*
ca. 1200	*Inca civilization emerges in Peru.*
ca. 1300	*Aztec civilization develops near Mexico City.*
1434–1519	*Aztec-dominated Triple Alliance gains control over Valley of Mexico and builds an empire.*
1460–1470	*Inca conquer the Chimu.*
1469	*Isabella of Castile marries Ferdinand of Aragon, uniting the kingdoms of Spain.*
1492	*Christopher Columbus reaches Caribbean islands.*
1493	*Columbus settles Hispaniola.*
1494	*Spain and Portugal sign Treaty of Tordesillas.*
1498	*Vasco da Gama sails around Africa to India.*
1500	*Pedro Álvares Cabral lands on the Brazilian coast.*
ca. 1500–1860s	*Approximately 12 million Africans are brought to Latin America as slaves.*
1507	*First world map showing "America" is published.*
1511	*First Spanish settlement is established in Cuba.*
	First audiencia in Spanish America is established on Hispaniola.
1512	*First Roman Catholic bishop arrives in America.*
1513	*Juan Ponce de León claims Florida for Spain.*
	Vasco Núñez de Balboa sees the Pacific Ocean from Panama.

Pachacuti (*ca. 1391–1473*)

Prince Henry the Navigator (*1394–1460*)

Christopher Columbus (*ca. 1451–1506*)

Amerigo Vespucci (*1454–1512*)

Moctezuma II (*ca. 1466–ca.1520*)

Bartolomé de Las Casas (*1474–1566*)

Diego de Almagro (*ca. 1475–1538*)

Vasco Núñez de Balboa (*ca. 1475–1519*)

Ferdinand Magellan (*ca. 1480–1521*)

Hernán Cortés (*ca. 1484–1547*)

Pedro de Alvarado y Mesía (*ca. 1485–ca.1541*)

Atahualpa (*ca. 1498–1533*)

Pedro de Valdivia (*1500–1553*)

Francisco de Orellana (*1511–1546*)

1519	*Hernán Cortés founds first Spanish city in Mexico.*
	Charles I is crowned in Spain.
1519–1522	*Ferdinand Magellan circumnavigates the globe.*
1521	*Cortés conquers Aztec empire.*
1522–1524	*Franciscan missionaries arrive in Mexico.*
1524	*Council of the Indies is formed to oversee Spanish colonies in the Americas.*
1527	*Civil war erupts in Inca empire between Huascar and Atahualpa.*
1531	*According to legend, the Virgin of Guadalupe appears in Mexico.*
1535	*Viceroyalty of New Spain is created.*
1536	*Francisco Pizarro and Diego de Almagro conquer Inca empire.*
1541	*Spanish settlement of Chile begins.*
	Pizarro is assassinated.
	Francisco de Orellana leads the first expedition down the Amazon.
1542	*Bartolomé de Las Casas speaks out against mistreatment of the Indians.*
	Spain revokes its grants to conquistadors' heirs.
1549	*Tomé de Sousa builds Brazilian capital at Salvador.*
ca. 1555	Popul Vuh *manuscript is created by the Maya.*
1556	*Philip II becomes king of Spain.*
1565	*City of St. Augustine is founded in Florida.*
	Jesuit missionaries arrive in Spanish America.
1570–1571	*Holy Office of the Inquisition is established in Lima and Mexico City.*
1571	*Manila galleon trade route is established between Mexico and the Philippines.*
1572	*Viceroy Francisco de Toledo of Peru captures Tupac Amaru I and destroys last Inca settlement at Vilcabamba.*
1580–1640	*Portuguese and Spanish monarchies are united.*
1598	*Juan de Oñate establishes a settlement at San Juan de los Caballeros in New Mexico.*
ca. 1609	*Santa Fe is founded in New Mexico.*
1621	*Dutch West India Company is founded to establish plantations in South America.*
1630–1654	*Dutch govern northeast region of Brazil.*
1637–1639	*Brazil's boundary expands to include the entire Amazon basin.*
1654	*Dutch are ousted from Brazil.*

Philip II of Spain *(1527–1598)*

John Hawkins *(1532–1595)*
Alonso de Ercilla y Zúñiga *(1533–1594)*

Garcilaso de la Vega El Inca *(1539–1616)*

Francis Drake *(1545–1596)*

Santa Rosa de Lima *(1586–1617)*

John Maurits *(1604–1679)*

Sor Juana Inés de la Cruz
(ca. 1651–1695)

1680–1692	Pueblo Rebellion temporarily ends Spanish control of New Mexico.
1700–1713	War of Spanish Succession brings Bourbon monarch to the Spanish throne.
1719	Viceroyalty of New Granada is established.
1730–1735	Comunero Revolt erupts in Paraguay over Jesuit land.
1739	Viceroyalty of New Granada is reestablished.
1756–1763	Seven Years' War in Europe gives Britain ownership of French colonies in the Americas.
1767	Jesuits are expelled from Spanish America.
1769	Spaniards establish settlements in California.
1776	Viceroyalty of Río de la Plata is established.
1777	Portugal and Spain sign the Treaty of San Ildefonso.
1780–1783	Tupac Amaru II leads Great Andean Rebellion.
1781	Comunero Revolt erupts in Colombia.
1791–1804	Haitian Revolution ends French colonial rule and abolishes slavery there.
1803	United States purchases the Louisiana Territory from France.
1807–1808	Napoleon invades Iberian Peninsula; Portuguese court flees to Brazil.
1810	Simón Bolívar joins revolutionary movement in Venezuela.
1811	Paraguay declares its independence from Spain.
1816	Argentina declares its independence from Spain.
1818	Chile wins its independence from Spain.
1819	Adams-Onís Treaty gives Spanish Florida to the United States. Gran Colombia is formed.
1821	Mexico becomes independent.
1822	Brazil declares its independence from Portugal.
1823	Monroe Doctrine prohibits colonization of the Americas.
1823–1824	United Provinces of Central America is formed.
1824	Battle of Ayacucho liberates South America from Spanish colonial rule.
1825	Bolivia becomes an independent nation.
1828	Uruguay wins its independence.
1835–1836	Battle of the Alamo spurs the movement for Texas independence; battle of San Jacinto results in Texas independence.

Junípero Serra *(1713–1784)*
Charles III of Spain *(1716–1788)*

Aleijadinho *(ca. 1738–1814)*
Tupac Amaru *(1738–1781)*
Toussaint L'Ouverture *(1743–1803)*
Francisco de Miranda *(1750–1816)*
Tupac Catari *(1750–1781)*
Miguel Hidalgo y Costilla *(1753–1811)*
Jean Jacques Dessalines *(1758–1806)*
José Bonifácio de Andrada *(1763–1838)*
Henri Christophe *(1767–1820)*
Josefa Ortiz de Domínguez *(1768–1829)*
Bernardo O'Higgins *(1778–1842)*
Simón Bolívar *(1783–1830)*

Antonio López de Santa Anna *(1794–1876)*
Antonio José de Sucre Alcalá *(1795–1830)*
Pedro I of Brazil *(1798–1834)*
Benito Juárez *(1806–1872)*

Juan Bautista Alberdi *(1810–1884)*

Juan Pablo Duarte *(1813–1876)*

Gabriel García Moreno *(1821–1875)*

William Walker *(1824–1860)*

Pedro II of Brazil *(1825–1891)*

Antonio Leocadio Guzmán Blanco *(1829–1899)*
Porfirio Díaz *(1830–1915)*

1836–1839	*War erupts between the Peru-Bolivia Confederation and Chile.*
1838	*Honduras and Costa Rica withdraw from the United Provinces of Central America.*
1846–1848	*Mexican-American War is fought over the territory of present-day Texas.*
1847–1848	*Caste War of Yucatán threatens the Creole government there.*
1848	*Treaty of Guadalupe Hidalgo ends the Mexican-American War and establishes the boundary between the two nations.*
1853	*Gadsden Purchase transfers 30 million acres of Mexican land to the United States.*
1856	*El Salvador becomes an independent republic.*
1856–1857	*Central American nations unite to defeat William Walker.*
1863	*French troops invade Mexico; Maximilian becomes emperor of Mexico.*
1864–1870	*War of the Triple Alliance is fought between Paraguay and the allied forces of Argentina, Brazil, and Uruguay.*
1865	*Dominican Republic becomes independent.*
1866–1867	*Napoleon withdraws troops from Mexico; Maximilian is executed.*
1868–1878	*Ten Years' War for Cuban independence is fought.*
1870–1930	*Waves of European immigration transform Brazil, Uruguay, and Argentina.*
1879–1884	*War of the Pacific pits Chile against Bolivia and Peru.*
1886	*Slavery is abolished in Cuba.*
1888	*Slavery is abolished in Brazil.*
1889	*First Pan-American Conference is held in Washington, D.C. Brazilian empire falls.*
1895	*Cuba begins a second struggle for independence from Spain.*
1898	*USS Maine blows up in Havana harbor; Spanish-American War begins. Cuba and Puerto Rico win their independence from Spain.*
1899–1902	*U.S. Army occupies Cuba.* *War of the Thousand Days brings violence to Colombia.*
1903	*Panama becomes independent of Colombia.* *United States passes the Platt Amendment protecting its interests in Cuba and limiting the island's sovereignty.*
1904	*Construction begins on the Panama Canal.*
1910–1920	*Mexican Revolution is fought to oust President Porfirio Díaz and to demand land reform.*

Joaquím Maria Machado de Assis *(1839–1908)*

Antonio Maceo *(1845–1896)*

Princess Isabel of Brazil *(1846–1921)*

Hipólito Yrigoyen *(1852–1933)*

José Julián Martí y Pérez *(1853–1895)*

José Batlle y Ordóñez *(1856–1929)*

Juan Vicente Gómez *(1857–1935)*

Francisco Indalecio Madero *(1873–1913)*

Francisco "Pancho" Villa *(1878–1923)*

Emiliano Zapata *(ca. 1879–1919)*

Mario Vargas Llosa *(1883–1954)*

Diego Rivera *(1886–1957)*

Gabriela Mistral *(1889–1957)*

Rafael Leónidas Trujillo Molina *(1891–1961)*

Juan Domingo Perón *(1895–1974)*

Miguel Ángel Asturias *(1899–1974)*

Fulgencio Batista y Zaldívar *(1901–1973)*

Pablo Neruda *(1904–1973)*

Salvador Allende Gossens *(1908–1973)*

1913	*United States ambassador plots with counterrevolutionary forces in Mexico; President Madero is assassinated.*	Jorge Amado *(born 1912)*
1914	*Panama Canal opens.*	Alfredo Stroessner *(born 1912)*
1915	*United States invades Mexican port of Veracruz.*	Augusto Pinochet Ugarte *(born 1915)*
1916–1924	*United States occupies the Dominican Republic.*	
1917	*New Mexican constitution is adopted.*	Oscar Arnulfo Romero *(1917–1980)*
1922	*Modern Art Week is celebrated in São Paulo, Brazil.*	María Eva Duarte de Perón *(1919–1952)*
1926–1929	*Cristero Rebellion erupts in Mexico as Catholics rebel against anticlerical measures.*	Fidel Castro Ruz *(born 1926)* Gabriel García Márquez *(born 1927)*
1929	*World is hit by a severe economic depression.*	Ernesto "Che" Guevara *(1928–1967)* Carlos Fuentes *(born 1928)*
1930	*Getúlio Vargas takes power in Brazil.*	Carlos Saúl Menem *(born 1930)*
1932–1935	*Chaco War breaks out between Bolivia and Paraguay.*	Derek Walcott *(born 1930)*
1939–1945	*Latin Americans support Allied forces during World War II.*	Mario Vargas Llosa *(born 1936)* Alberto Keinya Fujimori *(born 1938)*
1940s–1960s	*La Violencia claims 100,000 to 250,000 lives in Colombia.*	Oscar Arias Sánchez *(1940)* Pelé *(born 1940)*
1945	*Gabriela Mistral is the first Latin American woman to win the Nobel Prize for literature.*	Isabel Allende *(born 1942)* Daniel Ortega Saavedra *(born 1945)*
1947	*Nations of Western Hemisphere accept responsibility for their mutual defense in Rio Treaty.*	
1948	*Organization of American States (OAS) is formed.*	Carlos Salinas de Gortari *(born 1948)*
1952–1986	*Bolivian Revolution brings political and economic change to the country.*	
1954	*Guatemalan coup, backed by the United States, forces President Arbenz to resign.*	Jean-Bertrand Aristide *(born 1953)*
1959	*Cuban Revolution, led by Fidel Castro, ousts Fulgencio Batista.*	Rigoberta Menchú Tum *(born 1959)*
ca. 1960	*Civil war begins in Guatemala.*	
1960	*Brasília replaces Rio de Janeiro as the capital of Brazil.*	
1961	*Bay of Pigs Invasion by Cuban exiles is defeated.* *United States launches the Alliance for Progress.*	
1962	*Cuban missile crisis threatens the balance of world power.* *Jamaica becomes independent.* *OAS imposes sanctions against Cuba.*	
1963	*Pan-American highway is completed, linking the Americas from Alaska to Chile.*	
1964–1985	*Brazil is under military rule.*	
1968	*Student protest in Mexico City ends in bloodshed.*	
1969	*Football War between El Salvador and Honduras erupts in a soccer stadium.*	

1973	Military coup ousts Chilean president Salvador Allende.
1974–1983	Argentina's Dirty War leaves thousands of political opponents dead or "disappeared."
1977	Panama Canal Treaty is signed, keeping the canal open to all nations, even during wartime.
1979	Sandinistas overthrow dictator Anastasio Somoza in Nicaragua.
1980	Mariel boatlift allows Cubans to leave for the United States.
1981–1995	Ecuador and Peru go to war over border dispute.
1982	Argentine military seizes British-owned Falkland Islands; Britain defeats Argentina in Falklands/Malvinas War.
1983	United States troops invade Grenada.
1988	Contras and Sandinistas sign cease-fire in Nicaragua.
1989	United States troops invade Panama and seize Manuel Noriega. Chile forces Augusto Pinochet to leave presidency. Paraguay ousts dictator Alfredo Stroessner.
1990	Alberto Fujimori is elected president of Peru. Violeta Barrios de Chamorro is elected president of Nicaragua.
1992	El Salvador's 12-year civil war ends.
1993	Changes to Argentina's constitution enable President Carlos Saúl Menem to run for re-election. Colombian army kills Pablo Escobar, boss of the Medellín drug cartel.
1994	North American Free Trade Agreement (NAFTA) goes into effect, sparking revolutionary activity in Chiapas, Mexico. United States troops return Jean-Bertrand Aristide to power in Haiti. Fernando Henrique Cardoso wins presidential election in Brazil.
1995	United States provides economic aid to Mexico.
1996	Guatemala's 35-year armed conflict ends. Tupac Amaru guerrillas seize hostages in Peru.
1997	Mexico's Institutional Revolutionary Party (PRI) loses its majority in congress for first time in 68 years. Peruvian troops kill Tupac Amaru rebels and free hostages.
1998	Hurricane Mitch devastates Central America. Ecuador and Peru end their border dispute.
1999	Panama takes possession of the Panama Canal.

Clothing

* **metropolitan** referring to a large city and its surrounding suburbs

See color plate 11, vol. 2.

The clothing of Latin America reflects a mixed heritage and varies greatly according to region and climate. People in cities and large towns dress much like people in the United States dress on warm days. In metropolitan* centers such as Buenos Aires, men and women wear the latest designer fashions. In some countries, such as Bolivia, wealthy and middle-class people dress in a Western style, while some workers and most farmers wear traditional clothes. In many places, traditional costumes are worn only for special celebrations and festivals. In a few regions, such as the highlands of Ecuador, the Indians have steadfastly retained their native dress.

Mexico and Central America. Mexican dress reflects a blending of the native Indian and Spanish heritage. Indian men usually wear Western clothes (such as jeans, shirts, and shorts) outside their villages but still dress in traditional clothing at home. *Calzoncillo,* or trousers, vary in style from region to region. A *cotón,* or shirt, is usually cut from a single piece of cloth and then folded at the shoulder line, with a neck opening cut into the center. It is worn tucked in, with a bright woven sash at the waist, or loose outside the trousers like a jacket. Over this is worn a vest or woolen serape, a cloak that opens down the front. As a sign of respect, men cover their heads outside the home with sombreros, wide-brimmed hats made of felt or straw. Men wear leather sandals called huaraches and carry handwoven bags called *morrales,* which are worn on the shoulder and are decorated with designs unique to each village.

Indian women wear a *huipil* (tunic dress) and a *quechquemitl* (triangular poncho), which covers the upper body. They have also adopted the blouse and skirt from the Spanish. Blouses with square necklines are embroidered with birds, animals, flowers, and geometric patterns. These designs have strong links to ancient AZTEC and MAYA religions. Skirts are full and gathered at the waistline. Indian women's hairstyles have remained unchanged for centuries—long and braided with ribbons and other trimmings. Women also wear a shawl, or rebozo, as a head cover in church and protection against the weather. Slung from the shoulder, a rebozo also serves as a baby carrier or as a shopping bag.

In Guatemala, men traditionally wore plain white garments—a shirt, trousers, and a shawl called a *tzute.* Women's clothing is entirely handwoven in narrow strips that are handsewn together and embroidered. Indians throughout Central and South America take great pride in the beautiful handwoven materials they produce on hand looms. Many towns are represented by distinctive weaving patterns. Traditionally, the weaving pattern of the woman's *huipil* identifies her origin or village. Nowadays, both men and women favor bright colors, such as red, purple, blue, pink, green, and orange.

In Belize, Honduras, El Salvador, Nicaragua, and Panama, traditional costumes are usually of a colonial style and are worn only on Sundays and festival days. A similar pattern has developed in the nations of the Caribbean, including Cuba, Puerto Rico, the Dominican Republic, and Haiti.

The South American Cowboy

Throughout South America, most cowboys at festival time wear a costume similar to the traditional Argentinian gaucho: baggy trousers tucked into boots; large silver spurs; a sash wrapped around the waist and topped with a decorated leather belt; a colored cloth, or *chirpa,* tucked under the belt; a neckerchief; and a black or white wide-brimmed hat.

The Chilean *huaso,* however, wears a costume with a distinctly Spanish influence: a flat-topped, narrow-brimmed hat with a chin strap and long, black, tassled leggings that reach well over the knees.

Countries of the Andes.   In the mountainous regions of Colombia, the classic Indian attire is blue cotton shirt, white woolen trousers, and white poncho worn under a darker poncho, or ruana. Women wear blouses, blue cloaks, and black pleated wraparound skirts woven in stripes. Both men and women wear warm felt hats.

In Peru, the Spanish prohibited the wearing of native dress in 1572. Men gave up the *uncu* (a sleeveless, knee-length tunic) for trousers and a short jacket. Women replaced the *anacu* (wraparound robe) with a blouse and skirt. However, like other Andean people, many Peruvian Indians still wear the pre-Columbian* accessories, such as a wrapping blanket, sash, and shoulder bag. For warmth, both men and women wear close-fitting, knitted caps called *chullas,* with a flat hat or felt hat on top. Peruvian Indian women favor dark-colored skirts, with black being the most popular color, although for weddings, brides wear red skirts.

Bolivian Indians have a similar style of dress. They decorate their *chullas* with images of suns and llamas, and they also wear bowler or derby hats, which they adopted from the British who worked on the railroads in the Andes during the 1800s. These hats of natural-colored beige, brown, gray, and black wool are worn by men and women. They form a sharp contrast to the colorful reds, pinks, blues, oranges, and greens of the other garments worn by Bolivian women.

In Chile, Indian women wear a *manto* draped over the head and shoulders and worn over European dress or Indian skirts. Silver jewelry is very popular, especially a *tupo* (a necklace decorated with silver coins) and a silver headdress for festival days. Fiesta clothes are reminiscent of Spanish colonial dress, with frills and lace-edged aprons.

Countries of the North and East.   Brazil is home to many different racial and ethnic groups as well as many different climates and environments. Various Indian tribes, living mostly in the tropical parts of Brazil, wear relatively little clothing because of the hot climate. Women wear cotton wraps or skirts made of palm-leaf fiber, and men wear loincloths*. The body is sometimes painted for ceremonial purposes. The juice of the urucu seed is used to make a red dye and the genipa plant to make black. Men also wear fantastic ceremonial headdresses made of macaw, egret, and duck feathers. In the Brazilian region of Bahia, a blending of European and West African culture is evident in the floral-patterned, long cotton skirts and turbans*, shawls, and beaded necklaces worn by women.

Paraguayan women wear skirts with gathers coming from a tight-fitting bodice* that reaches to the hips, a style worn by Spanish flamenco dancers. The favorite colors are bright red, blue, and pink. Uruguay, where large numbers of Italians and Spaniards settled in the 1800s, developed new garments based on European styles. A woman's working outfit is usually white with a colored sash at the waist. The dress of the people of Suriname and French Guiana reflects a rich mix of cultures, particularly after many people migrated there from Dutch- and French-held territories in Southeast Asia. (*See also* **Fiestas; Textiles and Textile Industry.**)

° **pre-Columbian** before the arrival of Christopher Columbus and other Europeans in the Americas in the 1490s

See color plate 10, vol. 2.

° **loincloth** garment that covers a person's hips and thighs

° **turban** cap attached to a long scarf which is wound around the head

° **bodice** upper part of a dress

Cochineal Industry

° **indigenous** referring to the original inhabitants of a region

*C*ochineal is a bright red dye made from the bodies of small insects that are found on the nopal cactus, a plant that grows in Mexico and Central America. In precolonial times, indigenous* people harvested the cochineal insect from wild plants and used it to dye cloth. They developed an extensive trade in cochineal, particularly in Mexico. During colonial times, the Spaniards raised the insects and produced cochineal on commercial estates, or *nopalerías,* where the work was done by Indian laborers. The process of extracting cochineal was extremely tedious and required great skill. It took approximately 25,000 live insects, or 70,000 dried ones, to make one pound of dye. By 1600, the Spanish were shipping annually between 250,000 and 300,000 pounds of Mexican cochineal from Veracruz to Spain, where it was usually sold to textile makers from the Netherlands.

The cochineal industry in Central America had a brief boom in the early 1600s in the western highlands of Guatemala and northern Nicaragua. But production ceased abruptly, probably due to plagues of locusts that attacked the crop. After 1621, the production of cochineal was centered almost completely in Mexico, mainly in the southeastern state of Oaxaca. The rich red dye was in such great demand by Flemish, Dutch, and English weavers that by the mid-1700s, cochineal had become Mexico's second most valuable export, after silver. It remained a vital export for Mexico into the 1800s, when it was replaced by cheaper synthetic* red dyes. (*See also* **Clothing; Textiles and Textile Industry.**)

° **synthetic** produced artificially

Codices

See *Manuscripts and Writing, Pre-Columbian.*

Coffee Industry

° **perennial** plant that lives from season to season

° **temperate** having a moderate climate

*T*he coffee industry consists of the growing, selling, and exportation of coffee, and it is of major economic importance in many Latin American countries. The coffee industry has also influenced other aspects of Latin American life, including patterns of land use and population distribution.

Coffee is made from the berries of the coffee plant. Each berry contains two beans, which are dried, roasted, ground, and then brewed with hot water to make the beverage coffee. The coffee plant is a perennial* shrub that grows best in a frost-free, temperate* climate with regular rainfall and fairly rich soil. The interior uplands of southeastern Brazil and the highlands of Colombia, Central America, southern Mexico, and the larger Caribbean islands are especially good coffee-producing regions.

Native to northeastern Africa, coffee was introduced into the Caribbean and northeastern South America in the 1700s. It did not become a major commercial crop until the 1800s, however. At that time, the demand for coffee increased in Europe and North America, and transportation connecting remote coffee-producing areas to seaports improved.

Juan Valdéz, Coffee Grower

Since 1959, Colombia's National Coffee Growers Federation has maintained a successful advertising campaign in the United States using a fictitious Colombian coffee grower called Juan Valdéz. Valdéz is depicted as a typical Colombian mountain grower. With his donkey in tow, he carefully scrutinizes each coffee bean before loading it into his bag.

In reality, the Colombian coffee harvest is fast-paced, employing tens of thousands of migrant laborers. However, small and medium-sized independent producers still dominate the coffee industry of Colombia—as opposed to the larger business operations of Brazil.

Brazil. In 1830, coffee replaced sugar as Brazil's most important export, and by the 1870s, Brazil had become the world's largest coffee producer. Coffee production spread south and west from Rio de Janeiro, with African slaves providing the labor force on large plantations. This pattern extended into western São Paulo. In the late 1800s, the industry grew, and after slavery was outlawed in 1888, European immigrants began to replace slaves as the laborers on the plantations in São Paulo. From 1900 to 1920, Brazil produced three-quarters of the world's coffee, with the state of São Paulo alone accounting for one-half of the world's supply. The coffee trade brought mass immigration from Europe. It also brought in high revenues and boosted economic activity in Brazil. São Paulo emerged as South America's largest industrial center.

Despite this success, coffee growing was, and remains, a risky business. Yields can vary markedly from year to year. While world demand changes slowly, there may be abrupt fluctuations in supply. This produces cycles of boom and bust in nations that are dependent on coffee for revenue. An unusually large crop in 1906 prompted the Brazilian government to institute a program of price supports and market controls. These have become a feature of Brazil's coffee policy ever since. During the 1930s, when world prices were depressed, Brazil purchased and destroyed large quantities of coffee. Since World War II, a series of

Latin America produces and exports more than half of the world's coffee. Brazil and Colombia alone account for more than half of Latin America's total output. The two most important types of coffee beans are *arabica* and *robusta*. Both types of beans are grown in Brazil, Ecuador, and Guatemala, whereas the other Latin American countries, including Colombia, produce only *arabica*. Of the two types, *robusta*, produced mainly in Africa and some Asian countries, is considered less flavorful and aromatic and is used mostly in instant coffee.

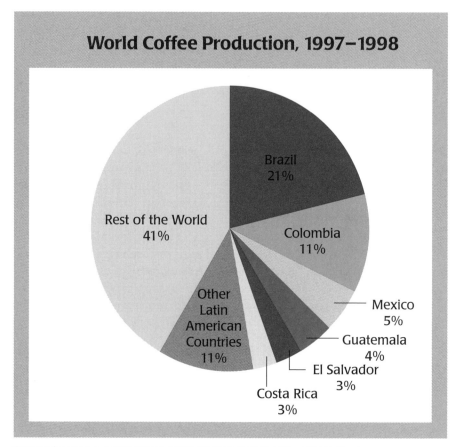

World Coffee Production, 1997–1998

Brazil 21%
Colombia 11%
Mexico 5%
Guatemala 4%
El Salvador 3%
Costa Rica 3%
Other Latin American Countries 11%
Rest of the World 41%

Source: Information Access Company, 1998; American Institute of Food Distribution Inc. The Food Institute Report, 1998.

international coffee agreements intended to regulate production levels and even out price swings has helped moderate these boom and bust cycles.

Colombia.   Beginning around 1835, Colombia exported only small quantities of coffee, but by the early 1900s, the country was second only to Brazil in coffee exports. The coffee industry in Colombia was strengthened by the formation of the National Federation of Coffee Growers in 1927. The federation* marketed the coffee of many small and medium-sized farms through what became a powerful political and financial organization that controlled the country's principal export. As Colombian growers concentrated on producing higher-quality varieties of coffee and developed an astute marketing strategy, Colombia's production steadily increased after World War II. By the 1980s, the value of its coffee exports rivaled the value of Brazil's and accounted for about 60 percent of the nation's exports.

Central America.   Coffee also became a large industry in Central America in the 1800s. Many formerly self-sufficient peasants were forced or drawn into the coffee industry's labor force as planters consolidated their power and took over village lands, either through privatization* laws or simply by seizing them. Guatemala and El Salvador have many large plantations, while Costa Rica, like Colombia, has a greater proportion of small and medium-sized farms.

Although coffee became a dominant export in several countries, no country has come close to Brazil in total production. The ups and downs of Brazil's annual crop have continued to influence world prices for coffee. However, since World War II, coffee production has expanded elsewhere in the world, particularly in central Africa. By the 1980s, Latin America accounted for 55 to 60 percent of world exports, down from nearly 90 percent in the early 1900s. (*See also* **Agriculture; Food and Drink; Slavery.**)

° **federation** political union of separate states with a central government

° **privatization** changing of a business or industry from public to private ownership

Coins and Coinage

° **mark** old European weight for measuring gold and silver, equal to about 8 ounces, or 248 grams

° **real** old coin of Spain and of Portugal; also, the modern currency of Brazil

*T*he first coins in colonial Spanish America appeared in Santo Domingo in the Caribbean in 1497. Called the *peso de oro,* each coin weighed about 4.6 grams and was worth one-fiftieth of a mark* of gold. These coins served as the standard monetary unit in the Indies until about 1535. In that year, Charles II of Spain ordered the founding of mints in Mexico City, Lima, and Santa Fe de Bogotá. In addition to gold pesos, the mints made the first silver peso, known as the *peso fuerte, duro,* or "piece of eight" (as it was known by the English). The silver peso became the standard monetary unit in the Indies for the next 300 years. The king also called for the minting of smaller silver coins. Of these new denominations, the two-real* coin, which was worth one-fourth of a silver peso or piece of eight, was the most commonly used.

Most pesos were circular. Inscriptions varied, with one side often depicting castles and lions, separated into four parts by a cross, and

The Guatemalan Quetzal

The currency of Guatamela is named for a beautiful, large, colorful bird—the quetzal—that perches on high branches in the dense forest of the country. The male of the species has emerald green feathers and a crimson red breast, with a long, graceful tail that can reach three feet in length. Ancient Mesoamerican chiefs used the quetzal's feathers as a symbol of authority. The quetzal cannot live in captivity and for this reason, it is a symbol of liberty and the national bird of Guatemala.

See color plate 8, vol. 1.

carrying an inscription of the value of the coin. On the reverse side were two columns representing the pillars of Hercules, the Greek mythological hero known for his great strength. Inscribed at the edge of the coin were the name of the monarch (in Latin) and a name or letter designating the site of the mint: *M* for Mexico City, *L* for Lima, and so on.

By 1600, improved technology and tighter controls over the mints resulted in coins of a more standard shape and weight. Silver quickly replaced gold as the only metal being minted at the three major mints. For most of the 1600s, the Spanish American piece of eight was considered the most reliable monetary unit in the world. (Its value remained unchanged from 1535 to 1728.) Merchants as far away as Asia often specified payment in pesos.

To ensure that the wide variety of coins circulating in Spain and the Indies could be easily converted from one to another, the Spanish crown also set an imaginary monetary unit of account, the maravedí. A real was valued at 34 maravedís, a peso fuerte at 272 maravedís, and the peso de oro at 450 maravedís. During the 1700s, the crown reduced the silver content of coins in America by about 5 percent, although this was slight compared to the devaluation of currency in Spain at the time. Moreover, many new mints were established throughout Central and South America. The Spanish king controlled and managed all mint activity, and mint officials were required to send samples of their coins to Spain every six months for inspection and weighing. In the hope of stopping the practice of shaving or clipping coins, new coins were made with ridged edges. At the same time, mints increased their production of gold coins and began stamping gold *escudos* of eight, four, two, or one *escudo*.

During the general devastation brought on by the wars of independence in Latin America in the early 1800s, mint activity sharply declined. The new independent nations that emerged continued to use the bimetallic (gold and silver) system of Spain. Eventually, all nations adopted the decimal system and the unit of the peso, although in several places it had a special name. In the late 1800s, the bimetallic system was replaced by the gold standard and in the 1900s, by paper money. Coinage was limited to smaller fractionary pieces or to "merchandise coins," trade tokens of little metal value.

Today the peso is still the unit of currency in several Latin American countries, where its value varies from country to country. Venezuela's unit of currency is the bolívar, named for independence leader Simón BOLÍVAR, while Ecuador's is the sucre, named for its liberator Antonio José de SUCRE. Nicaragua uses the córdoba, named for Spanish explorer Francisco Hernández de Córdoba, and Panama has the balboa, named for Spanish explorer Vasco Núñez de BALBOA. The colón of Costa Rica and El Salvador is named for explorer Cristóbal Colón (Christopher Columbus). Brazil uses the real, named for an old Portuguese currency, while Haiti uses the gourde, an old American-French currency. The Suriname guilder reflects that region's Dutch influence. Several nations, including Belize, Jamaica, and Trinidad and Tobago, use the dollar. Other currencies in Latin America reflect the region's Indian heritage. Paraguay's guaraní is named for the Indian tribe who originally inhabited the region. Honduras uses the lempira, named for an Indian chief of the 1500s, and Peru uses the inti, taken from the Quechuan word for "sun." (*See also* **Gold and Silver; Mining; Trade and Commerce.**)

Colombia

Colombia is a large country in the far northwestern corner of South America. It was one of the first parts of the South American mainland to be visited by Spanish explorers, and it has developed into one of the most important countries on the continent.

The Geography of Colombia

Colombia is the fourth-largest country in South America, after Brazil, Argentina, and Peru. Its geography is dominated by the ANDES mountains, which divide the country into several regions. Colombia's largest and most populous cities are BOGOTÁ, CALI, and Medellín, all located in the central Andes. Its most important ports are CARTAGENA and Baranquilla, located on the lowlands of the Caribbean coast. East of the Andes lie the LLANOS, or plains, and to the southeast are vast tropical RAIN FORESTS.

Colombia's climate is mostly tropical, with much rainfall and an average temperature of 74 degrees Fahrenheit. However, much of this rain falls in the remote rain forests and the high Andes, leaving only about 5 percent of Colombia's total land arable*. Most of this land is devoted to growing COFFEE, Colombia's main cash crop* and one of its most important exports. The climate and terrain are also suited to marijuana plants and coca shrubs (used to make cocaine), and both are grown illegally on a large scale.

Colombia is rich in mineral resources, including copper and fuels such as petroleum, coal, and natural gas. It has large reserves of precious metals—gold, platinum, and silver—and it also produces most of the world's supply of emeralds. FORESTS cover about half of Colombia's total land area, making the LUMBER INDUSTRY and paper products important parts of its economy. About one-third of its people are employed in industries that depend on the land and its products, including agriculture, MINING, hunting, and fishing.

Precolonial History

Historians estimate the number of INDIANS in Colombia before the arrival of Europeans was anywhere between 850,000 and about 4 million. Recent studies suggest that the larger number is probably more accurate, with most indigenous* peoples living in the valleys of the central and western Andes.

Organization and Decline of the Indians. Colombia's indigenous cultures ranged from simple hunting and gathering societies to very complex civilizations. The two most advanced cultures were those of the Taironas, who lived in the mountains in the northeast,

° **arable** suitable for producing crops

° **cash crop** crop grown primarily for profit rather than for local consumption

See map in South America, Pre-Columbian History (vol. 4).

° **indigenous** referring to the original inhabitants of a region

and the Chibchas, who lived near present-day Bogotá. Most Indians, however, were organized into smaller tribal groups that the Spanish called *cacicazgos*. Although very different in culture and social structure, all Colombians suffered the same fate during and after the Spanish conquest. Within 50 years of the Spaniards' arrival, warfare, DISEASE, and persecution* had reduced the Indian population to a fraction of its original total.

* **persecution** harassment of a group of people, usually because of their beliefs, race, or ethnic origin

The Spanish Conquest of Colombia. In 1499, Spaniards Alonso de Ojeda and Juan de la Cosa became the first Europeans to land on the shores of Colombia. When they returned to Spain with Indian treasures, Cosa and Ojeda inspired other explorers to set out in search of gold and slaves. In 1508, Cosa and Ojeda returned to establish a settlement at Cartagena, but they were driven off by Indians and suffered heavy losses. Two years later, they founded Spain's first settlement in Colombia at San Sebastián de Urabá. During the next 15 years, this and other nearby settlements served as the starting points for conquest and colonization.

Serious exploration of the Colombian interior began after Francisco PIZARRO conquered the wealthy INCA civilization of Peru in 1533. Other explorers, inspired by the prospect of finding riches in the regions that lay between Peru and the Caribbean, entered Colombia from several directions. Sebastián de Belalcázar, the conqueror of Quito, came from the southwest in 1535 and founded Cali and Popayán in the next two years. Gonzalo Jiménez de Quesada moved southward from the Caribbean coast in 1536 and found the rich Chibcha civilization. In 1539, the two explorers, joined by German Nicholas Federmann, founded the town of Santa Fe de Bogotá. By the mid-1500s, Spanish explorers had penetrated much of Colombia and carved out the areas in which colonial settlements developed.

Colonial Colombia

During the early colonial period, Spanish settlements in Colombia were separated by long distances and rugged terrain, and they tended to be very independent of one another. The population was quite small: by 1560 there were about 7,000 Spanish colonists, about 6,000 blacks and mestizos*, and 1.26 million Indians. The large percentage of mestizos later became an important factor in Colombia's social development. Although the widespread mixing of Spaniards and Indians made Colombian society less segregated*, great inequality of wealth existed between the rich settlers and the majority of the people.

* **mestizo** person of mixed European and Indian ancestry

* **segregated** set apart or separated from others in the community

* **tribute** payment made to a dominant power

* ***encomienda*** right granted to a conqueror that enabled him to control the labor of and collect payment from an Indian community

The Colonial Economy. Spanish settlers relied on tribute* and the *encomienda** system to obtain goods and services necessary for their subsistence. They established cattle raising and a mining economy throughout Colombia, and they exploited the Indians. Gradually, the Spanish appropriated the lands and began to cultivate commercial crops. These landholdings slowly replaced the *encomienda*, which was undermined because of the falling Indian population. Gold mining

Women in Colombia

As elsewhere in Latin America, progress for women has been slow in Colombia. It was not until 1930 that women gained the same property rights as their husbands. They were granted voting rights as late as the mid-1950s. Although women accounted for more than 15 percent of the workforce in the mid-1960s, and more than 30 percent by 1985, their wages have remained low and their working conditions poor. However, the situation is changing for women in Colombia. One of the best-liked politicians in Colombia is a woman, Noemí Sanín. Although she lost the presidential elections in 1998, Sanín overcame traditional barriers against women in politics, receiving about 25 percent of the vote.

° **conquistador** Spanish explorer and conqueror

° *audiencia* highest regional court in a Spanish colony; also, the district under its jurisdiction

° **Creole** person of European ancestry born in the Americas

° **graft** illegal or unfair gain by using one's political position or connections

° **dynasty** succession of rulers from the same family or group

° **viceroyalty** region governed by a viceroy, a royally appointed official

also played an important role in shaping the colonial economy. At first, Spaniards acquired gold by looting indigenous communities and burial sites. As permanent settlements and towns were established, mining replaced looting. Serious mining began around 1550, when gold deposits were discovered in the north and northeast of Colombia. Production dropped off in about 1580 as the Indian workforce around Bogotá declined dramatically. However, new deposits were soon found in western Colombia. These deposits were so rich that miners could afford to buy black slaves to work the mines. Gold was essential to the colonial economy because it enabled settlers to purchase goods from Europe, thus inspiring the development of TRADE within Colombia.

The gold boom continued until about 1640, when the miners had extracted all the gold they could. With the decline of gold mining, agriculture also diminished. The Spaniards and mestizos moved away from the mining towns to the Colombian countryside. Gold continued to be used sparingly in trade as the colonial economy turned to the manufacture of essential products. By the early 1600s, Indian workshops set up by the Spanish were making woolen CLOTHING and blankets that were sold within Colombia and in neighboring Venezuela. Cotton grown in central Colombia was used to produce TEXTILES that were sold in regional markets. Although gold mining picked up in the 1700s, the colonial economy expanded and became very diverse. Colombia came to rely less on gold and European imports and more on its own agricultural and textile industries.

Colonial Politics. Rodrigo de Bastidas, Jiménez de Quesada, Sebastián de Benalcázar, and other conquistadors* were the earliest Spanish political leaders in Colombia. In return for conquering new territory for Spain, they were named the first governors of territories within Colombia. They soon established CABILDOS (town councils), whose members were nearly always the powerful *encomenderos* (large landowners). *Cabildo* members chose new officers from among their friends and business associates, so that the *cabildos* came to be controlled by wealthy landowners, miners, and merchants.

The Spanish crown wanted to strengthen the government in the conquered areas, so it established the Audiencia of Santa Fe de Bogotá in 1550. The *audiencia** was intended to improve tax collection for Spain and enforce Spanish laws protecting Indians. However, most of the *audiencia* presidents were unable to control the Spanish settlers and their Creole* descendants. Despite some successes in the early 1600s, colonial government was plagued by fraud, graft*, and tax evasion. The colony's defenses against foreign attacks and invasions were also neglected. Cartagena fell to the French in 1697, and the following year, the Scots established a colony on the coast at Darién. Spanish control over the *audiencia* was weakened.

In 1713, the Bourbon dynasty* took control of the Spanish throne and set out to change conditions in Colombia. The Viceroyalty* of NEW GRANADA was established in 1719 to regain control over the colony, but the first VICEROY was so inept that the viceroyalty was dissolved four

Colombia

The towering Andes mountains separate Colombia's coastal region from its vast, nearly uninhabited southeastern lowlands. Nearly three-fourths of Colombia's people live in the valleys of the Andes, which contain rich mines, fertile farmland, and many cities. However, the Colombian Andes are also part of the "Ring of Fire"—an area around the Pacific Ocean that is prone to earthquakes and volcanic eruptions.

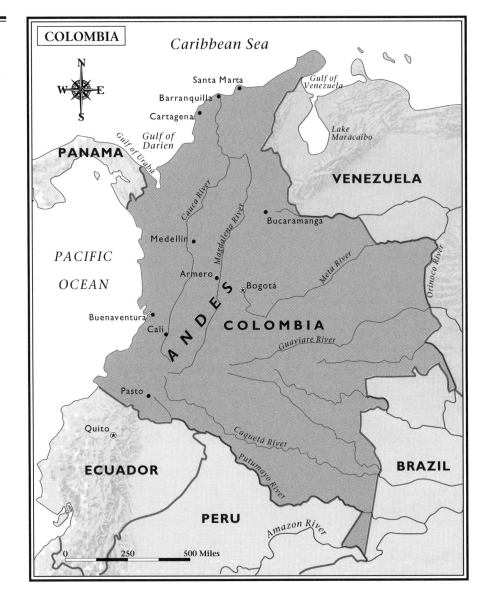

years later. It was reestablished in 1739 to oversee the area that now includes Colombia, Ecuador, Panama, Venezuela, and the Guianas. However, it concentrated its efforts on the provinces of New Granada and Popayán (the area that makes up modern Colombia). In the late 1700s, the Spanish crown again attempted to overhaul the colonial government and improve tax collection, but these measures led to an uprising in 1781 known as the COMUNERO REVOLT. The Spanish authorities were forced to retract their plans, and the reforms were never implemented.

The Comunero Revolt was the first sign of increasing opposition to the Spanish crown. In 1794, several Creoles, including Antonio NARIÑO, leader of Colombian independence, were arrested for plotting to overthrow Spanish rule. Although the small group was not considered a threat to the crown, it indicated a growing dissatisfaction with the way in which the European-born Spaniards, who held power, treated the Creole population.

The 1800s: Independence and Political Turmoil

When French emperor Napoleon captured the Spanish throne in 1808, the leaders of the Colombian independence movement sprang into action. As Spain's authority over the colony weakened, several revolts against the Viceroyalty of New Granada occurred. By July 1810, a group of Creole leaders overthrew the government and established a "Supreme Junta*" that ruled in the name of Ferdinand VII, the Spanish king captured by Napoleon.

° **junta** small group of people who run a government, usually after seizing power by force

Struggling with Independence.

In December, the junta called on all the provinces in the viceroyalty to send representatives to a congress in order to form a new government. The six members who came forward were unable to reach an agreement, so the congress disbanded and each province went its own way. Three separate states were formed: Cundinamarca, headed by Nariño and located near present-day Bogotá; the Federation of New Granadan Provinces, made up of other provinces in the colony; and Cartagena, which proclaimed itself an independent state. In 1814, the Federation defeated Cundinamarca and overthrew Nariño.

While Colombian leaders fought among themselves, Ferdinand VII regained the throne in Spain, and forces loyal to him began recapturing lost territories in Colombia. In 1815, a military expedition was sent from Spain, and by the following year, it had reconquered all of New Granada. Although opposition to the crown was dealt with harshly, a resistance movement developed that kept alive the hope of independence. In 1818, some of the Spanish troops in Colombia were sent to fight against Venezuelan rebels led by Simón BOLÍVAR. Bolívar responded by sending Francisco de Paula SANTANDER into New Granada to rally support for his cause. In August 1819, Bolívar attacked from Venezuela and defeated the Spanish forces in the Battle of BOYACÁ near Bogotá. He went on to capture New Granada and established the Republic* of Colombia, generally known as GRAN COLOMBIA.

See color plate 5, vol. 3.

° **republic** government in which citizens elect officials to represent them and govern according to law

Disunity and Regionalism.

The constitution for the new nation united the separate provinces, created a strong presidency (held by Bolívar), and gave voting rights to men with property who could read and write. Almost immediately it met opposition from those who wanted more power for the individual provinces. In 1826, Venezuela broke away from the union to form an independent nation, followed by Ecuador in 1830. The remaining provinces formed the basis of the modern Republic of Colombia. However, these provinces were divided, and their differences were reflected by the two main political parties that emerged in Colombia. The Conservative Party consisted of influential men who had connections in the religious, political, and educational centers of power, while men from secondary provincial towns formed the Liberal Party.

Colombia's political divisions became polarized during the presidential election of 1837, won by the Liberal Party's candidate in a bitter contest. In 1839, the National Congress ordered the closing of several

° **conservative** inclined to maintain existing political and social views, conditions, and institutions

° **federalism** distribution of power between a central government and the member states

° **coup** sudden, often violent overthrow of a ruler or government

° **liberal** person who supports greater participation in government for individuals; one who is not bound by political and social traditions

convents in the conservative* Pasto region of the southwest. This sparked the War of the Supremes, in which regional rebellions were fought throughout Colombia. The revolt was finally suppressed in 1842, and over the next 20 years, many reforms were put in place. SLAVERY was abolished, taxes reduced, and the Constitution of 1853 separated church and state, allowed civil marriage and divorce, and gave the right to vote to men over the age of 21. The two political groups still disagreed over several issues, particularly the role of the church in the state and the issue of federalism*. These disputes led to a coup* in 1854 and to civil war in 1859. A new constitution, enacted in 1863, established semi-independent states with their own governments and military and reduced the power of the president.

Social Tension and the Regeneration. During this time, many small farmers in search of land moved into south-central Colombia. They took over much public land as well as vacant land claimed by wealthy landowners. This movement led to the growth of thousands of small family farms that supported Colombia's coffee industry well into the 1930s. But it also alarmed conservatives and church leaders who considered the farmers a threat to public order. Their attempts to control the actions of the farmers led to another civil war in 1876. Social unrest, and a poor economy caused by weak demand for Colombia's exports, led to greater tensions between and within the political parties. In 1885, the Liberal Party split, and one faction joined the Conservative Party.

In 1886, the newly enlarged Conservative Party drew up a constitution that reestablished a strong central government, weakened the power of the states, and restored Catholicism as the state religion. This movement, known as the Regeneration, eventually resulted in the formation of the National Party, which promoted cooperation between political rivals to support the national government. However, disputes between the conservatives and liberals* led to the WAR OF THE THOUSAND DAYS in 1899 that claimed the lives of some 100,000 people. Taking advantage of the turmoil, Panama separated itself from Colombia and became an independent nation in 1903, with help from the United States.

Colombia Since 1900

The growth of the coffee industry was perhaps the biggest factor shaping Colombia after 1900. The small farmers who moved south in the second half of the 1800s greatly expanded the coffee-growing region, and production boomed. In 1913, Colombia exported about 132 million pounds of coffee; by 1953, it was exporting six times that amount. Coffee became Colombia's most important product, with small growers owning three-fourths of the farms.

Coffee, Industrialization, and Urbanization. Money from coffee exports brought new prosperity to small farmers, who could now afford to purchase more goods and services. This led to the development of local industries, particularly textiles, and encouraged

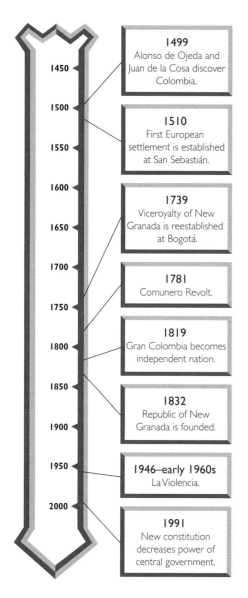

1450
1500
1550
1600
1650
1700
1750
1800
1850
1900
1950
2000

1499
Alonso de Ojeda and Juan de la Cosa discover Colombia.

1510
First European settlement is established at San Sebastián.

1739
Viceroyalty of New Granada is reestablished at Bogotá.

1781
Comunero Revolt.

1819
Gran Colombia becomes independent nation.

1832
Republic of New Granada is founded.

1946–early 1960s
La Violencia.

1991
New constitution decreases power of central government.

° **guerrilla** referring to a group that uses surprise raids to obstruct or harass an enemy or overthrow a government

FOREIGN INVESTMENT in the country. In 1922, the United States paid Colombia $25 million for its role in the separation of Panama, and a number of American companies—such as UNITED FRUIT COMPANY and several oil companies—set up operations in Colombia. As INDUSTRIALIZATION increased, HIGHWAYS and RAILROADS were built to bring the country together. The population grew rapidly, and the number of city dwellers increased sixfold between 1900 and 1930. Since 1918, Bogotá has grown from a city of 150,000 to one containing more than 6 million people, and four other Colombian cities boast populations of at least 1 million.

The growth of cities created new types of job opportunities, leading to a larger middle class. Urban growth was also accompanied by workers' strikes between 1900 and 1930. The government often responded with force, arresting and frequently beating large numbers of strikers. Laws were passed that weakened workers' unions and outlawed strikes in certain industries, such as transportation. By the late 1920s, foreign companies were less willing to invest in Colombia. The already weakened economy was devastated by the collapse of the world economy in 1929.

La Violencia and the National Front.
The 1930s were a time of continued political struggle between the liberals and conservatives. Liberal governments passed laws that tended to favor small farmers and workers, expand presidential power, and reduce the influence of the church. In the 1940s, conservatives regained control of the government, but the disputed presidential election of 1946 led to LA VIOLENCIA, a wave of violence that lasted almost 20 years and claimed hundreds of thousands of victims.

In 1956, troubled by the bloodshed, the two parties agreed to set aside their differences and share power in an arrangement called the National Front. Under the agreement, the presidency alternated between liberals and conservatives for 16 years, and all government positions were shared equally. The National Front managed to end the political violence, but it did not bring true democracy to Colombia. Most of the wealth and power was still held by a very small number of people, and several guerrilla* groups rose to challenge the government.

Colombia Since 1970.
Despite continuing guerrilla violence, Colombia has prospered, developing perhaps the most balanced and profitable export economy in Latin America. Coffee, though still important, accounts for less than one-third of Colombia's exports; petroleum, coal, and agricultural products all contribute significantly to the economy. Over half the population now works in the SERVICE INDUSTRY based in the cities. In recent years, the booming DRUG TRADE has had a damaging effect on Colombia, leading to widespread violence among those trying to control the Colombian drug market. The government has waged an aggressive war against growers and dealers but with little success.

The war on drugs has also weakened the government's attempts to make Colombia a more democratic country. Many of the poor who have been left out of power for so long are dependent on the money they receive for raising drug crops. They see the government's efforts to wipe out drugs as an attack on their livelihood.

Despite these difficulties, some progress has been made in bringing political and social equality to Colombia. Peace agreements with several guerrilla groups have ended some of the political violence in the country. A new constitution, drafted in 1991, reduced the power of the president, and new political movements are forming to challenge the liberals and conservatives. Economic and social improvements seem likely to continue, as do social tensions caused by inequality of wealth and power. (*See also* **Cities and Urbanization; Class Structure, Colonial and Modern; Copper Industry; Geography; Gold and Silver; Petroleum Industry; Spain and the Spanish Empire; United States–Latin American Relations.**)

Columbus, Christopher

ca. 1451–1506
Genoese explorer

See
color plate 2,
vol. 3.

* **viceroy** one who governs a country or province as a monarch's representative; royally appointed official

On a quest for a western water route from Europe to Asia, seaman and navigator Christopher Columbus landed in the West Indies in 1492. His voyages began Europe's intense and long-lasting interest in the Western Hemisphere.

Columbus was born in the Italian republic of Genoa on the western Mediterranean, the son of a wool weaver and merchant. He went to sea at an early age and settled in Lisbon, Portugal. As a young man, he sailed to England and Ireland and possibly as far as Iceland. He visited the Madeira Islands, the Canary Islands, and the African coast as far south as present-day Ghana. He returned to Portugal, where he married a woman from a prominent Italian-Portuguese family and had a son, Diogo. Through his marriage, he gained important connections to the Portuguese court.

In 1485, Columbus tried to interest the Portuguese king Dom João II in a plan to reach the fabled riches of Asia. Columbus based his ideas on rumors of unknown Atlantic islands, unusual objects drifting ashore from the west, and his readings of the most learned geographers of the time. Although Columbus knew that the world was spherical, he underestimated its circumference. When his plan was rejected by the Portuguese king, Columbus went to Spain to appeal to Queen Isabella I of Castile and her husband, Ferdinand II of Aragon. Six years later, they contracted to sponsor a voyage and granted Columbus noble status and the titles of admiral, viceroy*, and governor-general for any lands he might discover for Spain.

With three ships, the *Niña,* the *Pinta,* and the *Santa Maria,* and a crew of 90 men, Columbus set sail on August 3, 1492, for Asia. The fleet dropped anchor at an island in what are now the Bahamas on October 12. The local people called the island Guanahaní, which Columbus renamed SAN SALVADOR. Believing they were in Asia, the Europeans called the islanders Indians. Columbus then sailed to CUBA and to the island they named HISPANIOLA before returning to Spain. Thirty-nine of his crew remained on Hispaniola after the *Santa Maria* ran aground.

Certain that the Asian mainland lay close to the islands he had found, Columbus was given permission for a second voyage. In 1493,

Columbus's Unheeded Warning

Although Columbus was specifically forbidden on his fourth voyage to land again at Hispaniola, he arrived there anyway. Columbus knew that Governor Ovando was about to send a fleet home and saw that a hurricane was brewing. He warned Ovando of the approaching storm and asked to anchor in the harbor. But Ovando refused his request and ordered the fleet to depart, just before the hurricane struck. Twenty-five of the Spanish fleet's ships were sunk.

° **monarch** king or queen

° **patron** special guardian, protector, or supporter

with 1,200 men and 17 vessels, Columbus returned to Hispaniola, sailing through the Lesser Antilles and the Virgin Islands and past Puerto Rico, only to find his men dead. Most of them had been killed by the islanders. Columbus and his crew marched through the island with horses, war dogs, and guns, seeking gold through barter but conquering and taking captives when they met with any opposition. He left his brothers in charge this time and returned to Spain in 1496.

Columbus set sail again on May 30, 1498, with six ships carrying provisions and 300 men and 30 women colonists. He reached the island of TRINIDAD on July 31 and then sailed to the mainland of South America, on the coast of Venezuela. Returning to Hispaniola, Columbus found a dismal situation. The colonists had mutinied, the Indians were hostile, and his brothers had lost control of the settlement. In 1500, Columbus and his brothers were arrested and sent home in chains, and the Spanish monarchs* appointed a governor for Hispaniola. They allowed Columbus to keep some of his titles and all of his property, but the titles no longer carried any authority. Not until 1502 was he granted permission for another voyage.

On his fourth and final voyage, Columbus sailed along the coast of central America. Hostile local Indians forced him to abandon plans for a settlement in PANAMA. Columbus landed in northern JAMAICA and awaited rescue for a year. He reached Spain in 1504, broken in health, never again to return to the Indies. In Spain, he appealed to the crown to have his grants and titles restored. He died a wealthy man, surrounded by family and friends, but still dissatisfied, feeling betrayed and slighted by his royal patrons*. (*See also* **Explorers and Exploration**.)

Commercial Policy

See *Trade and Commerce.*

Communism

Communism is a political philosophy that maintains that a society's wealth and the means to produce that wealth should be shared among all the people in the community on the basis of need. When Communists took control of Russia in 1917, they established an organization called the Comintern (short for Communist International) to spread their doctrine throughout the world. Communism gained immediate support in LATIN AMERICA, where great differences in wealth between the upper and lower classes made its principles appealing to many poor people.

Communism Before World War II. In 1918, the first Communist party in Latin America was formed in ARGENTINA. Another party was established in MEXICO in 1919, with the aid of many foreigners—including United States citizens who had fled to Mexico to avoid the draft during World War I. In 1922, CHILE and URUGUAY also joined the Comintern, and a Communist party arose in BRAZIL. By the early 1930s, there were Communist parties in nearly every Latin American republic.

Communism

° **radical** favoring extreme changes or reforms

° **guerrilla** referring to a group that uses surprise raids to obstruct or harass an enemy or overthrow a government

° **militant** aggressive, willing to use force

The 1930s were a difficult time for Latin American Communists. Fear of communism led many governments to outlaw Communist activities. The Communists, who had few allies because they isolated themselves from other political groups, were driven underground and virtually disappeared. But in 1934, the Comintern decided to support the creation of popular fronts, movements in which Communists joined forces with other groups in society to consolidate their political power. The popular front in Chile won the 1938 presidential election, but the Communists refused to join the government because the president did not support their policies strongly enough. Popular fronts also enjoyed political successes in Mexico and CUBA.

From World War II to the 1980s.   When World War II began in 1939, the Soviet Union and Nazi Germany signed an agreement not to attack each other. Because of this agreement, the Comintern urged Latin American Communists to keep their countries out of the war. However, when Germany broke the agreement and attacked the Soviet Union in 1941, the nature of the war suddenly changed for the Comintern. It now portrayed the war as a crusade against the Nazis that all workers must support, and Communists worked closely with anti-Nazi governments throughout Latin America. In the mid-to-late 1940s, Communists entered government for the first time in Cuba, ECUADOR, and Chile. During the 1950s, however, their influence declined in most Latin American countries except GUATEMALA, where they held many key government positions and controlled the labor unions. At this time, Communist parties also arose in the BRITISH WEST INDIES.

During the late 1950s and 1960s, communism in Latin America developed a more radical* approach. In 1959, guerrilla* leader Fidel CASTRO seized power in Cuba and quickly made it a Communist state. The success of the CUBAN REVOLUTION gave rise to Latin American Communist groups that favored using violence to gain power. The most notable of these were the SANDINISTAS, who overthrew the ruling SOMOZA FAMILY in NICARAGUA in 1979, after nearly 20 years of guerrilla warfare. In the 1960s, Chinese leader Mao Zedong led the Chinese Communists out of the Comintern and called for a more militant* type of communism. Maoist groups soon split off from many Latin American Communist parties, preaching and often practicing violence. Although the Maoist movement weakened during the 1970s, it inspired the SENDERO LUMINOSO (Shining Path) that has been waging a violent guerrilla struggle against the Peruvian government since the early 1980s. The Trotskyists—followers of the Russian revolutionary Leon Trotsky—also had successes in many countries, particularly BOLIVIA.

Communism in Modern Latin America.   The rise of democratic governments throughout Latin America in the 1980s enabled Communists to operate more freely than they had in the past. However, when the Soviet Union collapsed in 1991, most Latin American Communist parties lost economic support and credibility with their followers and ultimately failed. In 1990, the Sandinistas were voted out of power in Nicaragua, leaving Cuba as the only Communist country in the region. Many Communist parties in Latin America have joined other political groups who share some of their philosophies. (*See also* **Class Structure, Colonial and Modern; Political Parties; Soviet–Latin American Relations; World Wars I and II.**)

Comunero Revolts

* **Jesuit** Roman Catholic religious order known as the Society of Jesus; also, a member of that order

* **mission** settlement started by Catholic priests whose purpose was to convert local people to Christianity

* **cash crop** crop grown primarily for profit rather than for local consumption

* **viceroy** one who governs a country or province as a monarch's representative; royally appointed official

*T*he Comunero Revolts were two separate popular uprisings in PARAGUAY and COLOMBIA during the 1700s. The name *Comunero* came from the word *común* (the people), because the leaders believed that true political power came from the people, who allowed the king to rule in their name. Although the two uprisings were unrelated, they had similar causes and outcomes.

The revolt in Paraguay arose from the Paraguayans' resentment of the Jesuits*, who owned much of the land and enjoyed greater economic privileges than ordinary citizens. Violence against the Jesuits began as early as the 1640s and resurfaced in the early 1720s. In 1724, Paraguayans defeated an army of GUARANI Indians who lived in the Jesuit missions*, and they expelled the Jesuits from the city of ASUNCIÓN. But in 1730, a pro-Jesuit governor, Ignacio de Soroeta, was appointed, and he allowed the Jesuits to return. Paraguayans expelled Soroeta the following year, and local elites from Asunción, the capital, governed the province. The Jesuits were thrown out again in 1732, and over the next few years, several leaders tried unsuccessfully to bring order to Paraguay. Finally, in 1735, the governor of BUENOS AIRES was ordered to bring peace to Paraguay. He did so ruthlessly, executing 4 of the rebel leaders, banishing 13 others, removing several officials from their posts, and forbidding public meetings.

The Colombian revolt was also triggered by economic inequality. In 1781, in the town of Socorro, an angry crowd led by a bold local woman named Manuela Beltrán protested against government policies that they considered unfair—such as the introduction of new TAXES, restrictions on growing TOBACCO (the region's only valuable cash crop*), and the government's practice of sending nearly all public money to the capital city, BOGOTÁ. The leaders of the uprising marched on Bogotá with between 10,000 and 20,000 men. In late May, they presented a list of demands, including improved living conditions for Indians and free blacks. On June 5, 1781, the viceroy* and archbishop of NEW GRANADA (which included the area of modern-day Colombia) both agreed to the demands. However, they revoked the agreements as soon as the *comuneros* returned to their homes. They pardoned most of those who had taken part in the revolt, including its leaders, then restored almost all of the taxes and other measures the *comuneros* had protested against. A few *comuneros* continued the armed struggle, but they were captured in October and their leaders killed in February 1782.

Although neither revolt was aimed at overthrowing Spanish rule, many modern-day Colombians and Paraguayans consider the Comunero Revolts to be the forerunners of independence movements and celebrate their leaders as early patriots who opposed imperial rule.

Confederates in Brazil and Mexico

After the United States Civil War, thousands of former rebels fled the South to seek new homes in LATIN AMERICA. Several important figures, including four former generals and two former governors, emigrated to Latin America. Most of these ex-Confederates settled in BRAZIL and MEXICO, where they became known as *confederatos*. Mexico attracted these settlers because it was nearby and because the Mexican emperor MAXIMILIAN welcomed them. However, lack of money and the hardships of pioneering in Mexico caused many *confederatos* to return to the United States. Many more left Mexico in 1867, when the overthrow of Maximilian caused political turmoil in that country.

Most of the former rebels—about 2,500 to 4,000—settled in Brazil. Fearing that Reconstruction after the war would be harsh, they fled to Brazil to replicate the PLANTATION way of life that they had previously enjoyed. Agents toured Brazil in 1865 and 1866, purchasing land for settlers and writing books and letters enthusiastically promoting settlement. Cheap land and labor, along with the existence of slavery, made IMMIGRATION attractive to *confederatos*. Brazil's government also made it easy for new settlers to pay off mortgages on the land they purchased. Even so, many settlers soon failed because their plantations were too far from markets and they lacked money and transportation to move their produce. Eventually, many *confederatos* relocated to the cities of SÃO PAULO and RIO DE JANEIRO or returned to the United States. The only successful *confederato* settlement was Americana, a cotton-growing enterprise that later switched to other crops, including watermelon. Today Americana is a city of 160,000, where descendants of the original *confederatos* still celebrate the Fourth of July.

Conquistadors

The conquistadors were Spanish adventurers who explored and conquered MEXICO, the Caribbean, and South and Central America for Spain during the 1500s. They all shared the same basic motivations for risking their lives in the remote jungles and mountains of LATIN AMERICA: wealth, honor, and the spread of Christianity.

Who Were the Conquistadors?   The conquistadors represented almost every class and type of people in Spanish society, except for the highest nobility. However, most of them were HIDALGOS, people from the lower ranks of the Spanish aristocracy. Often they were the sons of minor noblemen and were looking for riches that would enable them to live in the grand style they believed they deserved. A few conquistadors were members of the clergy*. Many of the very famous conquistadors came from the Spanish province of Estremadura, a dry and rugged region in west-central Spain.

The primary motivation of most conquistadors was the prospect of great wealth. They wanted to lead successful campaigns in America, become rich, and return to Spain to a life of leisure. However, in addition to riches, the conquistadors also sought personal honor through their

° **clergy** priests and other church officials qualified to perform church ceremonies

See color plate 3, vol. 3.

military exploits. For hundreds of years, Spanish Christians had fought to drive out the Moors (Spanish Muslims) who had controlled Spain since the early 700s. This was finally achieved in 1492 by the Spanish monarchs Ferdinand and Isabella. When the first conquistadors sailed across the Atlantic, Spain's long struggle against the Moors had instilled in the nation's culture a desire for honor and a deep respect for military values. The Spanish concept of honor maintained that the noblest way to achieve wealth was through struggle rather than through commerce or inheritance. Thus, both material gain and the hope of winning honor inspired the conquistadors.

A third motivation was the desire to spread Christianity among the indigenous* peoples of America. According to international law at the time, the conversion of pagan* peoples to Catholicism was the only legitimate reason for conquest. Bernal Díaz del Castillo, a foot soldier who participated in the conquest of Mexico under Hernán CORTÉS, expressed the conquistadors' mixed motives. He wrote that he and his companions went to Mexico "to serve God and His Majesty the King, to give light to those who were in darkness, and also to get rich—which all of us came looking for."

indigenous referring to the original inhabitants of a region

pagan referring to a belief in more than one god

Expeditions of Conquest. Although the Spanish monarchy and the CATHOLIC CHURCH had a large stake in the expeditions of the conquistadors, they did little to prepare or finance the voyages. Royal participation was often limited to granting a charter, or license,

The conquistadors were generally master strategists and able leaders. This manuscript illustration shows Hernán Cortés and the Indian allies he enlisted to help him defeat a much larger army of Aztec warriors.

See color plate 4, vol. 3.

Andalusian Spoken Here

Because Spain was busy fighting wars on several fronts in Europe in the 1500s, no regular Spanish troops participated in the conquest of America. Most of those who followed the conquistadors were lower-class Spaniards, including many craftsmen from the southern province of Andalusia. Many of these men settled in America. As a result, the regional dialect of Spanish spoken in Andalusia became the basis for the Spanish spoken in much of Latin America.

that gave the conquistadors permission to claim a particular territory for the king. Most conquistadors had to raise money themselves to buy ships and supplies for their expeditions and to pay the men who accompanied them. Many individuals who served under the conquistadors were also offered a share of any wealth that was captured as a further incentive to join the expedition. The parties rarely had access to warships and usually sailed in any privately owned vessels they could find.

The Spanish monarchy gave the conquistadors great freedom to conduct their operations as they saw fit. They were often granted the title of *adelantado,* or captain-general, which gave them absolute authority over their men during the expedition and control over the conquered land and its inhabitants. The conquistadors were typically very harsh with the Indians they conquered, looting their villages as well as torturing and often killing them. Some were just as cruel to their own men. Many conquistadors were recalled to Spain after their expeditions to answer charges that were brought against them for their actions in America.

The conquistadors were not mindless killers, however. Many were educated men who were master strategists and able leaders. Such skills were critical because many expeditions were quite small. For example, Francisco PIZARRO conquered the mighty INCA empire of PERU with a force that numbered only about 150 men. Some conquistadors were also skilled negotiators and managed to enlist the aid of some Indians. Cortés, for example, landed in Mexico with only 600 men, but he found indigenous groups who were enemies of the AZTEC leaders. He used these Indian allies, particularly those from the city of Tlaxcala, to help him defeat the much larger Aztec forces.

The Fate of the Conquistadors. The most successful conquistadors achieved their goals of wealth and power but rarely in the way they had planned. Those who conquered fabulously wealthy lands, such as the empires of the Aztecs and Inca, became instantly rich from the GOLD, silver, and gems they seized. However, most conquistadors failed to find such riches. Instead, they were rewarded with an ENCOMIENDA, the right to control the labor of the Indians who lived in a particular area. The *encomiendas* could be quite profitable if the conquistador established large PLANTATIONS and ranches on the land or discovered and mined precious metals. But obtaining wealth in this manner took many years, and most conquistadors never returned to Spain.

Although most were unable to fulfill their dreams of joining the nobility in Spain, the conquistadors achieved many of their other goals. Those who survived were able to afford large houses and expensive personal possessions, to marry a Spanish wife, to entertain their friends and family in style, and to live off the labor of the Indians they held in *encomienda.* They were often named governors of the territories they conquered, and their descendants inherited their power and wealth. Even their quest for honor and status was somewhat successful, because the conquistadors formed a large part of the early Spanish American aristocracy. (*See also* **Explorers and Exploration; Spain and the Spanish Empire; Tenochtitlán.**)

Conselheiro, Antônio

1830–1897
Brazilian religious leader
and missionary

° **doctrine** principle, theory, or belief presented for acceptance

Antônio Conselheiro spent much of his life wandering the backcountry of BRAZIL and preaching Christian doctrine*. He became a favorite figure among poor rural laborers, and he established a religious community in a remote part of BAHIA that attracted thousands of followers.

Antônio Vicente Mendes Maciel was born in a small town in the Brazilian state of Ceará and was raised by his stepmother. She imposed strict religious discipline on the household and frequently punished her children and her slaves. Although his father wanted him to become a priest, he was instead forced to take over his father's failing business in order to support the family. After Mendes's wife ran away with a soldier, he sold his house and went off to wander the backcountry.

By the 1880s, he had acquired a reputation as a *conselheiro,* or religious counselor. He wandered throughout the northeastern part of Brazil, living on handouts and sleeping on the floors of houses and barns. He dressed simply, fasted, and spent his time repairing old churches and cemetery walls and preaching to the poor. In 1893, he established a religious community in Bahia called Canudos that attracted more than 25,000 followers from all racial and economic backgrounds. Local landowners, however, were angry that so many of their laborers had abandoned their work to move to Canudos. In 1897, the Brazilian army attacked and destroyed Canudos, the second-largest city in Bahia, even though Conselheiro had died several days before and had been buried. The soldiers dug up his body, mounted his head on a pike, and paraded it through SALVADOR and other cities along the coast. (*See also* **Catholic Church; Missions and Missionaries; Religious Orders.**)

Conservative Parties

See *Political Parties.*

Consulado

° **monopoly** exclusive control or domination of a particular type of business

Consulados were institutions formed to protect the interests of Spanish merchants and traders. They enabled Spanish merchants to control trade with America. Through the *consulados,* merchants in the Spanish cities of Seville and Cádiz enjoyed a monopoly* on Latin American trade for more than 200 years.

The *consulados* grew out of local merchant GUILDS that had operated in Italy, France, and Spain since the Middle Ages*. They were responsible for settling disputes over contracts, shipping, insurance, and other

Contraband

° **Middle Ages** period between ancient and modern times in western Europe, generally considered to be from the A.D. 500s to the 1500s

commercial matters. They also determined who could trade in certain areas and under what terms. In 1543, the Spanish monarchy authorized a *consulado* for the merchants of Seville that gave them a monopoly on trade with America. The *consulado* worked closely with the CASA DE CONTRATACIÓN (Board of Trade) to protect that monopoly. In the early 1600s, *consulados* were established in MEXICO CITY and LIMA. They were run by the main importers in those cities, most of whom were representatives of the Seville merchants. This further strengthened Seville's control over Spain's trade with America. In the 1790s, the monarchy attempted to break up the Seville-Cádiz trade monopoly by establishing eight new *consulados* in Latin America. Their primary purpose was to protect and promote American commerce, and they eventually played important roles in the ECONOMIC DEVELOPMENT of the countries in which they operated. Because the *consulados* usually acted in the interests of Spanish merchants, most Latin American countries abolished them soon after independence. A few *consulados* survived into the late 1800s, but eventually all fell as Latin American nations adopted more liberal economic policies. (*See also* **Fleet Systems, Colonial; Trade and Commerce.**)

Contraband

See *Smuggling.*

Contras

° **guerrilla** member of a fighting force outside the regular army that uses surprise raids to obstruct or harass an enemy or overthrow a government

See
color plate 12,
vol. 4.

*T*he contras were a military force that opposed the SANDINISTA government of Nicaragua during the 1980s. They were supported by the administration of United States president Ronald Reagan, which provided them with arms, money, and training. Created in 1981, the contras began as a 500-man force intended to stop arms shipments from Nicaragua to antigovernment guerrillas* in El Salvador. Eventually, the contras numbered nearly 12,000 men with a new objective of overthrowing Nicaragua's Sandinista government. The contras represented several diverse political groups, including supporters of former Nicaraguan dictator Anastasio SOMOZA, dissatisfied Sandinistas, MOSQUITO INDIANS, and other Nicaraguans who were unhappy with the government.

Because the contras frequently attacked civilian targets and violated HUMAN RIGHTS, the U.S. Congress soon opposed them. When Congress cut official aid to the contras in 1984, President Reagan turned to the U.S. National Security Council to find other sources of support. Lieutenant Colonel Oliver North raised money for the contras by arranging the illegal sales of United States missiles to Iran and by obtaining donations from the leaders of several oil-rich nations. Although the contras continued to raid Nicaragua from bases in HONDURAS, they never controlled any territory or gained widespread support. In 1989, the presidents of the Central American nations signed an agreement to hold free elections in Nicaragua and to disband the contras. When the

Sandinistas were defeated in the elections of February 1990, the reason for the contras' existence disappeared, and they disbanded in June under the supervision of UNITED NATIONS peacekeeping forces. Some former contras remain in Central America, while their wealthier supporters live in the United States. (*See also* **Counterinsurgency; El Salvador; Guerrilla Movements; Nicaragua; United States–Latin American Relations.**)

Copán

Copán, the site of a major MAYA cultural center, is located on the western border of HONDURAS, near GUATEMALA. Dated monuments there indicate that Copán was occupied as early as A.D. 455 and as late as 790. During that time, Copán marked the eastern boundary of Maya territory and controlled trade between the Maya and the rest of CENTRAL AMERICA.

The site surrounds a large open plaza containing huge stone stelae—monuments with the carved images of Copán's rulers. The southeast corner of the plaza is occupied by a ball court and a stairway containing the longest carved Maya inscription known to exist. To the south, numerous ceremonial buildings stand on a large, elevated platform that is 120 feet high. A causeway, or earthen bridge, leads to an area of fine houses with elaborately carved inscriptions. Copán was one of the great intellectual centers of the Maya, especially in the astronomical sciences. Evidence suggests that the Maya developed a method of calculating the length of a lunar month based on observations made at Copán. Major activity at Copán ended suddenly after A.D. 800. The Maya center remained lost to history until 1576, when its ruins were discovered and reported by Don Diego García de Palacios. (*See also* **Archaeology; Architecture; Astronomy; Ball Game, Pre-Columbian; Cultures, Pre-Columbian.**)

 See map in Mesoamerica, Pre-Columbian History (vol. 3).

Copper Industry

South American INDIANS mined copper in the ANDES mountains at least 2,500 years before the first Europeans arrived. Since then, copper mining in Latin America has grown from an activity that served mainly local rulers and priests to one that serves a worldwide market and is vital to modern industry and TECHNOLOGY.

Early Copper Mining. By about 1000 B.C., the production of copper objects was common among the CHAVIN people of Peru. In addition to using pure copper, the Chavin developed alloys (mixtures of metals) that combined copper with GOLD AND SILVER. They also mastered techniques such as silver plating and gilding, in which copper objects were coated with silver or gold so that they appeared to be made of those precious metals. The use of copper and copper alloys eventually spread as far north as MEXICO. Many pre-Columbian cultures used copper to create objects that symbolized political power, social status, and religious beliefs.

° **conquistador** Spanish explorer and conqueror

° **by-product** something produced in the making of something else

° **nationalize** to bring land, industries, or public works under state control or ownership

The Spanish conquistadors* valued copper for use in WEAPONS, and they began mining it soon after they arrived in America. In 1494, on the Caribbean island of HISPANIOLA, Christopher COLUMBUS opened gold mines that reportedly produced copper as a by-product*. The first European copper mine in Latin America began operation in 1522 in Taxco, Mexico. However, CHILE has long been the region's leading copper producer.

Copper Mining in Chile. Copper mining became increasingly important in Chile during the 1800s, and the nation soon became the world's top copper producer. During the WAR OF THE PACIFIC, from 1879 to 1883, Chile gained rich copper mining regions from Peru. However, in 1882, the United States took the lead in copper production. In the early 1900s, United States companies began to invest in Chilean copper mines and to bring new mining technology to Chile. These new methods enabled Chile to make use of copper porphyry—a low-grade ore that had previously been considered worthless. Chile has several major deposits of copper porphyry, including a mine at Chuquicamata that produces nearly 600,000 tons of copper per year. This single mine produces more copper than the entire country of Peru, which is the second-largest copper producer in Latin America.

United States companies owned most of the larger copper mines in Chile until 1971. On July 16 of that year, Chile nationalized* its copper industry, taking control of all the country's mines. Today Chile is again the world's leading producer of copper, mining more than 1.6 million tons each year. The U.S. Bureau of Mines estimates that Chile holds more than one-fifth of the world's reserves of copper—more than any other nation.

Copper Mining in Other Latin American Nations. Peru and Mexico are also significant Latin American producers of copper. Peru controls about 6 percent of the world's copper reserves and produces about 400,000 tons per year. Mexican copper mines produce about half that much and contain around 4 percent of the world's supply. Many other Latin American countries produce copper, but in much smaller amounts. In total, Latin America currently produces one-quarter of the world's copper and controls more than one-third of the world's known supply.

Córdoba

° **Jesuit** Roman Catholic religious order known as the Society of Jesus; also, a member of that order

Córdoba is the name of both the central province of ARGENTINA and the province's capital. The mountains of the Sierras de Córdoba run through the middle of the province, and flat grasslands, called PAMPAS, lie to the east and west. MINING for minerals is the main industry in the mountains, while cattle and grain are raised on the eastern pampas. The western pampas comprise a dry, desertlike area containing large salt flats.

The city of Córdoba was founded on July 6, 1573, along the trade route from Upper Peru (now BOLIVIA) to BUENOS AIRES. The town grew quickly and attracted many RELIGIOUS ORDERS. The Jesuits* established a

° **mission** settlement started by Catholic priests whose purpose was to convert local people to Christianity

See map in Argentina (vol. I).

mission* there in 1599, and the University of Córdoba was founded in 1623. Córdoba became wealthy from AGRICULTURE and cattle ranching and soon rivaled the city of Tucumán as the area's major trading center. In 1783, it was named the seat of the Intendancy of Córdoba, which ruled several provinces in the RÍO DE LA PLATA (now Argentina). Córdoba gained prestige as one of the wealthiest, most cultured, and pro-Spanish settlements in the region. In 1810, when officials in Buenos Aires declared Argentina's independence, Córdoba voted to remain loyal to the king of Spain. Córdoba led the interior provinces in resisting the new leadership of Buenos Aires, and it was many years before Córdoba fully became a part of Argentina. In 1955, the city demonstrated its independent spirit again, when a local army commander led the uprising that overthrew dictator Juan PERÓN. In 1969, Córdoban workers and students launched the rebellion that ended the military rule of General Juan Onganía. Today Córdoba is a thriving city of more than a million people, with a strong industrial economy and excellent RAILROAD, HIGHWAY, and air connections to nearby and distant regions.

Corn

See *Maize.*

Coronel

A *coronel* was a local Brazilian political boss during the time when BRAZIL was mainly a rural agricultural country, from about 1870 to 1940. A *coronel* was part of the local economic and social elite—usually a landowner, merchant, lawyer, or even a priest—who rose to power because of his social standing. The title itself was a military rank associated with Brazil's National Guard, although many political *coronéis* (the plural of *coronel*) never held an official rank in the guard. *Coronelismo* was the term used to describe the political rule of a *coronel*. This system was especially dominant in the agricultural backwaters of Brazil's north, northwest, and far west.

A *coronel*'s power came from his control over economic and social resources. The *coronel* provided food and work for a large local population that, in turn, obeyed his orders and wishes. During Brazil's First Republic, from 1889 to 1930, the *coronéis* made promises to state and national politicians to deliver the votes of the local people in exchange for political favors. Influential *coronéis* brought public works such as roads, dams, and RAILROADS into their territories. These improvements connected remote rural areas to the urban centers and ports and increased TRADE between the cities and the countryside. *Coronéis* also appointed all local and state officials in their towns and ensured that those officials remained loyal. After 1930, thousands of Brazilians moved to the cities in pursuit of industrial jobs, and the political importance of the agricultural regions declined. *Coronelismo* gradually faded away as political power became concentrated in the urban centers. (*See also* **Caciques; Caudillos; Jefe Político.**)

Cortázar, Julio

1914–1984
Argentine writer

*J*ulio Cortázar was one of the main contributors to the explosion of notable and innovative Latin American literature that occurred in the mid-1900s. Like the Colombian novelist Gabriel GARCÍA MÁRQUEZ, Cortázar blended fantasy and realism in his stories to challenge traditional Western ideas of reason and reality in fiction.

Born in Belgium to Argentine parents, Cortázar and his family moved to ARGENTINA in 1918. In the 1940s, Cortázar taught literature at the University of Cuyo in Mendoza but resigned after publicly demonstrating against Argentina's dictator, Juan PERÓN. In 1951, Cortázar moved to Paris, where he wrote most of his works and served as a translator for the United Nations. He also traveled widely and lectured in support of Latin American political reform.

In his books, Cortázar experimented with the process of writing. His most famous work, *Rayuela (Hopscotch),* has 155 short chapters and may be read in several ways. One may read the chapters consecutively, or one may follow the instructions at the end of each chapter that tell the reader which chapter to read next. Another of Cortázar's unique novels includes two sets of pages that tell different stories, and the reader must determine which to read first. Cortázar used these devices to encourage creativity and stir the imagination of his readers. Some scholars believe that the international success of Cortázar's innovative novels sparked greater interest in works by other Latin American authors as well. (*See also* **Literature.**)

Cortés, Hernán

ca. 1484–1547
Spanish conqueror of Mexico

* **conquistador** Spanish explorer and conqueror

* **tribute** payment made to a dominant power

*H*ernán Cortés is best known as the man who conquered the AZTEC empire of central MEXICO. A charismatic leader, Cortés was often at odds with other Spanish conquistadors* and officials who disapproved of the methods he used to achieve his goals. He is also known for his written account of the conquest.

Early Life and Adventures.   Cortés was born in Medellín, Spain, and studied law at the University of Salamanca. Although he probably never received a degree, his activities and writings show that he acquired considerable knowledge of the law. In 1504, Cortés sailed to HISPANIOLA in search of wealth and power. Six years later, he joined Diego Velázquez in the conquest of CUBA, where he became an ALCALDE (mayor). By 1517, Cortés had married and acquired an ENCOMIENDA—a grant giving him the right to demand labor and tribute* from the local Indians—and several gold mines.

In late 1518, Cortés was chosen to lead an expedition to search for a missing explorer, Juan de Grijalva. By the time Cortés was ready to begin the search, Grijalva had returned. Instead, Cortés and 508 soldiers set out on a voyage to the YUCATÁN. His main mission was to establish trade, but he was also commissioned to convert the Indians to Christianity and to claim for Spain any new lands he discovered. Soon after his arrival in Mexico in April 1519, he learned of a rich and powerful

Noche Triste

The night of June 30, 1520, when Cortés and his troops retreated from Tenochtitlán, became known by Spaniards as the *noche triste* (sad night). Greatly outnumbered by the rebelling Aztecs, Cortés tried to sneak his army out of the island city during the night. The only escape was across a narrow bridge, but many Spaniards were loaded down with stolen Aztec gold. As Cortés and his army crossed the bridge, the Aztecs pelted them from all sides with thousands of arrows, spears, and stones. Only half of Cortés's forces escaped that night, and most were wounded. The Spaniards lost more than 400 men and all of their horses and treasure.

See color plate 1, vol. 3.

* **blockade** to close off a port, preventing ships from entering or leaving, and thus cripple trade

* **siege** prolonged effort by armed troops to force the surrender of a town or fort by surrounding it and cutting it off from aid

Aztec ruler named MOCTEZUMA II (also known as Montezuma) who controlled a vast empire that stretched from the interior of Mexico to the coast.

Conquest of the Aztecs. Cortés also learned that Moctezuma had many enemies who could be enlisted to fight against him, and he decided to make alliances with these Indian groups. At this time, he acquired an Indian interpreter, MALINCHE, who spoke two languages—the Mayan language of the Yucatán and the Nahuatl language of central Mexico. He founded a town called Villa Rica de la Vera Cruz and placed it under the authority of the king of Spain. This act challenged the authority of Velázquez, who raised an army to move against Cortés. In August 1519, Cortés marched inland to find Moctezuma and his capital city of TENOCHTITLÁN. A month later, he reached the city of Tlaxcala and defeated the Tlaxcalans in a fierce fight. He then formed an alliance with the Tlaxcalans. In early November, he reached the majestic city of Tenochtitlán and met with Moctezuma.

To intimidate the Aztecs, Cortés imprisoned their ruler. Shortly thereafter, Cortés learned that forces sent by Velázquez were preparing to attack him. He left his lieutenant, Pedro de ALVARADO, in charge of the Aztec capital while he and most of his soldiers went to meet the opposing army. Cortés won the battle and convinced the defeated Spaniards to join his forces. But when he returned to Tenochtitlán, he found it in chaos. Alvarado had slaughtered hundreds of Aztec nobles in the main temple, and the Aztecs were rebelling. Seeking to appease the Indians, Cortés released Moctezuma's brother Cuitlahuac. However, Cuitlahuac immediately led an uprising against the Spaniards, in which Moctezuma was killed. In July 1520, Cortés was forced to retreat to Tlaxcala, during a night of fighting that cost the lives of many of his soldiers. In the next few months, the Spanish attacked several towns around Tenochtitlán to control the region and gain more allied Indian forces. They also built 13 ships to blockade* the capital, which was built on several islands in a lake and could be reached only across bridges. The final siege* of Tenochtitlán lasted several months and destroyed most of the city. Thousands of Aztecs—including Cuitlahuac—died of starvation and DISEASES as well as from the constant fighting. Cortés's forces finally defeated the Aztecs in August 1521.

After the Conquest. The Spanish monarchy recognized Cortés as the conqueror and governor of NEW SPAIN, and he sent two of his lieutenants to conquer GUATEMALA and HONDURAS to expand his territory. When one of them, Cristóbal de Olid, rebelled against him, Cortés left Tenochtitlán (already renamed Mexico City) to confront Olid. While he was gone, Cortés's enemies convinced the monarchy to strengthen its control over New Spain. In 1529, King Charles V granted Cortés the title of *marqués del Valle de Oaxaca* and gave him 22 Mexican towns in *encomienda*, but Cortés never regained the governorship. Instead, he spent much of the rest of his life defending himself against lawsuits and investigations that arose from his activities in New

Spain. Although he had conquered the largest single community in America, Cortés died still seeking the status and riches he believed he had been denied. (*See also* **Imperialism; Spain and the Spanish Empire.**)

Costa Rica

Costa Rica is the third-smallest country in CENTRAL AMERICA, but despite its limited size and population, it has become one of the most prosperous, educated, healthy, and democratic nations in all of Latin America. It has achieved this without the benefit of resources such as oil, gold and silver, or precious gems.

The Geography of Costa Rica

See map in Central America (vol. I).

Although all of Costa Rica lies within the tropics, its varied geography creates areas in which the climate ranges from hot and humid to cool and dry. Among its most important geographical features are the mountain ranges that run from the country's northwestern border with NICARAGUA to its southeastern border with PANAMA. These ranges include several active VOLCANOES that have deposited much rich volcanic soil. This fertile land benefits local AGRICULTURE, especially the COFFEE INDUSTRY, which is Costa Rica's main source of revenue. Those living in the high valleys within the mountains enjoy a mild, springlike climate.

Costa Rica's heartland is the great Central Valley, and the country's first important cities—SAN JOSÉ (the capital), Cartago, Heredia, and Alajuela—grew up in the valley's Central Plateau. Most of the colonial population lived in and around these cities, and the national culture, character, and values, such as democracy, liberty, equality, peace, and EDUCATION, came from this region. Costa Ricans brought these values with them as they gradually occupied other regions of the country following independence in the 1800s.

The coastal areas on either side of the mountains differ in climate and geography. To the north, tropical RAIN FORESTS have heavy rains and high temperatures most of the year. The climate in this area is ideally suited to growing BANANAS, the country's second most important crop. Along the Pacific coast the climate is much drier, especially in the northwest.

Early History: From Independence to the National War

Costa Rica was part of the Spanish empire in America until the early 1820s. In 1823, the former Spanish provinces of GUATEMALA, EL SALVADOR, Nicaragua, HONDURAS, and Costa Rica declared their independence from Spain and formed the United Provinces of Central America. Meanwhile, the city of San José was establishing its dominance over the other cities of the Central Plateau. In 1835, San José defeated the other three cities in the War of the League and emerged as the nation's

Leading the Way

One of Costa Rica's first civilian presidents, Ricardo Jiménez Oreamuno, was also one of its finest. During his three separate terms as president, between 1910 and 1928, he ran the country according to its constitution and supported civil rights, economic growth, and education for all citizens. His skillful handling of foreign affairs kept Costa Rica safely apart from the political strife that was raging elsewhere in Central America. Indeed, Costa Rica gained international praise as a progressive and orderly state.

capital. Because of Costa Rica's relative political stability, the province of Guanacaste chose to join Costa Rica rather than Nicaragua in 1824.

Carillo and Coffee Transform Costa Rica. An important figure in Costa Rica's early history was Braulio Carrillo Colina, who served as president from 1835 to 1837 and again from 1838 to 1842. His two main achievements were to separate Costa Rica from the United Provinces and to promote the growing of coffee, for which the moderate climate and soil of the Central Valley were ideal. By separating Costa Rica from the United Provinces in 1838, Carillo helped his country avoid the deep divisions and violent uprisings that plagued other Central American nations. By encouraging coffee production, he played a key role in Costa Rica's economic development and modernization.

One of the most notable aspects of the new coffee industry was the way in which Carillo promoted it. Instead of giving large grants of land to wealthy growers, he gave young coffee plants to peasant farmers. This ensured that many more people would benefit from the new crop and prevented the serious resentments over land distribution that troubled other Latin American nations. Also unlike other Latin American countries, the Costa Rican government welcomed FOREIGN INVESTMENT and TRADE. British investors paid to grow and ship Costa Rican coffee. The government's openness to foreign capital contributed to Costa Rica's remarkably even and sustained economic development.

During the 1840s, coffee growing expanded dramatically, aided by Carillo's ambitious program to build roads. A coffee elite emerged, made up of both foreigners and ordinary Costa Ricans who invested in the coffee trade. They grew wealthy during the boom years of the 1840s and purchased their own land for coffee production. But they did not exploit or drive the independent peasant farmers out of business as happened in many other areas of Latin America. This new elite became the nation's dominant group, and they played a major role in Costa Rica's development.

The National War. In 1855, a troublesome United States adventurer named William WALKER conquered Nicaragua and sent troops into Guanacaste. In response, Costa Rica sent a force that succeeded in pushing Walker back into Nicaragua. In another battle against Walker, at the town of Rivas, a soldier named Juan Santamaría singlehandedly destroyed Walker's stronghold. He was killed in the effort, but he became a national hero. This so-called NATIONAL WAR gave Costa Ricans a strong sense of nationhood. However, it came at a price. An outbreak of cholera* struck the Costa Rican forces, who brought the DISEASE back to the Central Valley. The epidemic that followed killed about 10,000 people—almost 10 percent of the population.

* **cholera** serious intestinal disease that causes diarrhea, vomiting, cramps, and often death

From National War to Civil War

Following the National War, Costa Rica was thrown into political turmoil until 1870, when General Tomás Guardia Gutiérrez seized power. Despite his antidemocratic rule, he contributed to the nation's political

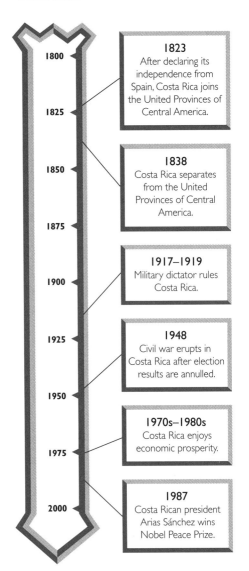

1800

1823
After declaring its independence from Spain, Costa Rica joins the United Provinces of Central America.

1825

1838
Costa Rica separates from the United Provinces of Central America.

1850

1875

1917–1919
Military dictator rules Costa Rica.

1900

1925

1948
Civil war erupts in Costa Rica after election results are annulled.

1950

1970s–1980s
Costa Rica enjoys economic prosperity.

1975

1987
Costa Rican president Arias Sánchez wins Nobel Peace Prize.

2000

* **Great Depression** period in the 1930s marked by low economic activity and high unemployment

* **Communist** referring to a social system in which land, goods, and the means of production are owned by the state or community rather than by individuals

and economic development in two important ways. In 1871, he introduced Costa Rica's first constitution, which, with some changes made in 1949, remains in effect. He also began the construction of Costa Rica's RAILROAD.

The Railroad and the Banana Trade.   The railroad was originally planned as a quick and inexpensive way to transport coffee from the interior to ports on the Caribbean coast. However, the tropical climate and diseases—such as malaria and dysentery—created problems for the builder, a United States investor named Minor Cooper Keith. Because Costa Ricans from the Central Valley did not want to work in such unhealthful areas, Keith imported workers from various Caribbean islands, particularly JAMAICA. These workers and their descendants became the main inhabitants of the Caribbean coastal area and gave it a character that was different from the rest of the country. Only since 1945 have other Costa Ricans moved there in significant numbers, and the Afro–Costa Ricans have moved to other regions of the country.

Another major problem for Keith was that he had to begin building the railroad from the coast, because there was no way to bring supplies to the interior coffee-growing regions. Meanwhile, because coffee could not reach the coast until the railroad was completed, coffee revenues could not pay for construction. Keith hit upon the idea of financing the construction by planting bananas on the land that ran alongside the tracks he was building. The plan was a huge success, and by 1880 bananas had become the country's second-leading export. The railroad and banana companies also built hospitals, schools, docks, and water treatment facilities in this previously undeveloped area.

Democracy and Reform.   In 1889, President Bernardo Soto Alfaro was defeated by challenger José Rodríguez Zeledón. This was the first time that power in Costa Rica had changed hands peacefully in a free election, and it marked the beginning of true democracy in the country. Except for the brief military dictatorship of Federico Tinoco Granados, from 1917 to 1919, Costa Ricans enjoyed democratic rule and domestic peace for the next 60 years. During that time, free public education was established, and several social reforms, such as the establishment of a minimum wage, were enacted. However, economic problems caused by World War I and the Great Depression* led to calls for greater social justice and economic opportunity for laborers and peasants. In 1931, the first Communist* party in Costa Rica was formed to push for additional reforms for farmers and workers.

The dominant political party, that of the National Republicans, met this challenge by electing the anti-Communist León Cortés Castro as president in 1936. However, Cortés had a poor record on HUMAN RIGHTS, and he angered many Costa Ricans by using political tricks to deny the Communists seats in Congress. In 1940, he was succeeded by Rafael Calderón Guardia. Unlike Cortés, Calderón undertook major reforms, such as establishing a social security system, national health insurance, retirement and disability pensions, and protections for workers—including the right to organize unions and to strike. He also founded the country's first university, distributed uncultivated land to anyone who agreed to develop it, and gave shoes to poor schoolchildren.

The middle class opposed many of Calderón's policies and the seemingly irresponsible way in which he spent money for his projects. They also opposed the Communists, and in 1940, they formed what later became the Social Democratic Party. The election in 1944 was marked by occasional violence and charges of fraud, and in the following two years, Costa Rica experienced numerous street protests, gang clashes, and terrorism. In this tense atmosphere, a man named José FIGUERES FERRER sought support to overthrow the National Republican government. Guatemalan president Juan José Arévalo Bermejo promised to provide arms and men if he needed them.

Civil War and Its Aftermath.

The elections of 1948 resulted in a victory for the opponents of the existing government. But the Congress, which was still controlled by the National Republicans, canceled the results and stayed in power. Figueres called for arms and men from Guatemala, and in March 1948, his forces seized several strategic locations in the south. The rebels were prepared to invade San José when the government called for a peace conference. The parties reached an agreement, overturned the election results, and declared the opposition candidate, Otilio Ulate Blanco, president. The rebels were pardoned, and Figueres organized a junta* that ruled along with Ulate Blanco.

The junta upheld the reforms of the previous years and attempted to make sweeping changes in the constitution. These included abolishing the army in favor of a national police force and creating an electoral tribunal* to ensure fair and open elections. Although most of these changes were overturned by the Congress, several of them, including the electoral tribunal, were kept. In the end, the junta made only minor changes to the existing constitution.

Costa Rica Since 1950

In a sweeping victory in 1953, Figueres was elected the first president under the new constitution. His party, the National Liberation Party (PLN) has since become the dominant political force in Costa Rica. It encouraged economic growth and the expansion of education throughout the country, and it delivered social, economic, and political development without resorting to either Communist or extremely conservative* governments. This helped Costa Rica maintain its democracy and its strong economy throughout the mid-1900s.

From the 1950s through the 1980s, Costa Rican leadership alternated between the PLN and various opposition groups, demonstrating that true democratic politics were to be a permanent feature of Costa Rican life. Economic prosperity continued unchecked until the late 1970s and early 1980s. At that time, concerns about the SANDINISTA revolution

* **junta** small group of people who run a government, usually after seizing power by force

* **tribunal** court of justice

* **conservative** inclined to maintain existing political and social views, conditions, and institutions

31

* **inflation** sharp increase in prices due to an increase in the amount of money or credit relative to available goods and services

in neighboring Nicaragua, low coffee prices, and high PETROLEUM costs led to high inflation* and a growing national debt. Costa Rica suffered economic setbacks that were compounded when the United States pressured the government to play a more active role in overthrowing the Sandinistas. Many refugees, especially from Nicaragua, added to the country's social and financial burdens. Costa Rica's difficulties led to the breakup of the PLN's main political opponent, Unidad, which had ruled the country from 1978 to 1982.

In 1986, Oscar ARIAS SÁNCHEZ was elected president. He worked to reduce the national debt and to eliminate Costa Rica as a base for United States anti-Sandinista activities. After winning the Nobel Peace Prize in 1987, Arias gained respect as a leading international figure, which helped him contribute further to political stability in Central America. His successor, Rafael Ángel Calderón Fournier, brought a new party, the Christian Social Unity Party (PUSC) to political power. The PUSC has become a strong rival for the PLN, ensuring that the PLN will not dominate Costa Rican politics and that the country's democratic tradition will continue. (*See also* **Geography; Spain and the Spanish Empire; United States–Latin American Relations; Universities and Colleges.**)

Council of the Indies

* **clergy** priests and other church officials qualified to perform church ceremonies

The Council of the Indies was the institution responsible for overseeing the affairs of the Spanish colonies in America. It was located in Spain's capital, Madrid, and dealt with all political, financial, legal, military, and commercial activities in Spanish America. The council also handled religious matters, appointing clergy* and deciding which papal decrees applied to the American colonies. No major project could be undertaken in America without the council's approval.

The council reached the peak of its power during the 1500s. During the 1600s, it lost authority to other councils and officials favored by the king. Eventually, many unqualified people purchased positions on the council—including a nine-year-old boy who was appointed as a reward for services performed by his father. In 1717, King Philip V reduced its power by appointing a minister of the Indies. In the late 1700s, the council was taken over by men with personal experience in America, and it regained much of its former power and prestige. By 1790, it was again the only institution in Spain devoted to American affairs. The council was finally abolished in 1834, after Spain lost most of its American colonies. (*See also* **Bourbon Reforms; Spain and the Spanish Empire.**)

Counterinsurgency

During the late 1950s and early 1960s, many developing countries, particularly in LATIN AMERICA, faced insurgencies (armed uprisings) that threatened to overthrow their governments. The leaders of these uprisings were often Communists*, and many of them received support from the Soviet Union. In response to the threat of Communist takeovers in these countries, United States president John

* **Communist** person who advocates communism—a social system in which land, goods, and the means of production are owned by the state or community rather than by individuals

F. Kennedy developed the policy of counterinsurgency to contain the spread of COMMUNISM.

The Rise of Nationalism.

Since achieving independence, Latin American countries have often been ruled by military DICTATORSHIPS. In many cases, the dictators were helped into power by foreign nations, especially by the United States. Such military governments were often challenged by armed groups within their country protesting inequality, injustice, and foreign influence. Most of these rebel groups called themselves nationalists because they considered the existing governments too closely tied to foreign nations. The goal of the nationalists was to establish governments that put the interests of the common people before those of the rich and the foreign investors and companies that seemed to wield so much power and influence.

After Communists overthrew the Russian government in 1917, the United States became more concerned about such armed uprisings. Concerned about possible Communist takeovers in developing countries, the United States enacted policies that would promote peaceful reform instead of violent revolution. United States concerns about political turmoil in Latin America peaked in 1959, when Communist Fidel CASTRO seized power in CUBA. Shortly after being elected in 1960, President Kennedy stated that "the most critical spot on the globe nowadays is Latin America, which seems made-to-order for the Communists."

Counterinsurgency During the 1960s.

The United States counterinsurgency policy was based on the idea that military action alone was not an effective way to defeat insurgencies. The conditions that caused people to oppose their governments were primarily economic and social, so the solutions must address these problems first. Economic assistance was to be provided by both private and public sources from around the world. The United States government also believed that economic reforms—such as better management of natural resources—would stimulate ECONOMIC DEVELOPMENT, enable people to improve their standard of living, and ultimately lead to greater democracy in Latin American countries.

Counterinsurgency also focused on fighting Communist attempts to undermine these reform programs. According to the plan, Latin American military forces would be encouraged to engage in civic action projects, such as LITERACY programs and the construction of medical clinics. It was hoped that these projects would improve conditions for the local people and in doing so, win their support. Local police and ARMED FORCES would be instructed to take military action against rebels who refused to accept a peaceful approach to reform.

In 1961, Kennedy created the ALLIANCE FOR PROGRESS to put his counterinsurgency plans into action. The Alliance offered a long-term plan for Latin American economic stability and political development while providing short-term military assistance against Communist guerrilla* activities. The United States established a school near the PANAMA CANAL

* **guerrilla** referring to a group that uses surprise raids to obstruct or harass an enemy or overthrow a government

33

Hunting Guerrillas

During the 1960s, the United States provided military training and equipment to several Latin American nations to help them fight guerrillas. This United States support was instrumental in the Bolivian army's defeat and capture of guerrilla leader Ernesto "Che" Guevara in 1967. In his diary, Guevara wrote that he was amazed at the ability of the Bolivian military to find and attack his forces despite their evasive maneuvers. Guevara did not know that the Bolivian troops were using airplanes with United States-made infrared sensors to track his every move.

See
color plate 12,
vol. 4.

to train Latin American military forces in the various aspects of counterinsurgency. United States military advisers and small teams of highly skilled Special Forces (the Green Berets) provided military instruction. Kennedy also changed the focus of the military assistance program from providing weapons and equipment to fight foreign invasions to targeting internal threats to the security of Latin American nations. Most of these United States counterinsurgency efforts focused on the countries of GUATEMALA, VENEZUELA, COLOMBIA, PERU, and BOLIVIA.

During the 1960s, Latin American governments were extremely successful in fighting Communist insurgencies. This seemed to prove that counterinsurgency was an effective strategy. However, their success was probably the result of factors other than the counterinsurgency program. For example, none of the Communist groups was able to duplicate Castro's *foco* model of insurgency, in which small, armed rural groups led resistance to the government and created the conditions for widespread revolution. Many of the rebel movements were torn apart by different factions competing for leadership. Moreover, many Latin American governments successfully responded to insurgencies either by using military force or by passing reforms when revolution became a real threat.

Counterinsurgency Since 1970. Despite the successes of the 1960s, the threat of Communist insurgency in Latin America reappeared in the late 1970s. The Communist-inspired SANDINISTAS took over NICARAGUA, and guerrillas became active in Guatemala and other nations. Participants in these insurgencies were better organized and better funded than earlier groups had been, and they enjoyed wider support from foreign countries, including the United States. These factors, combined with its new emphasis on HUMAN RIGHTS, prompted the United States to limit its counterinsurgency efforts. Even so, the United States government provided considerable aid to some countries, particularly EL SALVADOR.

Most insurgencies in Latin America seemed under control by the 1990s. Because the fall of the Soviet Union removed the major source of funding for most insurgencies and because democracy has arisen in many Latin American countries, there is hope that peaceful political solutions will replace violent ones. However, the conditions that led to insurgencies still exist in most Latin American countries, and money from the drug trade has added a new dimension to the problem. In addition, Latin America's long history of insurgency invites caution about assuming that armed uprisings there are a thing of the past. (*See also* **Contras; Cuban Revolution; Drugs and Drug Trade; Guerrilla Movements; Nationalism; Soviet–Latin American Relations; United States–Latin American Relations.**)

Coups

See *Dictatorships, Military;* **individual leaders.**

Cowboys

See *Gauchos.*

Crafts

° **pre-Columbian** before the arrival of Christopher Columbus and other Europeans in the Americas in the 1490s

° **indigenous** referring to the original inhabitants of a region

° **artisan** skilled crafts worker

Peruvian woman weaves a brightly colored, striped skirt for her daughter. A man in Guatemala carves a long-horned mask that depicts the Tzultacae, the ancient devil gods of his people. In Brazil, a family makes small dolls to sell to tourists. All of them are crafts workers. Crafts—including weaving, wood carving, pottery making, leather working, and metalworking—have played an important role in Latin American cultures since pre-Columbian* times. Some of these handmade goods, such as tools, furniture, clothing, and toys, are intended for everyday use. Others are works of art or objects of special religious significance.

Folk art is the name for crafts based on the cultural, ethnic, religious, and ceremonial traditions of ordinary people within a culture. In Latin America, those traditions reflect a blend of indigenous*, African, and European influences. The indigenous heritage is especially strong in rural areas, particularly the Andes, northeastern Brazil, and certain regions of Mexico, Guatemala, Panama, and the Amazon basin. Jewelry, dolls, baskets, paintings and sculptures, textiles, and other items that artisans* create using traditional materials and methods are called *arte popular, arte folklórico,* or *artesanías* in Spanish and *artesenato* in Portuguese.

Weaving is one of Latin America's oldest and most important crafts. Although modern metal looms and knitting machines are widely available, many Indians, such as this man, prefer to practice the traditional weaving methods of their ancestors.

° **archaeologist** scientist who studies past
human cultures, usually by excavating ruins

Sleeping in the Air

One Latin American craft item now
known to people around the world
is the hammock—a long, narrow,
woven net in which to sleep. With
its ends tied to the walls of a house
or to two trees, a hammock keeps
the sleeper off the ground, offering
protection from snakes, insects, or
dampness. At first, the Europeans
were astonished by this lightweight,
easy-to-move bed used by the
Brazilian Indians. However, they
soon learned that it was the most
comfortable way to sleep in Brazil's
hot climate. Brazilian and other
weavers still make hammocks of
cotton thread or other plant fibers,
decorating them with special
stitches and dyeing them bright
colors, such as yellow and orange.

° **loom** framework on which threads are
stretched for weaving

° **synthetic** produced artificially

See
color plate 10,
vol. 2.

In pre-Columbian cultures, the most skilled and gifted artisans
made high-quality jewelry, cloth, and stonework for their rulers and
gods. Other crafts workers made goods for the ordinary people. Few
everyday items from these cultures have survived. That is because many
of them were made of perishable materials, such as fiber, straw, or wax.
However, many items made of baked clay have endured, and these pottery pieces have given archaeologists* much important information
about early cultures.

The arrival of Europeans in the Americas in the late 1400s had a major
impact on the indigenous peoples and their crafts. Some craft traditions
were lost when Indian tribes were killed by European diseases and warfare. In addition, the colonists often prohibited Indian artisans from representing their own gods and designs in their crafts. Instead, some of
these artisans were directed to make works representing Christian images.
For instance, the wood-carvers of Guatemala became famous among Europeans for their beautifully carved and painted statues of Catholic saints.

Today many Latin Americans practice a blend of Christian and indigenous religions, which is reflected in their craft work. Both indigenous gods and Roman Catholic saints are now represented in the masks
and carvings made by Guatemalan artisans. Similarly, Peruvian wax
workers create special objects for use in both Christian and indigenous
religious ceremonies. To celebrate Catholic Holy Week, they build altars
called *andas* covered with candles in the shape of birds, flowers, bells,
dancers, national symbols, and crosses. For *el pago de la pachamama*, the
festival of the earth goddess, wax workers make candles of animal fat to
ask the goddess to protect their animals.

Since the mid-1900s, modern industry, technology, and global trade
have brought more changes to Latin American crafts. Manufactured
goods have become widely available, and these have taken the place of
some handcrafts. For instance, people living around Lake TITICACA in the
southern Andes mountains make rafts and other objects from a local
plant called *totora*. It takes a raft maker a month to build a raft, which lasts
only one year. This ancient craft is slowly vanishing, as the local people replace their rafts with motorboats, which cost more but last much longer.

Modern technology has also brought many changes to Latin American weaving, one of the region's most ancient and important crafts.
Many early cultures, especially those of the highly skilled MAYA and
INCA, wove patterned cloth on lightweight, portable wooden looms*.
Today, some Latin American weavers use modern metal looms and knitting machines. The designs of their woven goods are changing as well,
as they incorporate new synthetic* colors and styles to make their
goods more appealing to tourists and other international buyers.
Weavers have also created new textile crafts to replace older arts that are
being abandoned. For instance, among the KUNA people of Panama, designs showing scenes from Kuna life were once painted on people's bodies. Now, these patterns adorn a type of blouse called a *mola* that is worn
by Kuna women. Other ancient Latin American weaving styles are now
admired and copied in other parts of the world—as in India and China,
where factories produce textiles with traditional Guatemalan patterns of
tie-dyed threads.

The growth of international travel and tourism has also affected the practice of traditional crafts in Latin America. Increased tourism has spawned vast quantities of "airport art"—goods that are produced to sell to outsiders. Some of these are authentic crafts, made by people working in their own traditions, but others are produced quickly, and sometimes shabbily, in workshops far from their places of origin. For example, some non-Indian workers in Mexico City produce "Mayan" carved-stone animal statues for the tourist trade, and weavers in southern Mexico churn out "Navajo" rugs.

In spite of these changes, the authentic crafts tradition remains strong throughout much of Latin America. Many artisans still make pottery and other items using the shapes, colors, and designs once used by their distant ancestors. As international contact expands and world cultures continue to blend, Latin American crafts are becoming more and more important, not only as trade goods but as expressions of their distinct cultures. (*See also* **Art, Colonial to Modern; Retablos and Ex-Votos; Textiles and Textile Industry.**)

Creole

*A*lthough the term *Creole* meant different things in different places, in the colonial era it generally referred to a person of European ancestry who was born in the Americas. In Brazil, the Portuguese word for Creole, *crioulo,* referred to a black person of African descent who was born in the colony. In the Spanish colonies, a Creole— or *criollo*—was usually an American-born person of Spanish descent. Because there were many unions between Spanish men and Indian or mixed-race women, not all *criollos* were of purely European ancestry. The *criollos* were a privileged group that owned much of the colonies' land and wealth. However, they often competed for power and privileges with the even more elite Spanish-born officials, who were called *peninsulares* for the Iberian Peninsula from which they came. Tension between *criollos* and *peninsulares* over political and economic privileges fueled the Latin American independence movements of the early 1800s.

Today Latin Americans often use the word *creole* to describe things that are native to a country or typical of it, such as "creole cuisine." In English-speaking places that were once ruled by France or Spain—such as Louisiana and the British Caribbean—Creoles are native-born people of mixed descent, often with some African ancestry. The mixed European-African language that people of the former Caribbean colonies speak is also called Creole. (*See also* **Race and Ethnicity.**)

Crime and Punishment, Colonial

*F*rom the beginning, crime and violence were part of the conquest and settlement of Latin America. Today some people consider the Spanish conquest itself a crime. It was certainly violent, at least much of the time. Over time, as the colonies became more settled and Spain established formal governments, the authorities' attitudes toward criminal or violent behavior changed. Brutalities that went unpunished during the early years of conquest were later treated as criminal actions. For example, branding and enslaving INDIANS were made illegal in Central America in the 1530s. However, the illegal trade in Indian slaves flourished for two reasons: because many government officials participated in the trade and because those who *were* punished received only light sentences. Later, however, the colonial authorities enforced the laws against enslaving the Indians more strictly.

Geography also played a part in colonial justice. Officials were much more concerned with controlling crime in the cities of Latin America than in the countryside. Also, as usual, justice did not apply equally to all people. The race, class, and sex of criminals and victims determined the nature and severity of the punishment. This was true throughout colonial Latin America and, to some extent, in the judicial systems that developed after independence.

Crimes and Criminals.

Colonial records include many references to crimes against property and against individuals. Crimes against the state, such as treason, were rare but were considered extremely serious. Officials regarded robbery, assault, and murder as more serious and therefore more deserving of punishment than such "lesser" crimes as the abuse of Indians or slaves. Murder was one of the few acts that almost everyone in colonial society considered criminal. For this reason, records of murders are more thorough than those of any other crime.

Statistics show that most rural murders took place after work or on Sundays. These crimes usually involved people who knew each other. Many offenders—especially those who used weapons, such as butcher knives—were young men. Crimes against women generally took place in the home and were committed by a family member or someone the victim knew. The most common of these crimes were physical abuse, wife beating, rape, and kidnapping.

Justice for Some.

Members of colonial society were not equal in the eyes of the law. Spanish officials believed that *castas,* or people of mixed race, had lower moral character than others. The authorities expected mixed-race people to engage in crime and violence, were slow to punish such behavior, and often put up with high levels of criminality. However, when the authorities *did* take action against criminal mestizos*, mulattos*, and others of mixed race, they dispensed severe punishments as warnings to others.

* **mestizo** person of mixed European and Indian ancestry

* **mulatto** person of mixed black and white ancestry

Indians had a special status under the law, which treated them as minors no matter what their age. The Spanish thought that the Indians lacked full reasoning powers and therefore would be inclined to commit wrongdoing. The authorities considered Indians' crimes less serious than those of whites and generally gave them milder punishments. Although it may seem that this leniency benefited the Indians, it did so at the cost of denying them full status in society.

Latin America had a large body of laws to control the behavior of black slaves. In Lima, Peru, for example, blacks could not carry weapons or leave the city without official permission, and they were

Crackdown on Colonial Crime

Spain's most successful attempt to control crime occurred in New Spain in 1710. The authorities set up the *acordada* to pursue and try criminals, especially bandits in the countryside. The *acordada* extended jurisdiction to include Mexico's cities. It functioned independently, with its own judge and prisons. Neither the government nor the citizens interfered with the sentences it accorded. A single judge at the *acordada* heard almost 43,000 cases between 1782 and 1808—an average of about 1,654 cases a year. The 1812 Constitution of Cádiz ended the *acordada* in Mexico.

° **viceroy** one who governs a country or province as a monarch's representative; royally appointed official

° **captain-general** title of provincial rulers in colonial Latin America whose main duty was the military defense of a territory

° **ecclesiastical** relating to a church

° **cleric** member of the clergy

° **republic** government in which citizens elect officials to represent them and govern according to law

compelled to observe a curfew, a law that required them to be home by a certain hour. Punishments for breaking these rules were meant to be harsh: 300 lashes with a whip, exile, or hanging. Well-connected slaveholders, however, often bribed officials to overlook the misdeeds of their slaves. The most common offense slaves committed was running away.

WOMEN were also ill-served by the colonial justice system. They were often victimized in their own homes, frequently by husbands lashing out in anger. Many women were afraid to file charges for fear of angering their abusers further. Those who did seek help under the law received little relief. Male judges questioned them closely, searching for any weakness in their reputations or behavior. If a judge found such a blemish on a woman's reputation, her husband's brutality toward her was excused. If a wife engaged in sexual activity with someone other than her husband, the husband could legally kill both his wife and her lover under colonial law. Only men of the lower classes, however, committed these acts of retribution. Upper-class men typically ignored their wives' indiscretions in the fear that any action they undertook would result in public knowledge of their wives' unfaithfulness. Legal acts of retribution applied only to men—if a wife killed an unfaithful husband, she could expect no mercy from the law.

Wives were not the only women who received a bad deal from the colonial system of crime and punishment. Crimes such as rape and kidnapping against unmarried women often went unpunished. The authorities regarded rape as a serious crime only when a married woman was raped—and then only because it damaged her husband's honor.

Courts and Punishments. Several types of colonial officials shared responsibility for dealing with crime. In terms of police action, Spanish colonial cities and towns had *alguaciles,* sheriffs who captured criminals and were paid a percentage of the fines that the courts collected from criminals. Officials called *alguaciles mayores* did the same thing on a larger scale for the regional courts, or AUDIENCIAS. After independence, the nations of Latin America developed police forces. One of the best-known of these forces was the RURALES, or rural policemen, of Mexico in the late 1800s and early 1900s.

Various colonial courts tried criminal cases and sentenced criminals. On the local level, civic officials called alcaldes tried cases. People who wanted to appeal the verdict of an alcalde's court could take their case to a provincial court, where an official called an *alcalde mayor* or a *corregidor* would hear the request. An appeal from the provincial court went to the high court of the *audiencia,* which was the final court of appeal for criminal cases.

Special courts outside the criminal justice system heard certain types of cases. Viceroys* and captains-general* held military trials for soldiers accused of committing crimes, and ecclesiastical* courts handled cases involving clerics*. (After the Latin American colonies achieved independence, founders of the new republics* encountered much resistance when they tried to limit the power and privileges of the military and ecclesiastical courts.)

Although formal judicial systems existed, colonial justice was handled informally, especially in rural areas. Often a hacendado, or plantation owner, took it upon himself to discipline workers and to punish theft and assault. People in the cities were much more likely to go through formal court proceedings before receiving punishment, especially if they were white or of mixed race.

Colonial authorities based punishment not just on the crime that had been committed but on the criminal's race, class, health, gender, and previous criminal record. Homosexual behavior was considered a serious crime and was certain to carry the death sentence. Otherwise, judges rarely ordered the death penalty, except for rapist-murderers and highwaymen who had robbed and killed their victims. Most other murderers were convicted and sentenced to labor in private homes. Many male criminals found themselves working in textile workshops. Women's punishments were lighter than men's, but they also received sentences of labor in workshops or in private homes. Whipping was a common punishment for Indians, black slaves, and *castas*. Spaniards, however, were not whipped.

A Colonial Pardon. Criminal justice in colonial South America had a distinctive feature: the pardon. From time to time, the Spanish crown declared general pardons to celebrate such events as the coronation of a new ruler, the birth of a prince or princess, or a royal marriage. On learning that a pardon had been declared, colonial officials threw open the jail doors and released many prisoners, although some crimes, such as robbery and fraud, were not excused by pardons. A pardon also meant that any criminal who turned himself or herself in to the law during these periods of amnesty could avoid punishment. In addition, viceroys had the power to lessen or cancel court-ordered punishments for individual criminals. (*See also* **Laws and Legal Systems.**)

Cristero Rebellion

° **mestizo** person of mixed European and Indian ancestry

° **anticlericalism** opposition to the influence of the clergy in the affairs of state

° **clergy** priests and other church officials qualified to perform church ceremonies

In the late 1920s, a peasant uprising called the Cristero Rebellion brought MEXICO to the edge of political chaos. The rebels, known as Cristeros, were rural Catholic Indians and mestizos* who often shouted *"¡Viva Cristo Rey!"* (Long Live Christ the King!) in battle. Most fought to defend their faith, although some joined the rebellion to fight for land reform.

The revolt was rooted in the growing anticlericalism* of Mexican government and business, especially in northern Mexico. One of the politicians most determined to limit the power of the CATHOLIC CHURCH was Plutarco Elías CALLES, president from 1924 to 1928. He placed severe restrictions on the church—such as forcing priests to register with the government and closing church schools. The clergy* responded by calling a strike, ending all church services. This threw faithful Catholic peasants into a panic and sparked the rebellion.

Although the government claimed that Catholic priests had organized the peasant uprising, only about 45 of the nation's nearly 3,600 priests took part in the Cristero Rebellion. By mid-1927, more than 20,000 Cristeros were operating in small guerrilla* bands. Although the government won some early victories against these bands, the rebels received strong popular support. In 1928, they moved to a new level of military action under the leadership of an army officer named Enrique Gorostieta.

At the end of 1928, the federal government had launched a major attack on the Cristeros in Jalisco, but the rebels escaped. The following spring, the Cristeros scored a victory when 900 of them defeated a federal force that was more than three times larger. It soon became evident that neither side would be able to win the conflict decisively. In mid-1929, at the urging of the United States ambassador, the Mexican government reached a peace agreement with Catholic officials in Mexico and Rome. The Mexican government loosened its restrictions on the church, the priests began holding services again, and the Cristero Rebellion was over. (*See also* **Anticlericalism.**)

Cuba

Cuba is the largest island in the CARIBBEAN SEA and one of the first places in the Americas that Spain claimed as a colony. After 400 years of Spanish rule, the people of Cuba achieved their independence only to find themselves bound by economic and political ties to the United States. After their victory in 1959, revolutionaries* in Cuba redirected those ties to the Soviet Union, establishing not only a new government but a new Communist* social order. Since then, Cuba has remained the only Communist state in the Americas, and the United States government has remained firmly opposed to it.

The Land

Cuba is a long, narrow island about 745 miles long and 120 miles wide at its widest point. The nation also includes several smaller, nearby islands. Cuba lies just 90 miles south of Florida and 75 miles east of Mexico's Yucatán peninsula. This convenient location and Cuba's fine natural harbors have shaped its history since the late 1400s. Cuba was an ideal starting point for Spain's voyages of conquest in North and Central America. Later Cuba's position at the crossroads of Caribbean and Atlantic shipping routes made the island a major marketplace. In the 1960s, when Cuba became a Communist state, the island's nearness to the United States caused United States leaders to regard it as a dangerous enemy on their very doorstep.

Much of Cuba consists of a fairly flat, grassy plain, dotted here and there with royal palms. Hills and low mountain ranges cover about 40 percent of the island's total area. The highest mountains are in the east in the range called the Sierra Maestra, where a peak called Turquino rises to 6,560 feet above sea level. Surrounded by shallow tropical waters, Cuba's picturesque coastline has many bays and beaches. The island nation also has fertile soil and a warm climate that are ideal for agriculture.

See map in Caribbean Antilles (vol. I).

The Pope's Historic Visit

In January 1998, Pope John Paul II spent five days in Cuba—the first visit by a pope to the island. The pope had long been a foe of communism, and Fidel Castro, Cuba's Communist president, had been an enemy of religion. But the pope came to Cuba hoping that Castro would allow the Catholic church to play a larger role in the lives of the Cuban people. Castro benefited too. The visit of an important world leader put Cuba at the center of the global stage and placed Castro on an equal footing with other international statesmen. At the end of his visit, the pope conducted an outdoor mass, attended by several hundred thousand Cubans, in Havana's Revolution Square.

History

Cuba's recorded history begins with the arrival of the Spaniards and is generally organized into four periods. The colonial* period was by far the longest. The second period, the time of the movement toward independence, began after the mid-1800s. Cuban independence in 1898 touched off a third period, one in which the United States had a large stake in Cuba's economy. In 1959, the CUBAN REVOLUTION ended that period in the island's history and created Cuba as it is today.

Colonial Cuba. On October 27, 1492, when Christopher COLUMBUS landed in Cuba and claimed this land for Spain, he believed that he was in Asia. The Spaniards soon learned otherwise and explored Cuba from their base on nearby HISPANIOLA. In 1510, the conquistador* Diego Velázquez led the conquest of Cuba and its Carib, Taino, and Arawak Indian inhabitants. Velázquez then ordered an Indian named Hatuey, who had headed the Indians' three-month resistance to the Spanish takeover, to be burned at the stake. Another conquistador, Pánfilo de NARVÁEZ, also massacred Cuban Indians. Within a few generations, war, enslavement, and European DISEASES killed most of the Indians on the island.

By 1515, the Spanish had established seven settlements in Cuba. One of them, HAVANA, later became the capital. Spain's first interest in Cuba was gold, which the Spaniards mined using Indian labor. Gold mining and plantation agriculture made some of the first Spanish colonists in Cuba very wealthy. Hearing of even greater riches to the west, Velázquez sent Hernán CORTÉS to conquer Mexico. By the mid-1520s, Cuba had been stripped of its meager supply of gold, and the island was overshadowed by Spain's grander and wealthier conquests elsewhere in the Americas.

For the next 250 years, Cuba was the gateway to the Spanish empire. Its primary business was to supply and repair Spain's ships for ocean crossings and to house those ships' passengers and crews. Although some colonists operated sugar plantations worked by African slaves, most Cuban farmers produced food for local use. From time to time, other European nations tried to take over Cuba, but Spain had built strong forts to defend the island. Only once did Cuba fall into other hands—the British captured Havana in 1762 but returned it to Spanish control the following year in exchange for Florida.

In the 1790s, dramatic events on another Caribbean island led to significant changes in Cuba. The black slaves of Saint Domingue (present-day HAITI) rose in a violent rebellion that destroyed that island's sugar industry. As the demand for sugar increased, Cuba became a major sugar producer—and a major importer of slaves. From 1790 to 1865, nearly 440,000 African slaves were brought to the island. Sugar produced enormous wealth, and the island's total population boomed along with its economy. The harbors of Havana and Santiago de Cuba bustled with trade, including business with the United States. Cushioned by their economic good fortune and fearful of slave revolt, Cubans remained loyal to Spain and did not join the other Spanish American colonies in the WARS OF INDEPENDENCE of the early 1800s. The cruelties of the plantation system, however, eventually drove the island's black population to revolt. Led by free blacks, Cuban slaves rebelled in 1810, 1812, and 1844, but without success.

Toward Independence. By the mid-1800s, Cuba and Puerto Rico were Spain's last colonies in the Americas. But the United States had long had its eye on this nearby island. In the early 1800s, Thomas Jefferson suggested that "Cuba would naturally be taken by the United States, or the island would give itself to us." Many United States citizens agreed with Jefferson that the United States should own, or at least influence, Cuba. Indeed, through trade and investment in Cuban railways and sugar refineries, the United States already had a powerful influence on the island's economy. Such strong economic ties with the United States made Cuba less dependent upon Spain.

° **Creole** person of European ancestry born in the Americas

At the same time, Cuban Creoles* were dissatisfied with Spanish rule, believing that Spain's regulations limited Cuba's economic development. In 1868, a band of Creole landowners proclaimed Cuban independence and launched the TEN YEARS' WAR. Other rebel leaders soon emerged to carry on the fight against Spain, among them Máximo GÓMEZ and the Afro-Cuban Antonio MACÉO, who called for an end to slavery. The young José Julián MARTÍ Y PÉREZ, who was jailed and exiled from Cuba for supporting the rebellion, was eventually honored as "the father of Cuban independence."

The rebels lost the Ten Years' War, which killed more than 200,000 people, including many Creole landowners. Investors from the United States came to Cuba to take their places. By the mid-1890s, the United States controlled the Cuban sugar industry and consumed most of Cuba's exports. However, Cuba remained in turmoil. In 1895, the Cuban independence movement—led by Martí, until he died in the fighting—launched a new guerrilla* war against the Spanish forces on the island.

° **guerrilla** referring to a group that uses surprise raids to obstruct or harass an enemy or overthrow a government

In 1897, Spain granted autonomy to Cuba, but by then, Cubans were demanding more. Many revolutionaries did not want the United States to become involved in their struggle. They shared the concerns of Martí, who wrote, "Once the United States is in Cuba, who will get her out?" However, people in the United States were moved by the Cuban struggle and pushed Congress to enter the fight. In 1898, these pressures and the explosion of the U.S.S. *Maine* in Havana harbor prompted the United States to take military action, launching the SPANISH-AMERICAN WAR. When the short but violent war ended, Cuba was independent from Spain—but the U.S. Army occupied the island.

Toward Revolution. United States military forces left Cuba in 1902, after the Cubans had adopted a constitution and installed a president. A trade agreement encouraged United States investment in Cuba and gave Cuban goods favorable treatment in the United States market. However, a section of Cuba's new constitution (called the PLATT AMENDMENT) gave the United States the right to maintain a military base on the island and to involve itself in Cuba's political and economic affairs. Several times in the following 20 years, the United

Cuba

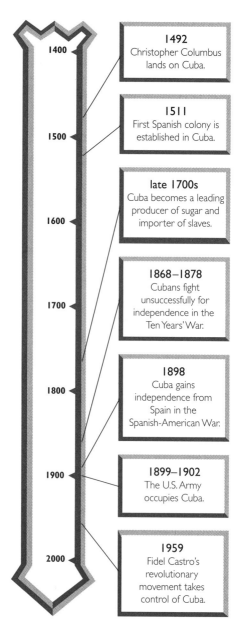

1492
Christopher Columbus lands on Cuba.

1511
First Spanish colony is established in Cuba.

late 1700s
Cuba becomes a leading producer of sugar and importer of slaves.

1868–1878
Cubans fight unsuccessfully for independence in the Ten Years' War.

1898
Cuba gains independence from Spain in the Spanish-American War.

1899–1902
The U.S. Army occupies Cuba.

1959
Fidel Castro's revolutionary movement takes control of Cuba.

° **regime** prevailing political system or rule

° **progressive** inclined to support social improvement and political change by governmental action

° **infrastructure** basic framework of a society and its economy, which includes roads, bridges, port facilities, airports, and other public works

° **coup** sudden, often violent overthrow of a ruler or government

States sent troops to Cuba to keep order or to prevent changes that might damage its interests there. The hand of American influence weighed heavily on Cuba.

In some ways, the United States presence in Cuba benefited the island and its people. Public health measures instituted by the United States greatly reduced the number of deaths from diseases, such as yellow fever. The United States sent engineers and money to build railroads, highways, and hotels, and encouraged the growth of a Cuban middle class of educated professionals, including lawyers and teachers. However, other aspects of the United States influence hurt Cuba. Havana became a playground for American tourists, where criminal elements from the United States operated casinos and nightclubs. United States companies dominated Cuba's sugar, oil refining, mining, railway, tourism, rubber, and chemical industries, and United States banks were so powerful that they often influenced the Cuban government.

In the 1920s, Cubans who rejected the United States influence in their nation founded several opposition groups, including the Cuban Communist party, called the PCC (Partido Communista de Cuba, whose name was later changed to the Partido Socialista Popular, or PSP). In 1930 and 1932, the PCC led workers' strikes, which were illegal under Cuban law. Dictator Gerardo Machado stopped the strikes with violence and had many of his critics killed. In 1933, after police killed several antigovernment demonstrators during a strike, Machado lost the support of both the army and the United States. He fled Cuba, and a mixed group of student revolutionaries and army officers took over the government in the Revolution of 1933. They turned the presidency over to a doctor named Ramón Grau San Martín, who had disapproved of Machado's regime°.

Grau passed many laws designed to help Cuba's working class and to reduce foreign influence on Cuba, which alarmed the United States. Grau's fellow Cubans also criticized him. His reforms angered the wealthy, who wanted Cuba to stay as it was, and those who wanted change but felt that Grau's reforms did not go far enough. In 1934, Fulgencio Batista y Zaldívar, one of the army officers who had led the Revolution of 1933, overthrew Grau's government. Later that same year, the United States signed a treaty with Cuba that eliminated the Platt Amendment.

For six years, Batista ruled Cuba through a series of puppet presidents, whom he placed in office. In 1940, Cubans elected Batista as their president and proclaimed a new progressive° constitution. Batista supported welfare legislation and improved public health, education, and infrastructure°. Then in 1944, Grau was elected president. To the dismay of those who viewed Grau as the voice of democracy and good government, his term in office was a time of widespread corruption, violence, and repression. His successor, Carlos Prío Socorrás, was no better. In 1952, before the scheduled elections took place, Batista emerged from retirement, overthrew Prío's government in a coup°, and appointed himself dictator of Cuba.

As dictator, Batista took a very different approach to ruling Cuba than he had taken as president. His administration was corrupt and brutal. An organized resistance movement began to develop. The rebels wanted the Cuban government to enforce the 1940 Constitution. On July 26, 1953, Raúl and Fidel CASTRO and others attacked the Moncada barracks in Santiago de Cuba. Many Cubans opposed not only Batista but also the United States, and Communists and non-Communists joined the rebel force. Fidel Castro emerged as the leader of this resistance movement.

Batista steadily lost support, including that of the United States, as the revolutionary movement gained strength. Seeing his defeat coming, the dictator fled Cuba on New Year's Day, 1959. Soon after, Castro and other rebels—who had led a guerrilla movement from their outpost in the mountains in the Oriente province—marched into Havana. With Batista gone and the rebels in charge, some people thought that the Cuban Revolution was over. Castro believed that it was just beginning.

See color plate 5, vol. 2.

Cuba Since the Revolution.
In place of the corrupt government they had driven out, Castro and the other revolutionaries wanted to offer something better. Historians disagree about Castro's original goals and plans. Some claim that, from the start, he was determined to set himself up as a Communist dictator. Others believe that he might not have led Cuba into communism if the United States had not been so hostile to him.

United States officials distrusted Castro's revolution for two reasons. First, the Communist PSP had played a large and visible role in the revolution, and the United States government was deeply concerned about the spread of communism. The United States and the Communist

Pope John Paul II's five-day trip to Cuba in 1998 was a historic moment full of memorable images. This photograph captures two icons of opposing forces: the pope, a long-time foe of communism, and on a building in the background, the image of Ernesto "Che" Guevara, the Communist revolutionary hero of Cuba.

superpower, the Soviet Union, were locked in a pattern of hostile rivalry called the Cold War, and the United States did not want to see a Communist state so close to its borders. Second, many Americans owned property or had other investments in Cuba, and they feared that reforms in Cuba might endanger these interests.

The United States struck against Castro's Cuba in several ways. Anti-Communist Cubans had fled the country during or soon after the revolution, many of them settling in southern Florida. These exiles were determined to topple Castro so that they could return to the Cuba they had known. In 1961, the United States government provided them with weapons and transportation for an invasion of Cuba. The BAY OF PIGS INVASION was a disastrous failure, but it convinced Castro that the United States would not hesitate to make war on Cuba. Castro asked the Soviet Union to help in its defense, which led to the CUBAN MISSILE CRISIS—a showdown between the superpowers. Around this time, Castro openly identified himself as a Communist and made Cuba an ally of the Soviet Union and the international Communist community. In the 1970s and 1980s, Cuba sent troops to Africa to support other leftist* governments and backed leftists in Central America during the 1980s.

Although the Bay of Pigs invasion had failed, the United States continued its efforts to end Castro's rule. The U.S. CENTRAL INTELLIGENCE AGENCY (CIA) participated in several plots to eliminate Castro. For years, the United States government supported anti-Castro activities among Cuban exiles in the United States. But the most successful strike against Cuba was economic. The United States government outlawed all trade between the United States and Cuba and declared that any foreign ship that did business with Cuba could not enter a United States port for six months. Some observers believe that these economic sanctions, as they are called, have hurt ordinary Cuban citizens more than they have weakened Castro's regime.

From time to time, the two countries have struggled to work out an agreement about immigration from Cuba to the United States. At first, Castro would not allow anyone to leave Cuba. Some fled anyway, risking their lives to make the 90-mile trip to Florida. In 1980, Castro permitted the MARIEL BOATLIFT, in which more than 100,000 Cubans emigrated to the United States. The boatlift caused problems and set back negotiations over the immigration issue, as well as the equally difficult question of how the United States should treat Cuban refugees.

Yet some of Castro's programs had improved conditions for the average Cuban—if only temporarily. His land reform programs ended rural unemployment by breaking up large estates and putting the government in control. The state, which owns all resources and administers the economy, guaranteed jobs to all. As early as 1961, the revolutionary government sent students into the countryside to teach people to read and write. Twenty years later, Cuba claimed to have wiped out illiteracy*, eliminated hunger and homelessness, and attained the highest standard of living in Latin America. It also had comprehensive health care—provided free to all citizens—and boasted new laws that attempted to end the racism that plagued Cuban society and to improve the status of WOMEN. By the end of the 1990s, however, many of

° **leftist** inclined to support radical reform and change; often associated with ideas of communism or socialism

° **illiteracy** the inability to read and write

46

its education, health, and welfare programs were struggling, and unemployment and other prerevolutionary problems had returned to Cuba.

Moreover, the Cuban Revolution failed to bring democracy to Cuba. The Constitution of 1976 modeled its economic and political system on that of the Soviet Union. It recognized the authority of the Cuban Communist Party, now known as the PCC, and only PCC candidates may run in elections. Cubans do not have the right to express their ideas freely. Those who have opposed or even criticized Castro and his regime have been arrested, and some claim to have been tortured. Cuban society is patrolled on a neighborhood level by the Committees for the Defense of the Revolution, or CDRs. While they perform many civic duties, the CDRs' primary purpose is to observe their communities and report any activities viewed as "counterrevolutionary." Most Cubans are CDR members because those who do not join are considered enemies of the revolution and potential threats to the community.

Cuba's economy has had varied success throughout the years, but its worst slump came in the early 1990s, after the Soviet Union collapsed. Three-quarters of Cuba's trade had been with the Soviet Union or its allies. When trade declined, Cuba entered a period of severe food and fuel shortages, unemployment, rising prices, illegal trade, and more refugees fleeing to the United States.

Some people thought that the Cuban government, like other Communist governments around the world, would crumble. It did not. Castro survived the difficult times, and by the late 1990s, Cuba's economy seemed to be improving as the nation attracted more foreign investment. However, many Cubans have lost confidence in communism, and some are demanding democracy and greater individual freedom. Some people doubt that the Cuban Revolution will continue when Castro is no longer alive to lead it. (*See also* **Asylum; Communism; Immigration and Emigration; United States–Latin American Relations.**)

Cuban Missile Crisis

*T*he Cuban missile crisis was a tense clash of wills between the United States and the Soviet Union in 1962. At the time, these two superpowers were engaged in a hostile global rivalry known as the Cold War, and some people feared that the Cuban missile crisis might explode into open warfare.

The crisis began when the United States learned—through photographs taken from spy planes—that the Soviet Union had installed nuclear missile sites and bombers in CUBA, which lies less than 100 miles off United States shores. President John F. Kennedy declared that Cuba and the Soviet Union would have to remove the missiles. Cuba and the Soviet Union replied that the missiles were intended to protect Cuba from a possible attack by the United States. Kennedy then ordered United States ships to encircle Cuba, cutting the island off from contact by sea with the rest of the world.

In secret talks, Soviet leader Nikita Khrushchev offered to remove the missiles if, in return, the United States government promised not to invade Cuba. Kennedy accepted the offer. Cuban dictator Fidel CASTRO, however, was angry and embarrassed that his Soviet allies had made a deal with the United States without including him in the discussions. Khrushchev had also promised that UNITED NATIONS inspectors could visit Cuba to oversee the removal of the missiles. Castro refused to allow this. Nonetheless, United States spy photographs eventually showed that the missiles had been removed. The Cuban missile crisis was one of several incidents during the Cold War that brought the superpowers close to the brink of armed conflict. But perhaps its most important long-term result was a cooling of relations between Castro's Cuba and the Soviet Union. (*See also* **United States–Latin American Relations.**)

Cuban Revolution

° **communism** system in which land, goods, and the means of production are owned by the state or community rather than by individuals

° **nationalist** patriotic person devoted to the advocacy of the nation's interests

° **protectorate** country under the protection and control of a stronger nation

*I*n 1959, the Cuban Revolution brought communism* to power in Cuba. When Fidel CASTRO, the leader of the revolution, marched triumphantly into Havana, he did more than overthrow the government. He declared that Cuba had won its long struggle for true independence.

During the TEN YEARS' WAR, from 1868 to 1878, Cuban nationalists* battled unsuccessfully for independence from Spain. They rebelled against Spain again in 1895, and by 1898, the United States entered the nationalists' fight. At the end of that year, Cuba became independent of Spain only to become a protectorate* of the United States. However, Cuban nationalist feelings remained strong, and new political ideas—including communism—gained a significant number of followers. In 1933, Cuban Communists initiated an illegal workers' strike and set up a revolutionary government. The 1933 revolution lasted only a short time, partly because the United States opposed it, but it served as a model for the much more successful Cuban Revolution of 1959.

During the 1930s and 1940s, upper- and middle-class Cubans benefited from a strong economy, while living conditions for rural farmers

In 1959, a revolution led by Fidel Castro (second from left) and Ernesto "Che" Guevara (second from right) brought communism to Cuba. Although the United States initially supported the Castro government, relations between the two countries declined sharply after American-owned property was seized by the new regime.

See color plate 9, vol. 3.

° **guerrilla** referring to a group that uses surprise raids to obstruct or harass an enemy or overthrow a government

° **regime** prevailing political system or rule

° **nationalize** to bring land, industries, or public works under state control or ownership

declined. In addition, United States companies owned most of the island's profitable sugarcane fields and processing plants, which angered many Cubans. One such irate nationalist was Fidel Castro, who with his brother Raúl and others attacked the Moncada barracks on July 26, 1953. They were captured, and Fidel used his trial as a platform to speak out against the government. A few years later, Castro fled to Mexico, where he formed a group called the Twenty-sixth of July Movement to overthrow Cuba's dictator, Fulgencio BATISTA Y ZALDÍVAR.

In 1956, Castro and his followers, including an Argentine doctor named Ernesto "Che" GUEVARA, returned to Cuba to wage a guerrilla* war against Batista. Other Cubans—Communists and non-Communists— also shared their goal. As the movement gained strength, Castro increasingly relied on Communist support. Although Castro agreed with the Communists' goal of reorganizing Cuban economic and social life, he did not identify himself as a Communist. When Castro communicated with the outside world, he gave the impression that his only goal was to end Batista's dictatorship. Despite its distrust of Castro, the United States government withdrew its support from Batista's corrupt, antidemocratic regime*. The Cuban army also turned against Batista, who fled Cuba on January 1, 1959.

The revolution was victorious, and Castro was clearly in charge. Within two years, he had exiled, executed, or removed from power most non-Communist members of the Twenty-sixth of July Movement. He also kept the revolution's promises. Castro nationalized* foreign-owned property, broke up private estates, and declared that all farmland on the island now belonged to the state. In response, a majority of the upper and middle classes fled the country.

The United States government secretly plotted to overthrow the Cuban Revolution. In 1961, it supported the BAY OF PIGS INVASION, an armed attack by Cuban exiles on Castro's government that failed disastrously. Afterward, Castro publicly declared himself a Communist and allied Cuba with the Communist superpower, the Soviet Union.

The Cuban Revolution did not end when Castro took power. Castro considers the revolution to be a continuing process, an ongoing struggle to create a new kind of society. By the 1990s, however, after the Soviet Union had collapsed, most of the world had given up on communism. Castro still had not succeeded in making the island's Communist economy prosper, and many Cubans were tired of the revolution. The aging Castro has named his brother Raúl to carry on the revolution after his own death, but some observers expect the Cuban Revolution to die with Fidel Castro. (*See also* **Communism.**)

Cultures, Pre-Columbian

*T*he ancestors of modern American INDIANS arrived in the Americas from Asia more than 15,000 years ago. Over the next few thousand years, they spread through the continents and formed hundreds of distinct cultures. Across Mesoamerica* and South America these cultures rose, flourished, and fell, some leaving behind them mighty monuments, others disappearing almost without a trace.

° **Mesoamerica** culture region that includes central and southern Mexico, Guatemala, Belize, El Salvador, and parts of Honduras, Nicaragua, and Costa Rica

° **archaeologist** scientist who studies past human cultures, usually by excavating ruins

See map in Mesoamerica, Pre-Columbian History (vol. 3).

° **egalitarian** favoring human equality with respect to social, political, and economic rights

° **hierarchy** division of society or an institution into groups with higher and lower ranks

° **iconography** pictures, symbols, or images illustrating a subject

° **pan-Mesoamerican** involving, or applicable to, all of Mesoamerica

The Spanish conquerors left vivid descriptions of the powerful and wealthy cultures they encountered, such as those of the AZTECS of Mexico and the INCA of Peru. These well-known peoples were related to peoples of other cultures that came before them and lived beside them. These pre-Columbian cultures—cultures that existed before Christopher COLUMBUS arrived in the Americas in the 1490s—were linked by a complex web of relationships that historians and archaeologists* are still unraveling.

Mesoamerica

Mesoamerica was home to many pre-Columbian cultures. At the time of the Spanish conquest, societies from northern Mexico to western Costa Rica shared many cultural traditions and characteristics. Among these were AGRICULTURE, including the growing of maize, beans, and chili peppers; ARCHITECTURE, including stone structures such as ball courts and pyramids; religion, including worship of DIVINITIES such as Tlaloc and Quetzalcoatl; ancestor worship; calendars; and human sacrifices. These characteristics and customs developed in various regions of Mesoamerica and spread as trade, war, and migration brought the cultures into contact with one another.

Before A.D. 250.   Between about 5000 B.C. and 2000 B.C., agriculture transformed Mesoamericans from wandering hunters and gatherers to full-time farmers. They lived in small permanent communities of about a dozen homes with cooking sheds and storage pits. Social and political relationships were egalitarian* and based on kinship. Trade, crafts, and agriculture were organized by extended family households. Between 1500 B.C. and 900 B.C., the population increased, and villages grew in size and importance. They became centers of political, economic, and religious activity. Mesoamericans built temples and marketplaces and traded in jade, seashells, fine pottery, and cacao. Soon, relationships began to be characterized by social inequality and political hierarchies*, and trade was no longer organized by households.

Mesoamerica's first major civilization was that of the OLMECS, which developed along the Gulf of Mexico around 1500 B.C. The Olmecs built monuments and maintained social and economic links with societies throughout Mesoamerica—Olmec symbols appear on pottery and monuments as far away as El Salvador. The widespread dispersion of Olmec iconography* suggests interactions between Mesoamerican cultures and the possibility of a pan-Mesoamerican* belief system. Although Olmec culture waned after about 400 B.C., other cultures, such as that of the ZAPOTECS, were rising.

Around 400 B.C., in the jungle-covered lowlands and mountains farther south, the MAYA culture began to develop. Large chiefdoms—or densely populated areas ruled by powerful rulers—were established at sites such as EL MIRADOR and TIKAL. Although these chiefdoms regularly fought against each other, they engaged in trade, shared religious beliefs and artistic styles, and fostered strong economic ties.

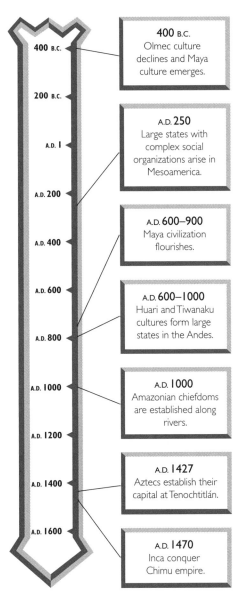

400 B.C.
Olmec culture declines and Maya culture emerges.

A.D. 250
Large states with complex social organizations arise in Mesoamerica.

A.D. 600–900
Maya civilization flourishes.

A.D. 600–1000
Huari and Tiwanaku cultures form large states in the Andes.

A.D. 1000
Amazonian chiefdoms are established along rivers.

A.D. 1427
Aztecs establish their capital at Tenochtitlán.

A.D. 1470
Inca conquer Chimu empire.

* **tribute** payment made to a dominant power

* **savanna** tropical or subtropical grassland with scattered trees and drought-resistant undergrowth

From A.D. 200 to the Conquest. An important change occurred in Mesoamerican culture and society around A.D. 250. Local chiefdoms became large states, with complex political organizations, ruling classes, craft specialization, distant colonies, and economies based on tribute*. TEOTIHUACÁN was at the heart of one such state, with colonies at Veracruz, Guatemala, and other remote sites. Around 750, Teotihuacán collapsed as a major economic and political power, and as a result, other centers grew in size and importance.

The civilization of the Maya flourished between 600 and 900, and Maya kings controlled large territories. However, the Maya population in the southern lowlands dropped, and the culture there collapsed around 900, possibly because of warfare, population pressures, and ecological disasters. Nevertheless, the Maya civilization did not entirely disappear. It remained vigorous in the lowlands of the Yucatán peninsula and in CHICHÉN ITZÁ.

The most powerful group in central Mexico after the collapse of Teotihuacán was that of the TOLTECS, who created a large trading empire with a strong central government. Toltecs dominated Mesoamerica until around 1200, when their capital at Tollán began to decline because of drought, famine, rebellion, and invasion. Central Mexico's next large urban center did not appear until the Aztecs founded their capital at TENOCHTITLÁN in 1427. It took the Aztecs less than a century to establish the greatest empire Mesoamerica had yet seen. That empire stretched from the Gulf of Mexico to the Pacific Ocean and from central Mexico to present-day Chiapas.

The Aztecs were not the only people in Mexico at this time. Among many others were the MIXTECS of western Oaxaca; the Zapotecs, who inhabited the Valley of Oaxaca; and the Totonacs of Veracruz, who were among the first to encounter the Spanish. The large Maya state of Yucatán fell apart into small city-states. Rulers who claimed to be Toltec descendants ruled the chiefdoms in the highlands of Guatemala. These chiefdoms fell to the Spanish in the 1520s, marking the end of the pre-Columbian period.

South America

The vast size of the South American continent, the Andes, and other physical barriers limited contact between its regions and its cultures. The two principal areas were the tropical rain forests and savannas* of the AMAZON REGION and the valleys and highlands of the Andes. These geographically different regions produced very distinctive cultures.

Amazonia. For many years, archaeologists and historians ignored the early cultures of Amazonia—the 2-million-square-mile area around the Amazon and Orinoco rivers in northern South America—because they had no large urban civilizations or empires. Some of these scholars believed that the people lived as primitive hunters and gatherers, with an undeveloped culture until the time of the European conquest. Other archaeologists and historians thought that the

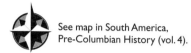

° **forage** to hunt or search for food

See map in South America, Pre-Columbian History (vol. 4).

° **conquistador** Spanish explorer and conqueror

° **quinoa** type of plant whose seeds have been a basic food source in the Andes region since precolonial times

rain forest's scattered food sources made it a poor environment for people who lived by foraging*. However, recent archaeological discoveries reveal that people have lived in Amazonia for a very long time and that some developed complex cultures.

Along the Orinoco and Amazon rivers, archaeologists have found tools and other human-made objects that date from around 9000 B.C. to 7000 B.C., predating agriculture. Pottery from several locations dating to the 3000s B.C. indicates that people in Amazonia were growing maize and other crops at that time. Similarities in pottery styles from far-flung regions suggest that by about 1000 B.C., the people of Amazonia had formed a trade network based on canoe travel. They also farmed and fished.

By 1000 B.C., complex chiefdoms existed in the region. The Marajoara culture at the mouth of the Amazon River is known for its colorful pottery and large earthworks. Archaeological constructions dating after 500 B.C. have also been found in the upper Amazon region. In the 1540s, conquistador* Francisco de ORELLANA and his companions, the first Europeans to cross Amazonia, reported large settlements and chiefdoms along the Napo and Amazon rivers. The Europeans, and the DISEASES they brought, soon wiped out many of these Indians and ended the development of their culture.

The Andes.   By 3500 B.C., people who lived in the Andean highlands shifted from hunting to herding LLAMAS. They also experimented with agriculture, growing potatoes, peanuts, squash, cotton, and quinoa*. Along the Pacific coast, people developed fishing industries, using cotton for fishing lines and gourds for floats. Agriculture brought population increases, a shift to permanent settlements, and the beginnings of civilization. These permanently settled farming communities first appeared in the northern Andes of Ecuador and Colombia.

The Valdivia culture of present-day Chile was among the first Andean cultures to develop pottery for cooking and food storage. Coastal cultures of this era produced some of the largest architectural constructions in Andean history, including massive pyramid platforms and other earthworks, built without the use of the wheel. Cultures in the highlands flourished later and lasted longer. The CHAVIN culture spread its religious influence and carried out trade over long distances, while the Cupisnique people on the northern coast and the people of Paracas to the south formed independent groups.

During the next phase of Andean history, from about A.D. 1 until A.D. 500, small states conquered the peoples of neighboring valleys. Between 300 and 500, the MOCHE gained much power and influence. Other characteristics of the time were the growth of an elite, or privileged, class of nobles and royal relatives and the appearance of cities such as the Moche capital of Cerro Blanco. Some Andean cultures, such as that of the NASCA of the south Peruvian coast, remained a society of farmers without any urban centers.

In the highlands around Lake TITICACA, people developed major political and ceremonial centers. Large highland states developed into

The Oldest Pottery in the Americas?

Pottery, which can last for centuries, is common to many cultures and can be dated fairly accurately, using special technology such as carbon-14 dating. Archaeologists use pottery artifacts to trace the history and practices of past cultures. They now believe that the first pottery in the Americas was made at a place called Taperinha, not far from the Amazon River near the present-day Brazilian city of Santarém. Some of the red-brown bowls that archaeologists found there date from around 5500 B.C.

empires. The first was based at the Bolivian site of Tiwanaku and controlled the region around Lake Titicaca. The Huari culture of southern Peru shared the religious tradition of Tiwanaku. The Huari expanded in all directions and brought the coastal and highland cultures under its control, creating a model for the Inca. By A.D. 1000, the Huari and Tiwanaku cultures had declined. For hundreds of years, Andean cultures remained small and separate, except on Peru's north coast, where Chan Chan became the capital of the Chimu empire around 1100. Cultures such as those of the Chancay on the central coast and the Inca on the southern coast coexisted with the Chimu, and some of them built very impressive centers, such as La Centinela in Chincha.

The region's last great pre-Columbian power, the Inca, inherited their empire-building tradition from the Huari. Through a succession of conquests, the Inca forged a unified state from a multitude of Andean cultures. They built several impressive administrative buildings and forts, including the temple-fortress at Sacsahuaman and the royal estate at Machu Picchu. However, their success was short-lived, lasting less than a century. In 1532, already weakened by European diseases, internal rebellions, and civil war, the Inca were defeated by conquistador Francisco Pizarro. (*See also* **Archaeology; Art, Pre-Columbian.**)

Cumaná

° **conquistador** Spanish explorer and conqueror

° **viceroyalty** region governed by a viceroy, a royally appointed official

Founded in 1520, Cumaná was the first permanent European settlement in Latin America. Located on the northeastern coast of Venezuela, Cumaná was a base for the exploration of the surrounding region. Its main economic activities in the early 1500s were fishing for pearls in nearby waters and raiding neighboring Indian villages to capture slaves. During these years, Cumaná was at the center of conflict between the Spanish and the Indians and between rival conquistadors*. By the end of the 1500s, Spain had established control over the region.

Cumaná became an important port for Spain's Caribbean colonies and a major link in the Caribbean defense network. During the 1700s, Cumaná developed an industry in cattle and hides and received annual subsidies from the treasury of the Viceroyalty* of Peru. Because of its coastal location, Cumaná fostered stronger political, cultural, and economic ties to the Caribbean than to the colonial capital at Caracas and to the rest of South America. Today Cumaná is a minor seaport, resort town, and the capital of the Venezuelan province of Sucre.

Cunha, Euclides da

1866–1909
Brazilian author

Euclides da Cunha is the author of a book that is considered a masterpiece of Brazilian literature—*Os sertões (Rebellion in the Backlands)*. Cunha emerged as a writer just as the Brazilian empire was collapsing and the country was struggling to survive as a republic*. The book, an account of a long and bloody revolt, deals with Brazil's struggle to find its national identity.

Cunha began his career as a journalist while attending military school. His first articles, published even before he graduated with a degree in engineering, attracted much attention. The articles dealt with the peasant rebellion led by Antônio CONSELHEIRO that had been raging in the backcountry of northeastern Brazil since 1874. Later, while on assignment on the battlefield, Cunha wrote *Os sertões* (1902). He argued that tragic misunderstandings and broken communications were responsible for the long war between rural peasants and the army of the newly formed republic. The book touches on a wide range of topics, including anthropology, geography, military history, literature, and philosophy, revealing Cunha's thorough understanding of Brazil, its history, and its deep-rooted social problems. It became a best-seller in Brazil and brought Cunha literary fame.

Cunha spent the next few years working for the Brazilian government, helping to map Brazil's northwestern borders. Before his death in 1909, he wrote two more books, *Contrastes e confrontos* (Comparisons and Contrasts) and *À margem da história* (On the Margin of History).

Curanderos

*T*hroughout Latin America, folk healers practice medicine outside the setting of hospitals and without formal Western medical training. These traditional healers are called *curanderos* in Spanish America (*curandeiros* in Brazil), and their brand of healing is known as *curanderismo*.

Indian healers are herbalists*, who prescribe medications made from plants. They are also expert at setting broken bones and giving massages. Much of their traditional knowledge has been handed down from pre-Columbian* times, when some Indian civilizations developed a body of knowledge about herbal remedies, the treatment of wounds, and other forms of medicine. Early European medical ideas that came to

Throughout Latin America, traditional healers called *curanderos* practice medicine using herbal treatments and magical rituals. In this photograph, a Venezuelan *curandero* practices a traditional healing ritual.

the Americas in the 1500s and 1600s made their way into traditional medicine. One such idea concerned the balance between hot and cold qualities. For example, in Guatemala, people classified peaches, chocolate, and honey as "hot" foods, while tomatoes, squash, and carrots were considered "cold," and they avoided eating too much of one kind or the other.

Today the typical Indian *curandero* is a shaman—a person who is believed to have contact with the spirit world and the ability to cure illness. Although many shamans describe powerful spiritual or magical experiences that gave them the power to cure, they generally acquire their skills from other shamans. Both men and women may become healers, but men are more common.

A healer's work often combines herbal and other treatments with magical rituals. As modern medicine becomes more successful in dealing with physical ailments, some healers have begun to concentrate on the mental and spiritual aspects of illness. Folk healers often divide their patients' problems into natural illnesses, to be treated by modern medicine, and illnesses believed to be caused by sorcery, which they treat with rituals. Healers sometimes take special drugs to induce a vision that will help them learn about a person's illness and how to treat it.

While Indian shamans practice within the traditional frameworks of their cultures, the urban *curanderos* have developed highly individual forms of *curanderismo*. Their healing practices are based on various religions and ideas from around the world, including Catholicism, Buddhism, African American and American Indian traditions, belief in ghosts and spirits, and theories about natural healing and medications. Urban *curanderos* treat both spiritual illnesses, such as *mal de susto**, and physical illnesses, such as obesity and cancer. Although each urban *curandero* develops a distinctive individual style, some regions are known for particular types of urban *curanderismo*. For example, some Brazilian cities are known for a ritual healing practice called Umbanda. (*See also* **Candomblé; Medicine.**)

* **mal de susto** illness resulting from intense and sudden fright that is believed to cause the soul to leave the body

Cuzco

* **department** province or administrative district of the government

See map in Peru (vol. 3).

Cuzco is a department* and a city in southeastern PERU, where the high Andes mountains descend into river valleys. Once the capital of the INCA empire and later captured by Spain, the city of Cuzco is more a blend of old and new, of Indian and European, than most Latin American cities.

According to legend, the Inca founded Cuzco around 1200. Located on a major north-south trade route through the ANDES, the city became the political and economic center of an empire that stretched from Ecuador to Chile. As the Inca empire grew in wealth and size, Cuzco boasted impressive buildings and imperial structures such as the Sacsahuaman, a stone fortress or ceremonial structure just outside the city.

In 1532, the Spanish, led by conquistador Francisco PIZARRO, conquered the region. Despite Indian resistance, the Spanish took control of Cuzco, destroyed Inca structures, and constructed new cathedrals and buildings on the ruins. By the time of the Tupac Amaru revolt in the

Cuzco, located in southeastern Peru, was once the capital of the Inca empire. After the Spanish conquered the city, they destroyed most Inca structures and built cathedrals, such as the ones shown here, and other new buildings—sometimes using the stones and foundations from the Inca ruins.

---

* **guano** excrement of seabirds that is used as a fertilizer

1780s, Cuzco became a place of complex ethnic and social relationships resulting from years of contact between the Europeans and the Indians.

Cuzco's cultural history includes many artistic and intellectual achievements. The city boasted great writers and artists and was the Andean center of the INDIGENISMO movement, a revival of Indian culture. After independence, Peru's economic activity shifted to the coastal guano* industry. Cuzco's textile-supported economy declined, and its population dwindled. However, railway links renewed development in Cuzco as did the rebuilding that followed a 1950 earthquake. Today Cuzco exports agricultural produce and textiles. With its preserved monuments and architecture, such as Sacsahuaman and the mountain-top ruins of MACHU PICCHU, Cuzco has also become a leading center of tourism in the Andes.

Dance

See *Music and Dance.*

Danish West Indies

See *Virgin Islands of the United States.*

Darío, Rubén

1867–1916
Poet and journalist

*R*ubén Darío was the leading Latin American poet of the late 1800s and early 1900s. He was the founder and a leading figure of *modernismo,* a literary movement that reshaped and "modernized" Spanish literature. His poetry is known for its bold innovative style, lush and exotic imagery, and lyrical beauty.

Born Félix Rubén García Sarmiento in NICARAGUA, Darío began writing poetry at an early age and was known as "the boy poet." By the age of 14, he was working at a local newspaper and soon established a career in journalism. Darío moved to CHILE in 1886 and immersed himself in poetry. Two years later, he published his first major work, *Azul (Blue),* a collection of short stories and poems.

Darío returned to CENTRAL AMERICA in 1889 and worked feverishly on poetry and newspaper articles. In the 1890s, he served as a diplomat in Spain and ARGENTINA. While in Argentina, Darío founded a literary journal dedicated to *modernismo* and published *Prosas profanas y otros poemas (Profane Hymns and Other Poems),* a collection that became a very influential modernist work.

Between 1898 and 1914, Darío lived in Spain and France, where he continued to work as a journalist. He also published many important books of essays and poetry. *Cantos de vida y esperanza (Songs of Life and Hope),* his first work to emphasize Hispanic culture, was considered by many to be his masterpiece. Darío left Europe in 1914 for a lecture tour of the United States. He contracted pneumonia in New York and died shortly afterward in León, Nicaragua. (*See also* **Literature.**)

D'Aubuisson, Roberto

1943–1992
Salvadoran army officer
and political leader

° **right-wing** very conservative

*R*oberto d'Aubuisson was an intelligence officer who left the army in 1979, when a new reform-minded government seized power in EL SALVADOR. D'Aubuisson opposed the social reforms proposed by the new government, and he played a sinister role in the civil war that raged in El Salvador in the 1980s.

After leaving the army, d'Aubuisson founded the Nationalist Republican Alliance (ARENA), a right-wing* political organization. Many Salvadorans hold this group responsible for violations of HUMAN RIGHTS during the civil war. D'Aubuisson's name was often associated with the activities of the death squads that terrorized the people of El Salvador. D'Aubuisson may have played a role in the assassination of archbishop Oscar Arnulfo ROMERO, a crusader for human rights.

D'Aubuisson served as president of the Salvadoran legislature from 1982 to 1984. However, the military and the United States prevented him from gaining a higher office because United States president Ronald Reagan feared that d'Aubuisson's reputation would jeopardize congressional support for military aid to El Salvador. Although d'Aubuisson lost the presidential election of 1984 to José Napoleón DUARTE FUENTES, he remained active in politics until his death in 1992. (*See also* **Counterinsurgency**.)

Death Squads

See *El Salvador; Guatemala.*

Debt Peonage

Sometimes called debt slavery, debt peonage refers to several types of forced or controlled labor that were common in Latin America up to the 1900s. It resulted from the advancement of money or goods to individuals who were unable or unwilling to repay their debts. The debtor was then obligated to work for the person who had advanced the money or goods until he or she repaid the debt. In doing so, the debtor often had to borrow more, going even further into debt and requiring an additional period of labor. The result was a kind of slavery. The workers under this system of labor are called peons.

Debt peonage is found in societies with deep class divisions in which the wealthy can restrict the movement of laborers through custom or law. This has been true in Latin America since colonial times. During the early years of Spanish rule in the Americas, the Spanish relied heavily on Indian and black slaves to meet their labor needs. Although debt peonage existed then, it became much more prevalent after the late 1600s because of the decline of the *encomienda** system and labor shortages resulting from declining Indian populations.

Several types of debt peonage developed in Latin America. In one type, recruiters offered money or goods to Indians and peasants who lived in the mountains and who agreed to work on the lowland PLANTATIONS during the harvest season. This gave the wealthy landowners a reliable workforce and gave the workers a source of income. Another type of debt peonage developed in secluded areas, where powerful landowners and political officials recruited workers to work on haciendas* and in mines. These landowners controlled the workers by forcing them to purchase goods at a "company store," where high prices for necessities caused them to go into debt. Private police forces—particularly on rubber plantations—often prevented the workers from escaping, and those who fled were pursued and punished severely.

Although debt peonage was harsh and allowed workers little freedom, it had some benefits. During the colonial period, for example, some peasants preferred debt peonage to the difficult lives they faced under the *encomienda* system or in their villages. In the 1800s, loans from employers offered one of the few ways for the poor to obtain money for items they needed. Moreover, in places where labor was scarce, peons had some bargaining power with employers. Recent historical research has shown that many peons in the late 1700s and 1800s considered themselves very fortunate to be working and feared being replaced.

In the late 1800s, employers and governments had limited political control in the countryside, making it difficult to enforce debt peonage.

* **encomienda** right granted to a conqueror that enabled him to control the labor of and collect payment from an Indian community

* **hacienda** large rural estate, usually devoted to agriculture

"Sharecroppers" of Latin America

In the 1800s, rural workers known as *colonos* provided labor to wealthy landowners in both Spanish America and Brazil in exchange for access to land or a small part of the harvest. This practice was associated with debt peonage and provided another source of labor on Latin American haciendas. The *colonos* were more than just indebted laborers. They were tenant farmers or "sharecroppers" whose labor benefited not only the landowners but also themselves. Many *colonos* were foreign immigrants who came to Latin America in search of land and better economic opportunities.

In areas that depended on only a seasonal labor force, it was still possible to attract workers. However, this type of peonage remained largely voluntary.

By the early 1900s, population growth and the greater need for cash encouraged more individuals into unforced, paid labor. As a result, debt peonage became increasingly uncommon. Today debt peonage has largely disappeared from Latin America, although some variations of it emerge from time to time in the poorer areas of the region. (*See also* **Sugar Industry.**)

Delgado, José Matías

1767–1832
Salvadoran independence leader

° **clergy** priests and other church officials qualified to perform church ceremonies

° **Enlightenment** intellectual movement of the 1700s that emphasized reason, progress, and modernity

° **bishopric** church district administered by a bishop

° **captain-general** title of provincial rulers in colonial Latin America whose main duty was the military defense of a territory

José Matías Delgado played an important role in the independence movement that freed CENTRAL AMERICA from Spanish rule. He also championed the separation of EL SALVADOR from the political influence of neighboring Guatemala in the years before and after independence.

Born in SAN SALVADOR, Delgado studied church law and became a member of the clergy*. Inspired by the ideas of the Enlightenment*, he resented Spanish and Guatemalan control over the province of El Salvador. In 1811, along with Manuel José ARCE and other Salvadorans, Delgado organized an uprising against Spanish authorities in the hope of gaining independence. The rebellion failed. Soon afterward, Delgado went to Guatemala and tried unsuccessfully to convince authorities to establish a separate bishopric* for El Salvador. He also played a leading role in convincing the captain-general* of Guatemala to declare Central America's independence from Spain in 1821.

After independence, Delgado presided over the assembly that prepared the constitution for the United Provinces of Central America. As a reward for El Salvador's help in the struggle for independence, the new government formed a separate bishopric there in 1825, with Delgado as the first bishop. Delgado died seven years later as civil war raged in Central America. (*See also* **Central America, United Provinces of.**)

Descamisados

Descamisados is a Spanish term meaning "shirtless ones." It refers to the urban lower-class supporters of Argentine president Juan Domingo PERÓN. From the mid-1940s to the 1950s, the *descamisados* provided much of the support Perón needed to remain in power.

In 1945, while serving as vice president of ARGENTINA, Perón was arrested by military rivals who feared his growing power. Hundreds of thousands of impoverished Argentine workers protested by gathering at the Plaza de Mayo, a large public square in the capital city of BUENOS AIRES. Perón had done much to improve the lives of workers, and he had become a favorite of theirs.

The huge protest forced the military to release Perón, who announced his candidacy for president. Newspaper reports of the protest referred to the "shirtless ones" who had rallied for Perón's defense. The *descamisados* accepted this label with pride, and it became a badge of honor that symbolized both their poverty and hard work.

Perón and his wife Evita garnered the support of the *descamisados* by identifying with them. The *descamisados* especially idolized Evita because of her own humble background and support for policies that benefited the poor. Throughout most of his presidency, Perón had strong support from the *descamisados,* who saw him and his wife as symbols of their hopes and dreams for a better life. (*See also* **Labor and Labor Movements; Perón, María Eva Duarte.**)

Dessalines, Jean Jacques

1758–1806
Emperor of Haiti

* **mulatto** person of mixed black and white ancestry

Jean Jacques Dessalines played a significant role in colonial Haiti's struggle for independence from France. Born on a plantation in Saint Domingue (present-day HAITI), on the island of HISPANIOLA in the West Indies, he ruled as emperor of Haiti from 1804 to 1806. However, his brutality and greed marred the achievements of his reign.

The child of black slaves, Dessalines experienced firsthand the horrors of SLAVERY and grew to despise whites, mulattos*, and authority in general. In 1791, he joined a slave rebellion led by TOUSSAINT L'OUVERTURE that erupted in Saint Domingue and went on to serve as a military commander in the Haitian revolution against France.

After Toussaint's death in 1803, Dessalines led Haiti to independence and proclaimed himself emperor. Historians believe that his fear that France might try to regain control may have triggered his mass slaughter of whites in Haiti. His brutality also extended to mulattos, whom he massacred by the hundreds.

As emperor, Dessalines instituted a system of forced labor marked by a severity that equaled or surpassed that of colonial times. He confiscated land, amassed great wealth and power, and ruled with cruelty and an iron hand. His hatred of mulattos threatened to erupt again in 1806, when the mulatto leader Alexandre Sabès PÉTION refused to marry Dessalines's daughter. The same year, Dessalines, while on horseback, was shot and killed by a crowd of soldiers angered by his economic and social policies. The rejoicing crowd shot him repeatedly and dragged his mutilated body through town for public display.

Dias, Henrique

died 1662
Black military leader in Brazil

* **literate** able to read and write

Henrique Dias, a black soldier, played a significant role in the Portuguese campaign against the Dutch in northeastern BRAZIL in the 1600s. He received many honors for his service to the Portuguese crown. In 1638, King Philip IV of Portugal honored Dias by making him a knight.

Although historians are unsure if Dias was ever a slave, they know that he was a free and literate* man when he joined the Portuguese military in 1633. Dias became involved in the Portuguese struggle against the Dutch, who were expanding their control over portions of northeastern Brazil. Initially the captain of a small force, Dias later commanded more than 300 blacks, both free and enslaved. His military skills proved invaluable in the defense and recovery of several Portuguese settlements, including SALVADOR and RECIFE.

Although Dias experienced racism during his long career, his achievements brought him honor and rewards. In 1639, he received a grant of land and authority over the colonists residing there. In 1656, he traveled to Portugal, where he requested and received the freedom of all the slaves who had served under him. His black troops also received the same rights and privileges as white soldiers. Dias died in 1662. To honor his memory, all black Portuguese military units were called "Henriques." (*See also* **Africans in Latin America; Slavery.**)

Díaz, Porfirio

1830–1915
President of Mexico

° **regime** prevailing political system or rule

° **mestizo** person of mixed European and Indian ancestry

° **seminary** religious school where priests are trained

Díaz and His "Scientists"

Among Porfirio Díaz's supporters was a group of young lawyers and journalists who believed that politics should be based on scientific principles. Known as the *científicos* (scientists), they, like many thinkers in the late 1800s, were more interested in creating strong government, social order, and economic growth than in protecting liberties. Although they sought to limit continuing dictatorial rule, they had greater influence on economic policy. Their economic strategies improved the nation's financial stability and success. After Díaz was overthrown in 1910, the term *científico* became an insult.

*P*orfirio Díaz controlled MEXICO for more than three decades in the late 1800s and early 1900s. During this period—known as the Porfiriato because of Díaz's prominence—Mexico experienced economic prosperity and progress. However, Díaz ruled as a dictator, and Mexicans suffered political repression under his regime*.

Early Life and Career.   Díaz, a mestizo*, was born in the city of Oaxaca in southern Mexico. As a child, he worked for a carpenter but also found time for his studies. At age 15, Díaz attended a seminary*. During the MEXICAN-AMERICAN WAR, from 1846 to 1848, he interrupted his studies to enlist in the national guard.

Díaz completed his studies at the seminary in 1849, but instead of entering the priesthood, he decided to study law. In 1854, he launched his political career when he became an administrative official in Ixtlán de Juárez, a town in Oaxaca province. Díaz joined the Oaxaca national guard in 1856 during the War of the Reform, an internal struggle in Mexico concerning the role of the CATHOLIC CHURCH. In 1861, Díaz was promoted to the rank of brigadier general and was elected to Mexico's Congress, in which he served only briefly.

Díaz first gained fame after the battle of Puebla on May 5, 1862, in which he played an important role in a military victory against French troops who had invaded Mexico. Over the next few years, Díaz continued the struggle against the French and was instrumental in their ultimate defeat in 1867.

Rise to Political Power.   Díaz supported Mexican president Benito JUÁREZ during the War of the Reform and the war against France. But in 1867, he opposed Juárez's attempt to increase the power of the presidency and change the country's constitution. In 1871, Díaz ran for president against Juárez. Defeated in the election, he claimed that the results had been falsified and demanded that the presidency be limited to a single term.

When Juárez died in office in 1872, Sebastián Lerdo de Tejada (head of the supreme court) succeeded to the presidency. Díaz ran against Lerdo in the 1876 presidential election. After another defeat, he planned a revolt against the government. Faced with mounting

Porfirio Díaz was president of Mexico for more than 30 years. He provided Mexico with a stable government and substantial economic development, but few political freedoms.

° **Creole** person of European ancestry born in the Americas

° **nationalism** devotion to the interests and culture of one's country

opposition, Lerdo resigned the presidency and went into exile. Díaz took over as president in May 1877.

During his first term in office, Díaz began consolidating his power. He did this by addressing the needs of various groups and by playing one group against another. He won the support of mestizos by giving them greater access to political office. He gained the cooperation of the Creole* elite by expanding economic opportunities and promising that the government would not interfere in the operations of their HACIENDAS (agricultural estates) and businesses. He deflected opposition from the Catholic Church by keeping the government out of church affairs.

The Porfiriato. Díaz chose not to run for reelection in 1880, but he did so in 1884 and was elected for four successive terms. Although the achievements of this long period, called the Porfiriato, were many, they were marred by several factors.

Díaz balanced the budget and created strong economic growth, but by encouraging FOREIGN INVESTMENT, he increased Mexico's reliance on other governments and subjected the country to greater foreign control. Moreover, most profits went to foreigners and to a few wealthy Mexicans. The vast majority of Mexicans continued to face extreme poverty.

Díaz provided Mexico with orderly and stable government by appeasing opponents and consolidating his own power. Over time, however, his rule became increasingly dictatorial and ruthless. Díaz blocked the formation of political parties, prevented the election of opponents, and maintained tight control over the courts. He also silenced the press and permitted few political freedoms.

Because of economic depression, increasing nationalism*, discontent over continued repression, and concerns about Díaz's age and that of his ministers, opposition to the leader grew rapidly during the last decade of his administration. At the same time, Díaz seemed increasingly unable or unwilling to maintain the balance between competing groups that had provided political stability during most of the Porfiriato.

In 1908, Díaz told a United States journalist that he would retire at the end of that term. However, he soon changed his mind and sought reelection in 1910. Díaz promised to restore greater democracy to Mexico, and he won the election. But his opponent, Francisco Indalecio MADERO, led a revolt against the government just as Díaz had done more than 30 years before. With little support left, Díaz was forced to resign from office in May 1911. He went into exile in France, where he died four years later.

Dictatorships, Military

*L*atin America has a long history of military dictatorship. From the 1800s to the present, many Latin American nations have been ruled, at one time or another, by powerful dictators. As in many developing nations in other regions, the intense struggles between rival political groups and social classes have made the tradition of military dictatorships dominant in parts of Latin America until quite recently.

° **conquistador** Spanish explorer and conqueror

° **Creole** person of European ancestry born in the Americas

Roots of Authoritarian Rule.   Authoritarian rule appeared in Latin America with the early conquistadors*, who established personal control over the areas they conquered and explored. They, or their representatives, generally ruled over the Indians with an iron hand—even though the Indians comprised a majority of the population.

When the Spanish monarchs colonized the Americas, they limited the power of the conquistadors and established a centralized system of colonial government based on the absolute power of the king. A small elite class controlled colonial administration, and there were few democratic institutions outside urban areas.

In the 1760s, the Spanish crown decided to permit Creoles* in the Americas to form local military units, or militias. Some were poorly trained and ineffectual, while others were capable of repelling foreign attack. For example, between 1806 and 1807, local troops in Buenos Aires successfully defended their territory against British occupation. The Portuguese colonies established local militias quite early, and they were strengthened during wars against the Dutch.

Dictatorship in the 1800s.   After Latin America gained independence in the early 1800s, various military dictators, called CAUDILLOS, emerged as rulers of the new nations. They gained and held power by means of personal qualities, strong loyalties, and ruthlessness. Because most Latin American nations were still developing political institutions and professional military establishments, many caudillos had no legitimate civilian or military rivals to challenge them. This was the case, for example, with José Rafael CARRERA in Guatemala and José Gaspar Rodríguez de FRANCIA in Paraguay. Most Latin American militaries remained unprofessional throughout the 1800s. One exception was Paraguay's military, which the dictator Francisco Solano LÓPEZ developed into one of the most disciplined and well-trained forces in Latin America.

Some caudillos of the 1800s, such as Ramón CASTILLA of Peru and Porfirio DÍAZ of Mexico, helped build and strengthen their nations. Both Castilla and Díaz modernized their countries and encouraged economic growth. Many others, however, concentrated on enhancing their own power and wealth and did little to improve their nations.

The Late 1800s and Early 1900s.   In the late 1800s, BOUNDARY DISPUTES and regional wars led many Latin American governments to begin training professional armies. These strengthened militaries played a major role in directing the course of their nations. By the early 1900s, the process of military professionalization had altered the nature of military dictatorship.

As the armies became more professional, military officers demanded greater independence from civilian political leaders. The new military elite considered themselves a special class that was both part of and separate from the rest of society. This attitude created a situation in which the old-style caudillos found it difficult to rule without the support of the military. Moreover, the military was more willing to overthrow civilian leaders it did not like.

63

A League of Dictators

In the late 1930s, the rise of European dictators—Adolph Hitler in Germany, Benito Mussolini in Italy, and Francisco Franco in Spain—was considered by many to be a serious threat to the world. At the same time, rumors circulated about a league of Latin American dictators who posed a threat in the Americas. This league was said to include Jorge Ubico of Guatemala, Maximiliano Hernández of El Salvador, Tiburcio Carías of Honduras, and Anastasio Somoza of Nicaragua. In reality, these dictators were rivals who tolerated one another only because none of them was capable of overthrowing the others.

* **communism** system in which land, goods, and the means of production are owned by the state or community rather than by individuals

The rise of professional militaries did not completely prevent the rise of powerful caudillos. For example, the Brazilian army supported Getúlio VARGAS as dictator of Brazil from 1930 to 1945, largely because of the stability his rule brought to the country. Other traditional caudillos, such as Juan PERÓN in Argentina and Augusto PINOCHET of Chile, were military men themselves. For the most part, however, professional armies resisted the rise of caudillos and sought reasons to establish military rule instead.

Dictatorship Since 1945.   After World War II, economic and social developments in Latin America expanded the political participation and influence of the growing middle and working classes. By the 1960s, peasants and the urban poor were also demanding a greater voice in government. However, this widespread participation increased political tensions among various social classes and groups. In some cases, class tensions and political unrest eroded democratic institutions and led to military intervention in government.

Since 1945, several Latin American nations have been controlled by military dictatorships, including Argentina (1966–1973 and 1976–1983), Brazil (1964–1985), Chile (1973–1990), and Uruguay (1973–1985). In such governments, the authority was typically shared among the military elite rather than placed in the hands of a single individual. One exception was the dominant leadership of General Augusto Pinochet in Chile.

Latin American military dictatorships often sought to maintain the political and economic stability of society. To accomplish this, military dictators sometimes used repression to silence opponents and rivals. They banned political party activities, destroyed labor unions, prohibited strikes, and imprisoned and tortured thousands of individuals whom they considered enemies of the state. Such repression was more typical of modern military dictators than of the caudillos who ruled in the 1800s.

Beginning in the late 1970s, military dictatorships throughout Latin America gradually relinquished power in the face of weak economies and increasing opposition. Another reason for their decline has been the decreased threat of communism*. In the 1960s and 1970s, many Latin American military leaders saw communism as a great danger to their societies, and they based their claim to power on the need to fight this threat. As communism declined throughout the world in the late 1900s, the perceived need for military rule faded as well.

Democratic institutions are now gaining a firmer foothold in most of Latin America. Nevertheless, the tradition of dictatorship remains strong, and the military continues to exercise enormous influence in Central America. Some Latin American nations may still experience authoritarian rule in the years to come. (*See also* **Armed Forces.**)

Diezmo

See *Taxes and Taxation.*

Dirty War

° **rightist** inclined to support conservative political ideas and to oppose reform or change

° **leftist** inclined to support radical reform and change; often associated with ideas of communism or socialism

° **Communist** person who advocates communism—a social system in which land, goods, and the means of production are owned by the state or community rather than by individuals

° **clergy** priests and other church officials qualified to perform church ceremonies

*T*he Dirty War was an internal conflict in ARGENTINA that lasted from 1974 to 1983. It pitted rightist* military governments against a leftist* opposition composed mostly of industrial workers, university students, young professionals, and intellectuals frustrated by political stagnation and economic decline in Argentina. The war created a period of terror in which thousands of Argentines died, were in exile, or simply "disappeared."

The Dirty War evolved from confrontations between the government and its opposition that began in 1969. In the early 1970s, leftist groups, either Communists* or supporters of Juan PERÓN, kidnapped and assassinated many military leaders and government officials. By 1974, the rightist groups retaliated with an unprecedented reign of terror carried out by government "death squads" and special military forces.

Activities against the leftist opposition included kidnapping, torture, rape, and murder. The families of victims often were unable to discover anything about loved ones unless a mutilated body turned up months after a "disappearance." Most victims were prominent journalists, union leaders, clergy*, and students, and some people "disappeared" for no apparent reason. A group of women called the Mothers of the Plaza de Mayo attracted international attention by demanding to know the fate of their children or grandchildren. Most Argentines, however, remained quiet because they were intimidated by the government.

The Dirty War ended in 1983 with the collapse of military rule in Argentina. A special commission investigated the past atrocities, and some individuals, including leading members of the military, were prosecuted for participating in crimes against the Argentine people. (*See also* **Counterinsurgency.**)

Diseases

° **colonial** period between the European conquest and independence, generally from the early 1500s to the early 1800s

° **indigenous** referring to the original inhabitants of a region

° **conquistador** Spanish explorer and conqueror

*D*iseases have played a significant role in the history of Latin America, especially during the European conquest and the colonial* period. The indigenous* peoples of Latin America had always had some diseases, but those brought to the Americas by conquistadors*, colonists, and African slaves had a devastating effect, killing perhaps millions of Indians. While some diseases were eventually controlled, others have remained a problem in Latin America.

The Pre-Columbian Period. Before Christopher COLUMBUS arrived in 1492, the Americas had a relatively healthy environment. One reason for the absence of diseases that plagued other parts of the world was the long isolation of the Americas. For thousands of years after the Indians' ancestors crossed the Bering Strait between Asia and Alaska, the Western Hemisphere was cut off from contact with the rest of the world. Moreover, people in the Americas were more widely scattered and lived in less crowded areas than people on other continents. These conditions were less supportive of diseases that thrive in densely populated areas. A third reason for the greater healthiness of

65

Diseases

Native Americans was the absence of domesticated* animals. The process of domesticating animals brought them into close contact with humans and introduced many illnesses to people.

However, the Western Hemisphere was by no means free of disease. The local Indians were subject to several illnesses, including tuberculosis, hepatitis, and various intestinal parasites. They also suffered from yaws (a tropical disease characterized by reddish growths on the skin) and encephalitis, which causes a swelling of the brain. But the Indians of the Americas did not suffer from many of the deadly diseases that affected people in Europe, Asia, and Africa, such as smallpox, chicken pox, measles, mumps, typhoid fever, cholera, typhus, diphtheria, scarlet fever, whooping cough, influenza, bubonic plague, yellow fever, and malaria.

Arrival of the Spanish.   By the late 1400s, the people of Spain and Portugal had been exposed to many diseases. Over the centuries, their homelands on the Iberian Peninsula of southwestern Europe had experienced wave after wave of invaders, from the ancient Greeks and Romans to the Moors*. These invasions exposed the Iberian people to the diseases of vast empires that extended throughout Europe and Asia. Spanish and Portuguese exploration of the African coast in the early 1400s also exposed the people of the Iberian Peninsula to many African illnesses. Although exposure to these different diseases brought sickness and death to the Spanish and Portuguese cities, it also increased the people's resistance and immunity to certain diseases.

The Indians of the Americas had no such resistance or immunity to these diseases. When the Spanish conquistadors and explorers arrived in the Americas, unwittingly carrying a host of diseases, epidemics* spread like wildfire through the Indian communities. As early as 1493, the Arawak Indians of the Caribbean islands were dying from an epidemic disease that might have been influenza. A typhus epidemic swept through the Caribbean a short time later.

By 1518, smallpox had arrived in the Caribbean. It swept through MEXICO between 1520 and 1524 and facilitated the Spanish conquest of the AZTECS. Smallpox reached the INCA of PERU even before the Spanish arrived there. Measles epidemics assaulted the Indians in the Caribbean in 1529, then spread to Mexico and Central America. Another killer that decimated the indigenous populations was diphtheria, and bubonic plague may also have appeared in the Americas in the 1500s. All of these diseases profoundly affected the Indians, weakening and killing thousands and making it easier for the Europeans to conquer those who survived.

The Fight Against Yellow Fever

In 1881, Cuban physician Carlos Juan Finlay proposed a theory that yellow fever was carried by mosquitoes. However, his theory was largely ignored until 1900. At that time, a United States military doctor, Walter Reed, who was investigating a yellow fever epidemic among American troops in Cuba, was ordered to test Finlay's theory. Reed's experiments confirmed that yellow fever was indeed transmitted by the mosquito. Efforts were made to eliminate the mosquito's breeding sites (typically areas of stagnant water), saving thousands of lives and ultimately enabling the building of the Panama Canal.

African and Asian Diseases.   Another round of fatal diseases arrived in the Americas with African slaves. Two of the deadliest were malaria and yellow fever. A lethal form of yellow fever reached the Caribbean island of Barbados in 1647, and yellow fever epidemics occurred in BRAZIL between 1685 and 1694. Because these are tropical diseases carried by mosquitoes, malaria and yellow fever primarily affected the people in warm, low-lying regions. Indians living in areas of higher elevation generally were spared these illnesses.

African fevers and other illnesses also afflicted white colonists in Latin America, while most blacks had acquired resistance and immunity in their African homelands. As the demand for African slaves increased, the ships that carried them to the Americas brought a host of other African diseases, most of which primarily affected tropical regions. Although the first new diseases in the Americas came from Europe, most of the illnesses that had reached Latin America by the 1800s originated in Africa.

Cholera, which struck whites, blacks, and American Indians alike, had neither European nor African origins. Several deadly cholera epidemics began in India and swept the globe in the 1800s. The first struck Cuba and North America in the 1830s. Three later cholera epidemics devastated much of the Caribbean and Latin America, leaving hundreds of thousands dead. A cholera epidemic that raced through Brazil from 1855 to 1856 killed as many as 200,000 people.

The Fight Against Disease. By the 1900s, programs were under way throughout Latin America to limit disease. Mosquito population control programs curbed yellow fever in the early 1900s, and the use of pesticides after the mid-1900s expanded these efforts. Various new

Indians had little resistance, or immunity, to the diseases unknowingly brought by European explorers. Diseases, such as smallpox and typhus, killed thousands, making it easier for the Europeans to conquer those who survived. This Aztec illustration shows the devastation caused by smallpox.

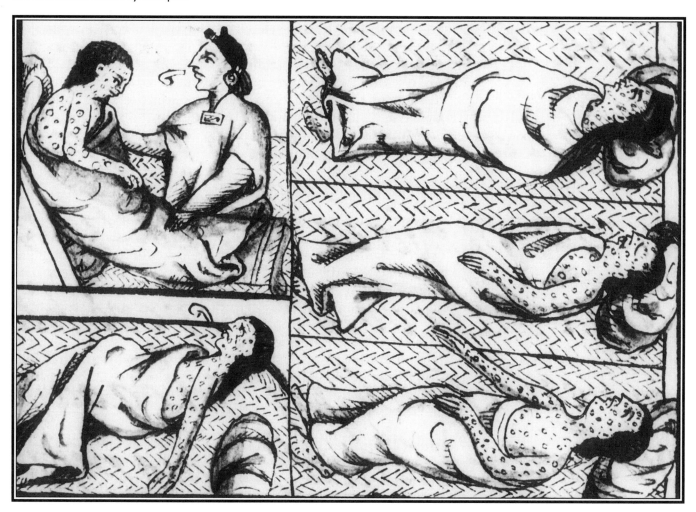

medications, improved health care, better NUTRITION, and increased sanitation also reduced the risk of many diseases.

Although such programs have done much to fight diseases, they have not eradicated them. New illnesses have emerged, such as AIDS*, which destroys the body's immune system. HIV (the virus that causes AIDS) and AIDS afflict about 1.5 million people in Latin America. Although the number of AIDS cases is far greater in Africa and Asia, the disease has had a major impact on Latin America. More people in Latin America die each year from AIDS than from traffic accidents. Incidence of HIV and AIDS is increasing among the poor and uneducated, and a significant portion of Latin Americans who test positive for HIV and AIDS are women. However, advances in AIDS treatments, as well as public education on its prevention, are beginning to yield some progress in fighting this disease.

Latin American nations face other threats to public health, as well. Many Latin Americans have little or no access to modern medicine or health care. Some nations—such as Nicaragua—lack the resources needed to detect certain illnesses in their early stages, making some diseases (such as cancer) very difficult to treat. Infant death rates remain high in Peru and other countries. In addition, the extreme poverty that exists throughout Latin America contributes to malnutrition*, which weakens people's resistance to illness. Inadequate housing, poor sanitation systems, and a lack of clean drinking water also create unhealthy environments in which diseases spread. As a result, many areas endure periodic outbreaks of serious illnesses, including cholera, malaria, Chagas' disease*, and dengue*. In an attempt to reduce such outbreaks, many Latin American nations have introduced health education programs to teach children and communities how to prevent disease by improving their diets, hygiene, and environment. (*See also* **Medicine**.)

* **AIDS** acquired immune deficiency syndrome—a condition that cripples the body's immune system, leaving the body vulnerable to disease and infection

* **malnutrition** lack of proper nutrition, often associated with various ailments
* **Chagas' disease** tropical disease that causes swelling, fever, and enlargement of internal organs and is carried by insects that live in the walls of thatched buildings
* **dengue** acute infectious disease that causes headache, severe joint pain, and rash and is spread by mosquitoes

Divinities

*T*he pre-Columbian* civilizations of Latin America had many divinities, or gods, associated with the natural world and its phenomena. The MAYA, AZTECS, INCA, and other pre-Columbian peoples worshiped these deities, built temples in their honor, and sometimes made human sacrifices to them. They looked to the gods for help, guidance, and understanding of the natural forces vital to agrarian* societies. Each pre-Columbian culture had its own pantheon* of gods. But many of these ancient societies also borrowed gods from other cultures—often changing their names—and assimilated* them into their own religious beliefs in a process known as SYNCRETISM. In some parts of Latin America, this resulted in a complex system of interrelated deities and religious myths.

Maya Divinities. The various Maya states each had several important gods, some of whom they may have adopted from the TOLTECS. The principal Maya deity was Itzamná, the god of heaven and of day and night. Along with his father, Hunab Ku, Itzamná played a major

* **pre-Columbian** before the arrival of Christopher Columbus and other Europeans in the Americas in the 1490s
* **agrarian** referring to farmland, its use, or its ownership
* **pantheon** group of gods and goddesses within a single religious tradition
* **assimilate** to adopt the beliefs or customs of a society

role in the creation myths of the Maya. He often appears as four serpent-headed gods called Itzamnás, who represent the north, south, east, and west. Closely connected with Itzamná are Kinich Ahau (the sun god) and Ix Chel (the moon goddess). The K'ICHE' Maya of Guatemala recorded their story of creation in the text called the Popul-Vuh.

The Maya practiced human sacrifice and ritual bleeding in some of their religious ceremonies. For instance, the Maya rain god Chac was linked to human sacrifice. Like Itzamná, Chac sometimes appeared as 4 gods, the Chacs, who were associated with the points on the compass. Another group of 4 gods were the Bacabs—brothers who held up the sky. A group of 13 gods, the Oxlahuntiku, ruled the heavens, while a group of 9 gods, the Bolontiku, ruled the underworld.

Several Maya gods were associated with death. The god of death, Ah Puch, is often depicted on Maya monuments as a skeletonlike being and is sometimes shown battling with Ah Mun, the corn god. Ixtab was the goddess of suicides, while Cizin was the god of earthquakes and ruler of the land of the dead.

See color plate 1, vol. 1.

Aztec Divinities.

The Aztecs had a large and complex pantheon of gods, each attended by its own priests and honored with special ceremonies and offerings. They believed that the gods required nourishment from still-beating human hearts to make the sun rise, and this practice was central to Aztec religion.

Among the most important Aztec deities were four powerful gods of creation and destruction: Tezcatlipoca, Huitzilopochtli, Coatlicue, and QUETZALCOATL. Tezcatlipoca was the god of majesty, destruction, the night, and magic. He could change his identity and take many disguises, including that of a JAGUAR. Tezcatlipoca had the power to bestow riches and fame and to punish wrongdoers with sickness and poverty.

Huitzilopochtli, the god of the sun and of war, was believed to have led the Aztecs from their original homeland to central MEXICO, where they founded the great city of TENOCHTITLÁN. He was also given credit for their military success, and the Aztecs often sacrificed prisoners of war to him.

Huitzilopochtli's mother, Coatlicue, was an earth goddess associated with reproduction and sacrificial death. According to Aztec myth, Coatlicue's children murdered her when they discovered she was pregnant with Huitzilopochtli. Upon her death, Huitzilopochtli sprang forth fully grown and killed his siblings.

Quetzalcoatl, or the Feathered Serpent, was an ancient deity worshiped by the people of TEOTIHUACÁN, by the Toltecs, and by the Maya, who called him Kukulcan. The Aztecs revered him as the god of the morning and evening star, a wind god, and a symbol of death and rebirth. Quetzalcoatl was thought to have transformed the bones of the dead into a new generation of people to inhabit the universe.

Another major Aztec god was Tlaloc, the god of rain, fertility, and agriculture. One of the most ancient gods of Mesoamerica*—and closely related to the Maya god Chac—Tlaloc was adopted by the Aztecs when they arrived in central Mexico and conquered the agricultural tribes

* **Mesoamerica** culture region that includes central and southern Mexico, Guatemala, Belize, El Salvador, and parts of Honduras, Nicaragua, and Costa Rica

there. Tlaloc was both greatly revered and feared. He and his assistants, called *tlaloques* (little Tlalocs), produced rain, lightning, thunder, and hail. Tlaloc could also cause drought and hunger and unleash devastating hurricanes.

Inca Divinities. The Inca assimilated several gods from the people they conquered. The greatest of the Inca gods was Viracocha, who created the other gods, as well as the earth, humans, and animals, and ruled over all. According to Inca myth, Viracocha gave other gods the responsibility of overseeing his creation.

Viracocha's most important servant, the sun god Inti, was the patron* deity of the Inca. They believed that he was the divine ancestor of the Inca rulers and referred to themselves as Intip Churin (Children of the Sun). Pachacamac, a pre-Inca creator deity, was another god of enormous prestige. He was a child of the sun and a god of fire. One of the most sacred places in the Andes was a shrine to Pachacamac.

The earth mother goddess, Pachamama, was an Inca agricultural deity worshiped for her role in fertility and the protection of crops. However, when the Inca needed rain and protection from drought, they prayed to Illapa, the thunder god who was believed to control the weather. Two other significant Inca deities were Mamacocha, goddess of the sea who created streams and springs, and Mamaquilla, the goddess of the moon and wife of the sun. (*See also* **Manuscripts and Writing, Pre-Columbian; Religions, Indian.**)

* **patron** special guardian, protector, or supporter

Divorce

See *Marriage and Divorce.*

Dollar Diplomacy

Dollar Diplomacy was a foreign policy created by the United States to ensure the financial stability of Latin America while protecting its business and economic interests in the region. Although the policy applied to all of Latin America, it focused mainly on CENTRAL AMERICA and the Caribbean.

Dollar Diplomacy grew out of the foreign policies of United States president Theodore Roosevelt's administration. In 1904, Roosevelt declared that the United States would intervene in Latin America to uphold the MONROE DOCTRINE, which had guided its foreign policy in the Western Hemisphere since 1823. The declaration became known as the ROOSEVELT COROLLARY to the Monroe Doctrine. The United States used the corollary to claim a financial and economic hold on the Latin American economies. This included seizing control of the finances of the DOMINICAN REPUBLIC in 1905 and sending troops into CUBA in 1906 to protect United States investments and interests there.

Roosevelt's successor, William Howard Taft, continued the efforts to expand United States influence in Latin America. Taft and his administration established a significant economic presence in the region. Their objective was to develop the political, economic, cultural, and strategic influence of the United States by substituting the power of investment and financial aid for diplomacy and military action. The United States also wanted to keep European powers out of the region by guaranteeing the repayment of foreign loans. The core idea behind this so-called Dollar Diplomacy was to manage the Latin American economies without direct military intervention, or in other words, to substitute "dollars for bullets." Taft believed that the policy would bring stability to the region and increase the influence of the United States without the need to send troops.

United States economic and security interests were greatest in Central America and the Caribbean, and these regions became the chief targets of Dollar Diplomacy. The United States government pressured Latin American leaders to accept United States customs collectors, financial advisers, tax administrators, and economic consultants. This gave the United States a great deal of financial and economic authority over those nations.

Despite claims to the contrary, Dollar Diplomacy resulted in many military interventions in Latin America because the United States felt compelled to protect its financial interests in the region. In 1912, for example, the United States sent troops to NICARAGUA when a revolution threatened the stability of the country. United States troops also occupied HAITI and the Dominican Republic for long periods and frequently intervened in Cuba, PANAMA, and HONDURAS.

In some ways, Dollar Diplomacy benefited Latin America. It attracted United States investment and provided financial aid to build roads, railroads, and seaports and to develop banks and other economic institutions. However, the intervention in Latin American affairs created a legacy of distrust and anti-Americanism that affected relations between the United States and Latin America for many years. The United States abandoned Dollar Diplomacy in 1912. However, future presidents continued to promote measures to ensure United States supremacy in Central America and the Caribbean. (*See also* **Foreign Investment; United States–Latin American Relations.**)

Domestic Labor

Domestic labor is an important part of Latin American society and economy. Since the colonial period, wealthy and middle-class families have employed servants in their homes. During the early colonial period, about half of these workers were male. Since the 1700s, most domestic servants have been female. In fact, domestic service has historically been the primary form of employment for women in Latin America.

During the colonial period, domestic labor was regulated by laws that stipulated the terms of employment. From the 1500s to 1700s, most domestic servants in BRAZIL were blacks or Indians. In MEXICO, most servants in the 1500s were Indians, but by the 1700s, most were mestizos*. Mulattos* and lower-class whites were also employed in domestic service.

Although domestic labor declined in importance in Europe and the United States during the 1800s and 1900s, it has remained important in

* **mestizo** person of mixed European and Indian ancestry
* **mulatto** person of mixed black and white ancestry

71

Latin America, primarily because of the presence of a large, unskilled, lower-class population desperately in need of jobs. This is particularly true for lower-class women, who have had few other opportunities for work.

In the 1980s, the demand for full-time, live-in domestic servants began to decline in Latin America. This was largely due to employers' desire for privacy, an increase in the number of day care and nursery schools, and the use of technology that simplified and reduced house-keeping chores. As a result, more domestic servants in recent years have been employed only part-time and for specific tasks. Part-time domestic work is less regulated and provides less secure employment than a live-in position. Nevertheless, it continues to attract those who have few other employment opportunities. (*See also* **Class Structure, Colonial and Modern; Labor and Labor Movements; Women.**)

Dominica

See *British West Indies*.

Dominican Republic

See map in Caribbean Antilles (vol. I).

*T*he Dominican Republic is the second-largest nation in the CAR-IBBEAN ANTILLES. This former Spanish colony occupies the eastern two-thirds of the island of HISPANIOLA, which it shares with HAITI. These neighboring nations also share closely linked, turbulent histories. The capital of the Dominican Republic, SANTO DOMINGO, dates back to 1496 and is the oldest permanent European settlement in the Americas.

The Colonial Period

Originally inhabited by the Arawak and Carib Indians, the island of Hispaniola was claimed for Spain by Christopher COLUMBUS on his first voyage to the Americas, in 1492. The Spanish established a colony and soon prospered from mining and agriculture there. For the next 50 years, Hispaniola served as the administrative center for Spain's growing American empire.

However, following the Spanish conquests of Mexico and Peru, which offered greater riches than the Caribbean, Hispaniola's importance diminished. By 1550, the island was a neglected backwater of the Spanish empire. In the 1600s, it suffered devastating raids by foreign BUCCANEERS (hired pirates) and continued to decline both economically and socially.

° **cede** to yield or surrender, usually by treaty

In 1697, Spain ceded* the western third of the island to France, which established the colony of St. Domingue (present-day Haiti). The history of the Spanish and French portions of Hispaniola remained intertwined. France gained control of the entire island in 1795, but Spain regained the eastern portion in 1809. In 1821, the Spanish colony declared its independence from Spain and became known as the Dominican Republic.

In a recent election, sign painters in Santo Domingo urged voters to elect more women to the congress and the government.

From Independence to 1930

For many years after the Dominican Republic declared its independence, the nation was in turmoil. It was dominated at various times by Haiti, Spain, and the United States. The nation also struggled with economic and political instability as well as with a long succession of dictators who prevented the development of democracy.

Haitian Rule. Within weeks after achieving independence from Spain in 1821, the Dominican Republic was seized by Haiti, which had gained independence from France several years earlier. In many ways, Haitian rule was harsh. The Haitians imposed high taxes, confiscated church property, and destroyed the Spanish educational system. They also forced out the traditional ruling class and placed their own people in all the highest administrative offices. However, the Haitians also freed the slaves in the Dominican Republic and governed efficiently.

In the 1830s, a Dominican leader named Juan Pablo DUARTE organized a secret society to fight the Haitians. After a long struggle, the Dominicans finally won their independence from Haiti in 1844. Because of his role in this struggle, Duarte became known as "the father of his country" and is regarded as the nation's greatest hero.

An Era of Dictators. Duarte's dream of establishing a democratic republic* soon vanished. Opponents forced him to flee the country, and the Dominican Republic was taken over by two powerful CAUDILLOS (military dictators)—Pedro Santana and Buenaventura Báez. For nearly 30 years, Santana and Báez battled each other for control of the Dominican Republic, alternating the presidency between them.

* **republic** government in which citizens elect officials to represent them and govern according to law

Dominican Republic

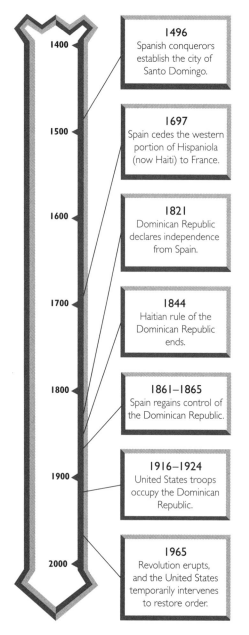

1400

1496
Spanish conquerors establish the city of Santo Domingo.

1500

1697
Spain cedes the western portion of Hispaniola (now Haiti) to France.

1600

1821
Dominican Republic declares independence from Spain.

1700

1844
Haitian rule of the Dominican Republic ends.

1800

1861–1865
Spain regains control of the Dominican Republic.

1900

1916–1924
United States troops occupy the Dominican Republic.

2000

1965
Revolution erupts, and the United States temporarily intervenes to restore order.

° **annex** to add a territory to an existing state

° **customs** government department that collects taxes on imports and exports

° **guerrilla** referring to a group that uses surprise raids to obstruct or harass an enemy or overthrow a government

° **caudillo** authoritarian leader or dictator, often from the military

Both leaders looked to foreign nations to help the country politically and economically, and the period of their rule was marked by great instability.

In 1861, Santana returned control of the country to Spain in an effort to end the continuing threat of invasion by Haiti. Most Dominicans objected to the reestablishment of Spanish rule. Their opposition led to the War of Restoration, which began in 1863 and resulted in Spain's permanent withdrawal from the Dominican Republic two years later. After Spain withdrew its troops, Báez approached the United States with a plan to annex* the Dominican Republic. United States president Ulysses S. Grant favored the idea and signed a treaty, but the U.S. Senate refused to approve it.

The frequent turmoil and instability that had plagued the Dominican Republic since independence ended temporarily in the 1880s and 1890s during the rule of Ulises Heureaux. This ruthless dictator dominated the country from 1882 to 1899. His rule was marked by assassinations, bribery, corruption, and surveillance of citizens by secret police. Yet at the same time, the country experienced substantial economic growth.

United States Intervention. Heureaux was assassinated in 1899, leading to renewed political and economic instability. The resulting chaos greatly concerned many in the United States who worried about their financial investments in the country. In 1905, the United States took over the administration of the Dominican Republic's customs* service, using the ROOSEVELT COROLLARY of the MONROE DOCTRINE as the basis for its intervention. The United States soon dominated the nation both economically and politically.

Between 1906 to 1911, the Dominicans enjoyed a period of stability and modernization under the presidency of Ramón Cáceres. However, his assassination in 1911 once again plunged the nation into turmoil. The United States responded by sending troops into the Dominican Republic and taking complete control in 1916.

The Dominican Republic remained under United States military control until 1924. During this time, the roads, schools, and sanitation systems were greatly improved. But United States rule also led to the suppression of Dominican guerrilla* movements, thus limiting the development of legitimate political opposition. The most harmful legacy of the United States occupation was the creation of a highly trained national guard under the command of Rafael Léonidas TRUJILLO MOLINA. This military force became the power behind Trujillo's long and brutal dictatorship.

The Era of Trujillo. In 1930, Rafael Trujillo and the national guard overthrew President Horacio Vásquez. For the next 31 years, Trujillo ruled the Dominican Republic as dictator, with powers far greater than those of the earlier caudillos*. His dictatorship was one of the longest and cruelest of modern times.

Trujillo was an authoritarian ruler, controlling the armed forces, the government, the economy, the church, and every other aspect of

Dominican society. Determined to acquire a great personal fortune, he seized most of the nation's land and industry. To ensure his control of the government, he gave important positions to members of his family. He silenced the opposition and maintained order through a secret police force. Although Trujillo himself was of mixed race, he was an extreme racist. In 1937, he ordered the massacre of nearly 25,000 black Haitians living in the Dominican Republic—including children.

For most of his rule, Trujillo maintained good relations with the United States. He repaid his nation's foreign debt and exported coffee, tobacco, sugar, cocoa, and other products that were in great demand in the United States. At the outbreak of World War II, Trujillo became a United States ally, and after the war, he opposed communism*, which ensured further support from the anti-Communist United States.

Trujillo's fortunes declined in the mid-1950s, when dictators throughout Latin America began falling from power. In 1959, some Dominican exiles invaded the Dominican Republic, but they were captured, tortured, and killed. Because the rebels had received support from VENEZUELA, Trujillo sent agents to assassinate the Venezuelan president, Rómulo BETANCOURT. The plotters injured Betancourt, and as punishment for the attempt on the president's life, the ORGANIZATION OF AMERICAN STATES (OAS) imposed economic restrictions on the Dominican Republic.

In desperation, Trujillo abandoned his policy of maintaining friendly relations with the United States. In 1956, Dominican agents kidnapped and murdered Jesús de Galíndez, a United States university teacher who had published a book criticizing Trujillo and his regime*. The Dominicans also murdered the North American pilot who had flown Galíndez to the Dominican Republic. These actions outraged the United States, which imposed an arms embargo* on the Dominican Republic as well as a special import tax on Dominican sugar. These policies crippled the Dominican economy and led to increased opposition to Trujillo. The dictator was assassinated in 1961.

Aftermath of Trujillo.
After Trujillo's death, his heirs and followers attempted to stay in power, but they were soon driven into exile by opponents of the regime, who had the support of the United States. The Dominican Republic then took its first real steps toward democracy. In elections held in 1962, a reformer named Juan Bosch became the first democratically elected president in the nation's history.

Conservative* forces remained strong, however, and Bosch was overthrown in a military coup* in 1963. Although the new government was run by civilian officials, the real power was wielded by the military. In 1965, tired of continued military corruption and repression, the Dominican people launched a revolution to restore democracy. The revolution was short-lived. Fearing that rebellion would bring Communists to power, the United States occupied the country until a new president was elected the following year.

Recent History.
During the 1960s and 1970s, the Dominican Republic made several important advances. Under the leadership of

° **communism** system in which land, goods, and the means of production are owned by the state or community rather than by individuals

° **regime** prevailing political system or rule

° **embargo** official order prohibiting the movement of merchant ships in or out of certain ports or countries

° **conservative** inclined to maintain existing political and social views, conditions, and institutions

° **coup** sudden, often violent overthrow of a ruler or government

75

Columbus Brings a Town to America

In 1493, on his second voyage to America, Christopher Columbus brought seeds, farm animals, and nearly 1,200 Spanish settlers. They built a town on the north coast of what is now the Dominican Republic and named it Isabella after the Spanish queen. However, the site was badly chosen; Isabella had a poor harbor and infertile soil. The Spaniards' crops failed, and they suffered hunger and illness. Weary and disappointed, many colonists returned to Spain. In 1496, Columbus's brother Bartolomé moved the settlement to a location on the south coast with a safe harbor and rich soil. Called Santo Domingo, this second town is now the capital of the Dominican Republic.

° **inflation** sharp increase in prices due to an increase in the amount of money or credit relative to available goods and services

° **infrastructure** basic framework of a society and its economy, which includes roads, bridges, port facilities, airports, and other public works

President Joaquín Balaguer, who served from 1966 to 1978, the nation's economy improved dramatically. Schools, hospitals, roads, bridges, and dams were built, and TOURISM and FOREIGN INVESTMENT grew. But the economic boom primarily benefited the upper and middle classes, and it produced much corruption, especially among the nation's top military leaders. In addition, foreign governments criticized the Balaguer administration for violations of HUMAN RIGHTS.

By the late 1970s, the economic boom was ending. Discontented Dominicans elected a new president, Antonio Guzmán Fernández, who promised to improve the lives of all Dominicans. However, the declining economy prevented Guzmán from achieving social reforms, and political corruption continued. His successor, Salvador Jorge Blanco, also faced economic problems and failed to improve living conditions for the average Dominican. In 1984, anger over rising prices led to protests and riots that were violently suppressed by the police and armed forces.

In 1986, Dominicans reelected former president Joaquín Balaguer. In an attempt to boost the nation's weak economy, Balaguer began a huge building program that included the construction of apartments, bridges, and highways. While this building boom relieved unemployment, it also increased the country's debt and fueled a period of severe inflation* that threatened the survival of many Dominicans.

Balaguer remained in office until 1996. During his time in office, the Dominican Republic continued to struggle with economic problems, including high unemployment and inflation, a lack of medical and educational facilities, and a crumbling infrastructure*. In 1991, the country also entered a bitter dispute with its old enemy Haiti, when Balaguer's government expelled thousands of Haitians from the Dominican Republic.

In 1996, Leonel Fernández Reyna was elected president of the Dominican Republic. Fernández promised to fight political corruption and reform the economy. But he and future presidents face a difficult task. Many wealthy, powerful Dominicans oppose change, and the nation has severe economic troubles. The country remains deeply in debt, many of its people live in extreme poverty, and increasing drug trade activity is compounding the nation's problems. (*See also* **Caribs; Economic Development; Geography; Spain and the Spanish Empire; Trade and Commerce; United States–Latin American Relations.**)

Dominicans

See *Religious Orders.*

Dowry

See *Marriage and Divorce.*

Drake, Francis

ca. 1545–1596
English privateer

° **privateer** privately owned ship authorized by the government to attack and capture enemy vessels; also the ship's master

° **indigenous** referring to the original inhabitants of a region

° **armada** fleet of warships

*S*ir Francis Drake was an English privateer* who terrorized Spanish ships and settlements in the CARIBBEAN SEA during the late 1500s. He was also a naval genius who developed a successful strategy to damage Spanish property and seize wealth intended for the Spanish treasury.

Drake was a member of English trader John HAWKINS's team that suffered a disastrous defeat at San Juan de Ulúa on the coast of MEXICO in 1568. Later Drake formed alliances with indigenous* warriors, and in 1572, he attacked a Spanish settlement in PANAMA and seized its wealth. After England and Spain signed a peace treaty in 1574, Drake stopped attacking Spanish interests in the West Indies (now the CARIBBEAN ANTILLES) for 11 years. His boldest move came in 1585, when he assembled more than 20 ships to attack SANTO DOMINGO, CARTAGENA, Panama, and HAVANA. He hoped to disrupt the flow of resources, especially silver, to Spain to hinder Spanish military efforts in Europe. He also hoped to establish an English stronghold in the West Indies. Drake succeeded in destroying much of Santo Domingo and Cartagena. However, bad weather and a sick crew forced him to return home. Although Spain's property and prestige were hurt, Drake's attack did not affect the empire.

Drake also played a key role in defeating the Spanish Armada* that was sent to attack England in 1588. In 1595, he led another raid in the West Indies, but the Spanish were well prepared to meet it. They defeated the English at SAN JUAN (in PUERTO RICO), Cartagena, and Panama. Drake was never able to break Spain's hold on the Indies, and he died shortly afterward. (*See also* **Buccaneers; Fleet Systems, Colonial; Piracy.**)

Drama

See *Theater.*

Drugs and Drug Trade

° **hallucinogenic** capable of distorting senses and feelings or altering one's awareness

° **divination** practice that looks into the future, usually by supernatural means

° **psilocybin** hallucinogenic substance found in certain mushrooms

*S*everal types of drugs have been used in Latin America for thousands of years for religious, medicinal, and recreational purposes. In recent times, some of these drugs have played an increasingly significant role in the economics and politics of many Latin American nations.

Drugs and Drug Use. Since about 3000 B.C., drugs have been a part of Latin American culture and RELIGIONS. Priests and healers have used them for meditation, curing the sick, predicting the future, or relieving hunger. The ancient MAYA used mushrooms, toad venom, rootstalk of water lilies, and other hallucinogenic* substances for healing and divination*. The AZTECS used "god's flesh" (psilocybin* mushrooms) in combination with other hallucinogens in ceremonial feasts, in rituals involving human sacrifice, and as payment of tribute*. Archaeological* findings indicate that the INCA chewed coca

° **tribute** payment made to a dominant power

° **archaeological** relating to archaeology, or the science of studying past human cultures, usually by excavating ruins

See color plate 1, vol. 1.

Mushroom Cults

Archaeologists have found several images sculpted in the shape of mushrooms in Guatemala, indicating the early use of mushrooms in Maya culture and religion. In the 1500s, Franciscan friar Bernardino de Sahagún also reported the widespread use of mushrooms in Mexican religions. Members of these groups believed that the hallucinogenic mushrooms purified their bodies and helped them have a direct experience with God. The visions that users experienced confirmed that the worshipper was in the presence of God. Others believed that these encounters enhanced their sexual appeal and improved their hunting skills.

° **Rastafarian** follower of Rastafarianism, a Jamaican religion whose members worship Haile Selassie and believe that Africa, especially Ethiopia, is the Promised Land

leaves as early as 500 B.C. and that the leaves were an important part of the religion and culture of the TIWANAKU empire.

The most important and widespread drug currently produced in Latin America is cocaine, derived from the leaves of the coca plant, which is native to the eastern slopes of the ANDES. When chewed, the coca leaves stimulate the central nervous system, induce feelings of elation and well-being, and relieve hunger. Other drugs native to Latin America include the peyote cactus and the San Pedro cactus. Grown mainly in MEXICO and along the western coast of South America, these cacti contain mescaline, a drug that induces visions enabling the user to experience a mystic state of being. Several types of mushrooms containing psilocybin are also grown in Central America and Mexico. Drugs not native to Latin America were brought by the Spanish and Portuguese in the 1500s (marijuana, or cannabis), and from Asia in the early 1900s (opium poppy). Marijuana relaxes the body and causes the user to undergo unreal and strange experiences. Opium relieves the user of pain, hunger, thirst, anxiety, and depression.

Drugs During and After the Colonial Period. Coca production and use in the Andes continued during the Spanish colonial period. The CATHOLIC CHURCH condemned the use of hallucinogens. Spanish rulers tried to stop the growth and use of coca for political and humanitarian reasons and because they thought its use in native religious activities encouraged Indian resistance to Spanish rule. However, their attempts were unsuccessful, and many Spaniards themselves began to chew coca leaves. By the late 1500s, the Spanish accepted the fact that coca was an integral part of Indian culture and the lifestyle of the workforce. Although they regulated the production and trade of coca, its demand continued to grow. Production increased to meet the demands from workers in the MINING industry who depended on coca to help them endure the difficult and demanding work conditions.

After the Spanish conquest, coca continued to play an important role in cultures such as the AYMARA and Quechua INDIANS of the Andean ALTIPLANO. Indians in the Andes and AMAZON REGION of PERU, BOLIVIA, and ECUADOR use coca in cultural and religious ceremonies. In Peru, healers use the San Pedro cactus and other hallucinogens to diagnose and treat illnesses believed to be caused by witchcraft. Marijuana, which was an unimportant drug in ancient Latin American cultures, is now popular in the Caribbean. Commonly called ganja, it is used in JAMAICA and some nearby countries, and it is associated with such groups as the Rastafarians*.

The Drug Trade. The Latin American drug trade is dominated by cocaine, marijuana, and heroin. Ever since the demand increased in the 1970s, the production and distribution of these drugs has influenced the economy, politics, and societies of Latin American nations. They have also affected UNITED STATES–LATIN AMERICAN RELATIONS because the United States is the main market for Latin American drugs. Although more than 80 percent of the coca is grown in Bolivia and

Peru, COLOMBIA leads the cocaine trade. Colombia has many refining plants and is strategically located between the main growing areas and the routes by which the drug is shipped to the United States and Europe. Recently, BRAZIL has also entered the cocaine trade.

Marijuana has been imported into the United States since the 1800s, mostly from Mexico. In the 1970s, Mexico decreased the amount of marijuana it shipped to the United States, while Colombia and nations in southern and central America and the Caribbean increased their production. Today marijuana is probably the largest cash crop* in Jamaica and BELIZE. Since the 1980s, Latin America has also exported heroin to the United States, supplying more than 40 percent of its market. Since then, Mexico has increased its share of the United States heroin market from 10 percent to about 30 percent in the late 1990s. GUATEMALA and Colombia have also begun to increase heroin production.

Drugs, Economics, and Politics.   Drug money has become an important source of income and foreign currency for many Latin American countries. Cocaine trafficking* produces profits estimated at more than $5 billion annually, and 10 to 20 percent of that money flows back into the economies of the producing nations. It is said that in the 1980s, marijuana trade supported Jamaica's economy when the country was short of foreign currency. Despite their efforts, governments have not been very successful in eliminating or minimizing drug production or in preventing drug trade. Various measures, such as encouraging farmers to shift to food crop production and fumigation and destruction of drug crops, have failed in most countries. Many farmers maintain that growing drug plants—such as coca— gives them a higher, more stable income than traditional AGRICULTURE.

In Colombia, drug cartels* such as the Medellín and CALI cartels, have become powerful political forces. The large amount of money they earn gives them considerable influence with the police, government officials, and judges. This has caused widespread corruption in drug-producing countries. Manuel Noriega, who controlled Panama's government for much of the 1980s, was accused of working with the Medellín cartel to smuggle drugs throughout the world and transferring drug money through his country. He was arrested by United States troops in 1990, tried, and sentenced to 40 years in prison. Drug lords also provide arms and money to terrorist and guerrilla* groups, such as Peru's SENDERO LUMINOSO (Shining Path), in exchange for the protection of the growers and dealers.

United States efforts to stop the drug trade have usually focused on eliminating the supply of drugs rather than on finding ways to prevent their use. For example, the U.S. National Drug Control Strategy emphasizes active measures at the sites of production and stricter border control. Since 1986, the United States government has annually certified those Latin American countries it feels are cooperating in the war against drugs and provides financial assistance for their efforts. Colombia recently lost its certification for the third consecutive year because the United States government felt the Colombian government was not

* **cash crop** crop grown primarily for profit rather than for local consumption

* **traffic** to engage or deal in an illegal trade

* **cartel** group of business organizations that join together to regulate the production, pricing, and marketing of the goods they produce

* **guerrilla** referring to a group that uses surprise raids to obstruct or harass an enemy or overthrow a government

79

aggressive enough in fighting its drug cartels, growers, and producers. Despite uneven progress in antidrug efforts, Mexico was recertified in 1998, a decision that many members of the U.S. Congress strongly opposed.

Most Latin American countries resent the United States drug certification process. These governments maintain that the United States, being the world's largest consumer of illegal drugs, lacks the morality to judge the actions of other countries. In response to United States actions, drug lords have adjusted their own strategies by spreading production over larger areas and finding new markets. Larger cartels have been replaced with smaller, harder-to-investigate trafficking organizations. Given the large sums of money involved, the economic and political conditions in Latin America, and the huge United States market for drugs, the drug trade seems likely to remain a problem for some time.

Duarte, Juan Pablo

1813–1876
Leader of Dominican independence

Although Juan Pablo Duarte never participated in his country's government, he is considered the father of Dominican independence. As a young man, Duarte studied in Europe while HAITI occupied the DOMINICAN REPUBLIC. He was influenced by the ideals of liberty and equality and, in 1838, formed a secret society called La Trinitaria, whose goal was Dominican independence.

After Haiti's president Jean-Pierre Boyer was overthrown in 1844, Duarte returned to the Dominican capital of SANTO DOMINGO to help form a new government. However, his ideas were too liberal for the Dominican military leaders, and he was exiled by General Pedro Santana, who became president. After spending 15 years in the jungles of Venezuela, Duarte returned in 1864 because Santana had agreed to return the Dominican Republic to Spanish control. But Duarte was unwelcome in the new government and was exiled again in 1865. He returned to Venezuela, where he lived the rest of his life in poverty, largely forgotten by the world. His role in Dominican independence remained unrecognized until his death in 1876.

Duarte Fuentes, José Napoleón

1925–1990
President of El Salvador

° **coup** sudden, often violent overthrow of a ruler or government

José Napoleón Duarte Fuentes was an important political figure in EL SALVADOR and twice served as the country's president. A civil engineer by training, Duarte became mayor of the capital at SAN SALVADOR in 1964 and ran for president in 1972. Although he claimed victory, the army tampered with the results and awarded the presidency to Colonel Arturo Molina, a military officer. Duarte then participated in an unsuccessful coup* but was captured, tortured, and expelled from the country. In 1979, after Molina was overthrown, Duarte returned from exile in Venezuela. He joined the ruling junta* and became the country's president in December 1980. Two years later, the national assembly voted him out of office. In the free elections held in 1984, Duarte defeated conservative* leader Roberto

° **junta** small group of people who run a government, usually after seizing power by force

° **conservative** inclined to maintain existing political and social views, conditions, and institutions

° **Communist** person who advocates communism—a social system in which land, goods, and the means of production are owned by the state or community rather than by individuals

D'AUBUISSON to become El Salvador's first elected civilian president in more than 50 years.

Despite receiving economic and military aid from the United States, Duarte had trouble ruling El Salvador, which was torn by a five-year-old civil war. His former political friends criticized him for working with the military, which had a long record of HUMAN RIGHTS abuses. The military considered him a Communist* because he met with rebels to try to end the war and supported reforms to benefit the poor. Duarte's efforts to end the war failed, and he lost his credibility when his government responded poorly to a major EARTHQUAKE that hit San Salvador in 1986. His greatest success may have come after losing the election of 1989. Despite the political turmoil in El Salvador at the time, he peacefully transferred power to the newly elected civilian president, Alfredo Cristiani.

Dutch in Latin America

*T*he first Dutch expedition to LATIN AMERICA did not occur until the early 1600s, more than 100 years after the first Spanish explorations of the CARIBBEAN SEA. From the beginning, the Dutch planned to invade, settle, and exploit the region's wealth. Dutch presence in America was brief, but it caused great difficulty for Latin Americans and their European rulers.

° **captaincy** governmental system established by the Portuguese monarchy for the settlement and colonization of Brazil

Dutch Jews and New Christians in Brazil

When Johan Maurits became the governor-general of Dutch Brazil in 1636, there were many Dutch Jews in the colony. There were also a smaller number of so-called New Christians, Jews whose ancestors had been forced to convert to Catholicism. Maurits increased protection for these Brazilian Jews and enabled the New Christians to openly return to their Jewish faith. In 1645, the Jewish community in Dutch Brazil was at its peak, numbering about 1,450 people, or almost half of the white civilian population in the colony.

The Dutch in Brazil. By the late 1500s, Catholic Spain had controlled the Protestant Dutch for many years. The Dutch rebelled against Spanish rule and, in 1596, raided Spanish possessions in South America and the Caribbean. In 1609, the Dutch gained independence, and the United Provinces of the Netherlands was born. The Dutch and Spanish signed a 12-year peace treaty, and the Netherlands began a profitable trade with Portuguese settlements in BRAZIL (at this time, Portugal was under Spanish control).

In 1621, two events occurred that renewed conflict between the two nations. First, the peace treaty expired, and second, the Dutch West India Company was founded. The Dutch West India Company was a private investment company that captured and controlled rich lands around the globe for the benefit of the Netherlands. The company paved the way for military conquests in Portuguese America. In early 1624, a Dutch force attacked and captured the Brazilian capital of SALVADOR. Although a combined Spanish-Portuguese force drove them out, the Dutch retained control of the seas off the coast of Brazil. In 1628, the Dutch captured the Spanish silver fleet in CUBA, and the West India Company amassed enough wealth for another Brazilian conquest.

In February 1630, the Dutch West India Company sent 76 ships and 7,000 men to attack the captaincy* of PERNAMBUCO in northeastern Brazil. Although they captured several settlements, the Portuguese, commanded by Governor Matias de ALBUQUERQUE, succeeded in restricting them to the coast. The two sides remained at a stalemate until mid-1632, when a deserter gave the Dutch valuable information about weaknesses in the Portuguese defenses. Over the next year and a half,

* **guerrilla** referring to a group that uses surprise raids to obstruct or harass an enemy or overthrow a government

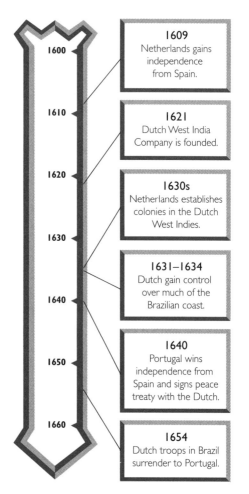

1609
Netherlands gains independence from Spain.

1621
Dutch West India Company is founded.

1630s
Netherlands establishes colonies in the Dutch West Indies.

1631–1634
Dutch gain control over much of the Brazilian coast.

1640
Portugal wins independence from Spain and signs peace treaty with the Dutch.

1654
Dutch troops in Brazil surrender to Portugal.

the Dutch gained control of a large portion of Brazil's coast and captured rich SUGAR lands in Pernambuco. Spain and Portugal sent reinforcements, and a bloody guerrilla* war raged for several years. In 1636, the Dutch sent Governor-General Johan MAURITS to Brazil to bring peace to the area and restore sugar production, which had been affected by the fighting. By 1641, Maurits fortified the Dutch presence in the region and thwarted Spanish and Portuguese attempts to recapture it.

In 1640, Portugal overthrew Spanish rule in Brazil and signed a ten-year truce with the Netherlands. However, the treaty did not go into effect immediately, and the Portuguese secretly plotted to throw the Dutch out of Brazil. In 1645, Portuguese troops attacked the Dutch and recaptured most of Brazil. The two sides continued to fight until 1652, when the Portuguese finally gained control of the sea. Unable to resupply their forces or prevent their enemy from receiving reinforcements, the weary Dutch troops surrendered in 1654.

The Dutch in Suriname and the Caribbean. Other centers of Dutch influence in Latin America were SURINAME, on the northern coast of South America, and the islands of the DUTCH WEST INDIES. The Dutch gained control over the Caribbean islands of Aruba, Bonaire, Curaçao, St. Martin, St. Eustatius, and Saba in the early 1600s and acquired Suriname from the English in 1667. Dutch involvement in this part of Latin America was less violent than it had been in Brazil.

The Dutch used the islands as centers for trade with North America, South America, and Europe. The islands became the center for a flourishing slave trade, and the Dutch took advantage of rich salt deposits and fertile PLANTATIONS. Suriname began as a profitable plantation colony, raising sugar for export to Europe. However, when slavery was abolished in 1863, the sugar industry became less profitable. Although the Dutch brought in paid labor from Asia, their efforts to keep sugar production profitable failed, and by the 1930s, it was no longer an important part of the economy.

The weakened economies of the Dutch West Indies hurt trade and immigration to the islands. The Standard Oil Company of the United States established a PETROLEUM refinery on Aruba in the early 1900s but abandoned it by the 1980s. In 1954, Suriname and the Dutch West Indies were made self-governing territories within the Kingdom of the Netherlands, and Suriname gained its independence in 1975. The Dutch heritage remains strong in the islands as they struggle to find their identity and place in the world economy. (*See also* **Caribbean Antilles; Portugal and the Portuguese Empire; Spain and the Spanish Empire.**)

Dutch West India Company

See *Dutch in Latin America.*

Dutch West Indies

See map in Caribbean Antilles (vol. 1).

° **indigenous** referring to the original inhabitants of a region

° **mulatto** person of mixed black and white ancestry

° **sack** to loot a captured city

> **Pawn in the Revolution**
>
> The tiny island of St. Eustatius played a major role in the American Revolution. Its free trade policy in the 1700s enabled North Americans to obtain badly needed European-made arms, ammunition, and other goods. St. Eustatius was also the first foreign government to recognize the United States as a nation. The British, who were unhappy with St. Eustatius's role in the Revolution, sacked the island in 1781, but they continued to fly the Dutch flag, luring American and other enemy ships into its port. St. Eustatius never regained its prosperity after the sacking.

utch West Indies is the former name of several islands in the CARIBBEAN ANTILLES that were once colonies of the Netherlands. They include Aruba and the Netherlands Antilles, which consists of Bonaire, Curaçao, St. Eustatius, Saba, and the southern part of St. Martin.

The Land and People. Although the Dutch West Indies are tropical islands, they have very barren soil and therefore support very little vegetation. The islands have low annual rainfall and almost no natural irrigation such as rivers. As a result, the Dutch West Indies were not a part of the SUGAR INDUSTRY that was so important to other islands in the Caribbean Antilles. However, the Dutch West India Company took advantage of Curaçao's excellent natural harbor and established the port city of Willemstad in 1634.

Like the other islands in the Caribbean Antilles, the Dutch West Indies were originally inhabited by Arawak and Carib Indians. When the Spanish arrived in the 1500s, they killed many Indians and brought DISEASES that devastated the indigenous* population. Very few descendants of the original inhabitants live in the region today. Most of the residents are blacks, the descendants of African slaves. There are also many mulattos* and a small white population.

Colonial History. St. Martin was the first of the Dutch West Indies to be discovered by Europeans. Christopher COLUMBUS first sighted the island on St. Martin's Day—November 11, 1493. Explorers Alonso de Ojeda and Amerigo VESPUCCI later discovered Aruba, Curaçao, and Bonaire while exploring the coast of present-day Colombia. The Spanish did little with any of these islands except Curaçao, which they settled in 1527 and used mainly for raising LIVESTOCK. After several wars with the Spanish in the early 1600s, the Dutch seized most of the islands.

The Dutch used the islands as a base for trade with South America, North America, and Europe. Willemstad became a rich trading outpost and a center for the Caribbean SLAVE TRADE. By the late 1700s, St. Eustatius became the commercial center of the eastern Caribbean, but it suffered great losses after the British sacked* the island and the 170 ships in the harbor during the American Revolution.

The Islands Since 1900. From the early 1800s to the early 1900s, the economy of the islands declined, but the discovery of oil in nearby Venezuela provided a much-needed boost. An oil refinery opened on Curaçao in 1918, and another began operation two years later in Aruba. The PETROLEUM INDUSTRY became the heart of the economy until the 1980s, and today SERVICE INDUSTRIES, such as TOURISM and BANKING, are important for all of the islands. Since the end of World War II, the islands have achieved a larger measure of self-rule than they had as colonies. They are still a part of the Kingdom of the Netherlands, but they have their own local governments. Although some islands have in the past announced their desire for full independence, all of them have, so far, decided to remain a part of the Netherlands. (*See also* **Caribs; Dutch in Latin America; Geography.**)

Duvalier Family

* **nationalist** patriotic person devoted to the advocacy of the nation's interests

* **mulatto** person of mixed black and white ancestry

* **oust** to remove from office

* **clergy** priests and other church officials qualified to perform church ceremonies

* **anti-Communist** referring to the opposition of communism

François Duvalier and his son, Jean-Claude, ruled the island of HAITI as dictators from 1957 to 1986. They were known for their cruelty, corruption, and disregard for the welfare of the Haitian people. François (Papa Doc) was a doctor who first gained attention during the 1940s for his work in fighting a tropical disease called yaws. In 1946, he joined the government as director of the yaws program and later became Haiti's minister of labor and public health. In 1950, the government was overthrown and remained under military rule until 1956. After a year of civil war, Duvalier, who was then very popular with the Haitian masses, was chosen president in an election that had been rigged by the military.

In the years that preceded his presidency, Duvalier had become active in Haiti's black nationalist* movement. Members of the movement had opposed the control and rule of Haiti by mulattos* and had supported the practice of VOODOO. Once in power, Duvalier destroyed his critics, ousted* mulattos from the government, and established a black nationalist state with himself as supreme ruler. He created the TONTON MACOUTES, or bogeymen, a terrorist group that imprisoned and killed his opponents, including members of the media. The Tonton Macoutes eventually replaced the army and became Duvalier's personal bodyguards. In 1959, Duvalier moved against the CATHOLIC CHURCH, arresting members of the clergy*, expelling officers of the church and JESUITS, and replacing them with Haitian clergy. He legalized voodoo and even used some of its priests as advisers.

Duvalier personally controlled the country; everyone took orders from him. Loyalty to Papa Doc became more important for his government officials than the ability to do a good job. He presided over a corrupt government, and his family and friends received shares of the profits from various government enterprises. The United States, which had supported Duvalier at first because of his anti-Communist* views, cut off most aid in 1963. Before his death in 1971, Duvalier chose his son, Jean-Claude, to be his successor and named him president for life.

Jean-Claude Duvalier, a failed law student and playboy, took office in 1971, but a council appointed by his father made all government decisions. In 1972, Jean-Claude (Baby Doc) dismissed his most powerful adviser and took control of the state. He instituted economic and political reforms that led to the renewal of United States aid and an increase in FOREIGN INVESTMENT, but the state was still extremely corrupt. Baby Doc married a mulatto divorcée whose shopping sprees in Paris and lavish parties at home led to riots and demonstrations in 1984 by the poverty-stricken Haitian public. Two years later, Duvalier, his family, and several close advisers fled the country aboard a United States cargo plane. (*See also* **Négritude.**)

François Duvalier, known as "Papa Doc," first gained popularity in Haiti as a country doctor fighting tropical diseases. After a military junta made him president, however, Duvalier imprisoned and murdered his opponents while gaining enormous wealth at the expense of the Haitian people.

Earthquakes

° **seismograph** device used to detect and measure the intensity, direction, and duration of movements of the earth, such as earthquakes

Earthquakes are a common occurrence in Latin America, especially along the Pacific coast. This photograph shows the devastation caused by an earthquake that struck the Pacific region of Mexico in 1995.

Seismic activity (movement of the earth) is common in Latin America, and many destructive earthquakes have shaken the region. Scientists believe that countries in Latin America and the Caribbean, especially those on the Pacific coast, are prone to earthquakes, accounting for about 17 percent of the world's total seismic activity.

At least ten major earthquakes struck CHILE between 1822 and 1965, and several were accompanied by destructive tidal waves called tsunamis. Central ECUADOR is also prone to earthquakes, and the capital, Quito, has been repeatedly devastated by them. COLOMBIA, PERU, ARGENTINA, and VENEZUELA have similarly experienced violent earthquakes. The damage from a massive earthquake in 1812 in Caracas, Venezuela, was not fully repaired for 50 years. Because of the frequency of earthquakes in South America, a seismograph* was installed in Santiago, Chile, as early as 1850.

Earthquakes are also common in CENTRAL AMERICA and the CARIBBEAN ANTILLES. JAMAICA's original capital, Port Royal, sank into the ocean following an earthquake in 1692. Colonial documents show that more than a dozen earthquakes occurred around GUATEMALA's capital city of Antigua, forcing the government to shift the capital to its present location, Guatemala City.

Earthquakes have even affected political fortunes in Latin America. Slow or inadequate reactions to earthquakes in NICARAGUA in 1972 and EL SALVADOR in 1986 contributed to the downfall of governments in those countries. Around that same time, a 1985 quake caused thousands of casualties in MEXICO CITY, one of the world's most densely populated cities.

Easter Island

° **archaeologist** scientist who studies past human cultures, usually by excavating ruins

° **missionary** person who works to convert nonbelievers to his or her faith

Easter Island is a small volcanic island in the Pacific Ocean about 2,300 miles west of CHILE. The island is famous for its enormous stone statues called *moai,* ranging from 10 to more than 30 feet in height. Polynesian peoples originally settled the island sometime between A.D. 400 and 750. The island's population and culture reached its peak around 1600, by which time most of the statues had been erected. Archaeologists* believe that the island's culture began to collapse in the late 1600s because of famine, overpopulation, and overuse of land resources.

The island was first discovered by Europeans when a Dutch sailor visited it on Easter Sunday in 1722, giving the island its name. The native names for the island are Rapa Nui and Te-Pito-o-te-Henua. The Spanish rediscovered Easter Island a few years later, and in 1862, Peruvians raided the island to capture more than 1,000 natives to work in the GUANO INDUSTRY. Some who survived the grueling work returned to the island, bringing with them a smallpox epidemic that killed all but 111 of the island's population. Missionaries* brought Catholicism to Easter Island in 1864. The island's population remains largely Catholic, although local traditions reflect Polynesian influences. In 1888, Chile claimed the island, and it has been a province of that country ever since.

See map in Chile (vol. I).

Archaeological excavations since the late 1800s have uncovered about 900 statues on Easter Island. Although their significance remains a mystery, local traditions suggest that the images may have represented important personalities or ancestors whom the people worshiped as gods after their deaths. The island, made popular by its statues, attracts thousands of tourists from around the world. By the late 1900s, the island's 2,000 people, frustrated with Chile's governance, began to seek autonomy and independent control of their archaeological sites, land, and internal affairs. (*See also* **Archaeology.**)

Eckhout, Albert

ca. 1607–1665
Dutch painter of Brazilian life

Albert Eckhout is best known for his portraits of the plants, animals, and people of BRAZIL. Little is known of his early life and career, except that he was appointed as an official artist to Johan MAURITS, the governor-general of Dutch Brazil. Eckhout's paintings are considered the best depictions of Brazil's people and wildlife during the early years of the European presence in the region.

The most famous and valuable of Eckhout's paintings are probably his life-size works showing members of different Brazilian tribes. German scientist and traveler Alexander von HUMBOLDT and Emperor PEDRO II enthusiastically praised Eckhout's paintings of Brazil. Hundreds of his paintings were used as the basis for woodcuts to illustrate Dutch books on the natural history of Brazil. The themes of some of Eckhout's later works suggest that he may have also visited Chile and West Africa. By 1645, he had returned to Europe and probably died in his hometown of Groningen (Netherlands) around 1665. (*See also* **Art, Colonial to Modern; Dutch in Latin America.**)

Ecology

See *Environmental Movements.*

Economic Development

Latin America is a region of great economic diversity where resources, although plentiful, are unevenly spread. Some countries have abundant resources and substantial wealth, while others struggle to meet the basic needs of their populations. Wealth is also spread unevenly, with elites enjoying great wealth while millions of others suffer crushing poverty. Because of these extremes and diversities, Latin American nations, like others in the developing world, have long struggled to expand their economies. This fight has sometimes been difficult. The region has experienced periods of dramatic change and progress as well as times of economic decline.

Colonial Times to the 1900s

Many conditions that affect Latin America's economic development today began during the colonial* era and in the years following

* **colonial** period between the European conquest and independence, generally from the early 1500s to the early 1800s

Many countries believe that searching for oil, as shown here in Colombia, can provide much needed economic development. But oil, like other exports, both helps and hurts Latin American economies. When the world price for oil is high, countries flourish; but when the price falls, they experience distress.

See color plate 6, vol. 2.

independence. The economic systems and institutions that evolved during those years greatly influence the continuing search for greater material development.

The Colonial and Independence Periods. During the colonial period, the European powers exploited the natural resources of Latin America for their own benefit. Spain, Portugal, and other colonial powers maintained their colonies primarily as a source of labor, riches, and raw materials and as a market for European manufactured goods. They adopted policies that prohibited the colonies from engaging in trade with other countries and limited the colonies' efforts to develop local industries. Such policies hindered economic growth and the development of stable economies.

When the Latin American colonies gained independence in the early 1800s, they took steps to stimulate economic growth and development in the newly formed nations. Every new country borrowed money from British merchant houses. Some new governments lifted colonial trade restrictions to encourage trade with other nations. Many countries sought FOREIGN INVESTMENT to help build and modernize their economies. These new policies led to dramatic changes in the economies of the region.

Prosperity and Problems. The period from the mid-1800s to the early 1900s was generally a prosperous time for Latin America. National economies grew, and AGRICULTURE, industry, trade, and other economic activities expanded. Economic growth brought increased revenue and contributed to a building boom. Governments financed the construction of RAILROADS, seaports, and other infrastructure*. Growth brought increased wealth to individuals, larger and more beautiful cities, and greater employment opportunities for many Latin Americans.

° **infrastructure** basic framework of a society and its economy, which includes roads, bridges, port facilities, airports, and other public works

° **cash crop** crop grown primarily for profit rather than for local consumption

Underlying growing prosperity, however, were a number of problems that would affect Latin America for years to come. Much of the region's economic growth and prosperity was based on primary exports: cash crops* and raw materials such as precious metals and minerals. The economies came to depend on these exports, which hindered the growth of other economic activities and discouraged the development of a varied agriculture. Countries dependent on natural resources typically experience boom-and-bust cycles, wild economic fluctuations that can quickly make and break fortunes, and Latin America was no exception. During the booms, people prospered, businesses grew, and foreign banks invested. But the busts brought financial panic, public and private debts, unemployment, and despair, creating a great deal of economic instability.

Latin America's economic growth also relied heavily on foreign investment—primarily from Europe and the United States—and on overseas markets. Foreign money and expertise helped Latin Americans build their economies, but it created dependent economies. The focus on overseas markets hindered the development of regional trade, crippled local manufacturing industries, delayed INDUSTRIALIZATION, and prevented the establishment of strong and stable economic relationships among the nations of Latin America.

Most of the economic growth and prosperity in the 1800s and early 1900s benefited the small upper and growing middle classes. Even in big cities in Argentina, Brazil, Mexico, Colombia, and Brazil, where production and exports flourished, domestic consumption remained concentrated among the affluent middle- and higher-income groups. Despite some growth in the middle class, the division between rich and poor remained great. Political leaders, especially those who relied on the wealthy for support, did little to improve the lives of the poor, increasing the threat of social unrest in many Latin American countries.

An Economic Turning Point

° **depression** period of little economic activity during which many people become unemployed

The worldwide economic depression* of the 1930s marked a major turning point in the economic development of Latin America. The region's exports declined dramatically, causing enormous losses of revenue. The depression revealed the dangers of relying too heavily on exports and on foreign markets. With the decline in income from exports, Latin American governments began to take an aggressive role in stimulating their national economies to create new and more varied economic activities.

° **tariff** tax on imported or exported goods

° **quota** a set number or proportional share of a total

Building National Economies. During and after the depression, many Latin American governments began to restrict foreign trade through tariffs*, quotas*, and other economic controls. These policies limited foreign imports and protected locally produced goods from foreign competition, which spurred more advanced industrialization in Latin America. Industries were soon making a greater number and variety of high-quality products than ever before. Some of the goods that were previously imported were now being produced locally, a phenomenon called import substitution.

Latin American governments took an active role in stimulating national economies in other ways as well. They regulated and monitored economic activities, often becoming directly involved by nationalizing* industries such as steel, and economic institutions such as banks. In general, government planning and control played the dominant role in economic development during this period.

These policies helped economic growth and resulted in a greater diversity of economic activities. However, many problems, such as the gap between the rich and poor, remained. Population growth placed increasing pressure on governments to provide more goods, services, and economic opportunities. Agricultural and industrial growth could not keep up with the demand for goods, resulting in shortages of food and other products. The mass movement of people from the countryside to the cities placed enormous pressures on public services, such as water, sewage, health, and transportation. These shortages resulted in the formation of slums in every major city and contributed to inflation*, which became a persistent problem throughout Latin America. Moreover, most nations failed to establish economic ties with their neighbors, preventing the development of a strong and integrated regional economy.

nationalize to bring land, industries, or public works under state control or ownership

inflation sharp increase in prices due to an increase in the amount of money or credit relative to available goods and services

privatization changing of a business or industry from public to private ownership

Latin America Looks Outward.

By the 1970s, it had become clear to most Latin American governments that their economic policies had significant drawbacks. Despite progress, they were suffering from inflation, rising debt, trade imbalances, and other economic problems, and these contributed to political and social unrest. Most nations in the region responded to this situation by reevaluating their economic policies and trying new approaches to aid economic growth and development.

In the 1980s, many experts believed that the region's problems were based on excessive government intervention and the tendency to focus economic policies inward. Thus, governments began relinquishing control of many industries and allowed privatization*. They also placed a renewed emphasis on exports and encouraged increased foreign investment in local industry.

Because most Latin American nations had rather small national markets for their products, the potential for growth in industries that provided domestic goods was limited. Some nations responded to this problem by emphasizing the need to place products in regional and foreign markets. This led to an interest in regional trade associations. Several such organizations were established in Latin America in the 1960s and 1970s, including the Latin American Free Trade Association, or LAFTA (1960); the Central American Common Market, or CARICOM (1960); the Andean Pact (1969); and the Caribbean Common Market (1972). The idea behind these organizations was to create a larger market for member nations and to encourage greater economic interaction among them. Although these associations were only modestly successful, the creation of MERCOSUR (Southern Cone Common Market) in 1991 and the signing of NAFTA (NORTH AMERICAN FREE TRADE AGREEMENT) in 1994 indicate that the interest to create integrated tariff-free regional markets remains.

Major Sectors of the Economy

Throughout the history of Latin America, the three most crucial sectors of the economy have been agriculture, MINING, and industry. Each has experienced the ups and downs that characterized the economic development of the region.

Agriculture. Agriculture has played a vital role in the economy of Latin America since its beginnings. Starting slowly in the 1700s, farming has generally taken place at two extremes. At one end are the small-scale farmers who work a few acres of land, producing enough for their own needs and perhaps a small surplus for local markets. At the other end are large PLANTATIONS, ranches, and haciendas* owned by wealthy individuals, the government, or private companies. These large-scale operations produce great quantities of food and other agricultural products, primarily for export. The emphasis on growing cash crops has often resulted in the need to import basic foods into Latin America. This situation has existed since colonial times, and it remains a serious problem.

° **hacienda** large rural estate, usually devoted to agriculture

Mining. The mining industry began in the early colonial period when conquistadors* realized that the New World contained large deposits of gold and silver. Until the 1800s, trade in mining products was restricted by colonial laws, and the mining industry primarily benefited the colonial powers. In the 1800s and early 1900s, the mining of minerals and metals became a major source of revenue and one of the most important economic activities in many nations, including Mexico, Chile, Peru, and Bolivia. Reliance on mineral exports, however, contributed to periods of economic "boom and bust" depending on world demand. When mining exports declined in the 1930s, governments shifted their attention to manufacturing and industrialization. Today mineral resources are exported by Latin American countries that have significant deposits.

° **conquistador** Spanish explorer and conqueror

Industry. Despite efforts to expand industry, Latin America does not have a strong industrial base. Before the 1930s, most Latin American nations focused on mineral and agricultural exports, and few forceful efforts were made to encourage industrialization until the 1950s. Latin American industry has grown substantially over the last several decades, but it remains hampered by several factors, including the need to import technology from other parts of the world. Perhaps the most important factor, however, is the limited domestic market for manufactured goods. Many Latin American countries have populations that are just too small to support large-scale industrial development. The demand for consumer products such as cars and television sets is low, especially in countries with low per capita incomes. Some

The United Nations and the Economy

In 1948, the United Nations created the Economic Commission for Latin America (ECLA) to study and resolve the region's economic problems. Led by several well-known Latin American economists, the commission has taken a variety of approaches to the region's economic problems. In the 1950s, for example, ECLA encouraged Latin American countries to begin manufacturing many of their own goods instead of importing them. In 1984, the United Nations renamed the group the Economic Commission for Latin America and the Caribbean (ECLAC) to reflect the economic and cultural ties between Latin America and the island nations of the Caribbean.

countries have tried to overcome this limitation by forming larger regional markets through trade agreements.

Future economic development in Latin America will require more attention to industry. It also will require efforts to create greater economic diversity and to resolve lingering social and political problems. Although Latin America trails the more developed regions of the world economically and much needs to be done to raise it to a higher level, the region is faring better than most countries in the developing world. (*See also* **Agrarian Reform; Cities and Urbanization; Class Structure, Colonial and Modern; Foreign Debt; Immigration and Emigration; Income Distribution; Labor and Labor Movements; Land, Ownership of; Taxes and Taxation.**)

Ecuador

*O*riginally part of the INCA empire, the South American nation of Ecuador was conquered by the Spanish in 1533. Since winning independence from Spain in the early 1800s, Ecuador has endured long periods of military rule, a series of costly border wars with the neighboring nation of PERU, and severe fluctuations in its economy. The nation's tradition of rule by a small elite class has made it difficult for democracy to take hold, and long-standing competition and rivalry among regions has hindered national unity.

The Land

Ecuador lies in northwestern South America, bordered by Colombia to the north, Peru to the east and south, and the Pacific Ocean to the west. It was named after the equator, which runs through Ecuador near QUITO, its capital city. About 600 miles offshore lie Ecuador's famous GALÁPAGOS ISLANDS, home to many unique species of animals that inspired British scientist Charles Darwin to formulate his theory of evolution in the 1800s. These remote islands are treasured and visited by scientists and tourists from around the world.

Regions. The ANDES mountains run through Ecuador from south to north in a high, rugged double chain of peaks. The mountains divide the country into three very different and isolated regions: the lowlands east of the mountains, the mountain highlands, and the coastal plain west of the mountains.

The Oriente, or eastern region, comprises almost half of the nation. The Oriente is a hot and humid plain that stretches from the Andes to the edge of the AMAZON REGION. Most of it is covered with tropical woodlands and rain forest. The Oriente has many navigable* rivers, but because they flow eastward toward the Amazon River and away from the rest of Ecuador, they are not particularly useful as trade routes.

Ecuador's mountain highland region, the Sierra, covers about one-fourth of the country. Most of the people in the Sierra live in 11 high, densely populated basins. Mountain walls separate each basin not only from the eastern and western regions of the country but also from the

* **navigable** deep and wide enough to provide passage for ships

° **cacao** bean from which chocolate is made

° **coup** sudden, often violent overthrow of a ruler or government

° **conquistador** Spanish explorer and conqueror

other basins. Each basin contains rolling, hilly plains and deep, narrow river valleys or gorges. Weather in the Sierra ranges from arctic cold above the snow line to tropical warmth far below in the deepest valleys. Within the basins, people graze livestock on the cooler plains and grow fruit and vegetables in the valleys.

The western coastal region has both low-lying plains and ranges of hills. The northern part of this area is wet and forested, while the southern coast is drier. Warm, well watered, and blessed with fertile soil, the lowlands are ideal for tropical agriculture.

Ecuador's fragmented geography has led to political, social, and economic regionalism—a tendency toward separations, differences, and competition among a country's regions that prevents national unity. In particular, the development of different social and economic systems on the coast and in the highlands often causes political conflict between these regions. Because the Oriente has few inhabitants—most of whom are Indians with little political power—this area has been less involved in Ecuadorian politics than the Sierra and the coastal region.

Resources. Although Ecuador's natural resources are limited, the country's economy has historically depended on the products of the land. The most important of these products have been wool from animals grazed in the high pastures and tropical produce grown in the lower regions. The area around the nation's main port, GUAYAQUIL, produces most of Ecuador's agricultural exports, including cacao*, BANANAS, and COFFEE.

The Oriente produced little of economic value until the 1960s, when geologists found oil there. Since then, the world's continuing demand for fuel has made Ecuador more willing to take on the high cost of developing this remote region. Many new plans for national progress focus on the Oriente.

History

Following the Spanish conquest of Ecuador in the 1500s, the colonial period produced a new society in Ecuador, one that felt considerable strain when Spain's rule ended almost 300 years later. Because Ecuadorians had no experience in governing themselves and seldom agreed on national goals, military strongmen often took control of the country. With a government that changed hands frequently in coups* and revolutions, Ecuador is an extreme example of the political crises that afflicted most Spanish American nations after independence.

Early Colonial History. When the Spanish armies of conquistador* Sebastián de Belalcázar invaded the northern Andes in 1533, they found Ecuador—then called Quito—in turmoil. Forty years earlier, the six Indian chiefdoms of Quito had been conquered by the Inca. Since that time, revolts and civil war within the Inca empire had kept the region in a state of disorder. Taking advantage of this turmoil, the Spaniards soon conquered the Inca and seized their territories.

See map in Audiencia (vol. I).

° **viceroyalty** region governed by a viceroy, a royally appointed official

° **Creole** person of European ancestry born in the Americas

However, political confusion continued under the rule of the conquistadors, who fought over the governorship of Quito. In 1563, the Spanish monarchy ended the conflict by setting up a formal administrative government. Quito became an *audiencia*—a district governed by a Spanish colonial high court—within the larger colony of the Viceroyalty* of Peru.

With a secure government in place, the Spaniards laid the foundation of a colonial society and economy. By the late 1500s, the *audiencia* of Quito was linked to a prosperous network of colonial economies throughout the Viceroyalty of Peru. To Spain, the colony's most important product was silver from the mines of Bolivia and Peru. Smaller regional economies, however, supplied food, labor, and other necessities to keep those mines operating. Because cloth manufacturers in Spain could not supply the growing need for TEXTILES in the mining districts, the Spanish colonists in Quito—known as *quiteños*—stepped in to meet the need. Using Indian labor and sheep imported from Spain to the rich grazing lands of the Sierra, colonists in the Ecuadorian Andes established *obrajes,* or textile mills, that produced wool for sale in the marketplaces of Colombia and Peru.

Throughout the 1600s, the textile industry brought the *audiencia* economic prosperity. Although the first *obrajes* legally belonged to the Indians who worked in them, in reality, the Spanish landowners controlled the mills and reaped their profits. Eventually, the most productive *obrajes* were privately owned on rural estates, and a small elite group of Spaniards and Creoles* who owned land and *obrajes* rose to economic and social power. By the end of the 1600s, a handful of leading families dominated the Quito *audiencia*. In spite of laws made to protect them, the Indians suffered constant abuse in the mills, where they worked long hours, received low wages, and sometimes were beaten. Indians tolerated these terrible conditions only because they desperately needed money to pay the *audiencia*'s high taxes.

Quito, the capital of Ecuador, has a long history. Founded by the Quitos Indians, the city was conquered by the Inca, who were, in turn, conquered by the Spanish. Buildings constructed by the Spanish still stand in the colonial quarter of the city.

Ecuador

Most of Ecuador's major cities are located in the Andean highlands, where European colonists first settled to raise livestock. Two other important regions of the country are the coastal plains west of the Andes, called the Occidente, and a sparsely populated area east of the Andes, called the Oriente. In 1998, a long-standing border dispute between Ecuador and Peru was settled. The new common border is to be defined.

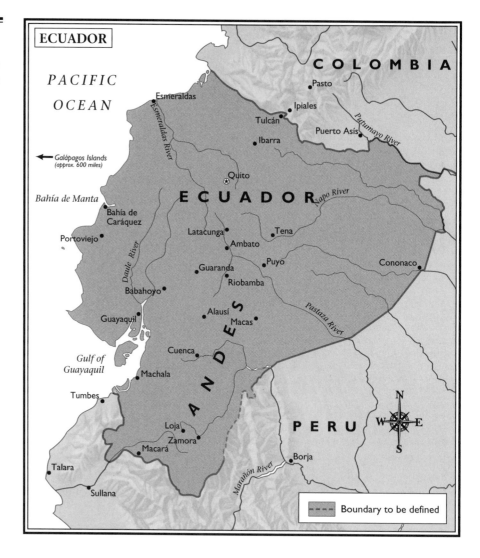

The 1700s.   After 1690, a decline in the mining industry in Peru and Bolivia lessened the demand for the *quiteños'* textiles. At the same time, droughts, earthquakes, and disease killed almost one-third of the Indians in Ecuador, ending the supply of cheap labor for the mills. Even more serious was the effect of Spain's new trade laws, which allowed the colonies to import foreign goods. Inexpensive cloth from Europe drove Ecuadorian wool out of the marketplace. The output of the *obrajes* decreased by more than half during the 1700s.

While the wool industry around Quito declined, new businesses arose. Indians in the southern highlands manufactured cotton cloth for Peruvian merchants. More importantly, the rise of agriculture on the coast began to flourish in the late 1700s, after changes in Spain's imperial policy allowed the colony to export its goods to Mexico and Europe. Quito's first major export crop was cacao. With demand growing around the world, cacao was the core of the coastal economy until the mid-1800s. Many Indians left the economically depressed northern and central highlands to seek a living in the more prosperous southern highlands and coastal regions.

Political life grew turbulent in the mid-1700s, when the Spanish crown tried to limit the power of the Ecuadorian elite by enforcing stricter tax collection and appointing outsiders to important positions. Ecuadorians of all classes resented these measures, and in the QUITO REVOLT OF 1765, they briefly overthrew the district's royal government. Although Spain quickly regained control of the *audiencia*, the *quiteños* continued to protest the acts of Spanish officials. By the end of the 1700s, the elite classes were disgusted with royal government, and poverty and hardship had spread discontent among the Indian and mestizo* population. Revolts broke out and were repeatedly put down by the Spanish authorities.

The 1800s.   In 1809, the *quiteño* elite formally challenged Spanish power by forming a junta*. Within a few months, however, royalists* overthrew the rebel government and killed most of its leaders. This defeat crushed the spirit of revolt in Ecuador. While independence movements gained strength throughout Spanish America, Ecuador's rebel movement remained small and generally ineffective.

Ecuador's struggle for independence from Spain strengthened after 1819, with the arrival of Antonio José de SUCRE, a Venezuelan military officer and South American liberator. In 1822, Sucre and his armies defeated the royalist forces at the battle of Pichincha. Sucre's followers made Ecuador part of a new country called GRAN COLOMBIA, which also included Venezuela and Colombia. Finally, in 1830, Ecuador withdrew from Gran Colombia and became an independent republic*.

Politics in the new nation were shaped by rivalry between different groups within Ecuador's elite classes. Elite groups in the highlands were strongly conservative*, while those living along the coast were liberal*. During the 1800s, the opposing political forces of these two regions struggled to dominate the national government, prompting four civil wars that nearly tore the country apart. Force became the usual means of transferring power, despite laws that called for free public elections. Throughout the 1800s, Ecuador's leaders ruled by military strength and often controlled the elections to make sure that they won. Two leading statesmen of that time, Vicente Rocafuerte and Gabriel García Moreno, achieved power through armed conflict and used force to stay in office.

The wealth and influence of coastal cacao growers and bankers brought the liberals into power in 1895. Despite bitter rivalries among themselves that sometimes led to rebellion, the liberals controlled the country for 30 years, during which they worked to modernize Ecuador and to encourage national unity.

The 1900s.   In the early 1900s, a drop in worldwide demand for cacao weakened the power of the cacao-producing coastal elites and crippled Ecuador's economy. As the economy declined, conservative politicians and journalists in the capital city of Quito grew ever more critical of the ruling liberals. In 1925, a group of young military officers overthrew the government and returned political power to the conservative Sierra region. This coup began a period of severe political, social, and economic distress in Ecuador, which worsened during the

* **mestizo** person of mixed European and Indian ancestry

* **junta** small group of people who run a government, usually after seizing power by force

* **royalist** supporter of the king or queen, especially in times of civil war or rebellion

* **republic** government in which citizens elect officials to represent them and govern according to law

* **conservative** inclined to maintain existing political and social views, conditions, and institutions

* **liberal** supporting greater participation in government for individuals; not bound by political and social traditions

Ecuador

° **depression** period of little economic activity during which many people become unemployed

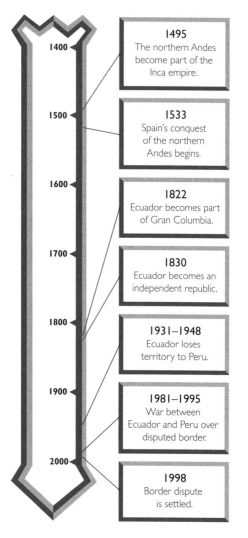

1495	The northern Andes become part of the Inca empire.
1533	Spain's conquest of the northern Andes begins.
1822	Ecuador becomes part of Gran Columbia.
1830	Ecuador becomes an independent republic.
1931–1948	Ecuador loses territory to Peru.
1981–1995	War between Ecuador and Peru over disputed border.
1998	Border dispute is settled.

° **guerrilla** referring to a group that uses surprise raids to obstruct or harass an enemy or overthrow a government

worldwide economic depression* of the 1930s. In the unstable years between 1931 and 1948, Ecuador had 19 different presidents, none of whom completed a full term in office.

Internal upheavals were only part of Ecuador's troubles. The country also went to war over a long-simmering border dispute with Peru. Both nations claimed an area of about 120,000 square miles of Amazon jungle, but Peru had sent more settlers into the disputed territory than had Ecuador. The standoff flared into open warfare in 1941, when Peru launched an assault not only on the Amazon territory but also on Ecuador's southern coast.

The Ecuadorian forces lacked basic supplies. They were unprepared for war, and their small force of about 1,600 men was greatly outnumbered by the Peruvian army, which contained well over 5,000 soldiers. The Ecuadorians retreated, and Peru captured El Oro, Ecuador's southernmost province. Ecuador sought peace, and in 1942, the two nations signed the Rio Protocol—an agreement that returned El Oro to Ecuador and gave two-thirds of the disputed Amazonian land to Peru. Under this treaty, Ecuador lost a huge chunk of territory as well as its main river outlet to the Amazon River.

After 1948, stability returned to Ecuador's internal politics. Three presidents completed their terms of office peacefully. Bananas replaced cacao as Ecuador's leading export crop and the mainstay of the nation's economy, and once again, people migrated from the highlands to the coast for a share in the agricultural prosperity. But when the economy weakened in the 1960s, this peaceful period ended. Frequent unscheduled changes of government again became common, and for three years a military junta ruled the country.

During the 1970s, Ecuador began exporting PETROLEUM, and the nation's economy grew rapidly. For most of that decade, Ecuador was governed by two military juntas that tried to bring about social and economic reforms. They failed to reduce the great gap between the rich and the poor, and Ecuadorians still lacked full democratic participation in government.

In 1979, Ecuador returned to civilian rule under President Jaime Roldós Aguilera, who wanted to use the income from petroleum sales to finance roads, dams, and other projects for rural development. This and other reform plans failed, however, due to lack of support from other leading politicians. Although Ecuadorian political life became more democratic in the early 1980s, it remained dominated by strong personalities, internal rivalries, and regional loyalties. Ecuadorians once again turned to violence to achieve political results. In the late 1980s, the government's failure to slow an economic decline led to coup attempts and clashes between government troops and students, workers, and guerrilla* fighters.

In addition, Ecuador continued to dispute its border with Peru. In 1960, Ecuadorian president José María Velasco Ibarra had declared the Rio Protocol invalid and an insult to Ecuadorian national pride. After that time, various skirmishes occurred along a 50-mile stretch of unmapped border. Peru won a brief border war in 1981, but Ecuador continued to fight, and in 1995, the Ecuadorians shot down several

° **diplomatic** demonstrating tact and skill at conducting negotiations among nations

Peruvian aircraft. Military observers from other nations, including the United States, worked to prevent further bloodshed over the issue and to encourage a diplomatic* solution. But the two countries remained at odds, with Peru seeking to uphold the 1942 agreement and Ecuador demanding—at the least—full access to Peru's Marañón River, which leads to the Amazon. The dispute was settled in 1998.

In the 1990s, Ecuador's leaders have also faced the difficult task of trying to bring about economic reform in a country where living standards have fallen steadily for more than a decade. However, attempts to limit government spending by turning state-owned industries over to private management or by cutting some government jobs have brought sharp objections from people whose interests are threatened by these measures. In 1996, Ecuadorians elected President Abdalá Bucaram, an eccentric individual known as El Loco (The Crazy One). Bucaram announced a plan to bring Ecuador's economic problems under control, although the necessary cuts in government spending would cause much hardship. However, the congress threw Bucaram out of office just six months after his election, when widespread corruption was discovered in his government. The nation's many competing political parties continue to struggle to form a government with broad enough support to survive and address Ecuador's pressing economic difficulties. (*See also* **Geography; Textiles and Textile Industry.**)

Education

° **literacy** ability to read and write; illiteracy is the inability to read and write

See color plate 8, vol. 2.

*T*he educational system in Latin America today is largely a product of the colonial Spanish system, although it serves a wider population than it did before. Since independence, Latin American nations have taken steps to resolve some of the region's serious educational problems, such as improving literacy* among adults and making schools accessible to those who were previously excluded—the rural poor and the Indians. Although Latin America has made great strides in education, especially in Brazil, several problems persist. Attendance in schools varies widely across the region, as does literacy. Schools, teachers, and books are in short supply in rural areas and city slums. Government and business leaders fear that without better education, Latin America will be unable to compete in the technological industries of tomorrow. Because traditional education has been unable to meet all of Latin America's needs, new approaches to teaching and learning—some of which have been effective—are being implemented. International organizations, local grassroots groups, and government agencies are also experimenting with new, nontraditional educational programs throughout the region.

Colonial Education. Formal education existed in the Americas long before the Europeans arrived. The three great civilizations native to the region—the AZTECS, INCA, and MAYA—all had educational systems. The Maya and Inca educated the children of their noble families. The Aztecs educated the children of the nobility and the commoners.

° **missionary** person who works to convert nonbelievers to his or her faith

° **evangelize** to preach Christian beliefs; to convert to Christianity

° **Creole** person of European ancestry born in the Americas

° **clergy** priests and other church officials qualified to perform church ceremonies

° **secular** nonreligious; connected with everyday life

The Europeans established their first schools in Latin America in the 1500s. The purpose of these schools was not simply to educate the Indians but to teach them Christianity and convert them to Catholicism. The schools were run by the CATHOLIC CHURCH, specifically by two RELIGIOUS ORDERS: the Dominicans and the Jesuits. Missionaries* instructed the Indians in reading and writing and taught practical crafts such as weaving and farming.

Although the original purpose of the colonial schools was to evangelize* the Indians, they soon began to serve other purposes. With the increasing Creole* population, several schools were dedicated to the education of the children of the colonists. Although the wealthier Europeans and Creoles sent their children to Spain for further education, by the 1600s, several universities were established in the larger cities of Latin America, including Santiago de Chile, La Plata, Cuzco, and Quito. Primarily religious schools, the universities trained members of the clergy* and educated doctors and lawyers. During the late 1700s, the ENLIGHTENMENT—a European intellectual movement that stressed the importance of science and reason—greatly changed education not only in Europe but also in the Latin American colonies. Officially, the church remained in control, but schools became more secular*. The universities began teaching science and languages, including some Indian languages.

Education Since Independence. Even after the Latin American colonies gained independence from Spain in the early 1800s, the Catholic Church continued to influence education. Gradually, however, church-run education lost in favor of secular schooling and technical training, especially in Chile, Argentina, and Uruguay—countries with large populations of European immigrants. Latin American leaders began to regard education as essential for progress. In 1870, Argentina established the Escuela Normal de Panama to educate future leaders of the nation. Mexico's president Benito JUÁREZ reformed his country's educational system to produce skilled, highly trained elites to serve as political and business leaders. Many Latin American countries drew inspiration from other systems—the British school system influenced Argentina, the German system influenced Chile, and the French system influenced many countries in the region. By the end of the 1800s, the Catholic Church had lost control of public education across Latin America.

After independence, education supposedly became accessible to *all* people. However, the rigid class barriers in society determined people's actual access to schools. Although literacy increased overall, the upper and middle classes had more opportunities for education than the poor and the rural peasants. Some nations took steps to change this. In postrevolutionary Mexico in the 1930s, students and teachers went into the countryside with the goal of establishing a school in every village. These volunteers considered themselves social reformers, not merely educators. Although the teachers faced indifference and hostility from the people, the program was successful in Oaxaca and other areas.

Despite the success of localized programs such as the rural outreach in Mexico, education in most Latin American countries remained formal, highly structured, and regulated by the government. National governments funded education and established centralized ministries of education to run the schools. Provinces, cities, and communities lost control of their schools to the central ministries, which trained and hired teachers and set the standards, curriculum, and rules for all schools. Latin American leaders firmly believed that centralized control and uniform education were key to the nations' development and to people's social identity.

By the mid-1900s, education had clearly not fulfilled its promise. More than half the people could not read or write. However, the second half of the 1900s brought substantial progress, Although progress was not uniform in all nations, school enrollments increased overall. In some countries, nearly all children between 6 and 12 years old were enrolled in school—although enrollment did not always guarantee attendance. Yet in countries such as Bolivia, El Salvador, and Guatemala, schools are still unable to provide even primary school education for all children. The picture is even bleaker for secondary school children, ages 12 through 17. In Cuba, Argentina, and Uruguay a high percentage of teenagers are enrolled in high school, but in Guatemala, Haiti, and Paraguay, that percentage is much lower.

In Brazil, there were 2.1 million students enrolled in school in 1932. By the mid-1980s, that number had risen to 30 million. However, numbers do not tell the whole story. Attendance, resources, and teachers remained problems, and although enrollment in some countries is high, the quality of education provided in rural schools is different from that provided in urban schools. Moreover, the urban poor, Indians, and other low-status groups have very limited opportunities to receive quality education.

Nevertheless, there are signs of change in Latin American education. International agencies such as the UNITED NATIONS and the ORGANIZATION OF AMERICAN STATES (OAS) advise and assist the national education ministries and bring new ideas to traditional education. Issues such as women's rights and HUMAN RIGHTS, environmental problems, the problems of the Indians, and the need to respect ethnic and cultural diversity are becoming part of teacher training and are making their way into the curriculum.

Schools have also begun to emphasize instruction in basic science and mathematics to close the so-called "knowledge gap" between the developed, industrialized nations and the poorer, developing nations. The information age has brought a growing demand for scientific and technical workers, and the Latin American ministries of education are trying to prepare their nations to compete in the job markets and economies of the coming years.

Like many other nations, Latin American leaders have long viewed the government's role in education as central to creating an educated population and workforce. Worldwide economic and political changes, however, have challenged this view of education. Many people now question whether education should remain entirely in the hands of national governments, and new approaches to education are appearing. In 1992, Chile's ministry of education launched a program to improve

> **Remember:** Consult the index at the end of this volume to find more information on many topics.

* **indigenous** referring to the original inhabitants of a region

the quality of primary schools by inviting communities to become involved in their children's education. Observers in Latin America see a trend toward democratic education, in which parents and communities help determine the curriculum and the methods of teaching used in their schools. Some countries are also trying to improve education for the indigenous* population by training Indian teachers in their native languages and establishing bilingual schools. Computer science as a subject and the use of computers are becoming prevalent in Latin America as schools in the region embrace scientific advancement and new technology.

Nonformal Education. Across Latin America, nonformal education is also an important force. Sometimes called alternative or experimental education, this includes a wide range of organized teaching activities that occur outside the formal school system. Mexico has experimented with many creative approaches to nonformal education. It was one of the first countries to have a people's university. Founded by teachers and intellectuals in 1912, the university was geared toward providing education in culture, health, and job training. Soon similar institutions were established in other Latin American countries. They adopted the methods of the grassroots education that Mexico established in the 1920s. They sent teachers, health professionals, and technical workers (such as engineers) into remote villages to teach and promote social change.

Since the 1940s, many Latin American countries have used nonformal education to confront social problems such as illiteracy, unemployment, and malnutrition. While some of these programs have been implemented on a national basis, others have been localized movements created by interested individuals, communities, or religious organizations. Examples of nonformal education are the recently developed programs that provide education, health care, clothing, and job training to the growing number of street children in cities such as Mexico City and Rio de Janeiro. These programs stem from the belief that the traditional school system can no longer meet all of Latin America's educational needs. (*See also* **Children; Literacy; Universities and Colleges.**)

From Teacher to President

Argentina's Domingo Sarmiento was an educational pioneer with many ideas that were ahead of his time. Sarmiento believed that universal education was key to progress. He founded a high school for girls in 1839 and "dreamed of founding schools and teaching the masses to read." As the director of education for Buenos Aires Province, Sarmiento worked tirelessly to implement his ideas. When he was elected president in 1868, Sarmiento founded several libraries and kindergartens and brought school teachers from the United States. His reforms placed Argentina's schools among the best in Latin America.

Ejidos

See *Land, Ownership of.*

El Dorado

El Dorado was a rumor of great South American wealth that haunted the imaginations of Europeans for hundreds of years. First said to be a mythical golden man, then a city of gold, El Dorado drew generations of adventurers and treasure seekers into the jungles of northeastern South America. The rumor they pursued may have contained some truth.

Early in the 1500s, European explorers in South America learned of an extravagant rite performed by the Muisca people in what is now

COLOMBIA. During the ceremony in which a chief becomes the recognized leader of the community, he covered himself with gold dust and then bathed in Lake Guatavita, northeast of modern Bogotá, while his subjects threw golden offerings into the water. This account may have been true, and hopeful Europeans wove tales about the "golden one" into the story of a jungle city of fabulous wealth. British explorer Sir Walter Raleigh, who came to South America seeking El Dorado in 1595 and 1617, was just one of many Europeans who hoped to find and conquer this city of gold. In addition, between 1562 and 1913, several unsuccessful attempts were made to drain the waters of Lake Guatavita in search of its legendary sunken treasure.

El Inca

See *Garcilasco de la Vega, El Inca.*

El Mirador

° **Mesoamerica** culture region that includes central and southern Mexico, Guatemala, Belize, El Salvador, and parts of Honduras, Nicaragua, and Costa Rica

° **archaeologist** scientist who studies past human cultures, usually by excavating ruins

*E*l Mirador was a large city built by the MAYA, whose civilization spread across southern Mesoamerica* centuries before the Europeans arrived in the late 1400s. Located in northern Guatemala near the Mexican border, El Mirador rose to prominence around 400 B.C. by controlling trade routes across the Yucatán peninsula between the Gulf of Mexico and the Caribbean Sea.

Because El Mirador is remote and difficult to reach, archaeologists* have not studied it as thoroughly as they have some other sites. However, they have learned that El Mirador was built on a grand scale. The center of the city was a cluster of large pyramids and other structures. They were made of piled rubble covered with stone slabs and stood on a platform that measured nearly 1,000 feet square. The main pyramid was 230 feet high, making it both the tallest and most massive of all known

El Mirador, shown here, is a Maya ruin located in the region that is now Guatemala. Once the leading center of power in the area, El Mirador contains the tallest and most massive Maya structures yet uncovered.

Maya structures. Walls and causeways, or raised walkways, link El Mirador's various groups of buildings, which are surrounded by low-lying areas that flood during the rainy season.

After several centuries of importance, El Mirador entered a period of decline. By A.D. 300, the Maya city of TIKAL, about 40 miles away, replaced El Mirador as the leading power in the area. (*See also* **Archaeology; Cultures, Pre-Columbian.**)

El Niño

*E*l Niño is a warm current that raises the surface-water temperature of the Pacific Ocean off the coasts of Peru and Ecuador. El Niño ("the child") received this name because the current usually occurs in December, the month of Christ's birth. El Niño is part of a large climate pattern that scientists call the Southern Oscillation, which refers to the natural change in ocean temperatures from year to year.

Normally, the waters off South America do not warm up very much, but during El Niño, the west-blowing trade winds relax over the central and western Pacific. Instead of being blown to the western Pacific, warm water sits on the surface of the eastern Pacific, preventing cold water from rising as it normally does. The warmth of El Niño brings very heavy rainfall to countries in the eastern Pacific, causes a drastic drop in marine life, and adversely affects commercial fishing in the region.

Because El Niño is part of the global weather pattern, its effects are not limited to South America. It causes heavier-than-usual rains and flooding in the southern United States and severe droughts (accompanied by crop failures and brushfires) in Australia, Indonesia, Africa, and eastern South America. Although experts are unable to attribute specific weather phenomena to El Niño, they are sure that the warm current increases the likelihood that certain *kinds* of weather events will occur.

Every century contains a few notable El Niño years. The Spanish colonial chroniclers recorded a strong El Niño as early as 1541. More recently, the strong El Niño of 1997–1998 brought rain and mud slides to Peru and California. It also brought severe droughts to eastern Central America and caused water levels in the PANAMA CANAL to drop so low that large ships were unable to use the canal.

El Salvador

*T*he Central American nation of El Salvador had to struggle to win its independence from Spain, Mexico, and Guatemala. Since becoming independent in 1856, it has faced many challenges, including border disputes, earthquakes, and a bloody civil war. By the 1990s, El Salvador was at peace, but many social and economic problems remained.

See map in Central America (vol. I).

The Land. El Salvador is located in western CENTRAL AMERICA, between Guatemala, Honduras, and the Pacific Ocean. It is the only Central American country without a Caribbean shoreline. It is also Central

Outdoor markets, such as the one shown here, are a common sight in El Salvador. People come to buy fresh farm produce as well as toys, clothing, and small appliances.

America's smallest country, measuring 200 miles from east to west and 50 miles from north to south.

El Salvador runs along a chain of volcanic mountains that are both a curse and a blessing. On one hand, their eruptions and earthquakes sometimes destroy areas of the central highlands, where the majority of the people live and where the capital city, SAN SALVADOR, is located. On the other hand, volcanic soil is rich, fertile, and easily farmed. Together with the warm tropical climate, the soil makes El Salvador very well suited to AGRICULTURE, which has long been the basis of the nation's economy.

*° **pre-Columbian** before the arrival of Christopher Columbus and other Europeans in the Americas in the 1490s*

Colonial Period and Independence.

In pre-Columbian* times, several Indian groups lived in El Salvador. Some were tribes of the great MAYA civilization that reached as far north as southern Mexico. Others came from central Mexico and spoke the Nahuatl language of that region. A third group, the Pipiles, are remembered as a hardworking and aggressive people, and many modern Salvadorans believe that they have inherited these qualities.

*° **conquistador** Spanish explorer and conqueror*

In 1524, soon after the Spanish had conquered Mexico, the conquistador* Pedro de ALVARADO marched south with a Spanish army. He overcame Indian resistance and added the territory that is now El Salvador to Spain's rapidly growing American holdings. As the Spaniards organized their new colonies into administrative units, El Salvador became a province within the Kingdom of Guatemala, which in turn was part of the Viceroyalty* of New Spain. The main Spanish towns in El Salvador were San Salvador, San Miguel, San Vicente, Santa Ana, and Sonsonate.

*° **viceroyalty** region governed by a viceroy, a royally appointed official*

*° **indigo** blue dye made from a plant of the same name*

In the 1700s, indigo* production became an important industry, and the indigo plantations of El Salvador supplied the textile mills of northern Europe. As its economy grew, El Salvador began to be recognized as a separate political unit. The first step toward El Salvador's emergence as a nation came in 1786, when the rulers of New Spain made it an intendancy*. Although El Salvador was still part of Guatemala, it had an official, the intendant, to promote its separate economic and political interests.

*° **intendancy** administrative district in Spanish America*

° **Creole** person of European ancestry born in the Americas

° **clergy** priests and other church officials qualified to perform church ceremonies

° **liberal** person who supports greater participation in government for individuals; one who is not bound by political and social traditions

° **confederation** group of states joined together for a purpose; an alliance

° **conservative** one who is opposed to sudden change, especially in existing political and social institutions

° **republic** government in which citizens elect officials to represent them and govern according to law

Blue Gold

El Salvador's most valuable product during the colonial period—and the foundation of many fortunes—was indigo, a dye that gives cloth a rich blue color. The Indians had made dye from wild indigo plants for centuries. In the late 1500s, the Spanish established indigo plantations. They used Indian and, later, African slaves for the dangerous work of dye making, exposing laborers to deadly plant poisons. El Salvador was the hub of the indigo trade, which flourished along with the European textile industry until cheaper human-made dyes replaced indigo in the 1800s.

Meanwhile, Salvadoran Creoles* grew resentful toward Guatemala for many reasons. Salvadoran indigo planters were bitter about the control that rich Guatemalan merchants held over the indigo trade. The Salvadoran clergy* disliked being led by the bishop of Guatemala and wanted to have their own bishop. Adding to the Salvadorans' frustration was a dispute over the location of the viceroyalty's capital. After an earthquake destroyed La Antigua Guatemala in 1773, Salvadorans pressed the government to move the capital city to San Salvador, but Guatemala City was made the new capital instead. In 1811, Salvadoran liberals* rebelled against Guatemala and sought independence for their province. The Guatemalan military put down the revolt, and the son of a powerful Guatemalan merchant family became the new Salvadoran intendant—further enraging the Salvadorans.

Ten years later, Guatemalan leaders joined Mexico in successfully declaring independence from Spain. Salvadoran Creoles immediately proclaimed their province independent of both Mexico and Guatemala, prompting a military conflict. The fighting ended in 1823, when the Salvadorans surrendered to a Mexican-Guatemalan army. However, that same year, Mexico's short-lived empire collapsed, and El Salvador led a movement to make Central America independent of Mexico. Guatemala, El Salvador, Honduras, Nicaragua, and Costa Rica joined together to form the United Provinces of Central America, a confederation* whose first president was Manuel José ARCE, a Salvadoran military officer.

In 1826, friction between El Salvador and Guatemala and between liberals and conservatives* led to a three-year civil war. The conflict ended in a liberal victory, and San Salvador became the capital of the confederation. However, in the mid-1830s, Salvadoran stability was threatened again, when the Pipil Indians rebelled violently against new taxes and other changes that endangered their traditional way of life. After similar peasant uprisings shook Guatemala in 1840, the confederation began to crumble, and one by one, the states withdrew from the union. In 1856, El Salvador formally declared itself a separate and fully independent republic*.

Modern History, 1856–1950s. In the late 1800s, El Salvador faced the prospect of renewed domination by Guatemala, which wanted to restore the Central American union. Although El Salvador had long favored the idea of a regional union, the Salvadorans were unwilling to tie themselves to their old rivals. The Salvadoran army defeated the invading Guatemalans in 1885.

Beginning with the presidency of General Gerardo BARRIOS in the late 1850s and early 1860s, El Salvador's government was led by many strong liberal leaders. The Liberal Party thoroughly dominated Salvadoran political life from 1871 to 1944 and, with its emphasis on economic development, brought important changes to the country. The volcanic soil of El Salvador's highlands produced high-quality COFFEE, and the liberal government encouraged an increase in coffee exports. As wealthy PLANTATION owners acquired ever more territory, they forced the rural peasants off their land and into jobs as hired laborers. By the late 1800s, coffee was the nation's leading export crop, and its success had given rise to a coffee elite—a small class of privileged growers whose political and economic power steadily increased. This group eventually became known as the "14 families." Several members of the families eventually became president.

With the support of the military, the liberal coffee oligarchy* stayed in power throughout the early 1900s. Its firm rule made El Salvador more stable than many of the neighboring countries, some of whom experienced frequent civil unrest and coups*. The liberal government built new ports and railways and the first paved highways in Central America. These improvements and the nation's prospering capital city gained El Salvador a reputation as the most progressive* country in the region. But under the surface, change and discontent were brewing.

The elite class became larger as more people gained wealth and status through the growth of the plantation economy, the rise of industry, and the increase in the number of military officers. There was also a rising middle class, centered in San Salvador, that began to play a significant role in the country's political, intellectual, and cultural life. However, the vast majority of Salvadorans remained poor, uneducated, and lacking in economic opportunities. In the 1920s, the lower classes formed political organizations—such as the Labor Party, founded by Alberto Masferrer—to challenge the ruling Liberal Party. Some of the strongest opposition to the liberals came from the Communist* Party of El Salvador and its leader, Agustín Farabundo Martí.

In the early 1930s, massive labor demonstrations and other antigovernment rallies broke out after the government refused to enact land reforms and to improve national health care and education. In 1932, Martí and the Communists led a short-lived rural revolt that pitted peasants with machetes* against soldiers with machine guns. In a massacre known as Matanza, government troops killed between 10,000 and 30,000 peasants—targeting Indians in particular. This peasant uprising and the slaughter it unleashed brought about two significant changes. It frightened the elitist rulers and made them hostile toward all political opposition, prompting them to rely heavily on military force for protection against the masses. The event also ended traditional Indian life in El Salvador, as those Indians who survived the massacre quickly adopted mestizo* clothing and customs to avoid further persecution.

Since the 1950s. During the second half of the 1900s, rapid population growth swelled the size of El Salvador's peasant class, increasing poverty and joblessness. With all the fertile land occupied by large plantations growing crops for export, the country could not produce enough food to feed its people. It became Latin America's most crowded nation, and its people were among the most poorly nourished in the world.

At the same time, the political climate in El Salvador became more open. Although military officers continued to run the government, they

° **oligarchy** rule by a few people

° **coup** sudden, often violent overthrow of a ruler or government

° **progressive** inclined to support social improvement and political change by governmental action

° **Communist** person who advocates communism—a social system in which land, goods, and the means of production are owned by the state or community rather than by individuals

° **machete** long-bladed knife used for cutting crops and vegetation

° **mestizo** person of mixed European and Indian ancestry

105

El Salvador

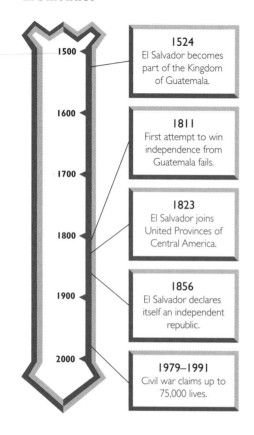

1524
El Salvador becomes part of the Kingdom of Guatemala.

1811
First attempt to win independence from Guatemala fails.

1823
El Salvador joins United Provinces of Central America.

1856
El Salvador declares itself an independent republic.

1979–1991
Civil war claims up to 75,000 lives.

* **right-wing** very conservative

* **guerrilla** referring to a group that uses surprise raids to obstruct or harass an enemy or overthrow a government

* **left-wing** very liberal

tolerated opposition parties and labor unions. The Liberal Party disappeared, and new organizations, such as the Christian Democrats and the Social Democrats, entered political life. A dynamic engineer named José Napoleón DUARTE FUENTES organized students, workers, and the Catholic clergy to support the Christian Democrats.

In 1969, war broke out between El Salvador and Honduras. The conflict was known as the FOOTBALL WAR because it was sparked by rioting among sports fans. However, the war was actually based on border disputes, trade disagreements, and the flood of poor Salvadorans who were migrating to Honduras and posing a threat to the availability of Honduran jobs and land. This brief but costly war prompted strict military rule in El Salvador during the 1970s. Salvadorans suffered HUMAN RIGHTS violations, including military and police death squads that murdered opponents of the government.

In 1979, a military coup began a long period of unrest and civil war. The following year, the military and the Christian Democrats formed a new government with Duarte as its leader. With support from the United States, Duarte tried to control the military and to make social and economic reforms, but he remained powerless against the right-wing* military chiefs. These right-wing forces carried out political assassinations, such as the murder of Catholic archbishop Oscar ROMERO. Romero was just one of many Catholic clergy who had been urging the Salvadorans to seek political and social change as part of a religious movement called LIBERATION THEOLOGY.

The government's opponents formed the Farabundo Martí National Liberation Front (FMLN) and began a civil war that dragged on for more than ten years. At least 75,000 Salvadorans were killed in the war, while many more fled to other countries for safety. As guerrilla* fighting raged in the countryside, the capital endured a devastating earthquake in 1986 and several changes of government. During this time, a right-wing group called the National Republican Alliance (ARENA)—headed by Major Roberto D'AUBUISSON—organized rural and urban voters into a powerful force by appealing to their fear of the left-wing* guerrillas and to their exhaustion with the war. The ARENA candidate, Alfredo Cristiani, became president in 1989, and in late 1991, Cristiani signed a peace agreement with the FMLN, ending the civil war.

El Salvador then began a process of economic recovery, aided by growing FOREIGN INVESTMENT. At the end of the 1990s, however, the countryside remained impoverished, and much of the nation's political power remained in the hands of the elite few. In addition, so many Salvadorans had fled the country to escape poverty that the city officials of San Salvador built a monument to *el hermano lejano* (our distant brothers). In the late 1990s, Salvadorans working in the United States sent an estimated $1 billion annually to family members in El Salvador—more than the country earned in foreign aid or exports. As in the past, El Salvador remains divided between a small, wealthy upper class and the impoverished masses. (*See also* **Central America; Central America, United Provinces of; Counterinsurgency; Dictatorships, Military; United States–Latin American Relations.**)

Emigration

See *Immigration and Emigration.*

Encomienda

° **tribute** payment made to a dominant power

° **conquistador** Spanish explorer and conqueror

° **indigenous** referring to the original inhabitants of a region

° **hacienda** large rural estate, usually devoted to agriculture

*T*he term *encomienda* refers to the right to control the labor of and to collect tribute* from an Indian community. This right was granted to Spanish subjects, especially the first conquistadors* and their descendants, as a reward for service to the Spanish crown. The person receiving such a grant was called an *encomendero.* In return for the grant, the *encomendero* promised to settle in the region, start a family, protect the Indians, and arrange for their conversion to the Roman Catholic religion.

The *encomenderos* used Indian labor to mine GOLD AND SILVER; build houses, churches, and other town buildings; cultivate crops for local use and for export; herd animals; and transport goods. With this unpaid labor, *encomenderos* became wealthy and influential, eventually controlling local government as well as the indigenous* population. Their wealth, influence, and prestige as conquerors and first settlers enabled them to ignore the wishes of the Spanish crown. To counter the power of the *encomenderos,* the crown enacted legislation to protect its interests in the Americas.

Although *encomienda* granted certain important rights, these did not include the legal right to own land or to exercise legal jurisdiction over the Indians. To break the power of the *encomenderos,* the Spanish crown regulated the amount of tribute that could be collected from the Indian community, abolished the unpaid service of the Indians, and encouraged the rise of an independent class of Spanish farmers. It was this landowning and mine-owning class that eventually replaced *encomienda* and may have led to the growth of the hacienda*.

Energy and Energy Resources

*L*atin America is rich in energy resources, but those resources are not distributed evenly among its countries. The countries have varying energy requirements, and Mexico and Brazil each consume more than one-fourth of the total energy. Moreover, the developing nations of Latin America are consuming more energy as populations and incomes rise, cities become larger, and industries develop. Nevertheless, some countries produce enough energy to sell their surplus to other countries.

PETROLEUM, or oil, is the primary source of energy in the region. While the rest of the world relies on oil for about 40 percent of its energy needs, Latin America and the Caribbean obtain almost 60 percent of their energy from oil. The smaller countries in the region are especially dependent on oil for their energy requirements. In the Caribbean, nearly three-fourths of all energy comes from petroleum, which not only provides electricity but also powers vehicles and fuels furnaces.

107

Harnessing the River's Power

For years, the two South American nations of Paraguay and Brazil argued about ownership of the Paraná River, which separates them. In 1966, they ended the dispute and agreed to share energy harnessed from the river. Together, the two countries built the Itaipú dam and power station on the Paraná. Completed in 1991 at an estimated cost of $18 billion, Itaipú is one of the world's most productive hydroelectric projects, turning the force of plunging water into electricity for the two nations.

° **monopoly** exclusive control or domination of a particular type of business

Latin America relies heavily on oil as a source of energy. Oil consumption is the highest in Latin American countries where growing cities and populations have created heavy demand for energy.

More than 90 percent of the oil deposits in Latin America are found in Venezuela and Mexico. Argentina, Bolivia, Brazil, Chile, Colombia, Ecuador, Guatemala, Peru, and Trinidad and Tobago also have oil deposits but in smaller amounts. Natural gas, another source of energy, is found in abundance in Mexico and Venezuela. Brazil also has a significant natural gas reserve, but the country lacks enough processing plants and gas lines to use this resource effectively. Therefore, only 2 percent of Brazil's energy is harnessed from natural gas.

Because several nations produce oil and gas in surplus, they trade these resources with other countries in the region. Petroleum dominates this trade in northern Latin America, while gas is the mainstay in the south. Argentina imports natural gas from Bolivia, for example, and Brazil has made a deal to buy electricity from a natural gas plant in a Bolivian border town. Throughout Latin America, governments closely monitor the exploration for oil and gas and the use of those resources. In the resource-rich nations of Mexico, Venezuela, and Brazil, the government has a monopoly* on oil and natural gas exploration, production, and distribution.

Coal, although an important source of energy, is used only in some parts of Latin America. Colombia, which has the region's largest reserves, gets more than 7 percent of its energy from coal. The El Cerrejón mine in Colombia is the largest in the region, exporting more than a

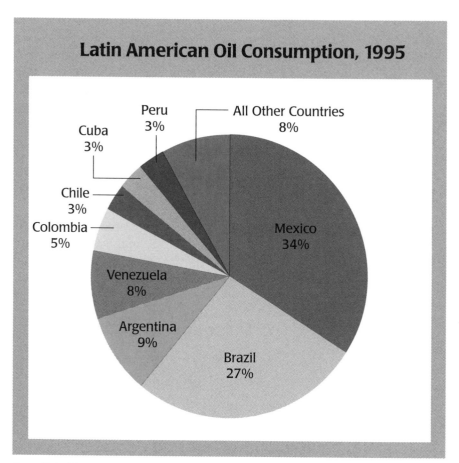

Source: United States Department of Energy.

108

million tons of coal each month. Brazil, Chile, Mexico, and Venezuela hope to increase their own coal production in order to supplement their growing energy requirements.

Hydropower* is the single largest supplier of electricity in Latin America. Argentina, Brazil, Colombia, Venezuela, and Paraguay all get substantial amounts of electricity from hydropower plants from dams located on their major rivers. Although the costs of building dams and hydroelectric* plants are high, some Latin American nations view hydropower as their best chance to become less dependent on imported oil or subject to oil's fluctuating prices. These countries have incurred large foreign and domestic debts in building their capital-intensive hydroelectricity plants.

Latin Americans also harness energy from other resources. Those in rural areas still use traditional fuels, such as wood, agricultural wastes, and dried animal dung, for residential applications. Firewood, which provided more than half the region's energy in the mid-1940s, is now used mainly in rural homes. In Cuba, Belize, and elsewhere, sugar mills burn sugarcane waste, or bagasse, to produce electricity. Argentina, Brazil, and Mexico tried to use nuclear energy but found that their enormously expensive nuclear plants were unable to compete with cheaper hydroelectric power.

Latin American countries are also exploring the possibility of harnessing energy from renewable* sources. The small island nations of the Caribbean, now dependent on imported oil, have launched projects to harness electricity from wind and solar energy. Another promising renewable resource is geothermal* energy, which can be tapped in areas that are prone to seismic* activity, such as Mexico, Central America, and the Caribbean. Since 1975, countries in these regions have been using geothermal power, and Mexico sells electricity from its geothermal wells to southern California. These sources of energy resources are becoming increasingly important as supplies of petroleum, natural gas, and coal dwindle.

° **hydropower** electricity harnessed from flowing water; the water turns turbines, producing an electric charge that is stored in huge batteries and transmitted through power lines

° **hydroelectric** referring to electricity harnessed from waterpower

° **renewable** not capable of being used up

° **geothermal** referring to naturally occurring heat beneath the earth's surface, caused by steam, hot water, or volcanic lava

° **seismic** referring to the movements of the earth, such as earthquakes and volcanic activity

Enlightenment

° **Middle Ages** period between ancient and modern times in western Europe, generally considered to be from the A.D. 500s to the 1500s

*T*he Enlightenment, sometimes called the Age of Reason, is the period of European history from the 1600s until the end of the 1700s when people gradually began to challenge the views of the world that were prevalent during the Middle Ages*. Medieval philosophy was based largely on the writings of the ancient Greek philosopher Aristotle and on the official teachings of the CATHOLIC CHURCH and such religious leaders as Saint Augustine. The works of European thinkers René Descartes, Jean Jacques Rousseau, Voltaire, and John Locke spearheaded the Enlightenment movement. These men believed that nature was orderly and that the world, including human behavior, could be explained through scientific principles. They rejected superstition and the blind acceptance of authority and were especially critical of the Catholic Church, which they believed maintained its power by keeping people in ignorance.

Ideas Put into Practice

The Enlightenment movement was not only about ideas but also the practical applications of those ideas. In an attempt to make Spain a prosperous, well-ordered, and unified state, King Charles III attempted to develop the economy through official action, including encouraging private enterprise. In addition, the inmates of asylums and orphanages were put to work. Town governments and governors had land drained and paved, established economic societies to discuss school reforms, and expanded agriculture to include new crops.

° **theology** study of religious faith

° **canon** regulation decreed by a church council

° **Jesuit** Roman Catholic religious order known as the Society of Jesus; also, a member of that order

In Spain and Portugal, where the church was strongly tied to every aspect of society, the ideas of the Enlightenment took hold more slowly than in the rest of Europe. In the late 1600s, early Latin American pioneers of the Enlightenment movement included Carlos de Sigüenza y Góngora in Mexico and Pedro de Peralta Barnueva y Rocha in Peru. From about 1720, the movement rapidly gained followers. The INQUISITION—a church tribunal that attempted to prevent certain books from circulating and to block the spread of new scientific ideas—was no longer effective. The writings of Spanish reformers, such as Benito Jerónimo Feijóo y Montenegro, circulated freely. These reformers supported education in mathematics and developed new scientific ideas based on the works of Descartes, Locke, and Sir Isaac Newton.

Such innovative concepts often came to the Americas with European scientific and technical missions. Groups led by scientists such as Aimé Jacques Bonplánd of France and Alexander von HUMBOLDT of Germany brought new books and scientific equipment and the latest scientific trends. These travelers generated enormous interest among American scholars. The Enlightenment received another boost in Spanish territories in 1759, when CHARLES III became king of Spain and officially supported the ideas of the Enlightenment.

In the late 1700s, many UNIVERSITIES, and even some religious schools, increased training in mathematics and modern physics. However, this process was gradual and still preserved fundamental Catholic values. Eventually, the old philosophies that had dominated these schools were taught only to those who were preparing for the priesthood.

The Spanish king demanded and won significant changes in the teaching of law and some aspects of theology*. Spanish law replaced Roman law as the dominant subject of study, and canon* law strongly emphasized the *regalias*—the rights of the monarchy over the church. In the late 1700s, the king dramatically asserted his control over the church by repressing the Jesuits* and by condemning their beliefs.

Some historians believe that the WARS OF INDEPENDENCE fought by Spain's American colonies in the early 1800s were sparked by the ideas of the Enlightenment. However, others insist that the wars were simply a result of the overthrow of the Spanish king by the French emperor Napoleon in 1808. These historians claim that the effects of the Enlightenment on Latin America are seen in the 1800s, as the new American nations struggled to establish their own governments and to determine balances of power and individual rights. (*See also* **Bourbon Reforms.**)

Environmental Movements

*E*nvironmental problems are often considered worldwide, not regional, concerns. Much of the international attention to Latin America's environmental problems focuses on global warming as it relates to the destruction of tropical FORESTS, especially in the AMAZON REGION and CENTRAL AMERICA. Many Latin American cities face pollution problems, including the need for adequate clean drinking water, sewage treatment, and cleaner air for the growing populations of SÃO

Since the 1990s, many Latin American countries have set aside land for preservation and reforestation. This photograph shows an area in Costa Rica that is undergoing reforestation.

° **sustainable** refers to development that meets people's present needs without compromising the ability of future generations to meet their needs

° **biodiversity** biological variety of an environment as indicated by the number of different species of plants and animals living there

A City Brought Back to Life

The Brazilian city of Cubatão, near São Paulo, was once called the most polluted site on Earth. However, the city cleaned up its act with the help of a loan from the World Bank, a special agency of the United Nations. By the mid-1990s, Cubatão had reduced pollution from chemicals and fertilizers to a fraction of their former levels. As a result, lush vegetation reappeared in once-devastated areas, and the overall health of the city's inhabitants dramatically improved.

PAULO and RIO DE JANEIRO, Brazil; MEXICO CITY, Mexico; and SANTIAGO, Chile; among others.

Since the 1980s, environmental issues in Latin America have had strong political and economic implications and have provoked much controversy. Development plans of the 1960s and 1970s were often blamed for many of the most serious environmental problems of the 1980s and 1990s. In the late 1980s, President Carlos SALINAS DE GORTARI of Mexico declared the health of the Mexican people to be a greater priority of his administration than development. Large sums of money were allocated to improve Mexico City's air quality, a major petroleum refinery was closed, and unleaded gasoline was introduced. By the early 1990s, many Latin American nations had established powerful government agencies to address environmental matters—often in combination with the development of natural resources or urban planning. For example, ECUADOR and GUATEMALA faced serious choices between opening new areas for petroleum production or preserving these lands as natural habitats. But environmental laws still varied greatly, and even where environmental measures existed, implementing or enforcing them was difficult or even impossible. Frequently, the measures were simply ignored.

Some countries have set aside tropical forest areas—known as extractive reserves—from which local residents are allowed to extract certain resources. The first, the Chico Mendes Extractive Reserve, was created in Brazil in 1990 and consists of more than a million acres of tropical forest. This reserve sought to save the forest from loggers and builders while supporting those who earned a living from the forest in the least destructive manner—in this case, rubber tappers. In other Latin American countries, new campaigns were inspired by the Brazilian model. Extractive reserves were formed for resin tappers in HONDURAS and nut gatherers in PERU. In COSTA RICA, foreign pharmaceutical companies encouraged the establishment of reserves in order to protect the forests as potential sources of new medications.

In 1992, the United Nations held a major international conference on the environment, popularly known as the Earth Summit, in Rio de Janeiro. More than 30,000 delegates from 178 nations attended, including 117 heads of state. The conference produced a plan outlining international measures for achieving sustainable* development. It also reached major agreements on regulating the emission of greenhouse gases—gases believed to cause global warming—and the preservation of biodiversity*. However, many critics believed that population, poverty, and development issues received too little attention and that the major agreements lacked serious substance.

Five years later, in 1997, Earth Summit II convened in New York City. Its report was not optimistic. Although the rate of world population growth had slowed and food production had increased, greenhouse gas emissions had risen since 1992. Freshwater supplies had been reduced, forest and agricultural lands were shrinking, poverty had worsened, and biodiversity had continued to decline. Tensions also arose between industrial and developing nations over financial aid for sustainable development programs. (*See also* **Economic Development; Forests; Industrialization; Population and Population Growth; Technology.**)

111

Ercilla y Zúñiga, Alonso de

1533–1594
Spanish poet

Although Alonso de Ercilla y Zúñiga was in Latin America for only a short period, he is considered one of the first Spanish American writers. As a young man, he served in the court of Spain's king PHILIP II, and for a brief period, he was a soldier. His experience fighting the Araucanian Indians in southern CHILE inspired him to write his epic poem *La Araucana*. Ercilla began writing the poem in Chile but completed it years later in Spain, adding several passages about important Spanish triumphs in Europe. The work—which Ercilla dedicated to King Philip II—praises the glories of the Spanish empire while also presenting a sympathetic and admiring view of the Araucanians. The poem does not have an individual hero, but it emphasizes the Indians' valiant defense against the Spanish invasion of their land. It even criticizes certain aspects of the war. In the work, Ercilla combines the imagination of a poet with the observations of a historian. The epic was widely read in its day, with at least 18 editions in circulation by 1632. Today *La Araucana* is considered a national classic in Chile. (*See also* **Literature.**)

Esmeraldas

See map in Ecuador (vol. 2).

° **cacao** bean from which chocolate is made

Located on the northwest coast of ECUADOR, Esmeraldas is one of the nation's most isolated and thinly populated areas. Most of Ecuador's black citizens live in the province, where traditional customs, such as the marimba dance and an oral literature known as the *décima*, have been preserved.

Esmeraldas was settled by a few Spaniards who were lured to the area by stories of gold and emeralds found during one of Francisco PIZARRO's early expeditions to South America. The region's first black inhabitants probably arrived in 1553, when a slave ship ran aground off the coast. These former slaves created a self-governing community, intermarried with the local Indians, and remained independent of the Spaniards for about 60 years. Throughout the 1600s and 1700s, black slaves brought to work the mines in Colombia also migrated to the region. In 1820—two years before Ecuador's liberation—residents of Esmeraldas declared their independence from Spain, but government troops sent from QUITO put down this early attempt at revolution. Violence also broke out from 1913 to 1916 in the bloody Concha War, in which the black population of Esmeraldas unsuccessfully rebelled against the government of President Leonidas Plaza Gutiérrez.

The province has experienced periods of growth and expansion—in the cacao*, rubber, balsa wood, and banana industries in the early to mid-1900s and in oil refining in the 1970s. Yet despite these booms, Esmeraldas remains geographically and politically isolated from the mainstream of Ecuadorian life. (*See also* **Africans in Latin America; Slave Trade.**)

Estancia

See *Land, Ownership of.*

Estrada Cabrera, Manuel

1857–1924
President of Guatemala

° **caudillo** authoritarian leader or dictator, often from the military

° **oligarchy** rule by a few people

° **impeach** to charge a government official with misconduct in office; sometimes results in his or her removal from office

Notorious for his cruelty, Manuel Estrada Cabrera was president of GUATEMALA from 1898 to 1920. His 22-year reign of terror still ranks as the longest uninterrupted rule in Central American history. When President José Reyna Barrios was assassinated in 1898, Estrada Cabrera was recognized as his legal successor. Although Estrada Cabrera was initially considered an undistinguished rural politician, he soon became a powerful caudillo*.

Estrada Cabrera was dedicated to the ideas of order and progress that were central to POSITIVISM, a philosophy that was widely favored at the time. He was careful to maintain the support of the nation's wealthy coffee growers. He encouraged the creation of large estates, supported forced labor and an economy based on exports, and favored a highly centralized government. As a result, Guatemala's lower classes became increasingly exploited and repressed, while the wealthy elite gained more and more privileges. It was soon obvious that the nation was run by a rich, landowning oligarchy* composed mainly of coffee producers. Although Estrada Cabrera modernized Guatemala somewhat during his presidency, his government denied the rapidly growing—and increasingly frustrated—middle and working classes the right to political expression. By 1918, his inability to adapt to the republic's changing political and social conditions, together with a series of devastating earthquakes that destroyed much of Guatemala City, rallied the opposition against him. Estrada Cabrera was impeached* in 1920.

Explorers and Exploration

° **conquistador** Spanish explorer and conqueror

° **indigenous** referring to the original inhabitants of a region

See color plate 2, vol. 3.

The European exploration of Latin America began with Christopher COLUMBUS's arrival in the Caribbean islands in 1492. Although other explorers may have arrived centuries before, Columbus's voyage marked the beginning of the age of exploration in the Western Hemisphere. It was the age of adventurers, conquistadors*, and discoverers who redefined the map of the world. That period ended by the 1700s, but exploration continued until the mapping of South America was complete in the 1900s. In many ways, Latin American exploration continues as scientists study the geography, wildlife, and indigenous* cultures of this vast and diverse region.

Europeans discovered the Americas by accident while searching for a sea route to the fabulously valuable spices, silks, and gems of Asia. Although they found these previously unknown continents and not Asia, their dream of finding great wealth prevailed. Everywhere the Europeans went in the Americas, they sought gold, spices, and other treasures. In its early stages, the exploration of Latin America was mostly a quest for riches and resources, and people to convert to Christianity. The explorations later became patriotic missions, spurring explorers to compete with one another to claim new territories for their home countries. Sometimes violent, greedy, and brutal, other times driven by religious or scientific goals, the explorers in Latin America encountered tremendous dangers and challenges as they searched for the secrets and hidden treasures of the continent.

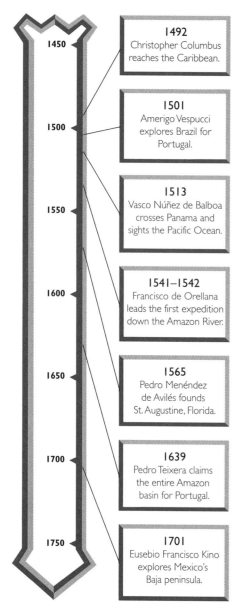

1450

1492
Christopher Columbus reaches the Caribbean.

1500

1501
Amerigo Vespucci explores Brazil for Portugal.

1513
Vasco Núñez de Balboa crosses Panama and sights the Pacific Ocean.

1550

1600

1541–1542
Francisco de Orellana leads the first expedition down the Amazon River.

1650

1565
Pedro Menéndez de Avilés founds St. Augustine, Florida.

1700

1639
Pedro Teixera claims the entire Amazon basin for Portugal.

1750

1701
Eusebio Francisco Kino explores Mexico's Baja peninsula.

First Explorations. The European Age of Discovery began in the mid-1400s, when Portugal sent several expeditions along the southern and western coasts of Africa in search of a sea route to Asia and the Far East. In the late 1400s, Columbus became convinced that he could reach the East by sailing westward, and he persuaded the Spanish monarchs to sponsor his voyage. Believing that he had reached the eastern edge of Asia, Columbus explored parts of CUBA and HISPANIOLA in the Caribbean. Upon Columbus's return to Spain, the Spanish and Portuguese rulers asked the pope to divide the world so that each kingdom would have a clear claim to future discoveries. According to the Treaty of TORDESILLAS, Pope Alexander VI drew a line down the middle of the Atlantic Ocean, cutting through present-day BRAZIL. Everything discovered east of that line would belong to Portugal and everything west of it to Spain. The treaty gave Columbus's new western discoveries to Spain. Portugal continued its efforts to sail around Africa.

Columbus made three more trips to the Americas. Until his death in 1506, he believed that he had reached Asia. By that time, other explorers probing the western shores realized that what Columbus had found was not Asia. It was not even included in their geography. They called it the New World. One of the first to understand that the Americas were a New World was explorer Amerigo VESPUCCI, who sailed along the Brazilian coast in 1501. Vicente Yáñez Pinzón of Spain, one of Columbus's former lieutenants, had already sailed along that coast, perhaps as far south as the mouth of the AMAZON RIVER, but Spain ignored his discovery because the coastline he had explored belonged to Portugal under the Treaty of Tordesillas.

Portugal's first encounter with Latin America took place in 1500. A fleet under Pedro Álvares CABRAL sailed from Portugal to India on Vasco da Gama's newly discovered route around the southern tip of Africa. Hoping to catch favorable winds, Cabral steered the fleet far west into the Atlantic—so far that it bumped into the eastern bulge of Brazil. Cabral thought he had landed on an island. He claimed it for Portugal and then went on to India. His voyage, like Columbus's, opened the way for other explorers and empire builders.

The Exploration of Spanish America. No sooner had Columbus established Spain's first American settlement on Hispaniola than a host of Spanish mariners began to explore the nearby coasts. Juan de la Cosa, a member of Columbus's first crew, captured Darién, Panama, in 1504. For the next 25 years, Darién and Hispaniola served as the launching points for Spanish expeditions to MEXICO and Central and South America. Each new territory became the starting point for further exploration. For example, in 1513, Juan Ponce de León set out from Puerto Rico for the first Spanish exploration of the FLORIDA coast. Florida then became the starting point for Hernando de SOTO's expedition into southeastern North America.

In 1513, Vasco Núñez de BALBOA made one of Spain's most important discoveries when he crossed Panama and found himself on the shores of the Pacific Ocean. Within a few years, conquistador Pedro

Arias de ÁVILA built an interoceanic road across Panama so that the Spanish could carry freight between their Pacific and Atlantic fleets. In the centuries that followed, hundreds of tons of silver from the Philippines and other goods traveled this road on their way to Spain.

A major landmark in the Spanish exploration and conquest of Latin America was the arrival of conquistador Hernán CORTÉS in Veracruz, Mexico, in 1519. Cortés conquered the AZTECS in 1521 and founded NEW SPAIN, which became one of the largest and most important colonies in Spain's overseas empire. New Spain sent many explorers north of Mexico to extend the Spanish empire. Among these were Francisco Vázquez de Coronado, whose men discovered the Grand Canyon in their search for the mythical SEVEN CITIES OF CÍBOLA, Pedro Menéndez de Avilés who founded St. Augustine (Florida) in 1565, and Juan de OÑATE, who founded a Spanish colony in present-day New Mexico in 1598. Spanish navigators also explored northward by sea, along the Pacific coast. Juan Rodríguez Cabrillo sailed from Acapulco (Mexico) to the present Oregon-California border in 1542.

The trek northward continued into the 1700s under explorers such as Father Eusebio Francisco KINO, who in 1701 discovered that BAJA CALIFORNIA in northern Mexico was a peninsula, not an island. The Spanish exploration of southwestern North America and CALIFORNIA continued into the late 1700s and produced several Spanish forts and missions throughout the region, including areas along the Pacific coast.

Spain also explored the South American interior and the regions to the south of Mexico and the Caribbean. Cortés's conquest of the Aztecs showed the Europeans that the Americas contained enormous wealth. While Cortés and his soldiers explored and conquered most of Central America, other conquistadors searched for other potentially wealthy civilizations to conquer. In 1528, Sebastian Cabot traveled up the Río de la Plata and its tributaries on the southeastern coast. Diego de ALMAGRO and Francisco PIZARRO overthrew the capital of the INCA empire in PERU in 1533, the same year that Sebastián de Belalcázar took the Inca city of QUITO, Ecuador. First Almagro, and then Pedro de VALDIVIA, explored CHILE. The discovery of silver in BOLIVIA in 1545 made that region the focus of intense Spanish exploration and colonization. In 1552, Juan Francisco de Aguirre crossed the Andes and founded the city of Santiago del Estero in ARGENTINA. Other explorers, some of them searching for the legendary treasures of EL DORADO (Golden One) founded colonies in COLOMBIA and VENEZUELA on the north coast of South America. By the 1550s, Spain claimed a huge American territory that stretched from northern Mexico to southern Chile and Argentina.

The Exploration of Brazil. Yáñez Pinzón and Cabral had seen parts of the Brazilian coast, but the real discovery of Brazil began in 1501, when Portugal sent Gonçalo Coelho and a fleet of three ships to examine Cabral's find. An unknown mapmaker on Coelho's expedition made the first known map that shows a section of the Brazilian coastline. Initially, Portugal was interested only in its eastern route to Asia, treating its American colony as little more than the source of novelties, such as parrots and monkeys. However, when other European

See color plate 1, vol. 4.

See color plate 4, vol. 3.

A Modern Explorer

Cândido Mariano da Silva Rondon was one of Brazil's greatest modern explorers. Between 1890 and 1915, Rondon led many military and scientific expeditions into Brazil's unexplored interior. His groups laid more than 1,350 miles of telegraph lines in the Amazon basin, mapped more than 20,000 square miles of territory, and discovered 12 rivers. A champion of Indian rights, Rondon convinced the Brazilian government to establish the Indian Protection Service in 1910 and served as its first head. In 1956, Brazil changed the name of the state of Guaporé to Rondônia in his honor.

Explorers and Exploration

The first European explorers to reach the Americas were searching for a new sea route to the fabulously valuable spices, silks, and gems of Asia. Although they failed to find Asia, their dreams of wealth did not die. This map shows the routes taken by four prominent explorers. Explorers such as Diego de Almagro and Francisco Pizarro were influenced by rumors of El Dorado—a city where according to legend, the king dusted his body with gold each day.

EXPLORATION OF SOUTH AMERICA

←	Diego de Almagro 1535–1537
◄- -	Francisco de Orellana 1540
◄····	Francisco Pizarro 1532
◄—	Amerigo Vespucci 1499–1500

0   500   1000 Miles

* **missionary** person who works to convert nonbelievers to his or her faith

powers started moving into northeastern Brazil, Portugal took action to establish a royal colony there.

One of the first great explorations of Brazil was led by Spanish conquistador Francisco de ORELLANA, who in 1541 commanded the first European voyage down the Amazon River. By the 1630s, both the Spanish and the Portuguese were beginning to explore Amazonia—the Spanish from the west and the Portuguese from the east. In the late 1630s, Pedro Teixera led a large Portuguese expedition up the river and claimed the entire Amazon River valley for Portugal. The Treaty of Tordesillas gave only the country's eastern bulge to Portugal, but Teixera's expedition later stood as the basis for Brazil's claim to its western territories in Amazonia.

While missionaries* and traders were exploring Amazonia, others worked their way into Brazil's interior from the coastal settlements of Bahia, Pernambuco, and São Paulo. From the 1590s until the 1730s, roving teams called BANDEIRAS searched the backlands for gold, gems, and Indian slaves. In doing so, they mapped the network of rivers that connected the interior to the coast. In 1648, Antônio Rapôso Tavares led a famous *bandeira* that covered 8,000 miles in the Andes, Amazonia, and western Brazil.

The scientific exploration of Brazil began in the mid-1700s, after the end of border conflicts with the Spanish colonies. The new surge of scientific exploration brought expeditions devoted to gathering specimens of plants and animals and to mapping the seacoast and the interior. In 1790, Brazilian-born José Mariano da Conceição Velloso published an 11-volume study of Brazilian plant life. Scientific explorers from France, Britain, and Austria flocked to Brazil to study the wonders of the RAIN FOREST. Dutch painter Albert ECKHOUT captured the beauty of the Brazilian landscape on canvas. Austrian Johann Natterer spent 19 years collecting specimens and founded a museum in Austria dedicated to Brazilian natural science. A few years later, Swiss scientist Jean Louis Rodolphe Agassiz headed an expedition up the Amazon. In the late 1800s and early 1900s, Brazilian explorers (such as Antônio Gonçalves Dias, who studied the Indians, and João Barbosa Rodrigues, who founded an important collection of Amazonia plants in the city of Manaus) carried out the mapping and scientific exploration of their country. (*See also* **Geography; Maps and Mapmaking.**)

Falklands/ Malvinas War

* **junta** small group of people who run a government, usually after seizing power by force

* **garrison** military post

See color plate 9, vol. 4.

*T*he Falklands/Malvinas War of 1982 arose from a long-standing dispute between ARGENTINA and Great Britain over possession of the Falklands/Malvinas, a group of islands located in the southern Atlantic Ocean about 300 miles off the coast of southern Argentina. The British had occupied the islands since 1833, when they displaced the few Argentines living there.

In 1982, the Argentine military decided the time was right to recover the islands. While the British had shown diminished military and financial commitment to the islands, Argentine interest in the territory was increasing. Argentina wanted to protect its commercial interests in the Antarctic and South Atlantic, and its ruling junta* needed a cause to unite the country under its leadership.

On April 2, 1982, an Argentine force of nearly 5,000 men attacked a small British garrison* and seized the islands. Many Latin American nations supported Argentina's claim to the islands, although not necessarily its use of force. However, the UNITED NATIONS Security Council passed a resolution that favored Britain. On April 25, the British navy retook the island of South Georgia. For three weeks, Britain and Argentina fought an air and sea battle that ended in a British victory on June 14.

Following the war, the 2,000 islanders remained British subjects, protected by a large British garrison. Meanwhile, the frustrated Argentines removed the military junta and elected a civilian president in 1983. Full diplomatic relations between Argentina and Great Britain remained broken for eight years. Postwar disagreements over control of foreign fishing vessels and reports of possible oil fields near the islands have added new issues to the dispute. (*See also* **British–Latin American Relations.**)

Family

The role of the family has always been very important in the economy and politics of Latin America. Both Spain and Portugal organized settlement, land distribution, and political power through the institution of the family. While modernization has changed the definitions and roles of the family, individuals of all economic and social groups continue to depend on the family network for support. It is still quite common for families of all classes to gather every week for Sunday dinner.

* **tribute** payment made to a dominant power

Colonial Families. Spain placed colonial power in the hands of certain families through the *encomienda* system. This system gave selected Spanish colonists—usually married men—the right to demand labor and tribute* from the local Indians. These men, called *encomenderos,* also received a seat on the city council. They were required to establish a *casa poblada,* a house on the town square that was large enough to house 35 people. They were also expected to supply horses and arms for 17 men. Many of the *encomendero*'s Spanish relatives and friends joined him in the Americas and became a part of his extended family and business.

In Brazil, the Portuguese *donatário* system also gave power to particular families. Land grants given to wealthy individuals led to a system of *latifundia,* in which a small group of families owned most of the land suitable for farming and ranching. The Brazilian city councils were comprised of *homens boms,* or "good men"—married landowners who were not of Jewish or Moorish* ancestry. Because there were only a few royal officials in the huge Portuguese colony, the *homens boms* and their families wielded considerable power in Brazil.

* **Moorish** relating to the Moors, the North African Muslim conquerors of Spain in the A.D. 700s

The elite Latin American families also took charge of much of the development in their colonies because the Spanish and Portuguese kings provided few resources for this purpose. The dominant families built public buildings, roads, and ports. They organized contributions of building materials and directed the labor necessary to complete the projects. Eventually, elite families intermarried with each other, creating clusters of relatives who controlled their region's politics and economy.

Colonial families, like those in Spain and Portugal, were patriarchal; the male head of the family had total authority over its members, and property was inherited through the male line. In addition, most men received a dowry* from their bride when they married, which helped them establish a household or business. Although most property was distributed through inheritance, men also kept wealth within the family by choosing cousins, brothers-in-law, and other male family members as business partners.

* **dowry** money or property that a woman brings to the man she marries

Kinship. In religious and legal terms, the Latin American family system was based on European practices. Kinship was traced from both the paternal (father's) side and the maternal (mother's) side, and individuals were known by both last names. A person's distant relatives—even seven or ten times removed—were also considered kin.

Ritual kinship, called *compadrazgo* in Spanish, was a special bond between two people of equal social standing that did not necessarily involve a blood relationship. It was a significant means of expanding family relationships within classes. The individuals in such a relationship relied on one another for mutual support in times of need. *Compadrazgo* was recognized by the CATHOLIC CHURCH, which required people linked by this type of kinship to seek special permission from the church to marry. Ritual kinship was sometimes also used to reinforce a blood relationship.

Latin American Indian and African families were also influenced by the European tradition of ritual kinship—often as a result of desperate circumstances. Indian families endured an extremely difficult period in the 1500s, when European diseases brought by the conquistadors* killed more than half of the Indian populations. Their populations recovered somewhat when the Indians cohabited* with Europeans and with Africans brought to the Americas as slaves. Gradually, the Indians and Africans adopted the European institution of ritual kinship in order to extend the base of mutual help and trust within their communities. For example, after Africans from different regions of Africa had suffered the perilous voyage to the Americas together in the same slave ship, they sometimes considered each other family members.

Households. The average Latin American household in the 1700s and 1800s was relatively small, with between four and six members, excluding slaves. The situation was similar in the city and in the country, and wealthier households generally were larger. Family size increased in the 1800s as households expanded their productive capacity. Because factories developed very slowly due to low levels of capital and poor communications, early industrialization was organized through the household. Goods were produced both to live on and to sell to markets, often for export.

In the 1800s, as farming became a large commercial venture, many men migrated to areas of agricultural employment, leaving women and children either to live on what they could grow themselves or to migrate to cities in search of better opportunities. Female-headed households became commonplace, especially in the lower classes. Women worked in textile or cigarette manufacturing, performed household services, such as laundering and ironing clothes, and prepared food to sell in the street.

Households often included nonrelated members, called *allegados* or *agregados,* who boarded with a family, either paying money or providing such services as housework or child care. Apprentices, clerks, cashiers, and others who worked in the family's business often lived with the family. Elite families also had *agregados,* including orphans, relatives, and in Brazil, captive Indians, in their households, where they usually worked as domestic servants.

Today many working-class families in Latin American cities earn too little to cover the needs of the household. Consequently, families often have several members who work for wages, as well as members of the family who hold multiple jobs. Families also rely on exchanges

° **conquistador** Spanish explorer and conqueror

° **cohabit** to live together as husband and wife

Family Size

Since the mid-1900s, the size of the average Latin American family has decreased. Rural families once needed to have many children so that enough would survive to adulthood to run the farm and take care of their parents. However, Latin American infant survival rates have increased, allowing such families to have fewer children. Greater access to education and the need for many urban parents to work several jobs in order to support a family have also led people to limit family size. Contraceptives are now available to most Latin Americans, although many choose not to use them because of their religious beliefs.

among relatives or neighbors for the things they need. Urban poverty has also contributed to the number of households headed by women. In some cases, men have abandoned their families because they were unemployed or too poor to provide for them. Families headed by women are among the poorest in Latin America and often rely on children to work and help support the family.

In rural communities, families are organized around labor and household production. Peasant families improve their economic and social standing through marriage, children, inheritance, and migration. Often several relatives work both on and off the family farm and combine their resources for the family's survival. (*See also* **Agriculture; Children; Cities and Urbanization; Economic Development; Fiestas; Industrialization; Marriage and Divorce; Women.**)

Farming

See *Agriculture*.

Farroupilha Revolt

* **regent** person appointed to govern while the rightful monarch is too young or unable to rule
* **ragamuffin** dirty, raggedly-dressed person of poor reputation, especially a child

* **republic** government in which citizens elect officials to represent them and govern according to law
* **caudillo** authoritarian leader or dictator, often from the military

* **federal** referring to a form of government in which power is distributed between a central government and the member states

*T*he Farroupilha Revolt, also known as the Ragamuffin War, was the longest and most dangerous of five major revolts that shook the Brazilian empire between 1831 and 1840. During this period, BRAZIL was ruled by a regent* until the young PEDRO II became old enough to assume the duties of emperor. The uprising occurred from 1835 to 1845 in Brazil's southernmost province of Rio Grande do Sul. At first, the rebels were ridiculed as *farrapos,* or ragamuffins*, for the fringed leather clothing they wore, but they later adopted the name as a banner of pride and defiance.

The revolt pitted Rio Grande do Sul's coastal city dwellers, who remained loyal to Brazil's central government, against the cattle ranchers of the interior, who felt that the central government neglected the province's needs. In 1836, the rebels declared the province an independent republic* and elected rancher Bento Gonçalves da Silva as president. They received support from Uruguay's caudillo*, Fructuoso Rivera, who hoped to form a new state unifying Uruguay, Rio Grande do Sul, and two Argentine provinces. In 1837, the Farrapos' successes inspired the outbreak of the SABINADA REVOLT in the northeastern province of Bahia.

However, in 1842, Brazil's most formidable military commander, Luis Alves de LIMA E SILVA, took command of the loyalist forces and of the administration of Rio Grande do Sul. The following year, the rebels drew up a moderate constitution for their republic, which retained slavery, kept Catholicism as the official religion, and provided for elections. Lima e Silva's considerable political skill and several military victories soon brought the rebellious province back under control, finally ending the conflict in 1845. Some Brazilians consider the revolt a forerunner of the formation of Brazil's federal* republic in 1889. (*See also* **Federalism.**)

Fascism

° **charismatic** having a special charm or appeal that arouses public loyalty and enthusiasm

° **patron** special guardian, protector, or supporter

° **anti-Semitic** referring to hostility or discrimination against Jews

° **conservative** inclined to maintain existing political and social views, conditions, and institutions

° **demagogue** leader who uses prejudice and emotional appeals to gain power

Appeal of Fascism Proves Limited

In Europe, fascism grew quickly in the atmosphere of sacrifice and disillusionment that followed World War I. By the 1930s, fascist governments had been established in Italy, Spain, Portugal, and Germany. The Mediterranean fascist regimes appealed to many Latin Americans who liked their grand, imperial style and support of Roman Catholicism. However, Latin Americans were less eager to embrace German Nazism because it opposed religion and declared that an Aryan race of white-skinned, blond, blue-eyed people was superior to all others.

*I*n Europe and elsewhere, the fascist movement has largely been associated with the absolute rule of a charismatic* dictator, strict government control of economy and society, powerful national identity, and often fierce and violent racism. The fascist movement in Latin America has few of these characteristics. Instead, Latin American fascism is rooted in populism, or the belief in the rights and wisdom of the common people. It is also closely linked to authoritarian NATIONALISM, or loyalty and devotion to a nation and especially to a particular national leader.

Latin American populist movements began in city politics before 1914. Many rural people had relocated to the cities in search of jobs, and city politics began to resemble rural politics in that they were characterized by strong patron*-client relationships. Soon, ambitious reformist politicians emerged, such as Uruguayan president José BATLLE Y ORDÓÑEZ. Between World War I and World War II, populism also embraced nationalism. People sought to establish a national identity, to modernize their nations, and to use government to achieve social equality. Nationalism included groups that previously had lacked a political voice, and it denounced the wealthy who invested in foreign-owned companies in Latin America instead of supporting the development of domestically owned businesses.

In the 1930s, several fascist groups were established in Latin America that sought to imitate those in Portugal, Italy, and Spain. The most important Latin American fascist movements were the Brazilian Integralistas, the Chilean Nacistas, the Mexican Sinarquistas, and the Movimiento Nacional Revolucionario (MNR) in Bolivia. In Argentina, authoritarian nationalist groups failed to gain a mass following and full support from politicians. As a result, they employed tactics of street fighting and anti-Semitic* terrorism.

European-style fascism failed to take hold in Latin America for many reasons. The major models for fascism—the German and Italian fascist regimes—were defeated in World War II. Furthermore, many Latin American countries had numerous, strong local and ethnic cultures that rejected the fascist belief in a narrowly defined national identity. Alternative political parties to fascism arose, such as the Christian Democratic Party, that supported nonviolent modernization and appealed to conservative* voters. In Argentina, Brazil, Chile, and Uruguay in the 1970s and in Central America in the 1980s, military regimes employed state terror to suppress dissent rather than the fascist method of using demagogues* to manipulate people's opinions.

The basic structure of fascism is sometimes taken to be an authoritarian, centralized state with a system of beliefs based on nationalism, a state-controlled economy, and a society having an organized mass following that supports the regime. According to this definition, there have been five fascist regimes in Latin America since the 1930s: Getúlio VARGAS's Brazil after 1937, Juan PERÓN's Argentina, the Bolivia of the MNR after 1952, Fidel CASTRO's Cuba since 1959, and the Mexico of the Institutional Revolutionary Party (PRI) after 1928. The first two—which included charismatic leadership and, in Argentina, anti-Semitism—most closely approximated European fascism. (*See also* **Caudillos; Dictatorships, Military.**)

Favela

See *Africans in Latin America; Brazil; Rio de Janeiro.*

Fazenda

See *Land, Ownership of.*

Federal War

° **regime** prevailing political system or rule

° **federal** referring to a form of government in which power is distributed between a central government and the member states

° **suffrage** the right to vote

See map in Venezuela (vol. 4).

*V*enezuela's Federal War, from 1859 to 1863, was a bloody civil conflict between the country's Liberal and Conservative parties. The Conservatives consisted mostly of wealthy businessmen who supported a strong central government, while the Liberals—composed mainly of elite landowners and artisans—desired greater regional independence. By the late 1850s, severe economic problems and social unrest were contributing to the tension between these groups.

On June 7, 1858, Venezuela's Conservative dictator, General Julián Castro, banished the most prestigious Liberal leaders from the country and imprisoned many other Liberals who opposed his regime*. The Liberals responded with armed uprisings and plots to drive the Conservatives from power and install a federal* system of government.

Open war broke out on February 20, 1859, when Liberal forces seized the military headquarters in the city of Coro and proclaimed the creation of a federation, an end to the death penalty, universal suffrage* for men, and the right of diverse political parties to participate in government. The fighting spread to many parts of Venezuela and lasted for four years. In April 1863, the war ended in a Liberal victory with the signing of the Treaty of Coche. Nearly 50,000 Venezuelans had been killed in the conflict.

The war did little to alter the lives of those who fought it because Venezuela's economic and social structures remained unchanged. However, it did result in the establishment of a federal system that is the basis for Venezuela's present national constitution. (*See also* **Federalism.**)

Federalism

° **liberal** person who supports greater participation in government for individuals; one who is not bound by political and social traditions

*F*ederalism is a form of government in which power is divided between a central (national) authority and regional (state or provincial) authorities. During the independence movement of the 1800s, several Latin American countries adopted a federal system of government based on the United States Constitution, the 1812 Spanish constitution, and various European models. Yet federalism remains a hotly debated political issue in Latin America.

Federalism appealed to many Latin American leaders of the newly-independent nations because it was compatible with their liberal* beliefs in individual rights. However, critics of federalism, such as the famous independence leader Simón Bolívar, condemned it as a dangerously weak system. They believed that its design would be unsuccessful in Latin America because it would give provinces with no prior administrative experience their own executive, legislative, and judicial branches that shared power with the national government.

Federalism has influenced several Latin American nations since the 1800s. In Mexico, it became a central doctrine of the Liberal Party and its successors. The three constitutions under which Mexico has been governed for most of its national history—those of 1824, 1857, and 1917—all gave the country a federalist organization. In 1853, the Argentine government adopted a federalist constitution that remains in force today. For a brief period under its Constitution of 1863, Colombia adopted an extreme version of federalism—a system in which the various Colombian states even had their own armies and postage stamps. In 1891, Brazil became a federation with the adoption of its first republican* constitution, which closely resembled that of the United States. Other Latin American nations, including Chile, Uruguay, Bolivia, Peru, and Venezuela, also experimented with federal or partly federal forms of government during the 1800s.

Latin America's three largest countries—Mexico, Brazil, and Argentina—are the only ones that still have a strictly federal constitution. Most small Latin American countries, such as Paraguay and the Dominican Republic, have maintained centralist* governments. However, many Latin American nations have included both centralist and federal features in their governments. For example, Argentina's federal constitution contains a centralist provision that allows the national president or congress to intervene in the government of the provinces or states under certain circumstances.

* **republican** referring to a government in which citizens elect officials to represent them and govern according to law

* **centralist** referring to a system that concentrates power in the central government

Feminism

See *Women.*

Festivals

See *Fiestas.*

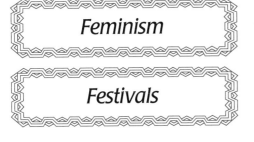

Fiestas

See color plate 9, vol. 2.

Throughout Latin America and the Caribbean, people celebrate many fiestas, including family events, saint-day parties, religious festivals, and national holidays. These festivals combine Indian, African, and European traditions, creating fiestas that are characteristically Latin American. More recently, North American holidays and customs have been gradually influencing festivals in Latin America. Celebrated with dancing and music, some fiestas also include parades with floats and elaborate costumes. People organize themselves into ethnic, occupational, or religious groups to build the floats and participate in the parades.

Fiesta Foods

Special foods are associated with many Latin American fiestas. On Independence Day, Mexican cuisine includes *chiles en nogada*, a dish made from stuffed green peppers, white sauce, and red pomegranate seeds, matching the colors of the Mexican flag. Holiday beverages include the *cuba libre*, a rum and cola drink to celebrate Cuban independence, and Noche Buena beer, brewed only during Christmas. Other foods include Virgin's Tears, a beet juice preparation for Holy Week, and a special bread made from egg yolks for the Day of the Dead. Three Kings' Bread, a sweet bread eaten on January 6, has a ring baked in it to bring luck to the person who finds it.

° **Lent** period of penitence and fasting before Easter

Fiestas serve many purposes in Latin American society. As community holidays, they are occasions for social interaction, political speech making and demonstrations, and for reenacting or celebrating historical events. They are occasions during which people enjoy the company of family, friends, and those with whom they share religious or national identity.

Private fiestas, organized by the women of the family, include gatherings to honor births, christenings, *quinceneras* (fifteenth birthdays for girls), marriages, and deaths. The most important festival in each country is usually that nation's independence day, celebrated with a nationwide fiesta. Other annual holidays commemorate historical or political events. For example, Mexicans celebrate Cinco de Mayo, or May 5, the date Mexican troops defeated an invading French army, and Cubans celebrate July 26, which marks Fidel Castro's first, and unsuccessful, attempt to seize power in Cuba.

Latin Americans also celebrate Jewish, Protestant, and traditional African religious festivals. The mostly widely celebrated religious holidays are linked to the CATHOLIC CHURCH, which played an important role in the colonization and cultural development of Latin America and the Caribbean. Until the 1900s, Easter was the most celebrated festival in the religious year, although Christmas later emerged as the more notable fiesta. CARNIVAL, a spring holiday preceding Lent*, is now one of the most celebrated and dramatic fiestas in Brazil and parts of the West Indies.

Other important religious holidays mark the anniversaries of the date on which the visions of the Virgin Mary or other Catholic saints

Fiestas are celebrated throughout Latin America to commemorate religious and community events. This photograph shows Zapotec Indians leading a fiesta procession through their village in Zaachila, Mexico.

first appeared. For instance, Mexicans honor their patron saint, the Virgin of GUADALUPE, on December 12, the day that she appeared to the peasant Juan Diego. Fiestas also celebrate saints' days, the days that the Catholic calendar assigns to the patron saints of countries and communities, such as the Black Christ festival in Guatemala (January 15) and the festival of Santiago, the patron saint of Chile (July 25).

Commercial holidays such as Mother's Day and Teacher's Day were created to honor special groups, while others were developed to encourage spending or to attract tourists. Among such fiestas are the Day of the Dead festival in Mexico's Michoacán state and Carnival in some Caribbean nations. Intended primarily for tourists, these events give outsiders an image of what government officials consider typical of local culture. Despite commercial or governmental motives, fiestas continue to play an important part in Latin American community life.

Figueres Ferrer, José

1906–1990
President of Costa Rica

*D*uring his three separate terms as president of COSTA RICA, José Figueres Ferrer shaped his country's course through the second half of the 1900s. His importance also extended outside Costa Rica. During the 1950s and 1960s, Figueres was an influential figure in Central American and Spanish Caribbean politics.

Born to Spanish immigrants in rural San Ramón, Figueres had little formal education after high school. He traveled to the United States intending to study electrical engineering, but instead he educated himself in political philosophy by reading books at the Boston Public Library. When Figueres returned to Costa Rica in 1928, he built a ranch and factory that became his model of rural reform. There he created jobs and provided social services and other benefits to employees and the community. Following a dispute with President Rafael Ángel Calderón Guardia, Figueres was exiled from Costa Rica in 1942. Upon his return two years later, Costa Ricans greeted him as a hero for having opposed the authoritarian Calderón.

During his exile, Figueres and other Caribbean political thinkers had formed a plan to rid the region of tyranny. Figueres seized his chance in 1948, when Calderón tried to steal Costa Rica's presidential election from the rightful winner, Otilio Ulate Blanco. With an army of citizen volunteers, Figueres seized control of the Costa Rican government. He established a constitution that abolished the army and included many social and economic reforms. He then turned the government over to Ulate.

Costa Ricans elected Figueres president in 1952 and again in 1970. During his first presidency, he expanded the role of government by creating agencies to administer banking, electrical power, health care, insurance, and other services. Figueres supported Fidel CASTRO in the Cuban Revolution but criticized other dictators in Nicaragua, Venezuela, and the Dominican Republic. He also endorsed United States president John F. Kennedy and the ALLIANCE FOR PROGRESS, a United States effort to bring political stability and democracy to Latin American nations. Figueres's second presidency was troubled by scandals involving his ties

to the U.S. CENTRAL INTELLIGENCE AGENCY and questions about investments in his ranch.

One of Figueres's key achievements was forming the National Liberation Party (PLN), which dominated Costa Rican politics after 1953. Throughout his political career, Figueres strengthened the democratic traditions and the economic and social well-being of his country. His influence helped Costa Rica avoid the bloodshed that occurred in many other Central American nations in the 1980s.

Film

See *Cinema*.

Fishing and Whaling Industries

*L*atin America's commercial fishing fleets are a major source of edible fish and other marine products for the world market. They contribute nearly one-fifth of the world's marine and freshwater fishery products. Since the 1980s, the Latin American catch has grown significantly to meet an increased demand for seafood in the United States, Japan, and Europe.

Stretching from the warm Caribbean waters north of the equator to the cold waters near Antarctica, Latin America has many diverse marine habitats and is close to the rich fishing grounds of the Pacific and Atlantic oceans. The region's leading fishing nations are Peru, Chile, Mexico, Brazil, Argentina, Ecuador, Venezuela, Cuba, Panama, and Uruguay. However, Chile and Peru, with their long Pacific coastlines, together produce almost three-quarters of the Latin American catch.

About 5 percent of Latin America's total catch consists of freshwater fish from the region's rivers and lakes—mainly tetras, tilapias, trout, salmon, catfish, and carp. The rest of the catch comes from the ocean and includes many fish that are not intended for human consumption. For example, Peru and Chile harvest vast quantities of pilchards and herrings that are processed into fish oil or fish meal, a leading ingredient in pet foods. More than two-thirds of the entire Latin American fishery catch is used to produce such industrial products.

On South America's Atlantic coast, Uruguay and Argentina harvest hake, a common and inexpensive fish. Countries in northern South America, such as Venezuela and northern Brazil, land a wider variety of food fish, some of which are prized on the international market. The catch in these countries includes shrimp, tuna, and sardines. Fisheries in the Caribbean produce lobsters, octopuses, groupers, snappers, oysters, and conchs. These highly valued seafoods are exported to fetch high prices in foreign markets. Nations such as Cuba and Mexico also land large numbers of mackerel, herring, and other less valuable fish that supply protein in the diets of local people.

The fishing fleets of the Latin American nations vary widely in terms of the number and size of their vessels. Commercial fishers in the Caribbean nations generally use small craft because most of their fishing is done in shallow waters close to shore. Chile and Peru operate

Who Owns the Ocean?

Nations and fishing fleets have often quarreled—and sometimes gone to war—over ocean fishing rights. In the 1970s, most modern nations adopted a policy that gives each country control of the ocean to 200 miles from its shore. Within this territorial limit, a country decides who may and may not fish in its waters. Except in cases of special agreements or treaties, the fishing vessels of one nation must respect the territorial limit of another. Venezuelan boats, for example, cannot catch fish within 200 miles of the Colombian coast. Today much fishing occurs far out at sea, beyond national limits.

Latin American countries bordering the Pacific Ocean have access to some of the richest fishing grounds in the world. This photograph shows fishermen on the Pacific coast of Mexico hauling in their nets to collect the day's catch.

See color plate 10, vol. 2.

* **monopoly** exclusive control or domination of a particular type of business

fleets of large vessels that can follow schools of deep-sea fish far out into the ocean and remain at sea for many days. The region's largest fishing fleets are owned by Mexico, Chile, Argentina, Cuba, and Peru. However, all Latin American nations have many small fishing boats—often handmade—whose owners use them to catch food for their families and sometimes a surplus to sell to local markets.

For many years, Latin America has been an important source of wild fish and shellfish. In recent years, however, the region has developed a different kind of fishing industry—aquaculture, or fish farming. Instead of catching fish in the wild, Latin Americans are beginning to raise them in controlled conditions and harvest them for export. Ecuador is a world leader in producing farm-raised shrimp, and Chile boasts large salmon- and scallop-farming industries. Latin American aquaculturists also raise oysters, catfish, rainbow trout, conchs, ornamental fish, and edible seaweed for export.

Commercial whaling—the harvesting of whales for oil—was once part of the economy of many seafaring nations. Brazil is the only Latin American country to have developed a significant whaling industry. In the early 1600s, European fishermen introduced whaling to Brazil, where gray, blue, humpback, and sperm whales gather along the coast each year to breed. The Portuguese crown made the capture of whales and the production of whale products into a royal monopoly*, and whaling stations spread from Pernambuco in the north to São Paulo in the south.

The royal monopoly on whaling ended in 1801. Around that time, the once-prosperous Brazilian whaling industry began to decline. As a result of 200 years of hunting, local whale populations were shrinking, and far-ranging American whalers soon drove the Brazilians out of the market. Some whaling continued into the 1900s, but changes in consumers' needs, as well as laws to protect whales, have ended the old-style whaling industry.

Fleet Systems, Colonial

In the 1500s, the voyage from Europe to the Americas was long and difficult. Bad weather, hostile foreign navies, and pirates could—and often did—bring disaster to ships carrying goods to or from the American colonies. Both Spain and Portugal developed fleet systems to protect their vulnerable cargo vessels. By sailing together in convoys at scheduled times, with the protection of armed warships, the cargo vessels stood a greater chance of making it safely across the Atlantic.

From 1543 to 1554, a single Spanish fleet sailed each year from Seville, Spain, to the Caribbean. Near the island of Dominica, it split into two parts, one bound for COLOMBIA and PANAMA and the other bound for SANTO DOMINGO and MEXICO. In 1554, the Spanish king ordered that two fleets would sail every year. According to the new system, the first annual fleet, called the *flota,* was to leave Spain in April and sail to Veracruz, the main port in Mexico. The second fleet, the *galeones,* was to leave in August bound for Panama, where it would unload goods to be shipped down the Pacific to Peru and pick up a waiting cargo of Peruvian silver and other products. In March or April of the following year, the ships were scheduled to meet in HAVANA, CUBA, and form a single fleet that would sail back to Spain before the hurricane season began. However, this system did not start operating until 1564—and then only with limited success.

In the late 1640s, most of the ships sailing between Portugal and BRAZIL were lost to pirates. To protect their ships, the Portuguese administrators of Brazil introduced a fleet system similar to Spain's. Beginning around 1650, two fleets a year crossed the Atlantic, each escorted by 18 military vessels. Departing from Lisbon, Portugal, in late fall or early spring, the fleets carried wine, flour, codfish and other goods to Rio de Janeiro, Brazil. The following spring, after a stop in Bahia, the ships returned to Lisbon loaded with valuable sugar and brazilwood, a tropical wood used to produce dyes.

In addition to these royal fleet systems, Spanish colonists on the west coast of South America created the Armada del Mar del Sur (Fleet of the Southern Ocean) in the 1570s. This small and poorly funded group of warships was intended to protect ports and shipping along the Pacific coast from French, Dutch, and English pirates and traders. By the late 1600s, however, the burden of defending the Pacific fell mostly on private shipping businesses.

Delays due to bad weather, PIRACY, warfare, and the unavailability of ships and cargoes created many gaps in both the Spanish and the Portuguese fleet systems. Sometimes several years would pass without a single fleet sailing from Spain to the Americas. Nevertheless, the fleet systems did serve their principal purpose: to protect the homebound

Daily Life

Plate 1

Throughout world history, the market has been a place where people gather to browse, chat with friends and neighbors, and shop for their daily needs. This painting shows the busy marketplace in La Plaza Mayor, or Zócalo, in colonial Mexico City in the 1700s. Before the conquest, the Zócalo was the center of the Aztec capital Tenochtitlán. During the colonial period, the central plaza became the seat of the government.

Plate 2

This photograph shows a shanty town located in the city of Salvador, Brazil. Known as favelas in Brazil, these settlements are established by the poor, who make the houses from scrap wood, sheet metal, and cement blocks. Because these communities are created illegally, favelas receive no city services. Desperate for land, the poor sometimes build their shelters on steep hills or dry river beds, where they often are destroyed by heavy rains and floods.

Plate 3

This photograph shows traders selling mangoes at a wholesale market on the banks of the Magdalena River in Colombia. European explorers brought mangoes to Latin America from India in the 1700s and 1800s. Today mangoes are grown in several countries including Brazil, Colombia, Mexico, and Peru.

Plate 4

A gaucho is seen here herding cattle on the Argentine pampas. In the early 1700s, gauchos were hunters who chased the herds of wild cattle and horses that roamed the pampas. Since colonial times, the reputation of the gaucho has gone from barbarian, to patriot, to ranch hand. Today gauchos still work seasonally on ranches rounding up and branding cattle.

Plate 5

Cars manufactured in the United States in the 1950s, such as the Dodge shown here, are fairly common in Cuba—left over from the pre-revolutionary era. Although the island nation has a highly developed network of roads, maintenance of the roads as well as fuel shortages have posed serious problems for many Cubans.

Plate 6

This 1835 engraving shows Brazilian slaves using a small, portable three-roller sugar mill to extract juice from sugarcane. The sugarcane is first placed between the rollers. As the bar at the top is rotated, the rollers crush the sugarcane, extracting the juice. This juice is then processed, refined, and converted into sugar.

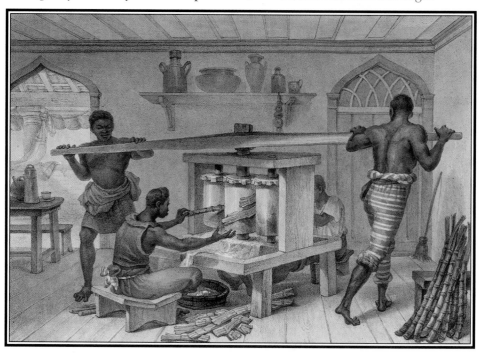

Plate 7

The city of Buenos Aires is the capital of Argentina and a busy seaport. Located at the mouth of the Río de la Plata, which empties into the Atlantic Ocean, the city became the colonial seat of government as well as a center for trade and commerce. The city remains the political, industrial, and commercial center of the country.

Plate 8

This illustration, from an early colonial manuscript, shows an Aztec girl learning to grind corn into flour, make tortillas, and weave on a staked loom. This codex—one of the few surviving painted books—contains information about the history, culture, and beliefs of the indigenous peoples of Latin America.

Plate 9

Latin Americans celebrate many festivals that combine elements of indigenous music and dance with the ceremonies of the Catholic Church. This photograph shows men and women celebrating during a festival held near Lake Titicaca in Bolivia.

Plate 10
The Aymara Indians live near Bolivia's Lake Titicaca (shown here), the highest navigable lake in the world. They use a dried reed called *totora* to make balsas, which are crescent-shaped boats built from bundles of reeds tied together. The Aymara use these boats for fishing and for travel between the islands in the lake, some of which are densely populated.

Plate 11
In this open-air market in Chichicastenango, Guatemala, K'iche'-Maya women are selling flowers. The market, which operates on Thursdays and Sundays, becomes filled with traders who bring their wares, textiles, and handicrafts. Like these women, vendors wear traditional *huipils* (blouses) decorated by hand in brilliantly colored designs that identify their village.

Plate 12

Haiti's network of roads deteriorated considerably during the reign of the Duvaliers. In the post-Duvalier years, the government has undertaken a program to improve the roads. However, relatively few Haitians can afford to own cars and most use buses, such as the ones shown here, some of which are converted trucks and school buses.

Plate 13

This mural in Mexico City depicts the conflict in the state of Chiapas. The conflict erupted in 1994 when several peasant organizations, inspired by the ideals of peasant leader Emiliano Zapata (1879–1919), rose in revolt against the government and NAFTA and demanded land reform, basic political rights, and relief from long-standing oppression by the government.

Plate 14

This illustration by Diego Rivera depicts an early pre-Columbian ball game, called *ulama* by the Aztecs, that was played in Mesoamerica. The ball court consisted of a rectangular stone enclosure. Players used a 15-pound rubber ball and the object of the game was to keep the ball in motion. The ball represented the sun, moon, or Venus—heavenly bodies that seemed to be always moving. The players, who wore protective gear, scored points when they knocked the ball through the ring seen in the center of the picture, and they lost points if the ball hit the floor.

Plate 15

There are many tales about how baseball came to Latin America—U.S. Marines brought it to Nicaragua; oilmen brought it to Mexico; or it may have been American sailors who brought the game to Cuba. One Latin American sports announcer noted that kids play it throughout the region, sometimes with only a stick and a bottle cap. These boys in Cuba take a break from their pickup game to pose for a photograph.

ships and their precious cargoes. The treasure of the Spanish fleet was lost only once—in 1628, when a Dutch privateer named Piet Heyn captured the fleet in a Cuban port. By the mid-1700s, the fleet systems had outlived their usefulness. The Portuguese system remained in place until 1765, by which time many private shipping fleets were serving Brazilian industries and regions. Likewise, the Spanish fleet system was abandoned by the 1770s, when free trade was established in Spanish America. (*See also* **Trade and Commerce.**)

Flores, Juan José

1800–1864
President of Ecuador

* **patriot** one who favored independence of the colonies in the Americas

* **liberal** supporting greater participation in government for individuals; not bound by political and social traditions

* **conservative** inclined to maintain existing political and social views, conditions, and institutions

Born in Puerto Cabello, Venezuela, Juan José Flores was a young man with little formal education when he was swept into the WARS OF INDEPENDENCE in the patriot* army of Simón BOLÍVAR. By 1826, he had risen to the rank of general and taken command of ECUADOR, which had won independence from Spain and formed the Republic of GRAN COLOMBIA together with Colombia and Venezuela. Flores urged Bolívar to make Gran Colombia a monarchy, although this did not happen.

In 1830, when Ecuador separated from Gran Colombia and became an independent nation, Flores was elected its president. He fought to establish Ecuador's northern border with Colombia and followed liberal* policies, such as reforming tax laws and creating a public education system with special schools for Indians. These policies turned conservative* Ecuadorians against the foreign-born president, who was forced to give up power in 1835, in the midst of a violent uprising.

Flores used his great influence over the Ecuadorian military to arrange his reelection in 1839. He secretly tried to turn Ecuador—as well as Peru and Bolivia—into monarchies. However, an uprising in 1845 drove him out of the region. For the next 15 years, in Spain and in various parts of Spanish America, Flores plotted to create an Ecuadorian monarchy. None of his plots succeeded. In 1860, Flores returned to political life in Ecuador at the request of President Gabriel García Moreno, who asked him to take command of the army and to end antigovernment opposition. Flores also defended Ecuador's northern border and put down a revolt in the coastal town of Guayaquil. Many Ecuadorians expected Flores to become president for a third time in 1865, but he fell ill and died aboard a warship.

Florida

The present state of Florida in the United States is only part of the territory that the Spanish once knew as La Florida. For several centuries, colonial Florida was the northeastern outpost of Spanish Latin America. Although hostile Indians, disease, pirates, and foreign invasions threatened Spanish control, the monarchy commanded at least a portion of this territory until 1821, when it became part of the United States. Today Florida continues to maintain its links with Latin America and is home to a large population of immigrants from Cuba and many Central American nations.

Indians may have settled in the area that is now Florida as much as 10,000 years ago. This European engraving shows Florida Indians bringing their crops to a public granary for storage.

° **conquistador** Spanish explorer and conqueror

° **adelantado** Spanish leader of a military expedition to America during the 1500s who also served as governor and judge

° **presidio** Spanish fort built to protect mission settlements

° **missionary** person who works to convert nonbelievers to his or her faith

La Florida. In 1513, conquistador* Juan Ponce de León, presumably searching for the mythical fountain of youth, undertook an exploration to settle the Bimini islands north of Cuba. He sailed northwest from Puerto Rico and sighted land that he later named Tierra La Florida (Land of Flowers). For the next 50 years, many Spanish expeditions that set out to explore and conquer the peninsula and the coastline surrounding the Gulf of Mexico were unsuccessful because of hurricanes or hostile Indians.

By the mid 1500s, Spain's rival France began establishing forts along the southern Atlantic coast of North America. In response, KING PHILIP II OF SPAIN appointed naval officer Pedro MENÉNDEZ DE AVILÉS as Florida's *adelantado**. Menéndez successfully drove out the French and built many fortified settlements. However, the settlements fell when attacked by angry Indians provoked by Spanish soldiers' raids on their food supplies. Only one settlement, ST. AUGUSTINE, received enough support to maintain the presidio* and its growing population of Franciscan missionaries*.

Missionaries traveled outward from St. Augustine to the Chesapeake Bay, exploring, converting Indians to Christianity, and annexing Indian provinces. These provinces spread along the Atlantic coasts of Florida

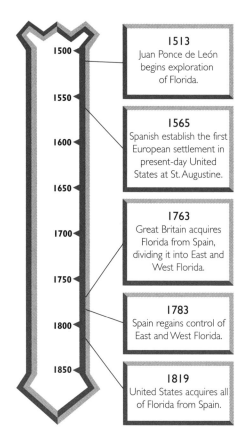

1500	**1513** Juan Ponce de León begins exploration of Florida.
1550	
1600	**1565** Spanish establish the first European settlement in present-day United States at St. Augustine.
1650	
1700	**1763** Great Britain acquires Florida from Spain, dividing it into East and West Florida.
1750	
1800	**1783** Spain regains control of East and West Florida.
1850	**1819** United States acquires all of Florida from Spain.

See map in Spanish Borderlands (vol. 4).

and Georgia, into interior central Florida, western Florida, and areas close to the Gulf. The Spanish first befriended the Indians and then required them to provide grain and labor for the soldiers, missionaries, and settlers. When war, famine, and disease took their toll on the Indians, the burden on those who survived increased greatly.

During the first half of the 1600s, the Spanish in Florida countered attacks by the Dutch and the French, salvaged shipwrecks off the coast, and put down Indian uprisings. Friars baptized thousands of Indians, extending the mission frontier. Ranching and agriculture expanded to supply food to the Spanish colony in Cuba. However, an outbreak of yellow fever killed Spanish and Indians alike and interrupted Florida's economic development. In 1656, the Indians of the central provinces rebelled, and harsh punishment by the Spanish caused the survivors to leave the area. By the 1660s, Florida was a largely deserted peninsula with a few Spanish settlements on the coast.

Around the same time, Florida faced renewed attacks. English pirates from Jamaica looted St. Augustine, English traders from Carolina stirred uprisings among the Indians to whom they also gave firearms, and the French began moving into Florida from the Gulf of Mexico. To protect its claim to Florida, Spain strengthened the fort at St. Augustine and built a new presidio at Pensacola on Florida's Gulf coast.

During the War of the Spanish Succession in the early 1700s, Spain and France became allies. Despite the formidable alliance, English colonists and Indian forces attacked in raids, and Spain's holdings in Florida were reduced to St. Augustine, Pensacola, and a trading post at San Marcos de Apalache. Although the former mission provinces in the interior were deserted, the abandoned ranches and wild cattle attracted runaway slaves and Indians who did not want to be Spanish allies. This mixed population became known as the Seminoles, from the Spanish word *cimarrón,* meaning "runaway." At the end of the SEVEN YEARS' WAR, when territories changed hands among the European powers, Great Britain gained control of Florida, which it divided into two colonies: East and West Florida.

East and West Florida. Under British rule, West Florida extended up to the Mississippi River and was the second-largest British colony in North America after Canada. However, the British did not control Florida for long. During the American Revolution, Spanish military officer Bernardo de GÁLVEZ recaptured West Florida for Spain. In 1783, the Treaty of Paris that formally ended the Revolution gave East and West Florida to Spain, much to the dismay of Americans who thought that the territories rightfully belonged to the United States. Spain administered the two colonies as military governorships. However, outlawry soon became a serious problem in East Florida, when Cuban officials dumped convicts into the area, and raids by armed bandits from Georgia only worsened the situation. Hoping to bring order to the area, Spain allowed British Protestants and American traders to move into East Florida. Although trade flourished briefly, Spanish control was threatened as the Florida settlers began to rebel.

Rebels and Pirates

In 1817, during the last days of Spanish Florida, a Scotsman named Sir Gregory MacGregor led the last attempt to set up an independent republic in the region. Backed by merchants in Savannah, Georgia, and other American ports, Mac-Gregor led a force of Georgians to Amelia Island and captured the port city of Fernandina, a smuggling center. But when the white settlers in East Florida failed to flock to his Republic of the Floridas, MacGregor left. On his departure, a French pirate and his band of free black Haitians took over the port and opened it to privateers and slave traders.

Moreover, the United States began to stake its claim to the area under its purchase of the Louisiana Territory from France in 1803. The United States maintained that it was entitled to most of West Florida, and it gradually acquired large portions of the colony. By 1813, West Florida was reduced to half its original size, and Pensacola was the only major settlement under Spanish control. Spain also began to lose its power in international affairs, and the Spanish empire in the Americas was beginning to crumble. Spain, swept up in a series of European wars, was unable to manage the Floridas. Finally, in 1819, Spain and the United States signed the ADAMS-ONÍS TREATY, which gave Florida to the United States.

Florida's Latin American Links.   Not only was modern Florida once part of Spanish America, but its geographic location also makes it the closest point in the United States to Cuba and some other parts of Latin America. For that reason, Florida has long been a destination for Latin American immigrants, many of whom have settled in and around the southern city of Miami. Along with Texas, California, and the Southwest, Florida is a center of Hispanic American population and culture.

The first wave of Hispanic immigrants to south Florida started in 1868, but the big shift occurred in the late 1950s, when refugees from Cuba fled to the United States after Fidel CASTRO's revolution. Other Cuban refugees have joined them in recent years, and new waves of immigrants continue to broaden Florida's Hispanic identity. Many Central Americans migrated to Florida in the 1980s, when their nations were torn by civil war and internal strife. The arrival of Costa Ricans, Nicaraguans, Hondurans, Guatemalans, and others greatly expanded southern Florida's Central American population between 1980 and 1989. Although Cubans outnumber other Hispanic immigrants in Florida, Nicaraguans and others have made their mark by establishing distinctive neighborhoods, stores, and restaurants.

As in other parts of the United States, the presence of so many immigrants in ethnic communities has sparked backlashes and controversies, including the belief that all public school education should be in English. Whatever the outcome of these controversies, Hispanic influence will surely remain a vital part of Florida's present and of its historical heritage. (*See also* **Immigration and Emigration.**)

Folk Art

See *Crafts.*

Food and Drink

*L*atin America is a huge and varied region, and its cuisines are just as varied. The food of Mexico is very different from that of Brazil, and even within Mexico and Brazil, regional and ethnic variations in food and drink prevail. This diversity in cuisines is attributed to the climate and environment, the influence of various cultures, and the region's history. Colonial agricultural practices, trade, and patterns of immigration and settlement have also influenced Latin American regional cooking.

Latin American foods, like other aspects of Latin American culture, reflect a blend of influences—traditional pre-Columbian* cooking of the Indians, foods introduced by the European conquerors and colonists, and foods brought in by African slaves and immigrants from Asia and elsewhere. Like a rich and savory stew, these influences simmered and bubbled over the centuries to produce the foods of modern Latin America. Those cuisines continue to change as foreign influences and new trends in food production and marketing alter the way people eat and drink.

Traditional Native American Foods.   The indigenous* peoples of Mexico and Central and South America developed dishes based on the resources available to them. Some of their staple foods, which form the foundation of their cooking, have their origins in the very beginnings of AGRICULTURE in the Americas. The three most important of these staples were MAIZE (corn), manioc (also called yuca or cassava), and the POTATO, all of which remain essential in Latin American cooking today.

Maize, the most widely cultivated of the staples, was at the center of a diet that also included beans, squash, CHILES, tomatoes, and fruits. Mexicans soak dried corn kernels in water and lime, grind them into flour, then add water to make dough that they bake to make tortillas. The versatile tortilla has long been the basis of Mexican cuisine, sometimes served as bread with fish, meat, or poultry dishes and at other times wrapped around meat, cheese, bean, or poultry fillings. Depending on the filling and the method of preparation, these meals-in-a-tortilla are called tacos, burritos, quesadillas, or enchiladas. Colombians

* **pre-Columbian** before the arrival of Christopher Columbus and other Europeans in the Americas in the 1490s

* **indigenous** referring to the original inhabitants of a region

Latin American foods vary greatly, depending on the region's climate, culture, and history. This photograph shows some of the vegetables for sale in a typical open-air marketplace in rural Mexico. From left to right are dried chilies, poblano peppers, several varieties of potatoes, onions, tomatoes, and fresh green peppers.

133

* **gruel** thin porridge made from grains cooked in water

See color plate 8, vol. 2.

* **jerky** sun-dried strips of meat

Salsa Preferred over Ketchup

Recent surveys suggest that salsa has begun to outsell ketchup in the United States. To make **Tomato Salsa,** coarsely chop **6 ripe tomatoes, 1 onion, 2 serrano peppers, ½ cup fresh cilantro leaves.** Combine these ingredients in a medium bowl. Add the **juice of 1 lime, salt,** and **pepper** to taste. Mix and serve with chips or as a sauce for scrambled eggs. For a hot salsa, substitute jalapeños for the serrano peppers.

and Venezuelans prefer *arepas,* roasted maize bread served plain or stuffed. Brazilians prepare maize in a variety of ways including a gruel* called *angu* and sweet corn biscuits. People in the highlands of the Andes mountains eat *macha* (roasted maize flour), *cancu* (loaves of maize bread), and *mote* (a maize gruel).

Since pre-Columbian times, manioc has been a staple in many lowland regions, especially Brazil. Prepared by grating the root and pressing out any poisonous juices, the nutritious gratings are then toasted and made into gruel or bread. Manioc's most common form, a dried toasted flour called *farofa* or *farinha,* is still widely consumed in Brazil today.

Potatoes, grown in the Andean highlands, were a basic food source for pre-Columbian peoples and remain an important part of the Latin American diet. Latin Americans also use frozen and dried potatoes to make *chuños.* Potatoes appear in such dishes as *papas a la huacaina,* which also has cheese, cream, peppers, and eggs. Beans—kidney, lima, black, wax, navy, and others—are also a key component of many regional diets. Several traditional Latin American dishes are based on beans. Among these are the Mexican frijoles refritos (beans mashed and mixed with fat, salt, and chiles) and the Brazilian *feijão* (beans cooked with coconut milk and vegetables).

The traditional cuisines of Latin America also include a great variety of other foods. Pre-Columbian diets included grains such as amaranth and quinoa; vegetables such as sweet potatoes, pumpkins, and peppers; and fruits such as papayas, pineapples, and guavas. These foods, found in abundance throughout Latin America, are eaten today as well. In pre-Columbian times, Indians ate the meat of alpacas and llamas, usually in dried forms as a kind of jerky*. They also ate turkeys, ducks, dogs, wild game (iguanas, rabbits, and armadillos), and birds and fish. Many of these meats are still widely consumed in Latin America.

Traditional Native American Beverages. Traditional Latin American beverages were based on maize. They include *atole,* a thin drink made from maize water; *pozole,* a heartier drink that sometimes contains chunks of meat or vegetables; and *pinole,* made from lightly toasted maize, ground into flour and mixed with water. Chocolate, mixed with coloring agents such as chiles or maize gruel, was consumed as a beverage. Cacao beverages had considerable prestige and were consumed only by the aristocracy in pre-Columbian Latin America. However, after the European conquest, cacao became a drink of mass consumption, especially in Central America.

Some drinks are made from grains or fruits, which when allowed to ferment become alcoholic beverages. For instance, *chicha de quinoa* (quinoa broth) is a nonalcoholic drink, but fermented *chicha,* made from palms, berries, sweet potatoes, or maize, is alcoholic. Pulque, another alcoholic drink, is made from the agave plant. Both beverages survived the European conquest, partly because the Indians could easily make them with locally available ingredients and partly because they were linked with sacred ceremonies. Indians also valued *chicha* and pulque for their medicinal qualities and used them to fight disease and infection.

Producing Pulque

The Indians of Central Mexico make an alcoholic beverage called pulque from the fleshy agave plant, or maguey. They cut a hole in the stem of the plant, use a long tube to remove the juice that collects there, and then store the juice in wooden or leather containers. The juice is fermented by adding pulque from a previously fermented batch. Nuts, fruits, and herbs are sometimes added as flavoring or sweetening agents. In the 1800s, the wife of a foreign diplomat in Mexico said of pulque that it is considered "to be the most wholesome drink in the world, and remarkably agreeable when one has overcome the first shock occasioned by its rancid odor."

Yerba maté, a highly caffeinated tea, was also well liked among the Indians. Cultivated even today in Paraguay and northern Argentina, these tea leaves are served in a pear-shaped gourd that is passed from person to person, each taking a sip of the hot drink. Although it is usually served "straight," maté may be mixed with milk as a sign of respect or with balm mint to denote displeasure, or it may be sweetened as a sign of friendship.

The Development of Latin American Cuisines.

The arrival of Europeans in the 1490s changed Latin American cuisines in three significant ways. First, the Europeans introduced new foods, some of which were widely adopted. Second, they introduced their own methods of food preparation by teaching these techniques to their Indian servants. Third, they brought African slaves, especially to Brazil and the Caribbean, creating a mix of Latin American, European, and African traditions. However, the influence was a two-way process—the Europeans assimilated indigenous foods such as corn, tomatoes, potatoes, and chocolate into their cooking.

The Spanish and Portuguese colonists cultivated wheat, their staple grain, wherever they could. In some places, bread made from wheat replaced the traditional staples, although Europeans in the Americas learned to cook with maize. They also relied on manioc as an inexpensive food, especially in Brazil. The Europeans also introduced rice. Rice consumption increased in Latin America in the 1800s for several reasons: the growing population sought new staples, rice-growing techniques improved, and immigrants arrived from India, China, and Japan, where rice has long been a staple.

Some other foods brought by the Europeans spread so quickly through Latin America that they soon seemed traditional. Bananas, brought from Africa in the 1500s, became important to diets in tropical and subtropical Latin America and were eaten raw, boiled, fried, or dried. In ranching areas, cattle became the mainstay of the colonial diet, and beef was eaten daily. Argentines and Brazilians cooked beef slowly over open fires or dried, smoked, and salted the meat. Animal fats, such as butter and lard, replaced oil in many cooking techniques, and by the 1700s, fried, fatty foods became common. Sugarcane, a commercial crop, soon became a part of the local diet as a sweetener for beverages, baked goods, and an alcoholic beverage called *aguardiente,* made from sugarcane juice.

Over time, the cuisines of Latin America found distinctive flavors thorough the combination of spices and herbs and different cooking techniques. For instance, chiles have come to dominate in the cuisines of Peru, Mexico, and Brazil, while cilantro (also called Chinese parsley) is widely used in Mexican food. Combinations of vanilla, black pepper, citrus, ginger, anise, cinnamon, nutmeg, and other spices are also used to flavor foods. Outside influences, especially from France in the 1800s, affected Latin American cooking but did not change the basic ingredients or techniques. In the second half of the 1900s, a major change altered the way Latin Americans regarded food. Mass-marketed foods and fast-food products from the United States began to appear in the Latin

American diet. Packaged cereals and snack foods, soft drinks, candy, and other commercial food products have greatly affected Latin American cooking. (*See also* **Nutrition.**)

Football War

*T*he Football War was a conflict between EL SALVADOR and HONDURAS that occurred in 1969, from July 14 to July 18. It started when violence broke out at the soccer (called football in Latin America) playoff games between the two countries' teams. But the real causes of the war lay deeper, and although the Football War was brief, it had a lasting effect on Central America.

Tension between the two neighboring countries began in the 1920s, when people had been leaving crowded and poverty-stricken El Salvador to settle in Honduras—often living illegally on public land. When the Honduran government decided to give some of this land to its own peasants, it drove some of the Salvadorans back across the border. Once home, they spread rumors of Honduran brutality that angered their fellow citizens. In June 1969, fans from the two nations fought each other at soccer games. People of both countries called for war, and the following month, Salvadoran troops invaded Honduras.

The war lasted only four days. Although El Salvador's army advanced rapidly toward the Honduran capital of Tegucigalpa, the strong and determined Honduran air force dropped bombs on the enemy's fuel supplies. Under pressure from the United States and the ORGANIZATION OF AMERICAN STATES (OAS), El Salvador agreed to a cease-fire. Nonetheless, the two countries did not reach a final peace agreement until 1980. The war hurt the Central American Common Market (CACM), an organization of Central American nations that promoted free trade in the region. It also worsened El Salvador's social and economic crises. When thousands of landless Salvadoran peasants returned from Honduras, the unrest and economic stress caused by their return led to political collapse and civil war in El Salvador during the 1980s.

Foraker Act

*T*he United States Congress passed the Foraker Act in 1900 to end military rule and to create a civilian government in PUERTO RICO. Although the Foraker Act ended the military rule that had governed the island since the end of the SPANISH-AMERICAN WAR, it did not give the people of Puerto Rico a voice in their government.

Under the Foraker Act, the United States appointed Puerto Rico's governor, cabinet members, and judges, while Puerto Ricans elected the 35-member house of delegates. The act also integrated Puerto Rico into the American economy, and the United States dollar became standard currency on the island. These measures were very unpopular among the Puerto Rican people, who felt that the United States was treating Puerto Rico as a colony. In 1917, the United States Congress softened the effects of the Foraker Act by passing the Jones Act. According to the Jones Act, Puerto Ricans were granted a bill of rights and the option to become citizens of the United States.

Foreign Debt

° **provincial** having to do with the provinces, outlying districts, administrative divisions, or conquered territories of a country or empire

° **debtor** one who owes money; borrower

° **creditor** one to whom money is owed; lender

See color plate 5, vol. 3.

See color plate 5, vol. 4.

° **depression** period of little economic activity during which many people become unemployed

Since independence, Latin American nations have borrowed from and thus owed money to foreign governments and banks. The size of these debts and the difficulties of repaying them have caused several debt crises in Latin America, generally coinciding with international economic recessions.

Until the early 1900s, national, provincial*, and municipal governments in Latin America took loans against bonds issued on capital markets in London, Paris, New York, and elsewhere. The governments pledged to redeem these bonds through repurchase—the loan amount was repayable in gold on a specified date, usually 10 to 30 years later. Since the mid 1900s, Latin American governments and private companies have borrowed directly from European, United States, and Japanese banks, promising to repay the loans—with interest—at the end of the loan period.

Latin America's history of foreign debt has followed a pattern. Each cycle began when the governments (and later the private companies) borrowed money from foreign banks. The next stage occurred when the countries experienced difficulties in repaying the debts or making the required interest payments. During these times, foreign money stopped flowing into the debtor* nations of Latin America and sometimes brought them into conflict with the creditor* nations. These debt crises signaled a time of economic distress for the debtor nations. Eventually, the creditors would come to an agreement with the debtor nations, perhaps by restructuring the loan or arranging new terms for repayment, including giving the debtor more time to pay, lowering the interest rate, or accepting a reduced repayment. Then, after a period of time, the cycle would begin again.

The leaders of independence—Simón Bolívar, Bernardo O'Higgins, Bernardo Rivadavia, and José de San Martín—obtained Latin America's first foreign loans from British bankers. The money was used to buy military equipment and warships for the newly formed nations. However, when international trade declined in the mid-1820s, the new nations had no money with which to repay the loans. This signaled the beginning of Latin America's first debt crisis. For 25 years, all the nations except Brazil failed to make their foreign debt payments. The situation improved only after 1850, when exports of coffee, sugar, leather, wool, silver, and other products invigorated Latin America's economy. The governments, then considered good credit risks, obtained about 50 new foreign loans to finance railroads and other public improvements. However, a slowdown in the world economy in 1873 led to another debt crisis. This cycle repeated itself in the late 1800s and several more times in the early and middle 1900s. After the worldwide economic depression*, and by the end of World War II, the countries that

Debt and Politics

During the 1800s, international debt often became entangled with war and politics. After its war with the United States in the 1840s, Mexico received large payments from the United States in exchange for California and other territories. Mexico used some of that money to repay debts to European bondholders. However, when Mexican president Benito Juárez suspended foreign debt payments in 1861, French, British, and Spanish troops occupied the port of Veracruz. After the British and Spanish left, French troops established an empire in Mexico. Thus, by defaulting on its foreign debt, Mexico sustained heavy political losses.

frequently defaulted on their external debt payments had restructured their foreign debts. In countries such as Mexico and Brazil, the creditors (pressured by the United States government), were forced to accept steep reductions in the real value of their debts.

During the 1950s and 1960s, international financial agencies such as the World Bank and the International Monetary Fund (IMF) began lending money to Latin American nations, hoping to reduce the severity of the region's debt cycles. After the world oil crisis of 1973, banks in the United States, Europe, and Japan began advancing large loans to Latin American countries, especially Brazil and Mexico, believing that these countries would be able to repay the loans with profits from oil exports. However, the amounts of debt were so large that by the late 1970s, some countries had to take out additional loans simply to pay the interest on the first loans—the sign of a debt crisis in the making. When oil prices fell in 1982, Latin America entered a severe and prolonged debt crisis. Under pressure from creditors to make debt payments, some governments cut their spending on vital services, such as health and education. These measures diminished the quality of life and caused widespread social and political discontent.

By the late 1980s, the governments in some countries gradually reduced their foreign debt deficits and the economic conditions began to improve. Mexico and some other countries renegotiated or restructured their loans. However, in 1995, Mexico found itself in another serious debt crisis, owing billions of dollars to lenders in the United States. The U.S. Congress voted to bail Mexico out of its debt crisis with loan guarantees worth $40 billion. The agreement enabled Mexico to obtain new loans to pay off its old ones and stipulated that the United States would repay the new loans if Mexico defaulted on its payments. The United States undertook this drastic step to prevent the Mexican economy from collapsing and simultaneously to protect its own economy, which gains billions of dollars from trade with Mexico. Since that time, the Mexican government has repaid the loan in full. More recently, in 1998, when the Brazilian economy was in a financial crisis, the IMF and the world's wealthy nations, led by the United States, voted to lend the government $42 billion as a rescue package. This bailout, considered one of the largest in history, was intended to prevent a devaluation of the country's currency, the real, and to avert a financial crisis that would affect other Latin American nations and the United States. (*See also* **Economic Development; Foreign Investment.**)

Foreign Investment

Latin America has a long history of investment from abroad. For centuries, investors from around the world have put capital into Latin American colonies, countries, and businesses, influencing its economies and societies. The first foreign investments were the ships, men, and supplies that Spain, Portugal, and other European powers sent to Latin America on exploratory expeditions. Thereafter, throughout the colonial period, the parent countries supplied Latin

America with human capital (colonists and laborers), physical capital (animals, tools, and supplies), and financial capital (money). The monarchies invested heavily, expecting great profits from their colonies in Latin America and the Caribbean.

After the WARS OF INDEPENDENCE in the early 1800s, capital investment from Europe dwindled. The newly independent nations of Latin America, which possessed abundant natural resources, looked to other foreign investors for capital. British merchant houses sold investment bonds to these investors, which Latin American governments promised to repay with interest. The first major investor was Great Britain, which bought bonds during the 1820s in exchange for increased trade rights in Latin America. Investors from other countries soon followed suit. However, political and economic instability in the decades following independence prevented the Latin American nations from repaying their debts on time. Britain and other creditor* nations resorted to threats or force to obtain repayment of loans, including sending armed troops into the defaulting countries or using warships to blockade* Latin American ports.

In the 1850s, the British and other foreigners again began to invest in Latin America. This time, instead of buying bonds, they invested in businesses, such as mines or other operations that required large amounts of capital to get started. British investment in the late 1800s was concentrated in Argentina, Mexico, and Brazil. At this time, Latin American nations were working to modernize and expand their economies and were spending foreign capital to build railways to facilitate the transportation of export goods. Thus, the foreign investors helped Latin American nations increase their earnings in the international market. However, the complete reliance on foreign investment seemed to suggest that foreigners owned Latin America's RAILROADS. Moreover, Latin Americans, outraged at the high rates charged by the railroads, insisted that the governments regulate or nationalize* the railways. By the early 1900s, Latin America became less attractive to European investors because of internal conflicts and harsh regulations.

By this time, the United States was emerging as Latin America's main source of foreign capital. The United States was not only wealthy enough to invest heavily, but it was also closely tied by geography and trade and therefore had an interest in ensuring the economic growth and stability of the region. By the 1980s, the United States accounted for more than 60 percent of all foreign investment in Latin America, followed by Western Europe and Japan.

Foreign investment during the second half of the 1900s was tied to the growth of large multinational corporations that built manufacturing plants or other operations in Latin America. Although some argue that such investment created jobs and improved health care, education, and the standard of living, others remained critical. Those who opposed this type of investment maintained that the mass-production methods used by these companies turned skilled artisans* into factory laborers and substituted foreign goods for local culture and products. They also claimed that the corporations reserved top-level jobs for foreign nationals, leaving only low-level positions for Latin Americans. In response to

° **creditor** one to whom money is owed; lender

° **blockade** to close off a port, preventing ships from entering or leaving, and thus cripple trade

° **nationalize** to bring land, industries, or public works under state control or ownership

° **artisan** skilled crafts worker

such criticism, companies doing business in Latin America revised their policies and appointed Latin Americans to high-level management positions.

Foreign investment remained a vital part of the Latin American economy in the late 1900s, and corporations continued to receive financing from abroad. Billions of dollars of capital entered the region each year in the form of foreign investments. In 1994, the NORTH AMERICAN FREE TRADE AGREEMENT (NAFTA) lowered trade barriers between Canada, the United States, and Mexico. Many believe that the agreement will eventually be extended to all of Latin America, facilitating foreign investment there. Yet the increasing speed with which the international money market operates and the growing interdependence of all parts of the world economy could cause dramatic changes almost overnight. For instance, if foreign investors become concerned about the economic stability of a region, country, or business, they can quickly withdraw their funds, perhaps causing an economic crash. Therefore, Latin American nations must balance their need for foreign capital against the dangers of falling deeply into debt or placing their assets in the hands of foreign nations, businesses, and lenders. (*See also* **Economic Development; Foreign Debt; Trade and Commerce.**)

Forests

*B*iologists call Latin America the Neotropical plant realm. This area contains several different kinds of natural forests as well as many species of plants that are found nowhere else in the world. One such plant, the rubber tree, became the basis of the modern RUBBER INDUSTRY. For thousands of years, the forests of Latin America have shaped human life in the region. Today, however, people and their activities are shaping the future of the forests.

When the first humans arrived in Latin America, the region's forests were expanding. RAIN FORESTS covered the hot, wet, tropical, and subtropical parts of northern South America, CENTRAL AMERICA, and the CARIBBEAN ANTILLES. On the fringes of the always green rain forests grew deciduous forests, whose trees dropped their leaves in the fall. The region also had large stretches of savanna, parklike plains dotted with occasional clumps of trees. Southern South America was covered with araucaria, cypress, and beech forests similar to those of New Zealand and Australia.

The earliest inhabitants of Latin America favored the open savanna and the edges of forests, bays, and rivers, where the fishing and hunting were ideal. After human beings began practicing agriculture, however, they moved into the forests, clearing land for planting by cutting down the trees and then burning them. This method—called slash-and-burn farming—worked well while populations were small. The burned-over forest soil lost most of its fertility after a few years, causing people to abandon their plots, enabling the forest to grow back. But as the human population grew and agriculture became more advanced, people farmed each patch of cleared land longer. Eventually, the soil on these plots became too depleted for the forest to reestablish itself when

A Fighter for the Forest

In the 1980s, a rubber harvester from the Brazilian rain forest became a hero to environmentalists around the world. Francisco Alves Mendes Filho, known as Chico Mendes, was born in 1944 and began working in the forest at the age of eight. He organized many projects to improve the welfare of local rubber tappers, but he gained international fame for his efforts to save the Amazon rain forest from destruction by ranchers, miners, and other developers. Mendes urged the government to support policies that would allow people to live in the forest and harvest its resources without destroying it. In 1988, he was shot to death by landowners who opposed his ideas.

This engraving shows the destruction of a forest in Brazil during the 1830s. The introduction by Europeans of cattle grazing, plantation farming, mining, and logging all led to mass deforestation in Latin America.

See map in Agriculture (vol. 1).

* **deforestation** removal of a forest as a result of human activities

the farmers moved on. After European settlers introduced livestock to Latin America, people began to graze cattle on this land, further preventing the regrowth of forests there. The Europeans also introduced PLANTATION farming, and much forestland was cleared to make room for profitable crops, such as sugarcane. Mining and logging also led to deforestation*.

During the 1960s and 1970s, many Latin American governments built roads and bridges in the forested interiors. Along with the expansion of railroads and the availability of heavy road vehicles, these new access routes enabled people to advance deeper into the forests and to clear them faster than ever before. The Latin American governments believed that developing and settling their remote forest regions was a form of progress. It allowed them to offer land to the poor and to attract foreign investment in their timber and cattle industries.

As a result of human activities, the Caribbean Antilles have lost all but a fragment of their forests, and Central America has lost nearly two-thirds of its rain forests. In Peru, policymakers have long desired to exploit and develop the *selva* (tropical rain forests) located east of the Andes. Nevertheless, tracts of undisturbed forest remain in many South American nations, including the world's largest rain forest, located in Brazil's AMAZON REGION. Although Latin America's timber industries place little value on conservation—sometimes cutting down 50 or 100 trees of lesser value to gain one prized specimen—an environmental movement has grown and spread throughout the region since the 1970s. Latin American environmentalists and their supporters around the world are pressuring the region's governments and businesses to protect what remains of its forests. Many countries have set aside areas of forest as nature preserves, and public and private organizations are seeking ways to harvest such forest products as woods, nuts, flowers, and medicinal plants while still allowing the forests to survive and flourish. (See also **Environmental Movements**.)

Forts and Fortifications

Almost as soon as the Spanish and Portuguese began colonizing the Americas, other countries began attacking these settlements. The most persistent assailants were the Dutch, French, and British. Sometimes their assaults took the form of naval invasions, while at other times they were simple PIRACY. To protect their colonies and property from such attacks, the Spanish and Portuguese monarchies built forts and other defensive structures at key ports in their American colonies. Although these costly, often massive fortifications never met the monarchies' expectations, they were the best defense against enemies who sought to plunder their treasures or seize their territories.

Spanish Fortifications. By the 1540s, Spain had fortified the ports it considered strategically important. The Spanish built forts at SANTO DOMINGO on the island of HISPANIOLA, Spain's first American colony, and at SAN JUAN on Puerto Rico, which rapidly became a center of Spanish power in the Caribbean. A fort at CARTAGENA in Colombia guarded northern South America, while forts at Nombre de Dios and Portobelo protected the Isthmus* of Panama, across which Spain transported treasures from its Pacific fleet to its Atlantic fleet. The fortress of San Juan de Ulúa on the shores of Veracruz guarded the gateway to Mexico, and the El Morro fortress in HAVANA defended the port where treasure fleets gathered before their voyage home to Spain. Despite these early fortifications, French raiders seized Havana in 1555.

In the late 1500s, English, Dutch, and French buccaneers* plundered Spanish ships and ports along the Pacific coast. Among the most notorious episodes were John HAWKINS's capture of VERACRUZ in 1568, Francis DRAKE's attacks on Pacific ports in the 1570s, and Drake's Caribbean raids in the 1580s. The Spanish responded by building new Pacific forts at Acapulco and by enlarging and strengthening their old forts. Italian engineer Juan Bautista Antoneli designed thick-walled fortresses with dry moats and gun platforms. When Hawkins and Drake renewed their attacks in 1595, they failed to take San Juan and Cartagena, and the new fortress at Havana resisted capture for almost 200 years.

These new forts should have withstood all assaults, but Spain did not always keep them properly staffed or maintained. As a result, buccaneers and their European allies captured several Spanish port towns and their fortifications. The poorly fortified Pacific ports of Mexico, Central America, and Peru were especially vulnerable, but even the larger Caribbean fortresses sometimes fell. In 1683, a buccaneer force assaulted the fort of San Juan de Ulúa and looted Veracruz, and in 1697, a French military force captured Cartagena—Spain's best-fortified outpost—because the city's fortifications were understaffed.

Although the threat from buccaneers was declining in the 1700s, the Spanish monarchy invested heavily in modernizing the fortifications at Havana, Cartagena, Veracruz, and elsewhere. The British military,

* **isthmus** narrow strip of land connecting two larger land masses

* **buccaneer** maritime adventurer who roamed the Caribbean between 1630 and 1700, attacking Spanish settlements and trade, and terrifying Spanish colonists

Spain's principal enemy during the last 80 years of the colonial period, attacked many of these improved fortifications. The modernized fort at Cartagena held off British attackers in 1741, and while the Spanish waited inside their fortress, the besieging British became ill and died of yellow fever, malaria, and other tropical diseases.

However, in 1762, a lightning-fast British attack caught the defenders of El Morro, the fortress at Havana, off guard. The British occupied the fort for ten months before returning it to Spain under the Treaty of Paris. The fall of Havana inspired Spain to strengthen its colonial fortifications once again, and the newly fortified stronghold at San Juan helped defeat British attacks on Puerto Rico in 1797. The fortress of San Juan de Ulúa in Veracruz remained the last stronghold of Spanish power in Mexico. Spanish troops and officers at Veracruz held out until 1825, after Mexico had declared its independence. During the 1800s, many of the colonial fortifications were converted into prisons.

Portuguese Fortifications. Colonial Brazil's major fort was the Fortaleza de Santa Cruz at the mouth of the Bay of Guanabara, very close to the city of RIO DE JANEIRO. Although little historical information is available on the fort, it is known that Santa Cruz commanded an enviable position and very easily repelled pirates and invaders during the colonial period, enabling the city to develop in peace. The fort's gray granite walls also served as one of Brazil's largest prisons and held both military and civilian convicts. The prison conditions were very harsh, often leading to rebellion among the prisoners.

In 1892, a dramatic chapter in Brazil's history unfolded at Santa Cruz when army sergeant Silvino Honório de Macedo led a mutiny at Santa Cruz in an attempt to topple Brazilian president Floriano Peixoto's government. He gave weapons to the prisoners, and it took a full-scale army assault on Santa Cruz to quell the revolt. Today Santa Cruz is much quieter. Still an army barracks, it also serves as a historical museum. (*See also* **Buccaneers; Fleet Systems, Colonial.**)

Francia, José Gaspar Rodríguez de

1766–1840
Dictator of Paraguay

* **theology** study of religious faith

* **liberal** supporting greater participation in government for individuals; not bound by political and social traditions

José Gaspar Rodríguez de Francia was the most powerful and well-liked politician in PARAGUAY during the three decades following the country's independence in 1811. Although Francia's enemies and some historians called him a ruthless dictator, others considered him an honest ruler who promoted Paraguay's economic growth and helped the peasants, who enthusiastically supported him.

Born in Asunción, Francia studied and taught theology* until he was fired for his liberal* ideas on religion and politics. He gained political experience while serving on Asunción's town council from 1807 to 1809. Later he became the head of the junta* that declared Paraguay's independence from Spain and neighboring ARGENTINA. Francia then wrote the country's first constitution, and in 1814, the National Congress elected him supreme dictator. Except for short periods when he shared power, Francia exclusively ruled the country until his death.

One of his greatest political accomplishments was preventing Argentina from absorbing Paraguay. Francia removed the CATHOLIC CHURCH

° **junta** small group of people who run a government, usually after seizing power by force

and the wealthy elite from their positions of power, and he supported the peasants. To promote the nation's self-sufficiency, he supported state-owned businesses, reduced taxes, improved roads and communication, and encouraged industry. He favored low rents for small farmers who produced food for local use, and many of his policies—such as care for orphans and food for prisoners—aided the poor. Francia's government was more stable, efficient, and honest than those of most Latin American nations after independence, but he ruled with an iron hand and was willing to use force against those who opposed him. Although his policies benefited Paraguayans, his rule laid the basis for dictatorship in Paraguay.

Franciscans

See *Missions and Missionaries; Religious Orders.*

Frei Montalva, Eduardo

1911–1982
President of Chile

° **right wing** conservative or reactionary members, especially of a political party

° **Communist** person who advocates communism—a social system in which land, goods, and the means of production are owned by the state or community rather than by individuals

° **agrarian** referring to farmland, its use, or its ownership

° **nationalize** to bring land, industries, or public works under state control or ownership

° **left wing** liberal or radical members, especially of a political party

° **coup** sudden, often violent overthrow of a ruler or government

*E*duardo Frei Montalva hoped to lead CHILE through social and economic change without revolution and bloodshed. Supported by Chile's right wing*, Frei served for a term as the country's president. However, he was unable to accomplish his goals.

Born in Santiago, Frei entered political life as a law student, founding what became the Christian Democratic Party. He held elected office in the Chilean Congress from the late 1930s, eventually representing the province of Santiago in the Senate. In 1958, Frei ran unsuccessfully for the office of Chilean president. Supported by the right wing, Frei ran again in 1964, defeating rival candidate Salvador ALLENDE, who was backed by the Chilean Communists*. In his election message, Frei proposed to solve Chile's problems of inequality and injustice without resorting to violent or unconstitutional means. As president, he tried to implement agrarian* and tax reforms and to nationalize* the COPPER INDUSTRY. Frei was unsuccessful in his efforts because of opposition from the right wing, which found him too liberal, and the left wing*, which felt that his reforms did not go far enough. Frei lost the 1970 election to his rival, Allende, by a narrow margin. Commenting on the results, Frei predicted that Allende's regime would end in "blood and horror."

As Frei had forseen, Allende's election resulted in political and social upheaval, bringing the country to the brink of civil war. In the bloody military coup* that followed, army officer Augusto PINOCHET UGARTE seized power. Frei spent the rest of his life trying to rebuild the Christian Democratic Party and resisting the dictatorship of Pinochet.

French Guiana

° **department** province or administrative district of the government

*F*rench Guiana, on the northeastern coast of South America, a former French colony, is now an overseas department* of France. Known as La Guyane in French, it is the only French territory in South America. The population is racially and ethnically diverse, reflecting a history of immigration from many countries.

Although the French had been around the Guianas since the 1400s, it was only in the mid-1600s that they founded the settlement at

Prisoners of the Devil

During French Guiana's years as a colony for prisoners, France built a large prison complex there that included prison camps on the mainland and on several offshore islands. The complex, called Devil's Island, became notorious for its harsh conditions and the difficulty of escape. In reality, however, Devil's Island was one of the milder prison camps. Alfred Dreyfus, a Jewish officer in the French army falsely accused of spying, was imprisoned there in 1895. His world-famous case drew public attention to the colony at La Guyane.

* **commodity** article of trade

Cayenne, now the capital of French Guiana. The French government formally took control of the colony in 1664, but persistent Indian attacks and rivalries with Spanish, English, and Dutch colonial ventures kept French Guiana from flourishing. It lagged behind the neighboring Dutch colony of SURINAME and the French Caribbean colonies of Martinique, Guadeloupe, and St. Domingue (present-day HAITI) in population and wealth. In the 1700s and 1800s, France unsuccessfully tried to boost the colony's fortunes by relocating French farmers to La Guyane. After 1802, when SLAVERY was reestablished, the PLANTATION economy improved slightly, producing cotton, sugar, spices, and hardwoods for export. However, when slavery was finally abolished in 1848, the freed laborers moved into the wilderness to establish their own farms, and the plantation economy slumped.

A gold rush that lasted from the 1870s until the late 1920s brought thousands of fortune seekers to Guiana. Gold became French Guiana's major export commodity* and pushed economic activity into the interior. Around the same time, France launched another plan to populate La Guyane—this time by sending inmates from France's overcrowded prisons to the colony. Although the French government intended to turn Guiana into a land of independent small farmers, the region became known as Devil's Island, a colony for prisoners that remained in operation until the late 1930s. In 1947, a year after France had made La Guyane an overseas department, the colony was officially closed.

As an overseas department, Guiana received large subsidies from France and the economic standard of living increased, but productivity declined. Today unemployment is high, and French Guiana continues to depend on economic support from France. Perhaps for this reason, there is little support in French Guiana for the idea of independence from France. La Guyane is particularly important to France today because of the large space station and rocket-launching base at Kourou, which was established in the 1960s. About four-fifths of French Guiana's people are black or racially mixed, many of them immigrants from Caribbean or South American countries. The remainder are white, Indian, or Asian. Most of the population lives on the coast, while the interior is largely undeveloped. (*See also* **French in Latin America.**)

French in Latin America

* **dyewood** wood from which dyes are extracted

*A*lthough France's colonies were far smaller than those of Spain and Portugal, it was involved in the exploration, conquest, and settlement of the Americas from the beginning. In fact, French forces often prevented the Spanish from penetrating many areas of the present-day United States. France has affected the course of events in Latin America through its political and military actions and through its cultural and financial influence.

As early as 1504, French ships were exploring the Brazilian coastline, looking for dyewoods* to trade. Rejecting Portugal's claim to Brazil, France established several colonies along the coast, one of which survived until 1615. In the early 1600s, French merchants founded a trading post on the coast of northeastern South America, which later

* **department** province or administrative district of the government

* **buccaneer** maritime adventurer who roamed the Caribbean between 1630 and 1700, attacking Spanish settlements and trade, and terrifying Spanish colonists

* **patriot** one who favored independence of the colonies in the Americas

The Pastry War

Newly independent Mexico was a turbulent place in the early 1800s. Civil disorder sometimes resulted in damage to the property of foreigners living in Mexico, and foreign governments tried to force Mexico to pay for these damages. In 1838, France demanded 600,000 pesos as payment for damages to the property of French citizens in Mexico. The claim included 800 pesos payable to a French pastry chef, to cover the losses suffered by his business. When Mexico refused to pay, a French fleet bombed the Mexican port of Veracruz in what was called the Pastry War. The French captured Veracruz, but in 1839, the two nations made peace and Mexico agreed to pay the sum of 600,000 pesos to France.

became FRENCH GUIANA (still an overseas department* of France). The French were also active in the Caribbean, founding colonies on the islands of Martinique and Guadeloupe in 1635. Today these islands form the FRENCH WEST INDIES. Martinique became an important sugar producer, and its PLANTATION elite produced important personalities, including Empress Josephine, the first wife of Napoleon Bonaparte, and revolutionary social theorist Frantz Fanon.

France's other major sugar colony was St. Domingue, founded by French buccaneers* in the 1640s on the uninhabited western end of HISPANIOLA (Spain's colony of SANTO DOMINGO occupied the eastern end). After a massive slave revolt in the 1790s and a failed French attempt to recapture the colony, Saint Domingue became the independent nation of HAITI.

French political ideas—especially the example of the French Revolution of 1789—and military practices greatly influenced Simón BOLÍVAR and other leaders of independence in Spanish America. Patriot* officers and troops copied French models in everything from fighting formations to uniform designs. In the 1820s and 1830s, during the troubled years after independence, France tried several times to interfere in the affairs of the new Latin American nations. The most notorious example of French interference came in 1861, when France, in concert with Spain and England, invaded MEXICO to force the nation to pay its outstanding foreign debts. After the other two nations withdrew, the French captured Mexico City in 1863 and established a short-lived empire ruled by the emperor Maximilian. Opposed by many in Mexican society, the new emperor relied greatly on French troops for support. When troubles in Europe caused France to recall its troops in 1866, the Mexicans overthrew and executed the luckless Maximilian. France's attempt to build an empire in Mexico ended in disaster.

Since then, France's influence in Latin America has been mainly financial and cultural. In the 1800s and 1900s, France was a major investor in Latin American industries and businesses, along with the United States, Great Britain, and Germany. France's cultural influence may have been even more profound, especially in Argentina and other countries with large populations of European immigrants. In the late 1800s, many Latin American capitals were rebuilt to resemble Paris, with wide boulevards and French-style architecture. French political and literary ideas have influenced Latin American thinkers, and French films are highly regarded. Although the status of France and French culture declined somewhat in the 1900s, Argentines and others still consider Paris the prime source of cultural trends and fashion. (*See also* **Maximilian and Carlota**.)

French West Indies

After Spain opened the door to the West Indies—the islands of the Caribbean Sea—other nations, including France, began to explore and colonize the region. France established colonies on several Caribbean islands that have remained under French control despite economic troubles and political changes. The Caribbean islands of Martinique and Guadeloupe are overseas departments* of France,

° **department** province or administrative district of the government

See map in Caribbean Antilles (vol. I).

See color plate 4, vol. 4.

° **by-product** something produced in the making of something else

Island Swapping with Sweden

Sweden, which seems far removed from the tropical sands and palm trees of the Caribbean, controlled the island of St. Barthélemy for more than a century. Christopher Columbus named the island after his brother Bartolomé. The French took control of the island in the mid-1600s, but after the Seven Years' War, they traded it to the Swedish in exchange for concessions on the Baltic island of Gotland. The Swedish renamed the island St. Barts Gustavia and initiated free trade. In 1877, the French regained control of St. Barts and maintained its free trade status. Today the island's architecture, culture, and road signs indicate its mixed French and Swedish influence.

and FRENCH GUIANA in South America is France's other Latin American territory.

The first French colonial settlement was established in 1625 on the island of St. Christopher (also called St. Kitts). France shared this island with Britain until 1713, when the entire island came under British control. In 1635, the French settled the islands of Martinique and Guadeloupe. The islands were supported by the Company of the Islands of the Americas, a French firm that supplied the islands with laborers, colonists, and missionaries in return for fees payable in tobacco and cotton. However, the settlers encountered resistance from the local Carib Indians, and without support from the government and merchants of France, the company became bankrupt and sold the colonies to private investors.

By the 1660s, the new owners converted these and other smaller French colonies into sugar PLANTATIONS worked by African slaves. They also planted sugar on St. Domingue, the unoccupied western end of Hispaniola. (Spain's colony of Santo Domingo occupied the eastern end.) The colonies prospered sufficiently to attract the attention of the French government. In 1664, French finance minister Jean-Baptiste Colbert arranged to repurchase the colonies, set up the French West Indies Company to control and tax their trade, and built slave-trading forts in West Africa to supply plantation labor to the French West Indies.

Colbert kept the island colonies under firm economic control, forbidding them to trade with any non-French territories or compete with French industries. The plantations simply produced the raw materials demanded by France and consumed only French-made products. Moreover, the colonies did not have assemblies to make laws. Instead, a French council passed their laws and appointed their officials.

In 1793, a massive slave rebellion signaled the end of plantation slavery in Saint Domingue, and the region became the independent nation of HAITI. By 1848, France had abolished slavery in all of its colonies. The freed slaves, then a segment of the French West Indian population, turned to farming for a living. The plantation owners imported laborers from India to work the plantations, and sugar and its by-products* continued to dominate the islands' economies through much of the 1900s.

In 1946, the French government accorded Martinique and Guadeloupe the status of overseas departments. Among Martinique's distinctive features are its capital city, Fort-de-France, which has one of the best harbors in the Caribbean, and the volcano Mount Pelée, which erupted in 1902, killing more than 30,000 people. Guadeloupe consists of two main islands, Basse-Terre and Grande-Terre, and the smaller islands of Marie-Galante, Désirade, Îles des Saintes, St. Barthélemy, and half of St. Martin. Basse-Terre is Guadeloupe's political capital, and Point-à-Pitre on Grande-Terre is the island's main port and business center.

The social structure of Martinique and Guadeloupe still reflects the islands' history as a plantation society. White landowners belong to the elite, while the middle class is composed of white immigrants, mostly from France, and people of mixed race. The middle class dominates business, politics, civil service, and professional life. The largest segment of the population, and the lowest economic group, consists of black and mixed-race people who live in rural areas and work in agriculture, either as small farmers or as hired laborers.

Although TOURISM is increasingly important to the economies of Martinique and Guadeloupe, unemployment is high, and both departments rely on France for education, health, and welfare funds. Like their economy, their culture (including their language) is closely tied to France. Although there is little desire for independence, some residents of the French West Indies would like to have more control over local affairs. (*See also* **Slave Revolts; Slave Trade; Slavery; Sugar Industry.**)

Fruit Industry

See color plate 3, vol. 2.

* **monopolize** to control exclusively or dominate a particular type of business

* **sovereignty** independence

*L*atin America's fruit industry began in the 1860s, when faster shipping and improved methods of storing and handling perishable foods made it possible for tropical fruit to be exported at a profit. Since then, BANANAS have come to dominate the Latin American fruit industry, although other tropical and nontropical fruits are also important.

Bananas are grown in the West Indies, Central America, northern Colombia, and Ecuador. Some economically important tropical fruits are the mango, papaya, passion fruit, and guava. Exports of these fruits from Latin America, especially Mexico, have increased since the 1960s. Chile, which does not have a tropical climate, exports nontropical fruits such as grapes, apples, kiwis, and citrus fruits. Chilean grape exports are an increasingly important part of the modern fruit industry.

Bananas first came to the Gulf coast of the United States in the mid-1800s, when shipping companies bought them from small independent producers in the Caribbean. In the 1870s, the United States–based Tropical Trading and Transport Company began importing bananas from Costa Rica. At the same time, a Boston sea captain started the Boston Fruit Company to import bananas to New England. In 1899, these two operations merged to form the UNITED FRUIT COMPANY (UFC), which eventually came to monopolize* the fruit industry, from PLANTATIONS to rail and sea transportation to distribution.

The UFC and other American fruit companies were good employers in that they paid high wages and provided benefits for employees such as schools and health care. However, these companies became deeply involved in the internal affairs of the countries, often bribing politicians and soldiers to ensure decisions in their favor. Many Latin Americans came to resent the power and influence of the fruit companies, especially when they threatened the sovereignty* of their country.

During the 1960s, a combination of plant disease and political problems reduced the profits of the banana industry in the West Indies and Central America, paving the way for Ecuador to become Latin America's largest producer of bananas. Ecuador's banana industry, launched by the UFC in 1933, is dominated by small and medium-sized producers who sell their produce to large corporations. In Ecuador and elsewhere in Latin America, the fruit industry no longer dominates politics as it once did.

Fuentes, Carlos

born 1928
Mexican author

° **diplomat** person authorized by his or her country to conduct international relations

Carlos Fuentes is a leading modern novelist whose works explore themes of Mexican history and identity. This photograph shows Fuentes happily singing after being awarded the Cervantes Prize for Literature in Madrid, Spain.

*C*arlos Fuentes is a leading modern writer and a spokesperson not only for MEXICO but for all of Latin America. His novels, stories, and essays explore Mexico's past and define its national identity. The son of a Mexican diplomat*, Fuentes was born in Panama and attended school in the United States, Argentina, and Chile. After receiving a degree in law from the University of Mexico, he served on the International Law Commission of the United Nations, and from 1952 to 1959, he was director of international cultural relations for the Mexican Ministry of Foreign Affairs.

Fuentes's literary career began in 1954 with the publication of *Los días enmascarados* (The Masked Days), a collection of short stories. His first novel, *La región más transparente (Where the Air Is Clear)*, published in 1958, brought him immediate fame. In 1962, he published one of his major works, *La muerte de Artemio Cruz (The Death of Artemio Cruz)*, a novel in which Fuentes comments on the corruption of the MEXICAN REVOLUTION through his portrayal of the final hours of a dying man reflecting on the crucial moments of his life. Since then, Fuentes has written many novels in which vivid stories and characters give life to ideas about civilization, desires, history, time, and identity. His works include *Terra nostra* (Our Land), a tale of the European discovery of America; *Burnt Water* and *The Orange Tree,* collections of short stories depicting the Spanish and Indian past; and *The Crystal Frontier,* an exploration of the complex relationship between Mexico and the United States.

Fuentes has also written important nonfiction works, including *The Buried Mirror: Reflections on Spain and the New World,* a history of Hispanic culture on both sides of the Atlantic Ocean (this book was made into a television series), and *A New Time for Mexico,* essays about Mexican government and society. Fuentes has frequently been a visiting lecturer on college campuses throughout the United States and Europe. He is also the winner of several international literary awards and is one of Mexico's best-known and most respected thinkers. (*See also* **Literature.**)

Fueros

See *Laws and Legal Systems.*

Fujimori, Alberto Keinya

born 1938
President of Peru

*A*lberto Keinya Fujimori, Latin America's first head of state of Japanese origin, was president of PERU during the 1990s, an eventful time in the nation's history. Born in LIMA to Japanese immigrant farmworkers, Fujimori earned degrees in agricultural science and mathematics before becoming the president of a Peruvian university. He hosted a television talk show on public issues that made him well known and well liked in Peru.

In 1989, Fujimori helped organize a political party named Cambio 90 (Change 90), and the following year, he was elected president of Peru. Fujimori took drastic steps to revitalize Peru's ailing economy, but

Fujimori, Alberto Keinya

Alberto Fujimori, Latin America's first head of state of Japanese origin, fought against terrorism during his time as president of Peru. This photograph shows Fujimori talking on a walkie-talkie moments after the Peruvian army stormed a building to free 72 hostages held by terrorists.

See color plate 13, vol. 3.

See map in Peru (vol. 3).

° **coup** sudden, often violent overthrow of a ruler or government

° **guerrilla** member of a fighting force outside the regular army that uses surprise raids to obstruct or harass an enemy or overthrow a government

more than half the population remained in poverty. He also took measures to minimize the political violence and terrorism associated with such groups as the SENDERO LUMINOSO (Shining Path) and Tupac Amaru Revolutionary Movement (MRTA). By 1992, Fujimori's government had captured key leaders of these organizations and greatly suppressed violence in Peru.

In 1992, Fujimori suspended Peru's congress and courts and took control of the government in what amounted to a coup*. Over the next 18 months, supported by most Peruvians, Fujimori organized elections for a new, smaller congress; rewrote the constitution to strengthen the authority of the central government; established the death penalty for terrorism; and allowed for the reelection of a sitting president. In 1995, Fujimori became the first Peruvian president to be elected for two consecutive terms. A year later, world attention focused on Peru when MRTA guerrillas* seized the home of the Japanese ambassador in Lima and took 72 people hostage. After a four-month standoff with the terrorists, Fujimori ordered the army to recapture the building. The guerrillas were killed in the raid, and one hostage died of a heart attack. After this dramatic incident, Fujimori's popularity fell. Peruvians also became concerned about the power of the military and about accusations that Fujimori may actually have been born in Japan, making it illegal for him to serve as Peru's president. Still, many Peruvians credit Fujimori with curbing terrorism in Peru, and their support may enable him to win a third term as president.

Gadsden Purchase

*T*he Gadsden Purchase was an agreement in which the government of MEXICO agreed to sell nearly 45,535 square miles of land—the southernmost portions of present-day ARIZONA and NEW MEXICO—to the United States. The agreement, signed in 1853, was named after James Gadsden, a railroad builder and United States minister to Mexico, who negotiated the transaction.

The purchase had a dual purpose. The negotiations developed from a dispute that existed from the time the two countries signed the Treaty of GUADALUPE HIDALGO at the end of the MEXICAN-AMERICAN WAR. According to Article XI of that treaty, the United States was required to protect Mexico from Native American raids on Mexico's northern border. However, the United States government did not fulfill its obligation. Moreover, BOUNDARY DISPUTES arose between the two countries because a map drawn at the time of the treaty questioned the exact location of the UNITED STATES–MEXICO BORDER. The United States was also seeking land in northern Mexico on which to build the southern transcontinental railroad. The plan further proposed to construct a port on the Gulf of California, which separates Mexico from Baja California.

In 1853, James Gadsden was appointed to negotiate the terms of the purchase. Although the United States initially sought to purchase much more land, several factors, including disputes about the status of slavery and over the control of the proposed railroad, reduced the territory finally purchased. In 1854, the agreement was approved by the U.S. Senate and the United States purchased the Mesilla territory from Mexico in exchange for $10 million. As part of the agreement, Mexican president Antonio López de SANTA ANNA also agreed to relieve the United States of its obligation to protect Mexico's northern border.

Galápagos Islands

* **islet** small island

See map in Ecuador (vol. 2).

*T*he Galápagos Islands, located in the Pacific Ocean about 600 miles west of ECUADOR, consist of 19 volcanic islands and many smaller islets*. The islands are famed for their many species of unusual plants and animals, including the giant tortoises from which the islands derive their name.

Thomás de Berlanga, the bishop of Panama, first discovered the islands in 1535. He named them Las Encantadas, or The Enchanted, because they were covered in mists that gave them an otherworldly appearance and because of the unusual animals he found there. During the 1600s, pirates took shelter in the islands. In the 1800s and 1900s, whaling vessels stopped there to capture the giant tortoises to provide fresh meat for the whalers' long voyages at sea. In 1832, Ecuador took possession of the islands, and in 1835, Charles Darwin visited the Galápagos to study the plant and animal life. In fact, Darwin's theory of evolution by natural selection is primarily based on his observations in the Galápagos. In 1892, the islands were renamed Archipiélago de Colón in honor of Christopher COLUMBUS.

Because the Galápagos are so isolated, many of the plant and animal species that developed there are unique. Among these are 80 species

The Galápagos Islands were called the "Islands of the Tortoises" by Spanish explorers who found giant 500-pound land tortoises living there. Sailors on long trips prized these tortoises as a source of fresh meat and slaughtered them to the point of near extinction.

of birds, several mammals, iguanas, and the giant tortoise, which is thought to be the longest-lived animal on Earth. Since the time of Darwin's study, this uniquely populated and isolated environment has been extremely important to scientists. They also attract thousands of tourists each year. Although large parts of the islands are now national parks and wildlife refuges, the environmental impact of TOURISM on the ecology of the region remains a concern.

Gálvez, Bernardo de

1746–1786
Governor and viceroy

* **New Spain** Spanish colony in Mexico

*B*ernardo de Gálvez, a Spanish military officer, held several key posts in the colonial government and played an important role in defeating the British in the AMERICAN REVOLUTION. He also led several successful military expeditions.

In 1765, Gálvez accompanied his uncle José de GÁLVEZ to New Spain*, where he gained experience fighting the Apache Indians on the northern border. Later he served in Spain's military campaign in Algeria. In 1776, King CHARLES III of Spain named him commander of the Louisiana Regiment. When Gálvez arrived in New Orleans, he replaced Luis de Unzaga as governor of LOUISIANA on New Year's Day, 1777. At this time, the American Revolution had just begun, and Gálvez was instructed to strengthen the colony and secretly help the Americans. Gálvez fortified the Spanish army in Louisiana and sent arms to American troops led by George Rogers Clark in the MISSISSIPPI VALLEY.

Once Spain declared war on England in 1779, Gálvez led military campaigns in which he defeated British forces at Baton Rouge, Mobile, and Pensacola. He also played a key role in keeping the British out of the northern Mississippi Valley. Gálvez's success enabled Spain to recover FLORIDA from the British under the Treaty of Paris. His military skills contributed significantly to the American victory over the British. Promoted to captain-general*, Gálvez served as governor of Cuba during the spring of 1785. That same year, he succeeded his father, Matías de Gálvez, as viceroy* of New Spain. He died the following year in Mexico City.

* **captain-general** title of provincial rulers in colonial Latin America whose main duty was the military defense of a territory

* **viceroy** one who governs a country or province as a monarch's representative; royally appointed official

Gálvez, José de

1720–1787
Spanish statesman

* **hidalgo** person of some means, but not an heir to great fortune or nobility

* **monopoly** exclusive control or domination of a particular type of business

* **intendancy** administrative district in Spanish America

* **Jesuit** Roman Catholic religious order known as the Society of Jesus; also, a member of that order

* **viceroyalty** region governed by a viceroy, a royally appointed official

José de Gálvez was responsible for reorganizing and strengthening Spain's control over many of its colonies in Latin America. Gálvez, a poor hidalgo*, was born in the hills of Andalusia, a province in southern Spain. He earned a law degree at the University of Salamanca and practiced law in Madrid. He handled many cases involving people in the Americas and attracted the attention of the ministers of the Spanish king CHARLES III. In 1765, the king instructed him to conduct a *visita*, or thorough investigation, in Mexico.

Upon arrival, Gálvez reorganized the collection of taxes, jailed corrupt officials, shifted control of trade with Spain from Mexican to Spanish merchants, and established a TOBACCO monopoly* that brought great wealth to the monarchy. He increased investment in MINING and took steps to make mining less costly and more profitable. In short, he overhauled the entire Mexican economy. Gálvez also reorganized the government by introducing the intendancy* system in Mexico and by establishing the PROVINCIAS INTERNAS (Internal Provinces) that created a separate government for the northern part of the country. To strengthen the monarchy's control over its colonies, Gálvez carried out the expulsion of the Jesuits* and put down several Indian revolts. In 1769, he began the colonization of CALIFORNIA, but because of his exhausting schedule, he suffered a physical and mental collapse and returned to Spain in 1771.

In 1776, Gálvez was named minister of the Indies and oversaw Spain's vast colonial empire. In this position, he tried to implement changes—similar to those he had introduced in Mexico—throughout the empire. *Visitas* were conducted in Peru, New Granada, Venezuela, and Ecuador, and a viceroyalty* was established in BUENOS AIRES. In 1780 and 1781, he brutally suppressed the TUPAC AMARU rebellion in Peru and the COMUNERO REVOLT in New Granada. After the American Revolution, Gálvez became the *marqés de Sonora* and played a major role in regaining FLORIDA from Britain and in expelling the British from Central America and Darién. Gálvez died shortly thereafter, before he had a chance to complete his reform of the empire. Although Gálvez was able and hard working, he angered many people by stripping them of their power and privileges. Nevertheless, many of his reforms remained in place throughout Spain's colonial period. (*See also* **Intendancy System; Spain and the Spanish Empire.**)

Gálvez, Mariano

1794–1862
Guatemalan chief of state

° **progressive** inclined to support social improvement and political change by governmental action

° **republic** government in which citizens elect officials to represent them and govern according to law

° **conservative** inclined to maintain existing political and social views, conditions, and institutions

° **liberal** supporting greater participation in government for individuals; not bound by political and social traditions

° **guerrilla** referring to a group that uses surprise raids to obstruct or harass an enemy or overthrow a government

° **cholera** serious intestinal disease that causes diarrhea, vomiting, cramps, and often death

During his seven years as chief of state, Mariano Gálvez attempted to establish a modern, progressive* republic* in GUATEMALA. Although he hoped that his plans would lead to social equality and prosperity, their ultimate failure caused the end of Gálvez's rule.

An orphaned child, Gálvez was adopted by an important family in Guatemala City and later studied law. He entered politics and was deeply involved in the negotiations that led to Guatemala's independence from Spain. After Emperor Augustín de ITURBIDE fell from power in 1823, Gálvez held public offices at the state and federal levels. In 1831, a devastating civil war destroyed the conservative* forces in Guatemala, and Gálvez was elected chief of state.

Gálvez immediately set out to reshape all of Central America through liberal* economic and social policies. He crushed the power of the CATHOLIC CHURCH by proclaiming religious freedom and putting education into the hands of the state. He introduced a new legal system, converted communal lands into private property, and promoted free trade. However, his trade policy hurt local industry, and peasants resented the taxes he imposed on them. His demand that peasants work on public works projects further fueled their resentment. They formed an alliance with the conservatives and the clergy, under the leadership of the guerrilla* fighter José Rafael CARRERA. Although Gálvez responded by modifying some of his programs, it was too late. When his modern measures to stop a cholera* epidemic failed in 1837, the peasants accused Gálvez's government of trying to poison them. He was overthrown in 1838 and was later forced into exile in Mexico.

García, José Maurício Nunes

1767–1830
Brazilian composer

° **mulatto** person of mixed black and white ancestry

José Maurício Nunes García was the most notable Brazilian composer of the early 1800s. Although he was a relatively unknown mulatto*, García won the attention of many important people, including JOÃO VI OF PORTUGAL, who decorated the composer with the prestigious Order of Christ award.

As a youth, García learned to play the harpsichord and viola and received voice training as well. He also helped found the religious Brotherhood of St. Cecilia. In 1792, García was ordained a priest in the Brotherhood of São Pedro dos Clérigos. Six years later, he was accorded the highest musical position at the cathedral in RIO DE JANEIRO, where he served as organist, composer, conductor, and music teacher. García gave free music lessons for almost three decades, during which he taught some of the most important Brazilian composers and musicians of the next generation.

In 1808, João VI arrived in Rio de Janeiro and soon heard of García's talents. João appointed him *mestre de capela* (music director) of the royal chapel, and in 1809, García composed 39 musical pieces for the king. That year, García received the Order of Christ. Two years later Marcos Portugal, the best-known Portuguese composer of the time, replaced García as *mestre de capela,* and García's career began to decline. However, in 1816, he wrote his most significant work, a requiem mass for the funeral of Queen Maria of Portugal. When João returned to Portugal as king in 1821, support for the arts was curtailed due a lack of funds. The state discontinued García's lifelong pension, leaving him in difficult financial circumstances until his death in 1830. (*See also* **Music and Dance**.)

García Márquez, Gabriel

born 1927
Colombian novelist and
short story writer

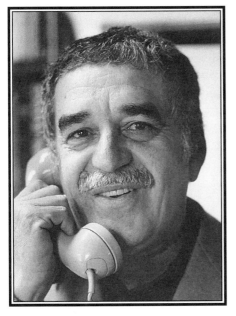

Gabriel García Márquez is a well-known Colombian writer whose works combine myth and fantasy with traditional literary forms. This photograph shows García Márquez talking on the phone after being informed that he had won the Nobel Prize for literature.

° **imperialism** domination of the political, economic, and cultural life of one country or region by another country

° **Communist** person who advocates communism—a social system in which land, goods, and the means of production are owned by the state or community rather than by individuals

Gabriel García Márquez is the best-known modern Colombian writer and a great figure in Latin American literature. By blending myth and fantasy with traditional literary forms, García Márquez created extraordinary novels based on the perceptions and imaginations of their characters rather than on logic or obvious reality. A Nobel Prize–winning author, his vision of the human experience has made him a celebrated writer throughout the world.

García Márquez was born in Aracataca, COLOMBIA, and studied law at the National University of Bogotá. In 1948, the assassination of a well-liked politician led to an outbreak of violence known as El Bogotazo that closed the university and interrupted his studies. García Márquez returned home and worked for several years as a journalist, a job that greatly influenced his writing. For example, one of his earlier novels, *Relato de un náufrago (The Story of a Shipwrecked Sailor)*, is based on an interview with a Colombian sailor who spent ten days on a raft in the Caribbean Sea.

García Márquez published his first novel, *La hojarasca (Leaf Storm)*, in Colombia in 1955. He moved to Mexico in 1961, and several years later, while driving to Acapulco, he had a vision of the fictional world that he had been trying to create for more than ten years. The result of this inspiration was *Cien años de soledad (One Hundred Years of Solitude)*, one of the greatest novels ever written in Spanish. It tells the story of his hometown through the eyes of a local family and includes history and fantasy, everyday events and fantastic occurrences, comedy and tragedy, the serious and the absurd. In some parts of the novel, García Márquez rewrites history to discredit government corruption and to tell what he believes to be the true story of Colombia's civil wars, its BANANA INDUSTRY boom, and United States imperialism*.

Shortly after the publication of *One Hundred Years of Solitude*, García Márquez moved to Barcelona, Spain. In 1975, he published *El otoño del patriarca (The Autumn of the Patriarch)*. This fictional portrait of a typical Latin American dictator is told in a unique style that features poetic language, humor, fantasy, and constantly shifting points of view. Some consider it the author's most significant literary achievement. He also wrote *El amor en los tiempos del cólera (Love in the Time of Cholera)*, considered one of the best love stories ever written. In recognition of his outstanding accomplishments as a writer, García Márquez received the Nobel Prize for literature in 1982.

From the late 1950s to the early 1980s, he was denied a visa to enter the United States because of his Communist* views and his friendship with Fidel CASTRO. However, these sanctions were lifted in 1991, and García Márquez was allowed to travel freely to the United States. (He had traveled to the United States in previous years with waivers from the United States government.)

García Márquez's books have been translated into many languages and published in many countries, and some books have been made into films. His later works include *El general en su laberinto (The General in His Labyrinth)*, *Del amor y otros demonios (Of Love and Other Demons)*, and *Noticia de un secuestro (News of a Kidnapping)*.

García Moreno, Gabriel

1821–1875
President of Ecuador

° **liberal** person who supports greater participation in government for individuals; one who is not bound by political and social traditions

° **conservative** inclined to maintain existing political and social views, conditions, and institutions

° **junta** small group of people who run a government, usually after seizing power by force

° **Jesuit** Roman Catholic religious order known as the Society of Jesus; also, a member of that order

° **machete** long-bladed knife used for cutting crops and vegetation

Gabriel García Moreno began his political career as a liberal* but later turned into a conservative* dictator who brutally repressed his opponents. As a young man, he opposed President Juan José FLORES and published three controversial newspapers that criticized Flores's regime. As a result, he was exiled from ECUADOR several times between 1850 and 1856. While abroad, he was attracted to conservative views and became a supporter of the CATHOLIC CHURCH.

In 1856, García Moreno returned to Ecuador, where he was named head of the University of Quito. Soon afterward, he won a seat in the Senate. In 1859, he joined a junta* that tried to take control of the government. The junta was unsuccessful, and García Moreno fled to Peru. He returned to Ecuador a few months later, and when peace was restored in 1861, he was elected president. As president, he reformed the treasury, improved the university and transportation systems, and defended Ecuador against threats from Colombia and Peru. He surrendered government control of church revenues and appointments and encouraged the Catholic Church to play a prominent role in the affairs of the state.

Although his term ended in 1865, García Moreno was able to manipulate his two successors and eventually seized power again in 1869. He allowed the Jesuits* to return to Ecuador, denied civil rights to non-Catholics, and gave large sums of state money to the Vatican. Despite improving Ecuador's roads, railroads, and schools, García Moreno's policies were unpopular among the people. In 1875, a group of young liberals killed him with machetes*.

García Robles, Alfonso

born 1911
Mexican disarmament specialist

° **diplomatic** demonstrating tact and skill at conducting negotiations among nations

Alfonso García Robles is a former Mexican foreign service officer who spent his professional life seeking ways to reduce the world's stockpile of nuclear arms. After studying at the University of Paris in France and the International Law Academy in the Netherlands, García Robles held diplomatic* posts in many foreign countries. Alarmed by the CUBAN MISSILE CRISIS of 1962, he masterminded a treaty that would make Latin America a nuclear-free zone. He played a key role in negotiating the Nuclear Arms Treaty of Tlatelolco in 1967 and later became Mexico's permanent representative to the UNITED NATIONS Committee on Disarmament*. He also coauthored the 1968 Nuclear Nonproliferation Treaty, which has since been signed by more than 155

* **disarmament** referring to the act of reducing or depriving of nuclear weapons and firearms

* **emeritus** honorary title accorded after retirement that corresponds to that held while engaged in active service

countries. From 1970 to 1975, García Robles served as Mexico's ambassador to the United Nations. In 1975, he was chosen as Mexico's secretary for foreign relations and was later named ambassador emeritus* to the United Nations. In 1982, García Robles received the Nobel Peace Prize for his efforts supporting disarmament in Latin America. He is the author of 20 books and more than 300 articles on foreign affairs.

Garcilaso de la Vega, El Inca

1539–1616
Peruvian author and historian

* **posthumous** occurring after the death of an individual

Historian Garcilaso de la Vega, born Gómez Suárez de Figueroa, wrote some of the earliest historical accounts of Spanish exploration in the Americas. Although his works often combine historical reports with sensitive imagination, El Inca, as he was known posthumously*, was the first American author to be widely read in Europe, and his writings have remained popular.

Garcilaso was born in Cuzco, Peru, to a Spanish officer and an Inca princess. In 1552, his father, Sebastián, married a wealthy Spaniard and turned Garcilaso, his mother, and his siblings out of the house. After his father's death in 1559, Garcilaso left for Spain, never to return to Peru. After a brief military career, he devoted his life to writing, taking the pen name Garcilaso de la Vega. He published his first historical text, *La Florida del Inca* (The Florida of the Inca) in 1605. The book was an account of Hernando de Soto's expedition to Florida and was based on published works and the testimony of a soldier who served on the mission.

Four years later, Garcilaso published a history of the Inca civilization describing the life and society of the Inca before the arrival of the Spanish. This work was based on recollections of what he learned as a youth and on written sources. His last work, *Historia general del Perú* (General History of Peru) published posthumously in 1617, covers the Spanish conquest of the Inca from the arrival of Francisco Pizarro in 1532 to the end of the Tupac Amaru rebellion in 1572.

Garcilaso's writings brought the Americas to life for many Europeans. His style and authority are powerful and his writings are still used as sources for histories of the Inca. (*See also* **Literature**.)

Gauchesca Literature

See *Literature.*

Gauchos

Gauchos (*gaúchos* in Portuguese) are the cowboys of Argentina, Uruguay, and Brazil. Gauchos once played a key role in the economy of the region, but they are now mostly cultural symbols. Their reputation in South America is similar to that of the cowboys of the North American West, and they enjoy the same kind of respect and romantic reputation.

Historical Origins of the Gauchos. When the Río de la Plata was colonized, vast herds of wild cattle and horses freely roamed the

Gauchos

See color plate 4, vol. 2.

* **monopoly** exclusive control or domination of a particular type of business

* **vagrancy** state of wandering from place to place without a permanent home or steady employment
* **royalist** supporter of the king or queen, especially in times of civil war or rebellion
* **epithet** descriptive word or phrase (often abusive) that accompanies, or is used in place of, the name of a person or thing

South America's cowboys were once feared and hated by government officials. Today, however, they have become a powerful symbol of freedom and individuality.

PAMPAS, the flat plains in South America. Colonial officials wanted to establish a monopoly* over the killing and use of these wild animals, but the gauchos believed that everyone should have access to the resources of the pampas. Therefore, the gauchos scorned colonial governments and fled from or resisted officials' attempts to control or dominate them.

The gauchos' culture was centered around the horse and the freedom of roaming the open plains. Much of their culture was borrowed directly from the Indians who inhabited the pampas. Gauchos dressed distinctively in ponchos, baggy pants *(chiripá)* held up by a strong leather belt *(tirador),* homemade boots *(botas de potro),* and iron spurs. They armed themselves with a swordlike knife called a *facón* and *boleadoras,* leather thongs tipped with rocks or metal balls. The gaucho would whirl the *boleadora* above his head and fling it at the feet of a fleeing animal, entangling its legs in the leather straps and bringing it down.

Colonial officials saw the gauchos as ignorant, uncivilized barbarians who were not much better than the Indians. The gauchos' familiarity with teachings of the CATHOLIC CHURCH was the only factor that separated them from the Indians. Nevertheless, the colonial governments persistently tried to end their free-riding lifestyle. They passed laws against vagrancy*, specifically targeting the gauchos, and often forced the gauchos to serve in the colonial armies. As soldiers, they fought against Indians, the British in 1806 and 1807, and royalist*

Vaqueros and Cowboys

Vaqueros—working cowhands from Mexico—herded cattle on frontier missions during the colonial era. Modifying Spanish equipment and riding techniques to fit their needs, Indian and mestizo vaqueros became skilled riders and ropers. During the 1800s, when the United States expanded into the Southwest, vaqueros came to work on ranches owned by United States citizens. These vaqueros taught the ranch hands how to round up wild cattle and to braid lassos and passed on the tradition of wearing leather outfits. From these lessons, the United States cowboy—the mythical embodiment of the West—was born.

forces during the wars of independence. Gauchos gained a reputation for valor and patriotism. The term *gaucho* became less of an epithet* and more of a description for a ranch worker who rode horses and tended cattle.

The "Civilizing" of the Gauchos.   During the 1800s, the landowning elite joined forces with the politicians to end the free gaucho lifestyle. New laws, new technology, and a rural economy that was much less dependent upon cattle signaled the decline of the social importance of gauchos. When much of the pampas was fenced in, the remaining gauchos were forced to find employment on the large *estancias,* or ranches.

Beginning in the late 1800s, the gauchos were slowly transformed from historical figures to characters in folklore and LITERATURE. Many important writers in Argentina and Uruguay made gauchos the focus of their work, and poets honored them in their verses. Today gaucho customs are preserved in music, dance, food, drink, and such traditions as the outdoor barbecue. In a turnaround from their origins as outlaws and barbarians, calling someone or something "very gaucho" is now considered a great compliment.

Gazetas

See *Journalism.*

Gems and Gemstones

° **pre-Columbian** before the arrival of Christopher Columbus and other Europeans in the Americas in the 1490s

° **archaeological** relating to archaeology, or the science of studying past human cultures, usually by excavating ruins

° **conquistador** Spanish explorer and conqueror

° **colonial** period between the European conquest and independence, generally from the early 1500s to the early 1800s

*L*atin America's rich deposits of gems and gemstones have been an important part of the area's economy and history for hundreds of years. The two most important gemstones mined in the region are emeralds and diamonds, although many others are produced in smaller quantities.

Emeralds.   Pre-Columbian* cultures in COLOMBIA used emeralds in jewelry and as offerings in religious ceremonies. Archaeological* finds in the area provide information about a ceremony in which offerings of emeralds and gold were thrown into the sacred Lake Guatavita, high in the Colombian Andes. After the Spanish conquistadors* arrived in the early 1500s, they took control of the sources of the gems. Colombian emeralds were soon being used in trade from the far north (Mexico) to the distant south (Chile). The Spanish later discovered new emerald deposits to the north of BOGOTÁ and forced thousands of Indian slaves to mine them. In the early 1600s, news of the brutal working conditions in the mines caused both the king of Spain and the pope to issue decrees forbidding Indian SLAVERY, and the mines were closed. The mining areas around Bogotá have had a history of violence ever since, with some 50,000 people killed in 1976 alone.

Many of the world's finest jewels, including the crown jewels of Iran, contain Colombian emeralds. During the colonial* period, the

Stone of the Gods

When archaeologists found beautiful artifacts—a human skull covered with a mosaic of small turquoise plates, necklaces, and ceremonial knives with turquoise inlays—in the Aztec capital of Tenochtitlán, they erroneously concluded that the Aztecs had produced those objects. In fact, archaeologists have only recently determined that the Mixtecs, not the Aztecs, created these beautiful objects. The Mixtecs produced many fine objects in gold and silver, but they placed great value on turquoise—a stone that they usually reserved for sacred uses. Many objects made from this blue-green stone have been found in tomb seven at Monte Albán in Mexico.

* **appraise** to determine the value or quality of an object

* **carat** unit of weight for precious stones; 1 carat = 200 mg

Spanish took large quantities of emeralds back to Europe. Many countries purchased Colombian emeralds from the Europeans, including Mogul rulers in India, among whom emeralds were very popular. However, when the Persians invaded India in 1739, they took many of these prized emeralds to the Middle East, where they remain today. Emeralds are still an important part of Colombia's economy. They are also mined in Brazil, the leading producer of gemstones in Latin America.

Diamonds. Until the early 1700s, India produced most of the world's diamonds. In 1725, diamonds were discovered in the Brazilian state of MINAS GERAIS. When Portuguese explorer Sebastino Leme do Prado first found the diamonds in BRAZIL, local miners were using the stones in their roughest form as chips in poker games. The Portuguese crown had some of these "chips" sent to Amsterdam to be appraised*, and when their value became known, the monarchy immediately took control over the diamond-producing areas. The diamonds were easily recovered by sifting gravel from riverbeds in a pan and were often accompanied by gold. Brazil became the center of the diamond industry for more than 150 years, and at one time, as many as 300,000 carats* of diamonds were mined each year. However, by the 1880s, Brazil could not keep up with the world demand for diamonds. Around the same time, diamond deposits were discovered in South Africa, which eventually replaced Brazil as the world's leading diamond producer. Diamonds and gold are still mined in Brazil, but only on a very small scale. Venezuela is also a minor producer of diamonds.

Other Gemstones. During World War II, mining for minerals such as quartz that were important to the war effort led to the discovery of many other gemstones in Brazil. Today most of the world's tourmaline, topaz, and garnet come from Brazil. Amethyst and opal are also mined in Brazil. Chile produces some lapis lazuli, and Uruguay has agate and amethyst deposits. Very few gemstones are mined in Central America, except for jade, which was mined in Guatemala before the Europeans arrived. The Dominican Republic is one of the world's major suppliers of amber. Mexico has produced fire opals since the late 1800s, but the AZTECS may have known about them hundreds of years earlier. (*See also* **Mining**.)

Gender Roles and Sexuality

After the Spanish conquest, gender roles in Latin America began to reflect traditional Iberian* attitudes and the teachings of the CATHOLIC CHURCH. Society was dominated by men (who controlled most public, economic, and political activity), and WOMEN had far fewer rights. Although women have since made significant progress toward achieving social and legal equality, traditional attitudes regarding "appropriate" behavior for the sexes continue to be held by most Latin Americans.

Gender Roles in Latin America

Anthropologists* and archaeologists* believe that before the arrival of the Spanish, gender relations among the Indians were mostly egalitarian, reflecting equality with respect to division of labor and to social and economic status. When the Spaniards settled the region, gender relations were redefined by *machismo, marianismo, hembrismo, maternidad, feminismo,* and *patria potestad*—concepts that delineated appropriate social roles for both sexes. Machismo, a distinctively patriarchal* attitude, refers to manliness and is measured by a man's ability to head a family, produce children, protect the virtue of his female relatives, and defend the family against other men. It emphasizes bravery, forcefulness, and aggressiveness, especially regarding sexuality, and rejects such traits as sensitivity, which are traditionally considered feminine. Men who exhibit machismo enjoy power and earn the respect of others. *Marianismo* refers to female purity and reflects values that are the opposite of machismo: submission to one's husband and acceptance of his infidelity for the sake of preserving the family. A submissive woman is thus both the object and the proof of a man's authority and power. The term *marianismo* comes from the Virgin Mary—a virgin and a mother—whose life Latin American women are raised to emulate.

Hembrismo and *maternidad* refer to a woman's role as a childbearer. *Hembrismo* implies that a woman is physically vulnerable and that her pregnancy *(maternidad)* is proof of her husband's virility. It also suggests that sex is the means of communication between men and women. *Feminismo,* or femininity, and *maternidad,* or motherhood, are essential to the traditional identity of Latin American women. They are closely associated with the Virgin Mary and together produce the symbol of a perfect woman who suffers all for the sake of her family. Women who are faithful to their families are considered morally superior to men.

Social Dimensions of Gender Roles. These ideas were legalized by *patria potestad,* an ancient Roman law that gave a man power over his family, preserving the patriarchal social order. Men were responsible for the family's economic survival, public conduct, and religious instruction. Thus, a man's position as head of a household was supported and reinforced by laws that preserved male dominance in Latin American society and was reflected in the teachings of the Catholic Church.

A woman's place was in the home, and her primary functions were childbearing and child rearing. Regardless of class or race, women were barred from professions and economic activity outside the home, although some upper-class women worked from their homes, managing property or lending money. Poorer women worked in the TEXTILE INDUSTRY or as domestic servants, peddlers, midwives, prostitutes, or slaves. Some women joined convents, where they could manage their affairs relatively free from male authority. Although they were ultimately under the guidance of priests, nuns enjoyed greater freedom and status than the average Latin American woman. The position of nuns aside, the Catholic Church reinforced traditional gender roles.

* **Iberian** from or related to Spain and Portugal, the countries that occupy Europe's Iberian Peninsula

* **anthropologist** scientist who studies human beings, especially in relation to origins and cultural characteristics

* **archaeologist** scientist who studies past human cultures, usually by excavating ruins

* **patriarchal** ruled or dominated by men

Heroic Women of War

The Latin American wars of independence affected the lives of women of all classes. Fleeing from advancing armies or forced to survive away from their homes, women, inspired by independence, overcame the restrictions placed on them. Gender lines blurred as women served as soldiers, spies, nurses, arms smugglers, writers, and fund-raisers. After independence, however, their efforts were forgotten. The only exception was in Cuba, where women's contributions were legendary and respected. In fact, José Martí, father of Cuban independence, remarked, "With women such as these, it is easy to be heroes."

° **indigenous** referring to the original inhabitants of a region

° **conquistador** Spanish explorer and conqueror

° **clergy** priests and other church officials qualified to perform church ceremonies

° **concubine** woman who lives with a man without being married to him

° **mestizo** person of mixed European and Indian ancestry

° **mulatto** person of mixed black and white ancestry

° **monogamy** having one wife at a time

° **ecclesiastical** relating to a church

Marriage, Sexuality, and Patriarchy in Colonial Times

When the Spanish and Portuguese first arrived in America, they encountered sexual practices that differed widely from their own. Polygamy (the practice of having multiple wives) was common among the INDIANS, and male homosexuality was acceptable behavior among the ARAUCANIANS and INCA. Greatly outnumbered by the indigenous* population, the Iberian conquistadors* used brute force to subdue the Indians and impose their own codes of morality and sexuality.

Marriage and Intermarriage. The first European settlers took Indian women as partners and often as wives. The Spanish and Portuguese monarchs, obsessed with *pureza de sangre,* or racial purity, accepted unofficial unions between Iberians and Indians but hesitated to recognize such marriages as legal. In contrast, the Catholic Church defended all marriages, regardless of race. By the mid-1500s, the church required all marriages to be approved by the Catholic clergy*. By this time, more Spanish women had emigrated to Latin America, and they became the preferred marriage partners for Spanish men. Nevertheless, the Spaniards continued to take Indian and African slave women as concubines*. Iberian men became powerful, aggressive, and sexually promiscuous, and they dominated the Indians, Africans, mestizos*, and mulattos*. Women were subordinate to Iberian men and to men within their own classes and races.

In 1728, in the hope of restricting sexual relations between races and classes, the Spanish crown passed a decree that stated that upper-class Spaniards, military men, and colonial officials were required to obtain official permission to marry outside their race or class. By 1805, all interracial marriages had to be approved by colonial authorities, regardless of the classes of the people involved. Despite these laws, interracial sexual relations continued. The Iberians also had sexual relations with their African slaves who worked on the plantations. African women were forced to become concubines for their Iberian masters, and although marriage was not a possibility, their living standards often improved in such relationships.

Meanwhile, the Catholic Church actively crusaded against promiscuity and sexual relations outside of marriage and promoted chastity and monogamy* among the Indians, mestizos, mulattos, and Africans. The church attacked Indian and African religions, which typically took a more practical and lenient approach to social issues such as infidelity, impotence, or unwanted pregnancies.

Prostitution and Homosexuality. Although condemned by the Catholic Church, prostitution was not uncommon in colonial Latin America. Women who engaged in prostitution belonged to the poorest classes and were generally scorned by society. Matters concerning prostitution were handled by the ecclesiastical* courts, which established correctional facilities to rehabilitate the women, usually nonwhites. Gradually, as the link between promiscuous behavior and sexually transmitted diseases became clear, the church severely reprimanded prostitutes. Male prostitution, on the other hand, was mostly ignored, unless it involved homosexual behavior.

Homosexuals suffered discrimination and violence because of traditional attitudes that favored machismo. During the colonial period, homosexuals were dealt with severely. Their "crimes" were punishable by imprisonment, or auto-da-fé*. During periods of leniency, homosexuals were allowed to live in the poor areas or with prostitutes. They were forbidden to work in the military, to work in public offices, or to hold government jobs.

° **auto-da-fé** death by burning

Gender and Sexuality Since Independence

The WARS OF INDEPENDENCE brought about a revolution in the status of women when they were forced out of their homes to join the men who were fighting against Spain and Portugal. As peace returned toward the end of the 1800s, many countries forgot the role women had played in the conflicts. However, after decades of struggle, women asked for a reevaluation of gender roles and became more militant in their demands for voting rights and equal educational and economic opportunities. Latin Americans also began to demand democratic rights for all, regardless of sex.

Independence promised prosperity and more rights for individuals, but most Latin Americans experienced neither. Men and women became politically active, and social reform movements swept across the region. Often women joined men in opposing repressive governments and policies that perpetuated poverty and injustice, but they rarely attacked the concept of machismo, which was the source of much of society's inequality. Many women believed that promoting better government and reducing corruption would lead to greater rights for women more quickly than emphasizing individual rights and freedoms. Female activists were key players in forcing governments to pass laws that led to gender equality in the home and in the workplace. In 1929, ECUADOR became the first Latin American nation to give the vote to women, and by 1933, URUGUAY, BRAZIL, and CUBA had done so.

Prostitution and Homosexuality Since Independence.
In the 1800s, prostitution came under the authority of the state. As modernization challenged traditional attitudes, prostitution came to be seen as a social, economic, and political problem that negatively affected women. In ARGENTINA, the state set up health clinics for prostitutes and restricted houses of prostitution to certain areas in each city. Former prostitutes were offered respectable jobs. In Cuba, Castro's government believed that eliminating poverty and integrating prostitutes into mainstream society would cause prostitution to disappear. In spite of the programs, prostitution persists in Cuba.

Since the 1800s, gays and lesbians have felt the greatest repression by Latin America's totalitarian* regimes. Homosexuals have rarely been accepted as members of society, although some liberal governments have ignored or neglected them. Gay and lesbian organizations have

° **totalitarian** referring to a government that exercises complete control over individuals, often by force

grown in number and magnitude, and they have united to fight machismo and to create a gay consciousness and identity. However, these organizations have had little success in achieving their objectives because they are generally forced to operate in secrecy to avoid persecution.

Contemporary Gender Relations.   Since World War II, women's rights advocates have been more militant and more willing to attack traditional gender roles. Women fought alongside men in the revolutions that spread across Latin America from 1940 to 1960, but they were frustrated by their unequal treatment at the hands of their male compatriots*. The revolutions inspired feminists to demand their own liberation and to resist efforts to continue treating them as second-class citizens. One result has been the widespread increase of divorce among the middle and upper classes.

° **compatriot** countryman

As political and economic liberalism* grows in the region, the status and role of women, homosexuals, and other suppressed groups will continue to evolve, but most societies remain patriarchal, and Latin Americans' attitudes toward gender roles and sexuality are still very resistant to change. (*See also* **Family; Marriage and Divorce; Suffrage Movement; Women.**)

° **liberalism** state of being liberal, or supporting greater participation in government for individuals; not bound by political and social traditions

Geography

atin America is a vast region, stretching over 6,500 miles, from the desert of northern MEXICO to PATAGONIA and the TIERRA DEL FUEGO archipelago* at the southern tip of South America. It is an area of immense geographical diversity that includes just about every type of climate and ecosystem found on Earth.

The Geography of South America

° **archipelago** group of islands

Three-fourths of South America lies within the tropics, but it also extends farther south than any other continent except Antarctica. Because of this, while some areas remain hot and humid year-round, others have frigid temperatures and even glaciers. Geographically, the continent consists of two distinct parts: the ANDES, along the Pacific coast from Venezuela and Colombia to Cape Horn, and the great river basins and plains that lie to their east.

The Andes.   The Andes mountains run about 4,500 miles down the entire western coast of the continent, from Trinidad to Tierra del Fuego. Many peaks reach heights of more than 20,000 feet, and the range has an average elevation second only to that of the Himalayas in Asia. The Andes, which are relatively young in geological terms, resulted from the collision of continental plates that came together near the Pacific coast. This accounts for their great height and the fact that they are very steep.

The Andes are, however, not one complete chain of mountains but consist of several closely joined structural units. In some places, the

Andes form two or more parallel ranges, divided by valleys or flat plateaus. The largest of these plateaus is the ALTIPLANO of PERU and BOLIVIA, which lies between 12,000 and 15,000 feet above sea level and extends about 125 miles at its widest. In spite of its altitude, the altiplano is very fertile and contains important agricultural lands and pasturage. Water collects in basins on the altiplano to form marshes and lakes, such as Lake TITICACA. Located on the border between Peru and Bolivia, Titicaca is the highest navigable* lake in the world. Farther south, the Andes form a single chain of peaks—including Mount Aconcagua (22,831 feet above sea level), the highest point in the Western Hemisphere—that have been deeply carved by glaciers. Glaciers still occupy more than 1,900 square miles of the mountains, feeding numerous lakes and the sea.

*° **navigable** deep and wide enough to provide passage for ships*

Rivers and River Valleys.   In addition to acting as a barrier between the Pacific coast and the rest of the continent, the Andes are also the source of many of South America's largest rivers. By far, the most important of these rivers is the AMAZON, the largest river system on the continent.

The Amazon rises in the central Peruvian Andes and runs across BRAZIL, about 3,900 miles, before emptying into the Atlantic Ocean. Although the Nile River in Egypt is longer, the Amazon carries more water—one-fifth of all the flowing freshwater in the world. The Amazon empties more than 6 million cubic feet of water into the Atlantic every second. That is more than ten times the outflow of the Mississippi River. The Amazon has more than 1,000 tributaries*, some of which are more than 1,000 miles long, and it drains about 40 percent of South America, more than 2.5 million square miles.

*° **tributary** stream or river that empties into a larger river*

The second-largest river system is formed by the Paraguay, Paraná, and Uruguay rivers, which flow east through the PANTANAL wetlands before emptying into the RÍO DE LA PLATA estuary*. This system drains about 1.6 million square miles and carries a volume of water that is second only to that of the Amazon. The other major Atlantic-flowing rivers are the ORINOCO in Venezuela and the São Francisco in Brazil. Because the Andes are so close to the Pacific, rivers draining into that ocean are shorter and carry much less water. The major Pacific-flowing rivers are the Guayas in Ecuador, the Santa in Peru, and the Aconcagua and Bío-Bío in Chile.

*° **estuary** wide part of a river where it nears the sea*

The Climate of South America.   Because of its geographical features and physical location, South America has a great diversity of climates. The continent falls into four climatic zones: tropical, temperate, arid, and cold. The northern and eastern parts of the continent experience a tropical climate that is hot and moist all year. The Chocó region of Colombia and parts of coastal Brazil average more than 100 inches of rainfall a year, and annual average temperatures are well above 80°F. The savanna region, characterized by high temperatures and lower rainfall, is found in the Orinoco basin, the Brazilian Highlands, and parts of western Ecuador.

Regions south of the Tropic of Capricorn and in the Andes are considered temperate. Paraguay, parts of Brazil, Bolivia, Argentina, and

Chile fall into this type of climate. On the Atlantic side, temperatures average between 77°F and 63°F, while regions in the south experience temperatures from 69°F in the summer to 9°F in the winter. Annual average rainfall is greater in the eastern parts because all the rivers on the eastern slopes of the Andes flow eastward. Thus, rain that falls only 100 miles from the Pacific coast is carried to the Atlantic, more than 2,500 miles away. However, in central South America, the high Andes prevent the moisture from the ocean from reaching the areas immediately to the east.

As a result, Patagonia, northwestern Argentina, and parts of the PAMPAS, which lie to the east of the Andes, receive little rainfall and are typically arid. Moreover, temperature fluctuations are great. Arid climates are also found to the north, near Peru, where the proximity of the Andes to cold ocean waters creates an almost continuous blanket of low clouds that block the sunshine for at least six months of the year. Other arid regions are the Atacama Desert—one of the driest places on Earth—and the deserts in northeastern Colombia and Venezuela. The southernmost parts of Argentina and Chile and regions in the high Andes are characterized by a cold climate. The annual average temperatures are low, about 50°F, and the rainfall is evenly distributed. These regions also experience sharp, violent winds that intensify the cold.

The Geography of Mexico, Central America, and the Caribbean

Mexico has a less diverse geography and climate than South America, but it features a combination of landscapes dominated by a desert in the north and tropical forests in the south. Central America and the Caribbean islands show the least geographical variation in the region.

Mexico. Northern Mexico is located in one of the world's great desert regions, where the terrain is dry and lacking in rivers or other sources of irrigation. The most important river in the area is the Rio Grande, which forms the border between Mexico and Texas. In the middle of the country, and stretching from the United States border to the area around Mexico City, lies the Mexican plateau. This is an area of high plateaus—4,000 to 8,000 feet high—separated by outcrops of mountains. The northern plateau region is quite dry, but toward the south, the climate becomes wetter and the soil more fertile. At the center of this plateau lies the Mesa Central, called Mexico's breadbasket because it is where most of the country's crops are grown.

Mexico's central plateau is separated from the Atlantic coast by the mountain range called the Sierra Madre Oriental and from the Pacific coast by the Sierra Madre Occidental. The Sierra Madre Oriental is the lower of the two ranges, averaging 8,000 to 9,000 feet in height, and sloping gently toward the Atlantic. The Atlantic coastal plain is about 100 miles wide near the United States border, but farther south, the mountains reach the sea. The Sierra Madre Occidental is higher and lies much closer to the coast. The Pacific coast is thus much narrower and has a more rugged coastline. In the southeast, the state of Chiapas,

See map in Mexico (vol. 3).

which extends from the Central American mountains, is covered by forests and surrounded by high valleys. North of Chiapas, the terrain flattens toward the YUCATÁN peninsula, a heavily forested area that seldom rises to more than 500 feet above sea level.

Central America. Central America stretches from southern Mexico to South America and includes the nations of Belize, Costa Rica, El Salvador, Guatemala, Honduras, Nicaragua, and Panama. The region lies at the meeting point of two continental plates that constantly move against each other, producing steep mountain ranges. These rugged ranges form the backbone of Central America and consist of mountains, plateaus, and valleys. The region experiences frequent seismic activity, such as EARTHQUAKES and volcanic eruptions. With more than half of its 40 volcanoes still active, Central America contains the Americas' most active volcanic belt. The mountain highlands have a moderate climate. More than three-fourths of the region's population and most of the major cities are found in the *tierra templada,* or temperate land, located at an altitude of between 3,300 and 6,500 feet. The highlands are also the agricultural center because of the fertile volcanic soils. Streams originating in the highlands flow swiftly into the Pacific and more slowly into the Caribbean.

On either side of the mountains, the coastal plains are narrow and shadowed by steep ranges. The weather is warm and humid, and the area is sparsely inhabited. The highlands and the coastal plains experience a wet season in the summer and a drier season during the winter, although the difference is more noticeable in the north. The Pacific plains receive less rainfall than the Caribbean coast and thus experience a longer dry season.

See map in Central America (vol. I).

The Caribbean. The Caribbean islands fall into two distinct geographical groups. The southern islands are small and rocky, and the nearby South American mainland prevents much rainfall from reaching them. As a result the climate is dry, the land is barren, and drought is common. The geography of the northern islands of CUBA, JAMAICA, HISPANIOLA, and PUERTO RICO is more diverse, featuring a mixture of mountains, plains, and beaches. The climate is much wetter, with abundant rainfall producing much more fertile land. (*See also* **Climate and Vegetation.**)

See map in Caribbean Antilles (vol. I).

Germans in Latin America

Germans played a modest role in the European settlement of Latin America. German colonists initially formed separate Germanic communities, but over time, they ended their isolation and became integrated within larger Latin American society.

German Presence Before 1900. Germans first came to Latin America in the early 1500s. Emperor Charles V had borrowed heavily from the Welser Bank in the city of Augsburg and was looking for a way to repay the money he owed. In 1528, he offered the Welsers a concession* in

* **concession** grant of land or property, usually for a specific purpose or in return for something else

German Criminals of War

In his book titled *Aftermath: Martin Bormann and the Fourth Reich* (1974), Ladislas Farago reports on many prominent German criminals who settled in South America after World War II. Among them was Josef Mengele, the notorious doctor from Auschwitz who performed gruesome experiments on concentration camp inmates and who later settled in Paraguay. In 1973, Farago also met with Martin Bormann, secretary to Adolf Hitler and the highest-ranking Nazi known to be alive. Bormann had just moved from Chile to Bolivia to Argentina, where he was enjoying the hospitality and protection of President Juan Perón.

° **nationalism** devotion to the interests and culture of one's country

° **deport** to expel a foreigner from a country

° **assimilate** to adopt the beliefs or customs of a society

VENEZUELA. The following year, the first German settlers arrived in Latin America and settled at Coro in northwestern Venezuela. However, the Germans mistreated the INDIANS and the colony failed to prosper. In 1548, Charles revoked the Welser Bank of Augsburg's concession.

German involvement in Latin America remained minimal until the WARS OF INDEPENDENCE during the early 1800s. At this time, German traders provided arms and shipping to Latin American rebels seeking to overthrow Spanish rule. By the mid-1800s, both BRAZIL and CHILE were recruiting German colonists to settle the frontier. Settling far from the mainstream population, these colonists created communities with a strong German flavor. The settlements were small and composed of well-to-do merchants, professionals, and many who worked for the government in EDUCATION and public service. Germans also served as military advisers in Chile, ARGENTINA, and BOLIVIA. Some Germans founded or joined agricultural communities in southern Brazil, Chile, Argentina, URUGUAY, and PARAGUAY. In GUATEMALA, they became prominent coffee producers. However, in spite of their involvement in state affairs and agricultural unions, the German colonists remained largely separated from the non-German population.

German Presence Since 1900. During WORLD WAR I, anti-German feelings surfaced in Argentina and Brazil. Rioters destroyed German-owned properties and attacked Germans. After the war, German IMMIGRATION into Latin America resumed. When the Nazis came to power in Germany in the 1930s, they rallied the support of these immigrants to stimulate German nationalism* and create an illusion of a worldwide German community. This resulted in armed uprisings and plots in South America, implicating the Nazis. Concerned about security, many countries, especially Brazil, restricted the freedom of German schools, churches, newspapers, and other institutions. When World War II broke out, many German businesses were forced to close, their property was seized, and many individuals were deported*.

After the war, many Germans once again settled in Latin America, despite United States attempts to prevent their immigration. Among the immigrants were scientists and technicians who greatly aided the industrialization of Latin America. These newcomers, especially those with a history of war crimes, were less inclined to draw attention to themselves by living apart from the native population. Since 1945, most Germans in Latin America have become assimilated* into mainstream society, and today only a few scattered German-speaking communities exist in Paraguay, Uruguay, and Chile.

Gold and Silver

*T*he pursuit of riches motivated the earliest Spanish explorers of Latin America. The explorers believed they would find this wealth by sailing west to reach the spices and silks of the Orient. Instead, they arrived at a new world whose riches of gold and silver profoundly affected the conquistadors*, the Indians, and much of the world.

° **conquistador** Spanish explorer and conqueror

° **indigenous** referring to the original inhabitants of a region

° **mestizo** person of mixed European and Indian ancestry

° **captaincy** governmental system established by the Portuguese monarchy for the settlement and colonization of Brazil

Gardens in Gold

In his commentaries, historian Garcilaso de la Vega described the extent and beauty of Inca wealth in great detail. He depicted the temple enclosures as "garden[s] of gold and silver as might be seen in the royal palaces of the kings." The plants, animals, pots, jars, fruits, and vegetables were all made of gold or silver. In the orchards of royal homes, where the Inca relaxed, decorative trees and plants were made of gold and silver and were adorned with fruits, flowers, and leaves. Birds and bird baths in gold and silver were also found in these orchards. He wrote that Peruvian gold was the finest, "with a fineness of twenty-four carats and ... even purer."

The Discovery of "El Dorado."   Indigenous* civilizations mined gold and silver long before the arrival of the first Europeans. Cultures from Mexico to Argentina used these precious metals for several purposes—to make masks and utensils; to decorate tools, jewelry, and adornments; and to signify rank. Spanish encounters with this native wealth was perhaps the greatest motivation for the continued exploration of Latin America. Discovery of precious artifacts among the AZTECS in Mexico, the Chibchas in Colombia, and the INCA in Peru contributed to the legend of Spanish America as El Dorado—the land of gold. Spanish explorers soon arrived in Latin America in search of these glittering treasures of the earth.

Although they obtained much gold from their new colonies, the Spaniards found silver in larger and more profitable amounts. By 1600, Spanish settlers had identified the main silver-producing areas in Latin America: the central ANDES (in present-day southern PERU and western BOLIVIA) and central and northern MEXICO. The silver ore in some of these places was located at high altitudes (up to 16,000 feet in the Andes) and required a considerable amount of labor to extract. In the Andes, the Spaniards used mostly Indian labor to extract the ore, believing that the Indians were accustomed to doing difficult manual labor in the oxygen-thin air at such heights. However, in Mexico, the Spanish employed wage laborers, who were often mestizos*.

Spain benefited greatly from the mining activities in America. Between 1560 and 1810, the Spanish monarchy recovered some 75,000 to 90,000 tons of silver from American mines. Gold and silver transformed Spain into a world power and financed the struggle against Protestantism in the Netherlands and England. Yet, despite this wealth, Spain was heavily in debt to foreigners and mortgaged silver shipments for years in advance by the mid-1600s.

Riches in Brazil.   Early Portuguese explorers found some gold in BRAZIL, but it was not until 1690 that they discovered major deposits. The gold rush of 1690 was centered in the southeastern part of Brazil, which became known as MINAS GERAIS, or General Mines. Most of the gold was found in rivers and streams or in land deposits close to the surface, making it easy to recover. Settlers flocked to the area, bringing African slaves to work their claims. By 1720, Minas Gerais was the most populous captaincy* in Brazil, and its population was mostly black. During the 1700s, Brazil produced more than 25 million ounces of gold, three-quarters of which was mined in Minas Gerais.

Gold transformed Portugal and Brazil the way silver had transformed Spain. SUGAR, once the main source of revenue in Brazil, declined in importance, and the center of the colony shifted from the northeast to the southeast. RIO DE JANEIRO went from a sleepy backwater town to the country's most important city almost overnight. Because colonial gold made the Portuguese crown less dependent upon support from the nobility, it became much more powerful and domineering.

Gold and Silver Since Independence.   The gold- and silver-rich countries in Latin America experienced a slump in production after

169

Magnificent works of gold and silver, such as this golden funeral mask, were created by pre-Colombian Indians. These artifacts led to the legend of "El Dorado" (The Land of Gold) and motivated many explorers to seek their fortunes in the Americas.

gaining independence in the early 1800s. By 1900, the industry had recovered and was expanding. Although mining for base metals such as COPPER and TIN has become more important to most Latin American countries, gold and silver still produce wealth for the region. Mexico and Peru remain two of the world's leading producers of silver, and gold mining has become an important activity in Venezuela, Chile, Ecuador, Costa Rica, and Honduras. (*See also* **Captaincy System; Mining; Potosí.**)

Gómez, Juan Vicente

1857–1935
President and dictator of Venezuela

Juan Vicente Gómez is credited with creating the modern nation-state of VENEZUELA. During his 27 years in power, he ended internal struggles, established a strong central government, and stabilized the economy by the wise use of Venezuela's PETROLEUM reserves. Gómez is one of the major figures in the political history of modern Venezuela.

Gómez was a butcher and cattle rancher until 1892, when he joined an ill-fated political movement led by Cipriano Castro. The group was forced into exile in Colombia but returned in 1899 to take power in Venezuela. Gómez played a major role in defeating groups who rose against Castro's rule, and he won support from both the military and the civilian population. In 1908, Castro went to Europe for medical treatment and named Gómez acting president. Gómez, taking advantage of Castro's absence, proclaimed himself president of Venezuela. He was supported by Castro's enemies, who thought they could control

° **regime** prevailing political system or rule

Gómez, and by foreign powers that had been poorly treated by the Castro regime*. The United States enjoyed particularly friendly relations with Gómez's government.

Gómez brought strong economic and political discipline to Venezuela. He encouraged FOREIGN INVESTMENT in the nation's petroleum industry by lowering TAXES on foreign companies and allowing them to hold unlimited amounts of Venezuelan land. His policies permitted the industry to develop rapidly, and he used the money from petroleum sales to build the national economy. He improved the collection of local taxes and cut government spending, and by the mid-1920s, Venezuela had no public debt. His economic policies also enabled him to begin construction of nationwide transportation and communication systems. In 1910, Gómez established a military academy to reform Venezuela's armed forces, and he raised salaries to attract qualified officers. By creating a professional army, he brought peace to a country that had been torn by fighting between rival groups seeking power.

Like most dictators, Gómez has been criticized for imprisoning and torturing his opponents and enriching himself and his friends at the public's expense. However, in recent years, Venezuelan scholars have begun to give him more credit for his economic and political achievements. Despite his abuses, many feel that, without him, Venezuela would have remained a divided nation dependent upon an unstable agricultural economy. Gómez died in Maracay, Venezuela. (*See also* **Dictatorships, Military.**)

Gómez y Báez, Máximo

1836–1905
Revolutionary leader

Máximo Gómez y Báez was a prominent military leader in the wars for Cuban independence in the late 1800s. He was born in SANTO DOMINGO and began his military career at age 16, fighting in the war against Haiti. In the civil war in Santo Domingo in 1866, Gómez lost all his property, and he fled to Cuba. When the TEN YEARS' WAR began in 1868, Gómez joined the rebel forces and became a close associate of rebel leaders Antonio MACEO and Calixto García. Together they believed that the revolution could not succeed without an expansion into Cuba's wealthy western sugar-growing provinces. In 1872, they marched west, burning PLANTATIONS and freeing slaves, thinking that the damage to Cuba's economic base would bring a quick rebel victory. However, they suffered heavy casualties and were forced to abandon the campaign due to a lack of supplies. When the war ended in 1878, Gómez was forced into exile.

While in exile, Gómez and Maceo joined forces with José MARTÍ, Cuban independence leader, to plan a second revolution. Gómez became the military commander of the Cuban Revolutionary Party, and in 1895, the men renewed the Cuban Revolution. Martí was killed shortly afterward, and Gómez became the commander in chief of the rebel movement. He banned sugar production, threatening to kill anyone who violated his orders. Cuba's economy was badly affected, but his tactics helped the rebels move into the cities of Matanzas and Havana by 1897. A Spanish counterattack the following year left the rebels seriously weakened, but the United States entered the war later in 1898 and ended Spanish resistance. When the United States withdrew from Cuba in 1902, the Republic of Cuba was created, and Gómez was urged to run for president. He declined, however, saying, "Men of war for war, and those of peace for peace." (*See also* **Spanish-American War; Wars of Independence.**)

Good Neighbor Policy

* **expropriate** to take forcibly
* **nationalize** to bring land, industries, or public works under state control or ownership

The Good Neighbor Policy was initiated by the United States government to improve relations with Latin America in the 1930s and 1940s. The policy, which went into effect during the administration of President Franklin Roosevelt, pledged that the United States would not interfere in Latin America's internal politics. In keeping with its pledge, the United States declined to send troops to CUBA during the Cuban crisis in 1933. Instead, Roosevelt sent Assistant Secretary of State Sumner Welles to negotiate an arrangement that allowed Fulgencio BATISTA to gain control in Cuba. The following year, Welles went to Panama to draft a new PANAMA CANAL treaty that appeased Panamanians and preserved United States interests there. In 1938, Roosevelt refused to join the oil companies in condemning Mexican president Lázaro CÁRDENAS for expropriating* United States–owned property and nationalizing* the country's PETROLEUM INDUSTRY. Roosevelt's actions were rewarded in 1942, when Mexico and the United States created a wartime alliance against Germany and its allies in World War II.

The Good Neighbor Policy restored United States trade with Latin America and helped the United States form a united economic and political front in the Western Hemisphere against Nazi Germany. Gradually, Latin America's commitment to a united hemisphere increased. After Japan attacked Pearl Harbor in 1941, efforts to present a unified front were stepped up, and the United States created the position of coordinator of inter-American affairs to promote understanding between the United States and Latin America. Despite the successes of the Good Neighbor Policy, United States efforts to oppose COMMUNISM after the war led to new interventions in Latin America and destroyed much of the goodwill that had been established. (*See also* **Inter-American Relations; United States–Latin American Relations; World Wars I and II.**)

Government, Local

See *Alcalde; Cabildo; Senado da Câmera.*

Gran Colombia

Gran Colombia was created when the Viceroyalty* of NEW GRANADA declared its independence from Spain in 1819. Although the country was originally called the Republic of Colombia, it later became known as Gran Colombia to distinguish it from modern-day COLOMBIA. It included the present-day countries of Colombia, VENEZUELA, ECUADOR, and PANAMA. In 1821, Gran Colombia

° **viceroyalty** region governed by a viceroy, a royally appointed official

See color plate 5, vol. 3.

adopted a formal constitution, even though Ecuador was not fully liberated at the time. By 1822, the Spanish were overthrown in Ecuador, which then became a part of Gran Colombia.

The creation of Gran Colombia was facilitated by Simón Bolívar, whose armies moved back and forth across the region during their campaign to liberate South America from Spain in the early 1800s. However, Gran Colombia was a weak union because of its vast size, the inadequacy of its transportation, and the lack of strong social, cultural, and economic ties among the regions. Rifts in the territory became obvious soon after independence, when Venezuela staged a revolt in 1826. In 1830, Ecuador and Venezuela formed their own separate republics, leaving Colombia and Panama to form the Republic of New Granada. Even after the breakup, the nations that were once a part of Gran Colombia continued to observe laws and regulations passed by the Republic of New Granada. They even kept the national colors of Gran Colombia (red, yellow, and blue) in their flags and continued to worship Bolívar as a hero. (*See also* **Wars of Independence.**)

Grenada

Grenada lies in the Caribbean Sea and consists of three small islands: Grenada proper, Carriacou, and Petit-Martinique. Located in the southern portion of the Windward Islands, Grenada was once an important sugar-growing country. Today its main industry is tourism.

Colonial History. The original inhabitants of Grenada were the Caribs, indigenous* people who fiercely resisted European settlement. In 1654, the last Caribs on the island committed suicide to avoid capture by French colonists. The French, who ruled for more than a century, brought African slaves to Grenada to grow sugar, which became the island's leading industry. Today the descendants of the slaves make up most of the island's population. The French also introduced the Roman Catholic faith, which remains the island's chief religion. When the British took control of Grenada in 1783, the slave population increased and their treatment worsened. In 1795, a mulatto* named Julien Fedon led a revolt to restore French rule. The uprising initiated a massive slave rebellion that took the British more than a year to put down.

When slavery was abolished in 1838, Grenadian plantation owners switched from cultivating sugar to growing cacao* and spices, particularly nutmeg. (Grenada has since remained one the world's leading producers of nutmeg.) By the late-1800s, Grenada's growing middle class began to resent the power of the British crown and the plantation owners. They demanded a voice in the government and gradually won more freedoms. By 1933, trade unions were legalized in the cities, but farmworkers were still poor and had no political power. In 1950, Eric Gairy, a trade union organizer, formed an agricultural union and founded a political party to represent the interests of farmworkers. He led a series of violent, yet successful, strikes that forced large landowners

° **indigenous** referring to the original inhabitants of a region

° **mulatto** person of mixed black and white ancestry

° **cacao** bean from which chocolate is made

to improve the working conditions on their plantations. However, Gairy gradually lost touch with his supporters as he became more concerned with promoting his popularity with the British colonial authorities and the Grenadian elite. Still, most Grenadians preferred the corrupt Gairy to his main rival, Herbert Blaize, who fought for the interests of the upper classes. When the New Jewel Movement (NJM) was formed in 1973 to represent those in the countryside, Gairy sent his militant Mongoose Gang to terrorize NJM supporters.

Grenada Since Independence.　In 1974, Grenada won its independence from Britain, and Gairy became prime minister. He soon established a dictatorship, but in 1979, he was overthrown by Maurice Bishop and the NJM. Now known as the People's Revolutionary Government, the NJM promoted education and health reforms. However, power had switched from one dictator to another; Bishop refused to hold elections, banned opposition newspapers, and arrested his political opponents. On October 19, 1983, Bishop and some of his close advisers were executed by his deputy, Bernard Coard. Six days later, troops from the United States and other Caribbean countries invaded Grenada and deposed* Coard. The following year, Herbert Blaize was elected prime minister. During his regime, Grenada developed close relations with the United States, received substantial aid from U.S. President Ronald Reagan, and expanded its thriving tourism industry. Blaize died in 1989 and was replaced by Nicholas Braithwaite in 1990. Although Braithwaite's government was less conservative* and more popular with Grenadians, he failed to improve the country's economy. Braithwaite resigned in 1995. In the elections that followed, the New National Party (NNP) led by Keith Mitchell came to power. Mitchell declared that his government would abolish the income tax. However, Grenada's economy continues to be plagued by problems, and the country relies greatly on aid from the United States. (*See also* **Geography; United States–Latin American Relations.**)

° **depose** to remove from office

° **conservative** inclined to maintain existing political and social views, conditions, and institutions

Grenadines

See *British West Indies.*

Gringo

*G*ringo is a slang term used in MEXICO, usually in a negative sense, to refer to Anglo-Americans or English speakers. Elsewhere in Latin America, the term is also used to refer to someone who speaks Spanish poorly. The origin of the term *gringo* is uncertain. According to one folk legend, the term may have originated during the MEXICAN-AMERICAN WAR, when Mexicans heard United States soldiers singing the popular song "Green Grow the Lilacs." Another opinion suggests that the word may be a corruption of the Spanish word *griego*, meaning "Greek"—the idea being that gringos spoke a strange language that the Mexicans could not understand—as in the expression "It's Greek to me."

Several related terms are also used in Latin America to refer to speakers of English, including *Anglo* and *yanqui*. The latter is the Spanish form of the word *Yankee,* which became popular before and during the American Civil War. Used by residents of the southern United States, Yankee referred to those who lived in the north, particularly in New England.

Guadalupe, Virgin of

° **mantle** loose, sleeveless cloak

$\mathcal{T}$he Virgin of Guadalupe is the patron saint of MEXICO and is also revered throughout the rest of LATIN AMERICA. According to legend, the Virgin Mary appeared to Mexican peasant Juan Diego at Tepeyac, a hill north of MEXICO CITY in December 1531. The Virgin instructed Diego to erect a church on the site, but the bishop of Mexico demanded to see proof of the Virgin's request before consenting to build the church. Diego appealed to the Virgin, who told him to gather roses from the hill in his mantle* and take them to the bishop. When Diego opened the rose-filled mantle before the bishop, the

According to legend, the image of the Virgin Mary appeared before a Mexican peasant in 1531 calling herself the Holy Mother of Guadalupe. Today images of the Virgin of Guadalupe, such as the one shown here, can be found throughout Mexico, where she is the patron saint.

Mother-Goddess of Mexico

Some believe that the Virgin who appeared to Juan Diego reflected Aztec religious traditions. Diego claimed that she called herself Tlecuauhtlacupeuh—or She Who Comes Flying from the Lake Like an Eagle of Fire. According to Aztec religious tradition, the gods lived in a region of light, and the eagle was a sign from the gods. The Virgin also identified herself as Tequantlaxopeuh—or She Who Banishes Those Who Ate Us. Some conquered Mexicans believed that the vision of the mother-goddess came to comfort them and bring them hope after their conquest by the Spanish.

Virgin's image was imprinted on the cloth. A cloak bearing an image of the Virgin, believed to be Diego's mantle, hangs above the altar in the Basilica de Guadalupe at the foot of the hill at Tepeyac.

The historical basis for the legend is weak. A chapel existed at Tepeyac as early as 1556, but the story of the Virgin was first made popular by Miguel Sánchez in 1648. The sources for Sánchez's tale are vague, and the story is probably a cult* legend dating from the early 1600s. Since then, the devotion of Guadalupe has had a major social, cultural, and political influence on Mexico. The Spanish rulers saw it as a sign of divine favor, and the legend soon spread throughout the empire. The devotion became popular across all boundaries, social classes, and races in Latin America. During Mexico's struggle for independence, the Virgin was used as a symbol of national liberation by revolutionary leaders. The Virgin of Guadalupe was named patroness* of Latin America in 1910. In 1945, Pope Pius XII called her the Queen of Mexico and Empress of the Americas.

° **cult** system of religious beliefs and rituals not officially approved by mainstream faiths; group following these beliefs

° **patroness** woman who supports or protects a person or a group of people; usually a saint or a religious figure associated with a particular place

Guadalupe Hidalgo, Treaty of

° **ratify** to give formal approval

° **cede** to yield or surrender, usually by treaty

The Treaty of Guadalupe Hidalgo is an agreement between the United States and Mexico that ended the MEXICAN-AMERICAN WAR, which had been fought from 1846 to 1848. The treaty transferred an enormous piece of Mexican territory to the United States and established the boundary between the two nations.

In 1848, after nearly two years of bitter fighting, representatives from the United States and Mexico met in the town of Guadalupe Hidalgo near Mexico City to sign a peace treaty. The agreement was signed on February 2 of that year and was ratified* by the United States and Mexican governments shortly thereafter. The treaty took effect on May 30, 1848.

By the terms of the treaty, Mexico agreed to cede* to the United States more than 525,000 square miles of land in the SPANISH BORDERLANDS, which included all or parts of the present-day states of California, Texas, Nevada, Arizona, New Mexico, Utah, and Colorado. In return, the United States agreed to pay Mexico $15 million as compensation for losses that Mexicans had suffered during the war. The treaty established the Rio Grande as the boundary between the two nations, and it guaranteed that the United States government would police its side of the border to prevent Indian raids on settlements in Mexico. It also promised to grant United States citizenship to the Mexicans living in the newly acquired United States territory and to protect their civil and property rights. The treaty further declared that Mexico and the United States would settle any future disputes peacefully. The U.S. Senate deleted Article X, which specifically promised that the United States would recognize and protect land grants.

Many historians note that the United States did not fully honor the terms of the Treaty of Guadalupe Hidalgo that pertain to the civil and property rights of Mexicans and CHICANOS (people of Mexican ancestry born in the United States). Over the years, the U.S. Congress and courts allowed many American ranchers and businessmen to seize land owned by Mexicans and Chicanos. In addition, Mexicans and Chicanos living in the territory were generally treated as second-class citizens.

The Treaty of Guadalupe Hidalgo remains in effect. During the 1900s, various disputes have arisen between the United States and Mexico over water rights and property rights along sections of the border. These disagreements have been settled peacefully through negotiation, according to the terms of the treaty. (*See also* **Boundary Disputes; United States–Mexico Border; United States–Latin American Relations.**)

Guadeloupe

See *French West Indies.*

Guaman Poma de Ayala, Felipe

ca. 1535–ca. 1615
Peruvian writer

° **indigenous** referring to the original inhabitants of a region

° **colonial** period between the European conquest and independence, generally from the early 1500s to the early 1800s

Felipe Guaman Poma de Ayala is one of the most admired indigenous* South American writers of the colonial* period. Although very little is known about his life, he probably was born in San Cristóbal de Suntunto, a small village in PERU, and lived for a time in CUZCO, the ancient capital of the INCA. He was educated in Spanish language and culture—perhaps by missionaries—and was also well versed in Quechua, his native language.

Around 1570, Guaman Poma served as an interpreter for the Spaniards during their campaigns in the ANDES. He may also have worked in LIMA, the Spanish colonial capital, where he became familiar with the writings of major Spanish historical and religious authors. These works, together with Indian oral tradition and Guaman Poma's own experiences, became the sources of his book *Primer nueva corónica y bien gobierno.* This extensive history is more than 1,000 pages long and contains 398 illustrations. In it, Guaman Poma chronicles ancient Andean times and life under both Inca and Spanish rule. He also criticizes colonial administration and offers a plan for "good government" to the Spanish king.

Primer nueva corónica is an important source of information on the history of the Andean region before the Spanish conquest and during the first decades of Spanish colonization. It is especially notable because it presents a native Andean version of history and of the cultural clash between the Spanish and indigenous populations. (*See also* **Literature.**)

Guano Industry

Guano is the dried excrement of seabirds. An excellent natural fertilizer, such bird droppings were PERU's main export product in the 1800s. When other types of fertilizer replaced guano toward the end of the 1800s, the industry fell into decline. The guano industry is a classic example of the boom-and-bust export experience that many Latin American nations have undergone.

Over the centuries, the seabirds that nested on the small islands off the southern coast of Peru deposited enormous quantities of guano there. In some places, these accumulations were hundreds of feet thick. Although the early Peruvian Indians used guano extensively as an

* **monopoly** exclusive control or domination of a particular type of business

* **inflation** sharp increase in prices due to an increase in the amount of money or credit relative to available goods and services

* **nitrate** mineral used in making gunpowder and fertilizer

agricultural fertilizer, the Spanish colonists rarely used it. However, in the early 1840s, when Europeans realized how effective guano was as a fertilizer, the substance suddenly acquired great value as an international export product.

Between 1841 and 1879, guano became Peru's most important export product. In those four decades, roughly 11.5 million tons of Peruvian guano were shipped to Britain, France, the United States, and other nations, bringing Peru about $750 million in revenue. Because of the product's economic value, Peru declared a national monopoly* over guano in 1841 and resisted efforts to open up the guano trade in the years that followed.

While the guano industry greatly benefited the economy of Peru, it took a toll on the people who mined the fertilizer. The extraction of guano was a primitive and oppressive business. Guano can be a toxic, or poisonous, substance if too much enters a person's lungs. Convicts, Chinese laborers, and other workers toiled under horrible conditions, digging up the guano by hand and hauling it by wheelbarrow to cargo ships.

While the use of guano increased the productivity of many European and United States crops, the enormous revenues generated by the guano industry revitalized Peru's economy and strengthened the nation's position in the world market. It also brought great wealth for a small minority of Peruvians. This wealth enabled Peru to stabilize its government and reduce political conflicts among the ruling classes. The majority of Peruvians, however, suffered from the effects of inflation*, increased dependence on expensive European imports, and political neglect.

In the long run, the guano industry did little to create sustained economic growth in Peru. Instead, dependence on this one industry increased the vulnerability of the Peruvian economy. In the 1870s, the guano industry fell into a rapid decline because of competition from other fertilizers. The collapse of the industry struck a devastating blow to the Peruvian economy and contributed to a political and social crisis. To make matters worse, from 1879 to 1884, Peru and CHILE went to war for control of another natural fertilizer—nitrates*, which were discovered in the Atacama Desert region of northern Chile and southern Peru. Peru's defeat in this WAR OF THE PACIFIC hurt the country further.

Over the years, the guano industry produced significant short-term gains for Peru. But its long-term effects on the nation were a weakened economy and a fragmented society—troubles that have persisted to the present day. (*See also* **Economic Development; Nitrate Industry; Trade and Commerce.**)

Guarani War

*T*he Guarani War was a series of armed engagements between combined Spanish and Portuguese forces and the GUARANI Indians in the region of present-day URUGUAY. The event that sparked the war occurred in 1750, when Spain and Portugal signed the Treaty of MADRID. This agreement gave Spain an important Portuguese settlement near the RÍO DE LA PLATA in exchange for a large wedge of Spanish territory east of the Uruguay River—an area that contained

° **mission** settlement started by Catholic priests whose purpose was to convert local people to Christianity

° **Jesuit** Roman Catholic religious order known as the Society of Jesus; also, a member of that order

See map in Uruguay (vol. 4).

several Guarani missions* run by the Jesuits*. The Guaranis strongly opposed the transfer of their lands to the Portuguese, who often raided Guarani territory to capture and enslave the Indians. The Guaranis resisted Spanish and Jesuit orders to leave their communities and organized a military defense led by a Guarani official named Sepé Tiarayú.

By the time the war began in 1753, the Guaranis were well prepared. In February 1754, the Indians captured the Portuguese fort of Santo Amaro. The following July, the Europeans launched a campaign to cut off the flow of supplies to the Indians. After four months of bloody resistance, several Guarani leaders surrendered. However, Sepé Tiarayú secured the aid of the Charrúa Indians, and the fighting continued.

Toward the end of 1755, a merciless European campaign against the Guaranis killed many Indians—including Sepé Tiarayú, who was replaced by a less-admired leader, Nicolís Ñeenguirú. On February 10, 1756, the Spanish and Portuguese surrounded the Indians during a major battle at Caaybaté. Ñeenguirú tried to negotiate, but the Europeans continued fighting. Although sporadic combat continued for several months, the battle at Caaybaté broke the main Indian resistance. Some Guaranis fled into the jungles and swamps, where they lived in isolation for decades. In the 1760s, the disputed territory was restored to Spain.

Guaranis

See map in Paraguay (vol. 3).

° *encomienda* right granted to a conqueror that enabled him to control the labor of and collect payment from an Indian community

° **mestizo** person of mixed European and Indian ancestry

° **mission** settlement started by Catholic priests whose purpose was to convert local people to Christianity

° **Jesuit** Roman Catholic religious order known as the Society of Jesus; also, a member of that order

*T*he Guarani Indians lived in the southeastern region of present-day PARAGUAY, between the Paraná and Paraguay rivers. Today, most of the people of Paraguay are descendants of the Guaranis, and many Paraguayan peasants speak a language based on that of the Indians.

Before contact with Europeans in the early 1500s, the Guarani population numbered about 300,000 and was organized into 14 subgroups called Guarás. They moved often to find fertile land for farming such crops as sweet potatoes and MAIZE. They also hunted and fished.

In the 1530s, the Guaranis sought an alliance with the early Spanish conquerors and settlers in order to strengthen their efforts against an enemy tribe, the Payaguá, who dominated the Paraguay River. Guarani chiefs gave women to the Spaniards to serve as wives or mistresses, believing that they would then regard the Guaranis as equals. The Guaranis also provided labor to the Spanish in exchange for iron tools. But eventually, the Guaranis realized that the Spaniards considered them inferior. As a result, some Guaranis revolted against the Spanish in 1545. This and later rebellions were unsuccessful, partly because many Guaranis continued to ally themselves with the Spaniards.

In 1556, Paraguay's governor, Domingo Martínez de Irala, attempted to limit the exploitation of the Indians by introducing an *encomienda** system that regulated Guarani labor. During this period, unions between Guarani women and Spanish men began to produce a mestizo* population and a distinct Paraguayan culture, both of which remain key features of modern Paraguay.

After 1610, some of the more remote groups of Guaranis joined missions* run by the Jesuits*. The missions provided them with a steady

source of Spanish supplies and some security from the Portuguese slave raiders, who came from nearby BRAZIL to capture and enslave Indians. In the mid-1700s, Spain's attempt to give the territory around these missions to the Portuguese led to the GUARANI WAR, fought from 1753 to 1756. When the Jesuits were expelled from Paraguay around 1767, many of the Guaranis who still lived in the missions relocated to northern Argentina, Uruguay, and western Brazil.

In 1848, the government of Paraguay granted citizenship to the Guaranis, which reduced some of the discrimination against them. However, citizenship also required them to serve in the military, and their formerly protected lands were made available for sale—leaving many of the Guaranis landless. In the 1900s, a few isolated bands of Guaranis in the forests of northeastern Paraguay continued to live as they had for centuries. However, the most important and lasting influence of the Guaranis lies in the Guarani-based Paraguayan language and in their cultural heritage, which is proudly preserved by the Paraguayan people. (*See also* **Encomienda; Missions.**)

Guatemala

° **pre-Columbian** before the arrival of Christopher Columbus and other Europeans in the Americas in the 1490s

° **conquistador** Spanish explorer and conqueror

° **captain-general** title of provincial rulers in colonial Latin America whose main duty was the military defense of a territory

Guatemala is the most populous nation in CENTRAL AMERICA. It is bordered on the north and west by Mexico, on the northeast by Belize and the CARIBBEAN SEA, on the east by Honduras and El Salvador, and on the south by the Pacific Ocean. Inhabited in pre-Columbian* times by the MAYA, Guatemala remains heavily populated by Indian peoples and influenced by their culture.

The Colonial Period

Spanish conquistadors* came to the region now called Guatemala in the early 1500s, searching for gold and silver. Led by Pedro de ALVARADO Y MESÍA, the Spaniards conquered the area around 1523. Alvarado was then named captain-general* of a region centered in Guatemala that included most of Central America.

Beginning in 1542, the region became part of various AUDIENCIAS—Spanish colonial administrative districts. Guatemala was first included in the Audiencia de los Confines, which stretched from the YUCATÁN in the north to Panama in the south, and in 1548, Guatemala's main city, La Antigua Guatemala, became the administrative center of this *audiencia*. In the 1560s, Spain abolished the Audiencia de los Confines and moved the region's administrative center to Mexico.

In 1570, Spain created the Audiencia of Guatemala, which also encompassed El Salvador, Honduras, Nicaragua, and Costa Rica. Guatemala and its capital—which was moved to GUATEMALA CITY in 1773 after severe earthquakes destroyed Antigua—remained the center of power in Central America until the end of the colonial period.

From Independence to 1850

In the early 1800s, Spain and France were engaged in a series of wars in Europe. During that time, Guatemala remained loyal to the Spanish crown. By 1820, however, Guatemala had been drawn into Mexico's struggle for independence from Spain. In 1821, Guatemala, led by the political activist Pedro MOLINA, declared its independence.

Guatemala and the United Provinces.

After independence, Guatemala and the other Central American states were incorporated into a Mexican empire established by Agustín de ITURBIDE. Within a year, however, the Central Americans declared their independence from Mexico and formed the United Provinces of Central America. As the largest province in the region, Guatemala played a leading role in this Central American federation*, but its prominence led to rivalries with the other Central American states.

Between 1826 and 1829, Guatemala became embroiled in a bitter civil war when the president of the federation, Manuel José ARCE, intervened in the Guatemalan state government and replaced its liberal* governor with a more conservative* one. The civil war touched all the Central American states, but it especially pitted Guatemala against El Salvador, its greatest rival for power. In the end, liberal forces under Honduran general Francisco MORAZÁN triumphed. They exiled most of the leading conservatives and restored Juan Barrundia to the governorship of Guatemala. Barrundia was succeeded by Mariano GÁLVEZ, who established a liberal agenda that dominated Guatemalan politics for much of the 1800s.

An Era of Reform.

In 1834, Gálvez launched major reforms in Guatemala and attempted to weaken the economic and social power of the conservative Creole* elite. Various new laws reduced the power of the Catholic clergy*, and many church lands were sold by the state. The new landowners were encouraged to develop export products that would stimulate economic growth. The COCHINEAL INDUSTRY, which involved the production of a red dye, gained importance at this time, and the Guatemalan economy became closely linked to textile manufacturing in Belize and Great Britain.

Gálvez encouraged immigration. But a plan to give land grants to English colonists was opposed by some Guatemalan leaders, who believed that Gálvez was too sympathetic to foreign interests. Gálvez also instituted political and judicial reforms, including the adoption of new civil and criminal codes in 1834. However, his attempt to replace the traditional Spanish legal system with a British-based system brought further criticism from many of the Guatemalan ruling elite.

In 1835, an outbreak of cholera* swept through Guatemala. While facing this disaster, the Gálvez government also encountered increasing opposition from the rural population, which was angered by many of the recent reforms. Under the leadership of José Rafael CARRERA, a former military officer, armed uprisings erupted in many rural areas. These revolts soon united into a powerful guerrilla* movement that brought down the Gálvez government in 1838. A successor government also fell to the peasants when it failed to meet their expectations.

From 1839 until his death in 1865, Carrera remained largely in control of Guatemala, although other men sometimes served as president.

° **federation** political union of separate states with a central government

° **liberal** supporting greater participation in government for individuals; not bound by political and social traditions

° **conservative** inclined to maintain existing political and social views, conditions, and institutions

° **Creole** person of European ancestry born in the Americas

° **clergy** priests and other church officials qualified to perform church ceremonies

° **cholera** serious intestinal disease that causes diarrhea, vomiting, cramps, and often death

° **guerrilla** referring to a group that uses surprise raids to obstruct or harass an enemy or overthrow a government

181

Guatemala

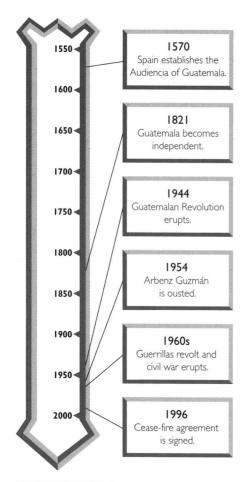

1550 — 1600 — 1650 — 1700 — 1750 — 1800 — 1850 — 1900 — 1950 — 2000

1570
Spain establishes the Audiencia of Guatemala.

1821
Guatemala becomes independent.

1944
Guatemalan Revolution erupts.

1954
Arbenz Guzmán is ousted.

1960s
Guerrillas revolt and civil war erupts.

1996
Cease-fire agreement is signed.

A Marginalized Majority

Although Indians—mainly of Maya descent—comprise more than half of Guatemala's population, they have suffered discrimination and persecution throughout the nation's history. Whites, ladinos (persons of partial Indian ancestry), and Indians who have rejected their native language and customs possess most of the wealth, land, and power. This cultural division, as well as rivalries and language differences among Indian communities, has made it difficult for Guatemala's Indians to unite to achieve greater political and social equality. Nonetheless, Indian activism has led to some progress. The government has begun to encourage programs (begun in the 1940s) that incorporate several Mayan languages into a national educational program.

The Carrera years represented a conservative reaction to the liberal ideas that had dominated the country's politics since independence. Carrera supported the clergy and restored many powers and privileges to the CATHOLIC CHURCH. He built a strong army and insisted on other conservative policies. In 1847, Carrera established the Republic of Guatemala, making the nation the fourth Central American state to declare independence from the United Provinces.

The Late 1800s

Carrera's rule marked the beginning of a long period during which Guatemala was ruled by powerful CAUDILLOS, or military dictators, associated with either conservative or liberal policies. Conservatives held power until about 1870, after which the liberals controlled Guatemala until the early 1900s.

Conservative Rule. Conservative rule was marked by the active participation of the clergy in government. Attempts were made to improve the Guatemalan economy by focusing production on agricultural exports, such as coffee. Under the conservatives, Guatemala had a heavy hand in the affairs of its Central American neighbors. It intervened directly in Honduras and El Salvador to maintain governments that benefited Guatemalan interests. In the mid-1850s, Guatemala also sent troops to fight alongside other Central American states in the NATIONAL WAR against William WALKER in Nicaragua.

By 1865, Guatemala had achieved considerable political stability and economic prosperity. But military repression and dictatorial rule had become notable characteristics of its government.

Liberal Rule. Liberal opposition to conservative rule grew in the late 1860s. It erupted in violence when coffee planters and liberal leaders in western Guatemala rebelled against the government. In 1870, Justo Rufino BARRIOS became the military leader of the rebellion. The following year, the rebels defeated the government forces, and in 1873, Barrios assumed the presidency.

Barrios was the first of several strong liberal dictators who emphasized economic growth, encouraged foreign investment, and sought to reduce the power of the traditional ruling elite. Barrios and his successors expanded the COFFEE INDUSTRY dramatically, modernized Guatemala City, and built railroads and modern ports. They promoted laws to reduce the power of the Catholic Church—seizing church property, reducing the number of priests in rural areas, and establishing civil marriage and divorce. In 1879, the Barrios government adopted a new constitution.

Despite such accomplishments, Barrios and the liberal leaders who followed him were no less oppressive than their conservative predecessors. They perpetuated a pattern of dictatorial rule, military strength, and harsh repression of opponents that has remained a part of the Guatemalan government.

Guatemala in the 1900s

During the early 1900s, Guatemala experienced great economic advancement. By 1930, however, repression and political corruption caused growing opposition to the liberal regime*. Economic problems arose as well, leading to greater instability.

regime prevailing political system or rule

Economic and Political Advances.

Under president Manuel ESTRADA CABRERA, who governed from 1898 to 1920, Guatemala's economy thrived. The UNITED FRUIT COMPANY developed a profitable BANANA INDUSTRY in Guatemala's lowlands. More railroads were built, including one that connected Guatemala City with the Caribbean coast. However, rural Guatemalans benefited little from this economic growth, and they became increasingly frustrated.

In 1920, Estrada Cabrera's opponents successfully removed him from office. During the next decade, the governments that ruled Guatemala were more democratic than earlier dictatorships. Although political participation was still limited, workers and other groups began to wield greater power.

depression period of little economic activity during which many people become unemployed

The worldwide depression* of the 1930s caused serious economic and social problems in Guatemala. As exports declined and revenues fell, public discontent grew. Amid these problems, general Jorge UBICO Y CASTAÑEDA was elected president in 1931. Ubico increased the power of the military, launched a crackdown on Communists* and labor groups, and created a system of laws that required peasants to work on coffee plantations. He also reduced Indian autonomy* by creating a new system of local government that replaced Indian mayors with officials appointed by the president.

Communist person who advocates communism—a social system in which land, goods, and the means of production are owned by the state or community rather than by individuals

autonomy independent self-government

The Guatemalan Revolution and Its Aftermath.

Opposition to the Ubico dictatorship increased during the 1940s and led to his overthrow in the Guatemalan Revolution of 1944. The revolution promoted a return to the more idealistic policies of the early 1800s. It encouraged broader political participation, especially among the middle and working classes, and emphasized a constitutionalist* system. In 1945, Guatemala adopted a new constitution that incorporated these ideas.

constitutionalist supportive of a government that is regulated by a constitution—a written document of established laws

One prominent leader in the period following the revolution was Jacobo ARBENZ GUZMÁN, who became president in 1950. Arbenz's election shifted the revolution toward the political left. He allowed Communists to organize a political party and maintained close ties with pro-Communist labor unions. His AGRARIAN REFORM laws redistributed some public lands and laid the foundation for a government seizure of large estates. These leftist* policies troubled the anti-Communist* United States government. In 1953, the United States launched a diplomatic offensive against Arbenz's government, and the CENTRAL INTELLIGENCE AGENCY (CIA) organized a plot that helped oust Arbenz in 1954.

leftist inclined to support radical reform and change; often associated with ideas of communism or socialism

anti-Communist referring to the opposition of communism

Growing Violence.

The overthrow of Arbenz marked the beginning of one of the darkest periods in Guatemalan history. A strong reaction against revolutionary reforms resulted in the suppression of the labor movement and the repeal of social and agrarian reforms. Communist and other leftist parties were outlawed, and the country experienced severe repression, intense rivalries among various military groups, and considerable corruption.

By the 1960s, rebels had launched a guerrilla war against the Guatemalan government that continued into the 1990s. During this period, violence soared as right-wing* government death squads murdered labor and leftist leaders and the guerrillas intensified their attacks on government forces. Guerrilla warfare spread from the cities to the countryside, where the guerrillas gained the support of the rural peasants.

* **right-wing** very conservative

In the period between 1950 and 1985, only one brief and essentially powerless civilian government ruled in Guatemala. For most of the time, the country remained under military control. Although the Guatemalan economy made impressive gains, the lower classes grew steadily poorer. The ruling military elite used their power to acquire private companies and large landholdings, greatly increasing their wealth at the expense of the rural population. Meanwhile, the government killed thousands of people—mainly Indians—who were suspected of supporting the guerrillas. Criticism by the United States and other foreign governments of Guatemala's HUMAN RIGHTS abuses had little effect.

Age-old practices still exist among the Maya people of Guatemala. The women shown here are using traditional backstrap looms to weave the colorful fabrics that are characteristic of their ancient culture.

Recent Years. By 1985, Guatemala was experiencing severe economic problems. Faced with growing discontent, the military decided to permit free elections, resulting in the first civilian government in decades. Yet the military still held tremendous power and resisted any serious attempts at reform. The economy continued to deteriorate, and corruption and violence became widespread.

The early 1990s were marked by frequent assassinations, kidnappings, conflicts over land, labor disputes, protests, and demonstrations against the government. The economy stayed weak, and social tensions remained high. In 1996, however, a new and much admired president, Alvaro Arzú Irigoyen, managed to remove several of the more corrupt military leaders from power. Arzú also negotiated with guerrilla leaders and persuaded them to sign an agreement ending the civil warfare that had raged for more than 30 years. By the late 1990s, Guatemala seemed to be making progress toward a more peaceful and democratic future. (*See also* **Anticlericalism; Central America, United Provinces of; Counterinsurgency; Guerrilla Movements; Political Parties.**)

Guatemala City

*T*he capital of GUATEMALA, Guatemala City, is the largest city in CENTRAL AMERICA. It is located in a broad highland valley about 50 miles inland from the Pacific coast. The landscape is one of great natural beauty, and the climate is mild and agreeable.

Originally named Nueva Guatemala de la Asunción (New Guatemala of the Assumption), Guatemala City was founded by the Spanish in 1776 to serve as the capital of the Kingdom of Guatemala. The city replaced the former capital of La Antigua Guatemala (Old Guatemala) after it was destroyed by a series of major earthquakes in 1773.

° **mestizo** person of mixed European and Indian ancestry

Many landless mestizos* flocked to the new city. Also among the early residents were Indians who had been forced to leave their own settlements in order to provide the city with a labor force and essential products. By 1778, the city had a population of more than 10,000. To encourage further development, Spain halted the collection of taxes from Guatemala City for a period of ten years. However, because the Catholic Church and other groups in Guatemalan society strongly objected to the relocation of the capital, the city grew slowly over the next several decades.

After the colonies of Central America gained independence from Spain in 1821, Guatemala City served first as capital of the province of Central America within the Mexican empire and then, from 1823 to 1833, as capital of the United Provinces of Central America. In 1829, internal struggles within the United Provinces brought fighting and destruction to the streets of the city. Living conditions for the city's residents finally improved in the late 1830s and 1840s, when Guatemala City experienced a period of modest growth and stability. It became the capital of the independent republic* of Guatemala in 1847. The successful export of various crops, including COFFEE, strengthened the city's economy, and various public works projects were completed, including the construction of a cathedral and a national theater.

° **republic** government in which citizens elect officials to represent them and govern according to law

In the late 1870s, coffee exports thrived, and government administration expanded to meet the demands of the country's growing industry. The number of public works projects grew, bringing new methods of transportation to the city, including an urban rail system. The nation's leaders also supported efforts to beautify the city through the construction of new buildings and avenues.

During the dictatorship of Manuel ESTRADA CABRERA, Guatemala City experienced one of its worst disasters. In 1917 and 1918, the city was almost totally destroyed by massive EARTHQUAKES. Many residents were forced to live in temporary camps until the end of the 1920s. The task of rebuilding Guatemala City proceeded slowly. Some of the most important projects, such as the construction of underground sewers and various government buildings, were not undertaken until the 1930s and 1940s.

At the Mercy of the Mountains

The highland region surrounding Guatemala City is known for its beautiful mountains, including Tajumulco, the highest summit in Central America. This beauty, however, is accompanied by danger. The region has several active volcanoes. While local farmers benefit from the rich volcanic soil, they live under the constant threat of eruptions. Area residents are also threatened by earthquakes. The quakes that shook Guatemala City in 1773 and 1917 were unusual only in their severity and in the amount of destruction they caused. The earth around Guatemala City trembles frequently, and major quakes may strike the city again.

Guatemala City experienced another major earthquake in 1976, followed by a new period of rebuilding. After this disaster, the government began selling inexpensive lots for new homes, and many low-income neighborhoods emerged. Since the 1970s, the city has grown rapidly, spurred by the concentration of industry there. In addition to serving as the center of Guatemala's government, the city also is the nation's main transportation hub and commercial center. (*See also* **Central America, United Provinces of; Cities and Urbanization; Coffee Industry.**)

Guayaquil

Guayaquil is the largest city in ECUADOR and the capital of Guayas Province. Situated on the Guayas River about 30 miles upstream from the Gulf of Guayaquil, the city has one of the best natural harbors along the Pacific coast of the Americas. This location has helped make Guayaquil Ecuador's main seaport.

Guayaquil is Ecuador's largest city and one of the best natural harbors along the Pacific coast of the Americas. This painting of the wharf at Guayaquil was created in 1884, when the city was a center for the export of cacao—the bean from which chocolate is made.

° **conquistador** Spanish explorer and conqueror

° **cacao** bean from which chocolate is made

° **epidemic** outbreak of a disease that affects a large number of people

Guayaquil was probably founded in 1531 by the conquistador* Sebastian de Belalcázar. Indians destroyed the settlement twice before Spanish explorer Francisco de ORELLANA reestablished the city at its present location in 1537. During the colonial period, Guayaquil was a major trading and shipbuilding center and was often attacked by BUCCANEERS, or pirates. Weary of paying taxes to Spain, the city declared its independence in 1820 and became a free city. Two years later, however, Venezuelan revolutionary Simón BOLÍVAR incorporated Guayaquil within his new republic of GRAN COLOMBIA.

In the 1800s, agricultural exports—particularly cacao*—dominated the economy of Guayaquil. With its hot, humid climate, the city was infamous as a DISEASE-infested port, and epidemics* of yellow fever and other illnesses struck repeatedly. In the 1900s, the city became the hub of Ecuador's international trade, as well as the nation's leading commercial and industrial center.

Guayaquil is the main rival and competitor of QUITO, Ecuador's capital. The two cities are culturally distinct, and each views the other with suspicion. The differences between the two cities are also reflected in Ecuadorian politics, leading to frequent clashes between them as each tries to gain political advantages over the other. (*See also* **Cacao Industry**.)

Guerra Grande

The Guerra Grande (Great War) was a civil war fought in URUGUAY from 1839 to 1851. It was the longest and hardest struggle in that nation's history. The war originated in a rivalry between two Uruguayan political parties—the Colorados and the Blancos—and their respective leaders, Fructuoso Rivera and Manuel ORIBE. In March 1839, Rivera overthrew Oribe to become president of Uruguay. Several days later, he declared war on the dictator of ARGENTINA, Juan Manuel de Rosas, who was Oribe's ally. This act marked the beginning of the Guerra Grande.

Early in the war, Rivera suffered several defeats at the hands of Argentina. In 1842, with the help of Rosas, Oribe and the Blancos drove Rivera into exile and began a nine-year siege* of the city of MONTEVIDEO, which was controlled by the Colorado Party. During this period, serious disagreements developed among members of the Blancos and the Colorados, and conflicts arose between those parties and their foreign allies. Tensions were especially bitter between the Colorados and the French and British, who tried to use the situation to gain advantages in the region.

In May 1851, a provincial governor in Argentina named Justo José de URQUIZA broke with Rosas, joined forces with the Colorados, and advanced into Uruguay. Faced with this new threat, Oribe and the Blancos agreed to make peace in October. The siege of Montevideo was lifted, the Guerra Grande was over, and Rosas was deposed the following year. However, the political rivalries that had intensified during the war lasted well into the 1900s.

* **siege** prolonged effort by armed troops to force the surrender of a town or fort by surrounding it and cutting it off from aid

---

Guerrilla Movements

* **regime** prevailing political system or rule

* **insurgent** person fighting against established authority in his or her own country; rebelling against authority

* **colonial** period between the European conquest and independence, generally from the early 1500s to the early 1800s

Guerrilla movements are armed struggles that use surprise raids to attack a nation's established authority. They are usually a means of protesting the perceived wrongs committed by a ruling government or foreign invader and are often aimed at overthrowing an existing regime*. Those who fight in such movements are called guerrillas. Opposition to guerrilla activity is sometimes called COUNTERINSURGENCY, meaning against the insurgents*.

Latin America has a long history of guerrilla movements that began in the colonial* period and extend to the present. These movements are primarily the outcome of local rebel traditions. Rebellions can be classified by period: colonial resistance movements, early independence-era revolts, revolutionary struggles of the late 1800s and early 1900s, and the modern guerrilla movements of the mid-to-late 1900s.

During the colonial period, renegade bands of fugitive African slaves, known as MAROONS, established guerrilla forces in remote areas throughout Latin America in order to resist European colonization. The Maroons offered sanctuary to runaway slaves and Indians, and together they raided many European settlements. These early guerrilla movements flourished in the mountains of Cuba, Nicaragua, El Salvador, Peru, and Bolivia; on the plains of Venezuela and Argentina; in the jungles of Guatemala and the YUCATÁN; and in the coastal regions of Brazil.

In the 1700s and 1800s, guerrilla-style Indian revolts had temporary successes in various parts of Latin America. In the ANDES, the Indian leaders TUPAC AMARU and TUPAC CATARI launched a rebellion against Spanish authority that lasted from the late 1770s to 1783, when it was put down by Spanish forces. The CASTE WAR OF YUCATÁN—one of the most violent and successful Indian revolts in Latin American history—enabled many MAYA to remain autonomous in parts of the Yucatán for many years.

In the 1800s and early 1900s, guerrilla forces staged rebellions in several Latin American countries. In Guatemala, former military officer José Rafael CARRERA headed a revolt that overthrew the government and withdrew the country from the United Provinces of Central America. In

Guerrilla Movements

° **revolutionary** person engaged in a war to bring about change

See color plate 9, vol. 3.

° **Communist** referring to a social system in which land, goods, and the means of production are owned by the state or community rather than by individuals

° **conservative** inclined to maintain existing political and social views, conditions, and institutions

° **right-wing** very conservative

"Many Vietnams"

In the 1960s, Cuban revolutionary Che Guevara sought to encourage guerrilla movements throughout South America, beginning in Bolivia. He believed that revolutionary success could be achieved only through an extended people's war against the authorities. Guevara used the civil war that was raging in Vietnam as a model for his strategy. He hoped to spark what he called "many Vietnams"—many revolutions based on peasant discontent, a weak economy, government failure to enact reform, and anxiety over increased United States interference in Latin American politics. However, before he could launch his plan, Guevara was captured and executed by the Bolivian army.

Cuba, a writer named José MARTÍ Y PÉREZ launched the struggle for independence from Spain in 1895. In MEXICO, revolutionaries* Francisco "Pancho" VILLA and Emiliano ZAPATA played important roles in the MEXICAN REVOLUTION.

The modern guerrilla era began in the late 1950s, with the successful revolution led by Fidel CASTRO against Cuban dictator Fulgencio BATISTA Y ZALDÍVAR. During the CUBAN REVOLUTION, Castro and his associate Ernesto "Che" GUEVARA developed tactics of modern guerrilla warfare that later were used throughout Latin America. The main features of modern guerrilla movements are a strong leader, the use of symbolism and myths focused on past revolutionary leaders and national heroes, and a core of guerrilla fighters who have the support of the local peasantry.

During the 1960s, Guevara and Castro urged other Latin revolutionaries to follow the example of the Cuban Revolution. A first wave of guerrilla activity aimed at overthrowing dictators in Panama, Nicaragua, the Dominican Republic, and Haiti. A second wave of guerrilla struggles, inspired by Communist* ideas, focused on reform movements and opposition to generally conservative* governments. The most prominent Communist-backed guerrilla movements of the 1960s occurred in Columbia, Guatemala, and Venezuela. Also in the 1960s, Che Guevara attempted to launch a third wave of guerrilla movements from Bolivia. This third wave was partly inspired by opposition to United States influence and interference in Latin America.

These waves of rebellion were centered primarily in rural areas and received most of their support from peasants. In the late 1960s, several guerrilla movements originated in urban areas, with a support base of middle-class and working-class people who wanted better economic opportunities. Urban guerrillas often organized protests and engaged in kidnappings and assassinations to further their goals. Major urban guerrilla movements erupted in Argentina and in Colombia in the 1960s and 1970s and in Mexico in the 1970s.

In the 1980s, two guerrilla movements in Central America attracted international attention. The first, in Nicaragua, pitted pro-Communist forces, known as the SANDINISTAS, against right-wing* guerrilla forces, called the CONTRAS. The other, in El Salvador, also focused on pro-Communist and anti-Communist sentiment as well as demands for political, economic, and social reform.

Three other guerrilla movements took center stage in the 1980s and 1990s, each claiming to represent the interests of Indian peasants. In Guatemala, a guerrilla movement that began in the 1960s merged with Indian activist groups in the 1980s, initiating a struggle that lasted for many years. Despite the signing of peace accords in 1996, Guatemala continues to experience political instability. In Peru, Indian discontent led to the rise of a guerrilla force known as the SENDERO LUMINOSO (Shining Path), one of the most extreme and violent rebel groups in Latin America. This group launched waves of terror in Peru from the 1970s to the mid-1990s. The third movement arose in CHIAPAS, a province in southern Mexico, where Indian peasants rose in armed rebellions against the government to demand land reform and political rights.

Outbreaks of guerrilla-related violence continue to threaten the stability of Chiapas and other regions in Latin America. (*See also* **Central America, United Provinces of; Communism; Labor and Labor Movements; Political Parties.**)

Guevara, Ernesto "Che"

1928–1967
Latin American revolutionary leader

° **guerrilla** referring to a group that uses surprise raids to obstruct or harass an enemy or overthrow a government

° **Communist** referring to a social system in which land, goods, and the means of production are owned by the state or community rather than by individuals

° **imperialism** domination of the political, economic, and cultural life of one country or region by another country

The Bones of the Martyr

For nearly 30 years, the body of Che Guevara rested in a secret mass grave in Bolivia. Then, in June 1997, the burial site was discovered. Guevara's bones were taken to Cuba and placed in a mausoleum at the Plaza Ernesto Che Guevara in the city of Santa Clara, which had been a guerrilla stronghold during the Cuban Revolution. That same year, leftist groups around the world commemorated the anniversary of Guevara's death with books, lectures, concerts, and other memorial activities. Many still revere Guevara as a sort of patron saint to the cause of revolution.

Ernesto "Che" Guevara was a guerrilla* leader who participated in the CUBAN REVOLUTION in the late 1950s and then worked to spread Communist* ideas throughout Latin America. In the 1960s, Guevara became famous for his opposition to imperialism* and his outspoken attacks on United States foreign policy. His book *La guerra de guerrillas (Guerrilla Warfare)* became an influential guide for aspiring revolutionaries.

Born to a middle-class family in Rosario, ARGENTINA, Guevara studied medicine and earned a medical degree in 1953. Both during and after his studies, he traveled throughout Latin America. Based on his observations there, Guevara became convinced that only violent revolution could bring an end to the region's extreme poverty.

In late 1953, Guevara traveled to GUATEMALA, where he joined an elected revolutionary government headed by President Jacobo ARBENZ GUZMÁN and met several exiled Cuban revolutionaries. When forces backed by the United States toppled the Guatemalan government in 1954, Guevara fled to MEXICO. Soon after arriving there, he met Fidel CASTRO and his brother Raúl, Cuban exiles who were plotting to overthrow Cuba's dictator, Fulgencio BATISTA. Guevara joined the Castro forces and accompanied them to Cuba in 1956.

For two years, the revolutionaries engaged in guerrilla warfare against Batista's troops. During that time, Guevara became one of Fidel Castro's closest aides, and he helped shape the strategy of the revolution. When Castro overthrew Batista in 1959, Guevara became a Cuban citizen. Over the next several years, he played a prominent role in Cuba's new government. He served as a director of the National Institute of Agrarian Reform, president of the National Bank, and minister of industry and centered Cuba's early economic policy on Communist principles. He also tried to inspire Cubans to dedicate themselves to the revolution and to become motivated by moral rather than material incentives.

Eventually, Guevara's influence in the Cuban government declined. In 1965, he resigned his government posts and dropped out of public life. Little is known about his activities during the next two years, other than that he participated in a civil war in the Congo in Africa along with some other Cuban guerrilla fighters.

By 1967, Guevara was in BOLIVIA, establishing a GUERRILLA MOVEMENT that he hoped would serve as the basis for Communist revolutions throughout South America. The movement suffered numerous difficulties, including a failure to win the trust of the local peasants, internal divisions among the guerrillas, and poor relations with the Bolivian Communist Party. Bolivian forces, assisted by United States military advisers, killed many of the guerrillas and wounded Guevara. On October 8, 1967, a Bolivian army unit captured Guevara and his remaining

Ernesto "Che" Guevara was a guerilla leader who participated in the Cuban Revolution in the 1950s and then worked to spread Communist ideas throughout Latin America. This photograph shows Guevara (second from right) in Havana, Cuba, welcoming a delegation from Communist China.

fighters. Guevara was executed the following day, and to prove that he was dead, his killers displayed his corpse to the press, who circulated photos of his body around the world.

Since his death, revolutionaries in many parts of the world have considered Guevara a martyr*, and his political ideas have continued to inspire Latin American leftists*. Guevara's writings have also endured and serve as both a practical and theoretical guide for those hoping to overthrow dictatorship and end foreign imperialism. (*See also* **Communism; Imperialism.**)

° **martyr** someone who suffers or dies for the sake of a cause or principle

° **leftist** person who is inclined to support radical reform and change; often associated with ideas of communism or socialism

Guilds

° **artisan** skilled crafts worker

° **Middle Ages** period between ancient and modern times in western Europe, generally considered to be from the A.D. 500s to the 1500s

° **colonial** period between the European conquest and independence, generally from the early 1500s to the early 1800s

Guilds (or *gremios*) are self-governing organizations of artisans* that regulate the production and sale of specialized goods as well as the training of skilled crafts workers. Modeled on the craft guilds established in Spain and Portugal during the Middle Ages*, guilds for shoemakers, silversmiths, carpenters, and other craftsmen flourished in Latin America during the colonial* era. They were organized to improve the social status of members and to limit competition from indigenous* artisans.

The first Latin American guilds were established between 1545 and 1560 in the major colonial cities of MEXICO and PERU. By the end of the 1500s, there were guilds in many secondary cities, and eventually, craft organizations existed in most cities throughout Latin America.

Often these colonial guilds were supported by city governments that sought to protect consumers from high prices and poor-quality

° **indigenous** referring to the original inhabitants of a region

° **monopoly** exclusive control or domination of a particular type of business

goods. Authorities gave guilds a broad range of regulatory powers, allowing them to maintain a near monopoly* on their products. Each guild also determined membership and training criteria for its craft, the goods that could be produced, the prices of those goods, and the wages and working conditions of artisans. Guild officers conducted inspections to make sure that proper price and quality levels were maintained. If a craftsman violated the guild's rules, the officers could impose fines, seize his goods, and even close his shop.

Guild members were organized into three ranks: masters, journeymen, and apprentices. Only masters could own shops and sell directly to the public. They also controlled all guild offices and the examination system that permitted journeymen and apprentices to move up in rank. Such powers allowed masters to limit competition and control advancement to master rank. Apprentices often lived with a master artisan, and the terms of their apprenticeships were defined in a written contract. Journeymen were promoted to master rank only after they had demonstrated a certain level of knowledge and skill.

° **solidarity** strong unity within a group, usually based on shared goals, interests, or sympathies

The Latin American guilds were generally weaker than those in Europe because of colonial prejudices and restrictions. Although colonial artisans often recruited and trained apprentices from local Indian, African, and mixed-race populations, such nonwhite guild members were often excluded from the rank of master and from guild offices. This discrimination led to racial divisions that undermined guild solidarity*. The American crafts organizations were also weakened by colonial authorities and powerful commercial interests that limited their ability to restrict imports and eliminate competition. Gradually, guilds became viewed as corrupt obstacles to colonial economic progress. By the 1800s, the economic powers once held by Latin American guilds had been eliminated almost completely. (*See also* **Crafts.**)

Guillén, Nicolás

1902–1989
Cuban poet

° **Communist** referring to a social system in which land, goods, and the means of production are owned by the state or community rather than by individuals

Nicolás Guillén was considered the national poet of CUBA. Of mixed European and African ancestry, Guillén was born in the city of Camagüey and developed an early interest in poetry. In 1921, he abandoned his law studies at the University of Havana and devoted himself to journalism and poetry. Beginning in the 1920s, Guillén explored African themes in his work and wrote many poems about Afro-Cubans. After his poetry collection *Motivos de son* (Sound Motifs) was published in 1930, Guillén gained fame among several literary movements that focused on Afro-American culture and heritage.

In the 1930s, Guillén began to write and speak out against poverty, racism, and oppression. He joined the Cuban Communist* Party in 1937 and traveled extensively in Europe and Latin America in the 1940s. In 1953, Guillén was exiled from Cuba because he publicly opposed the dictatorship of Fulgencio BATISTA Y ZALDÍVAR. In 1954, he received the Lenin International Peace Prize. Guillén enthusiastically supported the CUBAN REVOLUTION and returned to his homeland in 1959, when revolutionary leader Fidel CASTRO overthrew Batista's government. Guillén later became president of Cuba's National Union of

Writers and Artists and served as an official in the Cuban Communist Party. Many of his later poems address themes of revolution and social protest. (*See also* **Communism; Literature.**)

Gulf of Mexico

The Gulf of Mexico is a large body of water on the southeastern coast of North America. Bounded by the United States, MEXICO, and the island of CUBA, it is linked to the Atlantic Ocean by the Straits of Florida and to the CARIBBEAN SEA by the Yucatán Channel. The Gulf measures nearly 1,100 miles across at its widest point and about 800 miles from north to south. The warm waters of the Gulf affect the climate of adjacent areas and contribute to the formation and intensity of hurricanes in the region.

Spanish explorer Sebastián de Ocampo became the first European to discover this body of water when he sailed around the western end of Cuba in 1508. Early Spanish maps of the region referred to the Gulf as the Golfo de la Nueva España (Gulf of New Spain) and as the Seno Mejicano (Mexican Bay). However, by 1569, it had become known as the Golfo Mexicano, or Gulf of Mexico. During the colonial period, Spanish ships passed through the Gulf, bringing colonists and supplies to Spanish America and returning to Spain with gold, silver, and other American riches. Located on the Gulf's Mexican shore, the city of VERACRUZ was a leading colonial port, and it remains one of the region's major ports today.

The Gulf of Mexico is a great source of food, minerals, and energy to both the United States and Mexico. Fishing is an important industry in many Gulf ports, and petroleum and natural gas are extracted along the edge of the North American continent, which extends under portions of the Gulf. (*See also* **Petroleum Industry.**)

Gutiérrez, Gustavo

born 1928
Peruvian priest

° **theology** study of religious faith

° **Communist** referring to a social system in which land, goods, and the means of production are owned by the state or community rather than by individuals

° **conservative** one who is opposed to sudden change, especially in existing political and social institutions

The Peruvian priest Gustavo Gutiérrez was the founder of a religious movement called liberation theology*. This movement attempted to involve the CATHOLIC CHURCH in the struggle for justice that was taking place among the poor and oppressed in Latin American society during the late 1900s.

Born in LIMA, Gutiérrez abandoned his medical studies to train for the Catholic priesthood in Europe in the 1950s. After returning to Peru, he taught theology at the Catholic university in Lima. In the early 1960s, Gutiérrez joined a network of church leaders who wanted to reform the church to make it more responsive to the needs of Latin Americans. Influenced by Communist* ideas, he began to write and speak out against social and economic inequality.

In 1971, Gutiérrez published *Teología de la liberación (A Theology of Liberation),* a work that became the foundation of the liberation theology movement. His ideas inspired some Latin American Catholics to defend actively the rights of the poor and the oppressed. However, conservatives* and church leaders in Rome have criticized Gutiérrez's teachings because they reflect Communist theories. (*See also* **Liberation Theology.**)

Guyana

° **indigenous** referring to the original inhabitants of a region

° **indentured servant** person who agreed to go to a new country and work for a specified period in return for passage on a ship

° **progressive** inclined to support social improvement and political change by governmental action

° **Communist** referring to a social system in which land, goods, and the means of production are owned by the state or community rather than by individuals

A South American Melting Pot

Guyana is a place of great ethnic, religious, and cultural diversity. Its population includes people of indigenous, African, Indian, Chinese, European, and mixed ancestry. Christianity, Islam, and Hinduism are all widely practiced, and distinct cultural traditions are often maintained at home or within family life. While many of these differences affect the nation's politics, Guyana's people are united by a common culture. They share a common language (English), a history of British rule, and a passion for the sport of cricket. Many also share the belief that racial and ethnic heritage should not interfere in one's public life.

Guyana is the only English-speaking country in South America. Its name means Land of Waters, and indeed, Guyana has numerous rivers and canals as well as some of the world's tallest and most spectacular waterfalls. Much of the country's interior is covered by lush RAIN FORESTS, and the nation has valuable resources of timber, gold, diamonds, and other minerals. Most of Guyana's diverse population lives near the fertile Atlantic coast.

Although the Spanish first sighted the coast of Guyana in 1498, they avoided the area—known as the Wild Coast—because of the hostile indigenous* people who lived there. In the late 1500s, the Dutch established friendly relations with the native people and founded several settlements along major rivers. By 1675, the Dutch had built profitable sugar, coffee, tobacco, and cotton PLANTATIONS that were worked by slaves brought from Africa.

In the late 1700s, Britain seized the Dutch settlements in Guyana. Over the next few decades, the British vied with the Dutch and French for control of the region, and it changed hands frequently until Britain finally gained permanent control in 1803. In 1831, the British united the various settlements in the region as the colony of British Guiana.

Several important developments occurred under British rule. In 1834, Britain freed the territory's slaves, who founded villages along the coast. Thereafter, labor needs were met by indentured servants* imported from Africa, India, and China. Gold was discovered in British Guiana in 1879, increasing settlement and sparking a long-term boundary dispute with neighboring VENEZUELA. This disagreement was partially resolved in 1899 by a treaty that awarded the Orinoco River to Venezuela. British Guiana became a crown colony in 1928, and all remnants of Dutch governmental structure were abolished. Complete power was given to a British-appointed governor and a Colonial Office staffed by British officials.

From the 1940s to 1960s, British Guiana was in turmoil while leading political parties struggled for power. The first general elections, held in 1953, resulted in victory for the People's Progressive* Party (PPP) and its leader, Dr. Cheddi Jagan. But the British, concerned that the PPP was pro-Communist*, suspended the constitution and sent in troops. Soon after, the PPP divided along racial lines. One group, headed by Jagan, consisted primarily of Indians (from India). The other, led by Forbes Burnham, had the support of blacks. Between 1961 and 1964, serious rioting between Indians and blacks resulted in much bloodshed.

In 1966, British Guiana gained independence from Britain and was renamed Guyana. The new government was headed by Prime Minister Forbes Burnham and the People's National Congress (PNC). Under PNC rule, Guyana sought to increase foreign investment and adopted programs to improve its economy. In the 1980s, however, demand for Guyana's main exports (bauxite and sugar) declined sharply, sending the country into economic crisis. Resulting shortages of food and basic supplies and reductions in public services caused considerable unrest. The PNC maintained control of the government until 1992, when the PPP and Cheddi Jagan won the national elections.

193

Guyana's economy improved significantly during the 1990s. Many private businesses emerged, foreign investment increased, and important resources were developed. Yet despite such improvements, the average standard of living in Guyana remains extremely low. Many of its best-trained professionals migrate to other countries seeking better opportunities—a situation that Guyana hopes to remedy as its economy continues to grow. (*See also* **Boundary Disputes; British–Latin American Relations.**)

Guzmán Blanco, Antonio Leocadio

1829–1899
Venezuelan president and caudillo

° **caudillo** authoritarian leader or dictator, often from the military

° **liberal** supporting greater participation in government for individuals; not bound by political and social traditions

Antonio Leocadio Guzmán Blanco held absolute power in VENEZUELA for nearly 20 years in the late 1800s. Under his leadership, the nation improved education, built many public works, and experienced substantial economic growth. However, ruling as a caudillo*, Guzmán Blanco often jailed those who criticized his government.

Born in CARACAS, Guzmán Blanco was the son of a prominent journalist and founder of the Liberal* Party. He studied law and medicine, and lived and traveled abroad—including a period in the 1840s when he served as a diplomat in the United States. In 1863, Guzmán Blanco helped negotiate an end to a five-year civil war in Venezuela. His success led to his appointment as vice president of the nation. In this position, Guzmán Blanco secured European loans that helped the Venezuelan economy and benefited him both financially and politically.

When civil war broke out again in 1867, Guzmán Blanco fled to the Caribbean island of Curaçao, where he became the leader of the Venezuelan liberal forces. In February 1870, he returned to Venezuela and marched with troops to Caracas. By the end of April, Guzmán Blanco had taken control of the capital city and the government.

Guzmán Blanco served several terms as president of Venezuela between 1870 and 1889. During most of his rule, Venezuela enjoyed peace and prosperity. The nation experienced strong economic growth, especially in agriculture. The economy also benefited from the extensive construction of roads and railroads, the improvement of seaports, and the establishment of telegraph communications. In addition, Guzmán Blanco launched a program to improve education and to make it free and available to all students.

An early challenge to Guzmán Blanco came from the CATHOLIC CHURCH, which resented his policies that established civil marriages, restricted church landholdings, and ended state contributions to the church. Although Guzmán Blanco eventually made peace with the church, he ensured that its power remained limited.

After 1876, Guzmán Blanco began to spend much time in Europe, where he enjoyed a luxurious lifestyle. He selected several people to rule in his place during his absence. However, Venezuela's economy deteriorated, and in 1886, the congress asked Guzmán Blanco to return. By 1887, the nation's economic crisis was causing serious public discontent with Guzmán Blanco's leadership. As he had done at other times during his rule, Guzmán Blanco attempted to eliminate such opposition by reducing civil liberties and arresting his critics. In 1888, he left Venezuela

° **coup** sudden, often violent overthrow of a ruler or government

in the hands of another successor, Pablo Rojas Pául, and returned to Europe. The following year, Rojas Pául led a coup* that permanently removed Guzmán Blanco from power. The former president never again returned to Venezuela. (*See also* **Caudillos.**)

Hacienda

° **conquistador** Spanish explorer and conqueror

° *encomienda* right granted to a conqueror that enabled him to control the labor of and collect payment from an Indian community

See color plate 3, vol. 1.

° **cacao** bean from which chocolate is made

A hacienda is a large rural estate in Latin America. One of the basic institutions of rural life, haciendas range in size from a few hundred acres to hundreds of square miles. These properties and the individuals who control them have dominated the politics and economics of Latin America since the 1500s.

Haciendas emerged soon after Spain conquered territories in the Americas, when the Spanish crown gave land grants to certain conquistadors* and colonists. These landholdings gradually were enlarged through additional land grants, purchases, and takeovers of unoccupied Indian lands. Some colonists who had *encomiendas* * also obtained Indian land. These properties often became farms that were later expanded into haciendas.

There are three main types of haciendas. One is the ranch, which developed from the *estancia,* or livestock ranch (called a *fazenda* in Brazil). The *estancia* held widespread appeal for early colonists because its establishment required relatively little money and few laborers. Before the 1700s, *estancias* generally were not very large. The owner, or *estanciero,* had legal title to only a few units of land on which he built a house, a storage shed or building, and corrals for holding livestock. Pastures were held in common by all the *estancieros* of an area. In the 1700s, Spain began selling these pastures to individuals, enabling owners to turn their *estancias* into large haciendas.

The second type of hacienda was the mixed farm, which raised both livestock and crops. The establishment of a mixed farm generally required more money than an *estancia,* and many more laborers were needed to tend and harvest crops. Over time, many mixed farms grew into large estates.

The specialized farm was the third type of hacienda. Usually dedicated to producing a single crop that was intended for sale in distant markets, specialized farms required a great deal of both money and labor. The crops most often grown on specialized farms included sugarcane, rice, cacao*, and wheat. These farms were the forerunners of PLANTATIONS.

All three types of hacienda relied on a varied workforce. Laborers included Indians who had left their own communities, community members working on a temporary basis, and wage-earning or salaried workers. Landowners sometimes forced workers to stay on the haciendas by keeping them in constant debt, and in tropical regions, some haciendas had large numbers of black slaves. Many of the biggest haciendas grew to the size and complexity of small towns, with a church, jail, and other buildings in addition to the home of the owner, housing for workers, and various buildings for the operation of the hacienda.

Although some haciendas were self-sufficient and produced only enough for their own needs, most haciendas produced goods for market

Large rural estates, called haciendas, emerged when colonial populations grew large enough to require a steady supply of basic foods, especially grains. As time passed, they also cultivated crops for export.

and generated profits for their owners. In some cases, the owners of large haciendas—who were known as hacendados—amassed great fortunes. Because hacendados were among the wealthiest people in Latin American society, ownership of a hacienda became a symbol of power and prestige.

The hacendados controlled the region's means of agricultural production and provided employment for farm laborers, skilled crafts workers, and professionals such as bankers and lawyers. Because of their wealth, they wielded considerable political power at various levels of government. Many wealthy professionals, businessmen, and merchants tried to imitate the successful hacendados by buying land for themselves. While some of these individuals acquired haciendas to raise food or livestock for their own enterprises, many simply sought the prestige that owning large tracts of land could provide.

In modern times, land reform has become a serious political issue throughout Latin America. Demand for governments to break up large estates and redistribute the land among the peasants has sometimes sparked violent revolts. In the 1960s and 1970s, several countries passed land reform laws to redistribute property, but few of these measures have proven effective. As a result, large estates and their owners continue to dominate the economy in many areas of Latin America. (*See also* **Agriculture; Economic Development; Encomienda; Land, Ownership of; Latifundia.**)

Haiti

A tropical, mountainous country in the CARIBBEAN ANTILLES, Haiti occupies the western third of the island of HISPANIOLA. Haiti is the only independent country in Latin America whose European cultural heritage is predominantly French. Although discovered by the Spanish, it became a French colony in the late 1600s and remained part of France's colonial empire until 1804. Today the country is one of the poorest in the Western Hemisphere, and most of its people—who are mainly of African descent—live in extreme poverty, due in part to Haiti's long history of political and economic instability.

Early History

Before Europeans arrived in the Americas in the late 1400s, Haiti was inhabited by various indigenous* peoples, including the Arawaks. By about A.D. 1000, the Indians had developed a complex system of chiefdoms headed by leaders called CACIQUES. These chiefdoms had an agricultural economy, and they also traded with other islands throughout the Caribbean.

*indigenous** referring to the original inhabitants of a region

European Discovery and Settlement.   The first Europeans to sight Haiti were the Spaniards. Christopher COLUMBUS reached the north coast of Hispaniola on his first voyage to the Americas in 1492. The Spanish invaders had a tremendous impact on the island. They introduced forced labor and—unintentionally—European diseases, both of which had a devastating effect on the native population. By 1514, the number of Indians on Hispaniola had declined from perhaps several hundred thousand to only about 30,000. Most of these survivors died soon afterward.

See map in Caribbean Antilles (vol. I).

The Spaniards settled the eastern part of Hispaniola (present-day DOMINICAN REPUBLIC), but they largely ignored the western part of the island. French pirates, or BUCCANEERS, invaded the western coasts in the 1550s, and by the 1600s, that area had become a base for both French and English buccaneers. Gradually, the French settlers became more numerous and established PLANTATIONS along the northern coast as well.

French Colonization.   In 1665, the arrival of a French governor brought stability to the western section of Hispaniola. Within a decade, the English pirates had been expelled, and a French planter society emerged, although officially, Spain still controlled the entire island. In 1697, Spain signed the Treaty of Ryswick, ceding* western Hispaniola to France. This area became the French colony of St. Domingue.

*cede** to yield or surrender, usually by treaty

St. Domingue soon developed into France's richest colony in the Americas, exporting huge quantities of sugar, coffee, and other agricultural products to Europe and North America. Because their plantation economy depended on a large supply of labor, the French colonists imported large numbers of African slaves. By the late 1700s, black slaves and free blacks comprised the majority of the colony's population.

Despite its economic success, St. Domingue was politically unstable. The mountainous interior sheltered many fugitive slaves called MAROONS, who raided plantations and harassed travelers. Efforts to overcome the maroons failed, and in 1784, the government agreed not to pursue them if they ceased their attacks. The colony also faced frequent slave resistance on the plantations. However, the main source of St. Domingue's instability was its divided society. The colony had a rigid caste* system based on ethnic categories, which led to tensions

*caste** rigid social class based on race, wealth, or occupation

* **mulatto** person of mixed black and white ancestry
* **Creole** person of European ancestry born in the Americas

* **republic** government in which citizens elect officials to represent them and govern according to law
* **autonomy** independent self-government

and rivalries between elite whites, middle-class whites, mulattos*, Creoles*, African-born blacks, free blacks, and slaves.

Revolution and Independence

In the 1790s, St. Domingue experienced violent conflict and foreign intervention. Between 1791 and 1804, the inhabitants of the colony struggled against France and against each other. The results included the abolition of SLAVERY and the independence of Haiti.

Beginnings of Revolution. In 1789, the people of France rebelled against the king and established a republic*. The French Revolution inspired the elite whites of St. Domingue to seek greater autonomy* from France. At the same time, middle-class whites and mulattos began to seek greater liberty and equality and inclusion in the colonial aristocracy.

In 1791, a group of mulatto leaders went to France to gain representation in the French National Assembly, but Creole planters opposed their efforts. When the mulattos returned to St. Domingue, they led a rebellion against the colonial government. This event marked the beginning of the HAITIAN REVOLUTION. Although the rebellion failed, mulattos in southern Haiti continued to resist colonial authorities. Meanwhile, black slaves in the north revolted against their masters, burning plantations and killing many whites. Sporadic fighting continued during the next two years. Meanwhile, Britain intervened in the struggle to help the whites, while Spain sided with the rebels, hoping to expel the French and regain control of western Hispaniola.

Black Leaders Rise to Power. Among the black rebels fighting in the north was a former slave named TOUSSAINT L'OUVERTURE, who rose rapidly to a high rank in the rebel forces. He was a masterful military and political leader and gradually eliminated all external and internal opponents. By the end of the 1790s, the Spanish and British troops had withdrawn from the struggle and Toussaint's forces turned their attention to a race war (War of the Knives) against the mulatto armies in the south. By 1801, Toussaint had conquered the entire island and abolished slavery. He did not declare independence from France, however, but accepted the post of governor for life.

In 1802, the French ruler Napoleon Bonaparte sent troops to Hispaniola to restore complete French control over the colony. Toussaint and two of his fellow black leaders, Henri CHRISTOPHE and Jean Jacques DESSALINES, battled the French fiercely. But eventually, all three surrendered. Despite agreements Toussaint had reached with the French, he was taken to France, where he died in prison. Christophe and Dessalines rejoined the rebel cause, winning a major victory in 1803 that prompted a mass evacuation of French soldiers and white colonists. The eastern part of the island remained under French authority, but on January 1, 1804, the western part was formally declared the independent republic of Haiti. Dessalines became the first leader of the new nation and proclaimed himself Emperor Jacques I. But his reign was brutal, and he was assassinated two years later.

An Independent Haiti

The Haitian Revolution created a black nation in which the overwhelming majority of inhabitants were the descendants of African slaves. It also brought to power a new elite of black and mulatto leaders who faced the enormous challenge of rebuilding an economy devastated by years of war.

A Divided Nation. After Dessalines's assassination, Haiti split apart. Henri Christophe established a black-controlled government in the north and declared himself king. Alexandre PÉTION, a mulatto leader who had fought against Toussaint, formed a separate republic in the south.

In the north, Christophe attempted to restore the plantations through a system of compulsory labor. He established friendly relations with foreign powers but prepared for the possibility of invasion by building fortresses. In the south, Pétion pursued a more moderate policy, breaking up many large estates and distributing the land to veterans of the revolution. Meanwhile, in 1809, Spain regained control of the eastern portion of the island.

The Nation Reunited. After the deaths of Christophe and Pétion, Haiti was reunified under mulatto leader Jean-Pierre Boyer. Boyer's lengthy presidency, from 1818 to 1843, was a formative period for Haiti. He reconquered eastern Hispaniola in 1822 and ended slavery there. He also opened negotiations with France to gain that nation's recognition of his government.

Boyer dreamed of creating a plantation economy geared to exports. To achieve his goal, in 1826, he issued the *Code Rurale,* a series of laws intended to restrict people's movement and to force them to work on plantations. However, his policies had very limited success and failed to prevent the further breakup of plantations into small landholdings.

Boyer's government was dominated by an elite group of mulattos who used their power and influence to gain personal wealth. Other mulattos and elite blacks agitated for greater democracy. But none of these groups made any attempt to include the masses of rural black peasants or to consider their needs. Discontent and political turmoil led to Boyer's overthrow in 1843. The following year, the eastern portion of Hispaniola permanently broke free from Haitian rule and became the Dominican Republic.

The Road to Foreign Intervention. For the remainder of the 1800s, Haiti experienced long periods of stability under strong dictatorships, followed by brief periods of instability and turmoil. Often a small group of mulattos governed behind a black figurehead who had the support of the peasants.

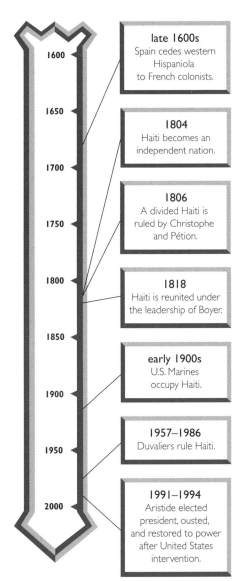

late 1600s
Spain cedes western Hispaniola to French colonists.

1804
Haiti becomes an independent nation.

1806
A divided Haiti is ruled by Christophe and Pétion.

1818
Haiti is reunited under the leadership of Boyer.

early 1900s
U.S. Marines occupy Haiti.

1957–1986
Duvaliers rule Haiti.

1991–1994
Aristide elected president, ousted, and restored to power after United States intervention.

1600
1650
1700
1750
1800
1850
1900
1950
2000

The Haitian "Boat People"

Between 1991 and 1993, as many as 43,000 Haitians attempted to escape economic hardship and political repression by sailing to the United States in small boats. Often called "boat people," some of these Haitians drowned when their flimsy or overloaded boats foundered at sea. Many were intercepted by the U.S. Coast Guard and returned to Haiti. Others were taken to the United States naval base at Guantánamo Bay in Cuba, where they applied for asylum in the United States. Fewer than one-third of the Haitian boat people eventually were granted asylum. The rest were returned to Haiti to face the tremendous problems they had tried to escape.

One of the longest and most damaging dictatorships of that century was that of Faustin SOULOUQUE, a former black slave who ruled as emperor from 1847 to 1859. Soulouque lived like an aristocrat. His economic policies almost completely destroyed Haiti's economy and put the country heavily in debt. He used urban terror squads to eliminate critics and massacred many mulattos. In his desire for more power, Soulouque attempted to reconquer the Dominican Republic, and his defeats there led to his overthrow.

By the late 1800s, the United States had established various military and commercial interests in Haiti. However, recurring unrest there posed a threat to United States interests and those of other nations who had invested in the island nation. In the early 1900s, when it seemed like France, Britain, and Germany might intervene to protect their interests, the United States stepped in and invaded Haiti.

U.S. Marines occupied Haiti from 1915 to 1934. The occupation brought political and financial stability and some material gains. Health conditions improved; roads, hospitals, and schools were built; and foreign investment increased. But United States interests were given priority over Haitian interests, and much Haitian land was sold to foreign investors. These practices angered the Haitians, as did the United States policy of favoring the mulatto elite over the black elite. Resentment of United States occupation persisted until the troops withdrew in 1934.

Haiti in the 1900s

After the United States occupation of Haiti ended, the nation once again began to experience economic problems and political instability. These problems have persisted to the present, leaving Haiti one of the poorest and most distressed nations in the Americas.

See color plate 10, vol. 4.

The Duvaliers. In reaction to the United States occupation of Haiti, several Haitian leaders who governed from the 1930s to the 1950s embraced a movement that rejected European traditions and emphasized Haiti's African heritage. One of these leaders was François DUVALIER, a black physician who won Haiti's presidential election in 1957. He presented himself as a reformer and as a supporter of African traditions.

Duvalier, known as Papa Doc, ruled Haiti for almost 14 years. He established an authoritarian regime, maintaining power by brutally eliminating or exiling his opponents and terrorizing the population with a private army of brutal ruffians called the TONTON MACOUTES. Although Duvalier spoke of revolutionary change, his policies were conservative*. He replaced foreign priests with Haitians and took away some of the privileges of the elites. But he did little to solve the economic and social ills that plagued Haitian peasants. In fact, their standard of living deteriorated more rapidly than ever before.

Upon Duvalier's death in 1971, he was succeeded by his son, Jean-Claude Duvalier, who became known as Baby Doc. His rule was less violent than that of his father, but he still relied on repression to control

* **conservative** inclined to maintain existing political and social views, conditions, and institutions

the population, and his regime was notorious for its corruption and inequality. Widespread discontent caused Duvalier to flee the country in 1986.

Haiti in Recent Years.   Since 1986, Haiti has made several attempts at democracy. Each time, however, civilian rule has been overthrown by a military coup*. One notable democratic presidency was that of Jean-Bertrand ARISTIDE, a former priest who was elected president in 1991. Within a year, a military junta* headed by general Raoul Cedras overthrew and exiled Aristide and began murdering his supporters.

The United States and other nations established a trade embargo* to try to force Haiti's military government to return power to Aristide. In 1994, extensive negotiations and the threat of a United States invasion finally persuaded the military leaders to step down, and Aristide was restored to the presidency. The United States and the United Nations sent troops to Haiti to ensure a peaceful transition to civilian rule. In 1995, Aristide agreed not to seek reelection, and René Préval was elected president.

Although the level of violence in Haiti has been reduced, the possibility of political turmoil remains great. Moreover, the country still faces enormous economic problems that will be difficult for any government to solve. (*See also* **Africans in Latin America; Class Structure, Colonial and Modern; Foreign Debt; French in Latin America; French West Indies; Port-au-Prince; Race and Ethnicity; United States–Latin-American Relations.**)

° **coup** sudden, often violent overthrow of a ruler or government

° **junta** small group of people who run a government, usually after seizing power by force

° **embargo** official order prohibiting the movement of merchant ships in or out of certain ports or countries

See color plate 12, vol. 2.

Haitian Revolution

° **mulatto** person of mixed black and white ancestry

° **republic** government in which citizens elect officials to represent them and govern according to law

*I*n 1791, on the island of HISPANIOLA, mulattos* and blacks in the French colony of St. Domingue (present-day HAITI) rose up in a rebellion against white authorities and wealthy planters. Inspired by the French Revolution of 1789 and its ideas of liberty and equality, the Haitian Revolution lasted for more than a decade. It finally ended in 1804, with the establishment of the independent republic* of Haiti.

As a result of the French Revolution, rich white planters in St. Domingue began to demand greater independence from France. However, they resisted efforts by the colony's mulattos and free blacks to gain their rights. Mulattos responded in early 1791 by rebelling against whites. The crisis escalated in August of that year, when tens of thousands of black slaves revolted against their masters, burned plantations, and killed many whites. War soon raged throughout much of St. Domingue, with many mulattos shifting sides between whites and blacks. Interference by Britain and Spain for political reasons added to the confusion.

Amid the bloody turmoil of the 1790s, a remarkable black leader named TOUSSAINT L'OUVERTURE arose and seized the initiative. A master of military tactics and political maneuvers, Toussaint gradually eliminated most of his opponents. By 1799, he and his rebel forces were engaged in a race war, known as the War of Knives, against mulattos in southern St.

° **siege** prolonged effort by armed troops to force the surrender of a town or fort by surrounding it and cutting it off from aid

° **revolutionary** person engaged in a war to bring about change

° **guerrilla** referring to a group that uses surprise raids to obstruct or harass an enemy or overthrow a government

Domingue led by André Rigaud. During that struggle, two of Toussaint's black commanders gained prominence. Henri CHRISTOPHE led Toussaint's forces in a siege* of mulatto strongholds in the south, and Jean Jacques DESSALINES terrorized mulattos with brutal massacres.

By 1801, Toussaint had defeated the mulatto armies, conquered the Spanish province of SANTO DOMINGO west of St. Domingue, and become ruler of all Hispaniola. A new constitution adopted that year made him governor for life and abolished slavery. It also maintained French rule over St. Domingue—at least in theory.

Toussaint's victories ended the fighting, but only temporarily. In January 1802, France invaded St. Domingue, hoping to restore complete colonial rule. At first, the French met with success, seizing all the main ports. But they had miscalculated the skill and fervor of the black revolutionaries*, who fought a continued guerrilla* war from the island's interior. Before long, however, Christophe surrendered to the French, and Toussaint and Dessalines soon followed. Although other guerrilla leaders continued to fight, the French seemed to have regained the island. Toussaint was taken to France, where he died in prison.

French attempts to disarm the black population led many former slaves to realize that France intended to restore slavery to the island. Many blacks thus fled to the interior and joined the guerrilla forces. Christophe, Dessalines, and some other black leaders, however, supported the French.

Renewed fighting broke out in the fall of 1802, and the war became widespread and marked by dreadful atrocities. By October, the tide had turned. Dessalines, Christophe, and mulatto leader Alexandre PÉTION abandoned the French and rejoined the rebels. Then, in May 1803, England declared war on France. The next month, the British began attacking French troops in St. Domingue. Guerrilla forces led by Dessalines took this opportunity to counterattack, burning plantations and executing whites. Many survivors fled the island.

In November 1803, a mass evacuation of local whites and French soldiers ended French rule in St. Domingue. Independence was formally declared on January 1, 1804, and the new republic was given the Arawak Indian name Haiti. The Haitian Revolution created a nation that was almost entirely black and mulatto. It also devastated the former colony's economy. The new ruling elite of blacks and mulattos faced a difficult struggle to rebuild a nation battered by nearly 15 years of brutal war. (*See also* **French West Indies; Wars of Independence.**)

Havana

*H*avana, a city of more than 2 million people, is CUBA's capital and principal seaport. Founded by Spanish explorer Diego de Velázquez in 1514 on Cuba's southern coast, the capital was relocated in 1519 to its present site on the northern side of the island. This new location gave the city certain advantages—a magnificent natural harbor and proximity to the Gulf Stream*.

Spain declared Havana the colonial capital in 1553. Known as the "Key to the New World," the city commanded the main exit from the

"The Havana Special"

In the 1920s and 1930s, Havana was the center of a busy tourism trade. Although many people traveled to Havana by cruise ship, vacationers could also take a luxury train known as "The Havana Special." The train journeyed down the east coast from New York City to Miami, Florida, then passed over a rail causeway—a raised railroad across the water—to Key West, Florida. From there, the cars were loaded onto ferries that took the vacationers to Havana and other Cuban coastal resort towns. However, in 1936, the train's heyday came to a sudden end, when the rail causeway collapsed into the sea during a violent hurricane.

° **Gulf Stream** major ocean current that forms in the Caribbean and flows through the Gulf of Mexico and into the North Atlantic Ocean

CARIBBEAN SEA to the Atlantic Ocean and the route to and from the busy port of VERACRUZ, Mexico. In the 1500s, ships carrying precious metals from Mexico and from Cartagena (in Colombia) stopped at Havana's harbor before returning to Spain. In the 1700s, Spain began trading not only in precious metals but in agricultural products from the tropics. Havana became an export center, especially of TOBACCO and SUGAR.

After international free trade was introduced in the early 1800s, demand for sugar and tobacco enabled Havana to become a major commercial center. As Cuba's trade increased, so did Havana's population—growing from about 40,000 in the 1770s to almost 100,000 by the 1820s and reaching nearly a quarter of a million by 1900. From 1898, when Cuba gained independence from Spain, until the CUBAN REVOLUTION in 1959, the island developed close economic ties with the United States. The city enjoyed a thriving tourism trade and was a major stop for cruise ships.

Because of its strategic location, Havana has long been a military as well as commercial center. In colonial times, Spain heavily fortified the city, and Havana became the most important stronghold of Spain's American empire. Morro Castle, a fort built to guard the entrance to Havana's harbor, still stands. During the 1700s, in addition to serving as a major naval base, Havana was also an important shipbuilding center. Despite the city's defenses, the British captured Havana in 1762 and occupied the city for nearly a year. Following this incident, Spain invested huge quantities of Mexican silver to rebuild its military strength there. Havana finally regained its historic role as a strategic military base after Cuba achieved independence.

Today Havana remains the hub of Cuba's political, cultural, and commercial activities. It is the nation's center of government, and it houses the University of Havana, several museums, hundreds of sporting facilities, and the national symphony and ballet. However, Havana

Havana was once called the "Key to the New World" because it provided access to the Caribbean Sea, the Atlantic Ocean, and the busy port of Veracruz, Mexico. This engraving shows Havana's magnificent natural harbor as it looked in colonial times.

° **Communist** referring to a social system in which land, goods, and the means of production are owned by the state or community rather than by individuals

° **subsidy** money granted by one state to another

° **persecution** harassment of a group of people, usually because of their beliefs, race, or ethnic origin

suffered hard times in the 1900s, particularly following the Cuban Revolution in 1959. Under dictator Fidel CASTRO, Cuba became allied with the Soviet Union and other Communist* nations. As a result, the United States broke all economic and diplomatic ties with Cuba in 1961. Although Havana received large subsidies* from the Soviet Union until the mid-1980s, much of the city was neglected. Many of its beautiful old buildings and streets became dirty and in need of repair. After the Soviet Union collapsed at the end of the 1980s, life in Havana and the rest of Cuba became increasingly difficult. Food and other supplies were strictly rationed, and the city endured frequent power outages.

In the late 1990s, increased foreign investment from nations other than the United States has improved Cuba's economy somewhat. New hotels, restaurants, and nightclubs have appeared, catering to tourists and the few wealthy Cubans who have United States dollars. Cars—rather than bicycles—once again dominate Havana's streets. However, most of Havana's citizens live in poverty, hunger, and fear of persecution* by Castro's repressive government. (*See also* **Soviet–Latin American Relations; Spain and the Spanish Empire; Spanish-American War.**)

Hawkins, John

1532–1595
English trader

See map in Caribbean Antilles (vol. 1).

° **armada** fleet of warships

John Hawkins of Plymouth, England, sought to establish himself as a legitimate trader with the Spanish empire, but Spain considered him a pirate. Between 1562 and 1568, he organized four trading voyages to the CARIBBEAN ANTILLES, three of which he led personally. His purpose was to exchange cloth and merchandise from England and slaves from Africa with the Spanish in return for SUGAR, hides, and silver. Hawkins tried to secure a license from the Spanish government to trade freely, but Spain refused.

Hawkins's first voyage, from 1562 to 1563, was made during a period of peace between Spain and England and proved to be a prosperous venture. However, his second and third voyages faced serious difficulties, as relations between Spain and England soured and Spain attempted to prohibit foreign trade with its colonies. Hawkins's second voyage, from 1564 to 1565, was directly supported by the English government but had little success in trading. His third voyage, from 1567 to 1569, met with disaster. On his way home, Hawkins encountered bad weather that forced him to dock at the port of San Juan de Ulúa just outside Veracruz, Mexico. The Spaniards, unwilling to allow open trading, had begun treating foreigners as pirates. When they encountered Hawkins's docked fleet, they destroyed most of it. Enduring great hardships, Hawkins and his 15 remaining crewmen managed to return to England.

After helping the English defeat the Spanish Armada* in European wars in 1588, Hawkins and another English explorer, Sir Francis DRAKE, gathered a large fleet and returned to the Caribbean in 1595. They intended to break Spain's power in the Americas. However, the Spaniards were well prepared. They defeated the English at San Juan, Puerto Rico; Cartagena, Colombia; and in Panama, bringing Hawkins's career to a humiliating end. (*See also* **Gold and Silver; Piracy; Slave Trade.**)

Hay–Bunau-Varilla Treaty

° **intermediary** go-between

The Hay–Bunau-Varilla Treaty was an agreement between PANAMA and the United States that provided the legal basis for United States construction of the PANAMA CANAL and the creation of the Canal Zone, an area of more than 500 square miles surrounding the canal and operated by the United States. The treaty was signed on November 18, 1903, just two weeks after Panama declared its independence from COLOMBIA.

The treaty was negotiated and signed by United States secretary of state John Hay and Philippe Bunau-Varilla of France, who served as an intermediary* between Panama, France, and the United States. (France was involved in the negotiations because the French company that had led a failed attempt to construct a canal in Panama retained property rights there.) Bunau-Varilla was committed to seeing the canal built in Panama rather than in another proposed location in nearby Nicaragua. One reason for his enthusiasm was his belief that the United States government would guarantee the success of Panama's revolution once that country had signed a treaty with the United States.

As Panama's first representative to the United States, Bunau-Varilla granted virtually every right and privilege the United States had asked for in an earlier treaty with Colombia, including the right to construct a canal, to fortify it, and to "act as if it were sovereign" in the Canal Zone. In exchange, the United States government agreed to pay Panama $10 million and a $250,000 annual rental fee. In 1936, the United States and Panama signed the Hull-Alfaro Treaty, which increased the annual fee to $436,000, permitted free passage to Panamanians, and made the Canal Zone Panamanian territory. In 1979, the Hay–Bunau-Varilla Treaty was replaced by treaties that established joint operation of the canal until December 31, 1999, when it will be turned over to Panama. (*See also* **United States–Latin American Relations.**)

Haya de la Torre, Víctor Raúl

1895–1979
Peruvian political leader

° **populist** appealing to the common people

° **nationalist** relating to devotion to the nation's interests

° **imperialism** domination of the political, economic, and cultural life of one country or region by another country

One of PERU's most important politicians of the 1900s, Víctor Raúl Haya de la Torre founded the Popular Revolutionary Alliance of America (APRA) in 1924 and the Peruvian Aprista Party (PAP) in 1931. His supporters, mainly from the lower middle classes of Peru, were attracted by his charming personality, his populist* and nationalist* views, and his unifying appeal among Peru's various Indian cultures.

Born into a prominent but not wealthy family in the coastal city of Trujillo, Haya studied law as a young man. In 1919, he rallied behind Peruvian workers in their fight for an eight-hour workday. He became president of the Student Federation and established the base for the future Aprista Party. In 1924, Haya was exiled for his political stance and went to Mexico, where he began the APRA movement. APRA sought to increase Indian pride, redistribute land and wealth, improve literacy, and fight imperialism*.

In 1930, Haya returned to Peru. The following year, he ran in the presidential election but lost to nationalist colonel Luis Sánchez Cerro. Claiming that the election had been a fraud, the Aprista Party organized an uprising in Trujillo that was brutally suppressed by the army. Haya was imprisoned but later freed after Sánchez Cerro died in 1933. Thereafter, Haya engaged in politics behind the scenes and did not openly campaign again until 1945, when Luis José Bustamante y Rivero, backed by the Aprista Party, was elected president. However, in 1948, another uprising led Haya to seek asylum in the Colombian embassy in LIMA. In 1963, Haya again ran for election but was defeated, and a military overthrow of the government later in that decade further delayed his ambitions. In 1978, Haya finally won the largely ceremonial post of president of the Constituent Assembly. (*See also* **Nationalism; Political Parties.**)

Healers, Folk

See *Curanderos.*

Henry the Navigator, Prince

1394–1460
Portuguese prince

*P*rince Henry the Navigator is one of the most controversial figures in Portuguese history. He is noted for promoting the voyages of discovery that led to Portugal's creation of an overseas empire, but historians differ in their views about the extent and motives of his leadership. Writers of Henry's day portrayed him in many very different ways—as a shrewd politician, as a practical man preoccupied with the idea of overseas expansion, and as a pious crusader.

Henry was the third son of King John I of Portugal and had a strong interest in mathematics and astronomy. Around 1415, he played a key role in the Portuguese expedition that captured the North African port of Ceuta, then believed to be a link to gold-producing lands south of the Sahara. When the Portuguese succeeded, Henry was made governor of the city. Henry planned and raised money for many other expeditions along the northwest coast of Africa, bringing mapmakers, astronomers, and mathematicians to his court at the southern tip of Portugal. By the time of his death in 1460, Portuguese exploration had reached the coast of present-day Sierra Leone in western Africa. Most importantly, by supporting these voyages, Henry had laid the foundation for the navigational skills and knowledge necessary for Portugal's later conquests in Africa, Asia, and the Americas. (*See also* **Explorers and Exploration; Portugal and the Portuguese Empire.**)

Hidalgo

*H*idalgo is a Spanish term that originally meant "son of some means" *(hijo d'algo).* The term indicated a person of some wealth, but not an heir to a great fortune or nobility. It applied to some of the leaders of Spain's conquest of the Americas who were members of the lesser nobility seeking their fortune overseas.

In the 1500s, Spanish hidalgos were identified by the title don and women by the feminine doña. Spanish leaders also addressed wealthy indigenous* peoples who collaborated with them as "don" as a form of

* **indigenous** referring to the original inhabitants of a region

flattery and in the hope of maintaining their support. After the conquest, Spaniards continued to use "don" in addressing indigenous political leaders.

Over the course of the colonial period, settlers ceased using the titles don and doña and the term *hidalgo* to identify members of the lesser nobility. Instead, these became general terms of respect used for an older person, a master craftsman, an employer, or someone in a position of authority. (*See also* **Class Structure.**)

Hidalgo y Costilla, Miguel

1753–1811
Priest and Mexican revolutionary

° **curate** priest in charge of a parish

° **Creole** person of European ancestry born in the Americas

° **militia** army of citizens who may be called into action in a time of emergency

° **mestizo** person of mixed European and Indian ancestry

See color plate 6, vol. 3.

Miguel Hidalgo y Costilla led MEXICO's revolution against Spain in 1810, but he did not live to see that revolution won. The son of an agricultural administrator from the province of Guanajuato in central Mexico, Hidalgo became a priest in 1778. Although he gained positive recognition for his forward thinking, Hidalgo found himself in trouble with his superiors. Finally, in 1803, he was appointed curate* to the prosperous town of Dolores. A landowner, educator, and reformer, Hidalgo devoted much of his time to stimulating industrial development. He introduced a pottery works, a tannery, a brick factory, vineyards, and mulberry trees for raising silkworms. Although he was highly respected in intellectual circles, some of his activities brought him into conflict with colonial and church officials.

It is not known exactly when Hidalgo began to support the idea of Mexican independence, but before the revolution, he befriended fellow independence fighter Ignacio Allende and associated with local Creole* leaders who were eager for revolution. The revolt started on September 16, 1810, when Hidalgo led his brother Mariano, Ignacio Allende, and a few others to free prisoners who were being held at the local jail. After gathering members of the local militia*, Hidalgo marched on the towns of San Miguel el Grande and Celaya, arresting Spaniards and threatening to execute them if they resisted. Many Indians and mestizos* from local villages and haciendas joined the rebellion. Armed with lances, knives, slings, bows, agricultural tools, sticks, or stones, they marched triumphantly from town to town, proclaiming Hidalgo their supreme commander. When Spanish troops at the city of Guanajuato fought back on September 28, Hidalgo's followers massacred the royalists (supporters of the Spanish monarchy) and looted the city. Hidalgo and his force of about 60,000 men then occupied the city of Valladolid in the province of Morelia. Hidalgo was declared generalíssimo (commander in chief), and the rebels marched toward the capital, Mexico City. However, Hidalgo abandoned his plan to occupy the capital, realizing that his forces needed better discipline and weapons.

During the autumn of 1810, the rebels suffered a series of defeats by the royalist forces. After each defeat, the rebel forces scattered, abandoning artillery and equipment. Their biggest loss occurred in January 1811, when an enormous rebel force of up to 100,000 men was defeated at Guadalajara.

Hidalgo failed to develop a strategic plan to fight the war. He also had no plan for the type of government that would replace the colonial

* **tribute** payment made to a dominant power

* **defrock** to take away a priest's right to perform the rites of his religion

administration. Nonetheless, he appointed a minister of justice and a minister of state and named an ambassador to the United States. He also abolished SLAVERY, eliminated the despised tribute* tax for Indians, and ended state control of paper and gunpowder. However, his dependence on the lower classes for support and his acceptance of the slaughter of Spanish prisoners divided public opinion. The great majority of Creoles supported the royalist cause.

Following their defeat at Guadalajara, Hidalgo and his senior commanders fled north to seek assistance in the United States. But as they marched across the province of Coahuila in northern Mexico, they were taken by surprise and captured. Hidalgo was sent to the city of Chihuahua for trial, where he was defrocked* and executed by firing squad. His head and those of Allende and other revolutionary leaders were sent to be displayed at the four corners of the Alhóndiga—a fortresslike granary in the city of Guanajuato. After Mexico won its independence, Hidalgo was greatly honored for leading the revolution, and his remains were reburied in Mexico City.

Highways and Roads

* **navigable** deep and wide enough to provide passage for ships

* **tribute** payment made to a dominant power

*H*ighways have always served as important links between otherwise isolated regions. They connect small towns to large cities, and producers to their markets. Roads promote change and growth by making it easier for people to communicate information and ideas. Vast open spaces, mountainous or jungle terrain, and a lack of navigable* rivers have made roads important in much of Latin America. However, until the 1900s, highway networks in Latin America had expanded very little since the time of the ancient AZTEC and INCA empires.

Ancient Highways. Both the Aztec and the Inca empires expanded along roads necessary for the movement of their armies. In Aztec Mexico, routes running north-south and east-west linked the principal towns in the Valley of Mexico. A primary east-west route linked the eastern coastal trading villages with the Valley of Mexico, and then ran down the western slope of the mountains to the Pacific Ocean near Acapulco. North-south routes went in many directions from the valley, funneling tribute* into the Aztec capital and carrying armies outward on marches of conquest. Control of roads was critical and was one of the first objectives of warfare. At the height of the Aztecs' power, their highways reached as far south as Central America and north of present-day Mexico City. The Spaniards later used these roads during their conquest of the Americas.

The capital city of Cuzco lay at the center of the Inca empire's sophisticated highway network. The Inca administered their roads strictly and efficiently. They enforced local maintenance of roadbeds and of rest houses, called *tambos*. The Inca network branched out from Cuzco, reaching as far north as present-day Ecuador and as far south as Santiago, Chile. One route, through the ANDES mountains, was a particularly spectacular feat of highway engineering. The road was often 25 feet wide, and it was sometimes cut into solid rock. The Inca built massive retaining walls to support portions of the road and wove suspension bridges of wool or plant fiber cables to span wide streams. This highway enabled the Inca to transport goods through difficult terrain by foot and by llama. They also used the route to convey messages swiftly, using couriers on foot and a system of visual signals sent down the road from one watchtower to the next.

Colonial Highways. During the colonial* period, the Indian highway networks changed little and, in some cases, fell into disrepair. Although the Spanish colonists extended some existing roads, they devoted most of their efforts to creating roads that reached new MINING areas. Most colonial roads were little more than unpaved trails, especially in the highlands.

In colonial Mexico, the main routes included the Veracruz–Mexico City–Acapulco road, linking the Atlantic and Pacific oceans and, therefore, connecting Europe with Asia. Another major trade route led north from Mexico City and through the mining towns of central and northern Mexico. These roads not only served the silver economies and regional trade of Latin America, but they also brought Iberian* culture to remote outposts.

The most important land route in Central America was the road across the Isthmus* of Panama. The difficult mountain trail channeled Peruvian silver from Panama City to the coast and then to Europe. Another major silver road traversed much of the Andes, serving the mines of Upper Peru. Peruvian roads were built on the Inca system that linked the capital of Lima with the mines of Potosí and then through the South American interior to the Atlantic ports of Buenos Aires and

° **colonial** period between the European conquest and independence, generally from the early 1500s to the early 1800s

° **Iberian** from or related to Spain and Portugal, the countries that occupy Europe's Iberian Peninsula

° **isthmus** narrow strip of land connecting two larger land masses

This photograph, taken in the 1930s, shows workers in El Salvador constructing a stretch of the Pan-American Highway. Completed in 1963, the highway connects the capitals of 17 Latin American nations and has become a major trade route in the region.

The Pan-American Highway

The Pan-American Highway system is an international project linking North and South America. First proposed in 1925, the Pan-American Highway extends 29,525 miles from the United States–Mexico border to southern Chile. It is interrupted in only one place—the Darién Gap, a stretch of jungle about 90 miles long near the Panama-Colombia border. The highway connects the capitals of 17 Latin American nations and links the west and east coasts of South America. It serves both as a major commercial route and as a unifying tie between American countries.

Montevideo. This was the dominant trade and communication route in South America, and it connected all the major cities.

During the colonial period, Latin America's highway systems remained largely unchanged, except for those of Brazil. There, by 1800, a dynamic system of mule trains, slave labor, and new roads was established to carry COFFEE from plantations to the ports of Rio de Janeiro and São Paulo.

Modern Highways. The wars of independence stifled road development in most of Latin America in the early 1800s, and later in that century, the expansion of RAILROADS and ports took priority over highway development. However, most Latin American nations began comprehensive highway construction programs in the early 1900s, when motor transportation made it possible to exploit previously unsettled lands. Argentina and Mexico especially improved their road systems. In the years following World War II, most Latin American countries expanded their highways. However, by the 1970s and 1980s, difficulties in financing slowed many highway programs.

Perhaps the most ambitious road construction program—the Transamazon Highway—occurred in Brazil. Begun in 1957, the highway connects Brazil's northeastern coast to remote regions of the Amazon basin as part of a long-term plan to develop Brazil's backlands. The highway stretches over 3,000 miles and was built in several phases. Similar projects, although on a much smaller scale, in Colombia, Ecuador, Peru, and Bolivia have also attempted to penetrate parts of the Amazon.

Hispaniola

* **garrison** military post

See map in Caribbean Antilles (vol. 1).

* **indigenous** referring to the original inhabitants of a region

Named by explorer Christopher COLUMBUS, the island of Hispaniola lies in the Caribbean Sea between CUBA and PUERTO RICO. Hispaniola was the site of the first recorded European settlement in the Americas. Today the island is divided into two nations: HAITI in the west and the DOMINICAN REPUBLIC in the east.

Columbus landed on Hispaniola during his first voyage in 1492 and left behind a group of men in the garrison* town of Navidad. Upon his return in 1493, he found the settlers dead and Navidad in ruins. Still determined to establish a colony on the island, he founded the town of Isabela to the east, but this settlement also was short-lived. In 1496, the Spaniards finally succeeded in establishing a permanent base of operations at the city of SANTO DOMINGO on Hispaniola's southern coast. For the next 20 years, Santo Domingo served as a strategic port from which they explored, conquered, and colonized the surrounding islands and mainland.

The Spaniards did not manage Hispaniola well. Their exploitation of the island's indigenous* people, the Taino, led to an uprising in 1494. Despite attempts at reform, continued abuse and exposure to European diseases soon killed most of Hispaniola's Indians. Meanwhile, the Spaniards had exhausted the island's limited supply of gold. When richer territories were discovered on the mainland, Spain quickly lost

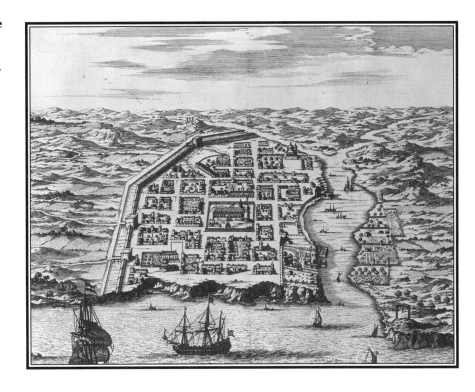

Santo Domingo, shown in this 1671 engraving, is located on the island of Hispaniola. Founded in 1496, Santo Domingo is the oldest European-built city in the Western Hemisphere.

See color plate 4, vol. 4.

° **cede** to yield or surrender, usually by treaty

interest in Hispaniola. France established a colony on the island's western coast, while the British and Dutch took possession of the surrounding islands. In 1697, Spain ceded* the western third of Hispaniola to France, which named the colony St. Domingue (present-day Haiti). The Spanish withdrew to the eastern two-thirds of the island, which became the Dominican Republic in 1844.

Honduras

° **federation** political union of separate states with a central government

Located in the middle of CENTRAL AMERICA, Honduras shares the cultural heritage and history of that region, and for long periods of time, it has been part of various Central American federations*. When it became an independent nation in 1838, Honduras was the least developed and poorest country in the region, and it has struggled to solve many social, economic, and political problems. Hondurans have suffered from frequent disruptive changes of government and from interference in their political affairs by the United States and its neighbors, especially Guatemala. Yet Honduras was spared the bloody civil wars that erupted in some other Central American countries in the late 1900s, and by the 1990s, it was enjoying political stability and economic development.

The Land.   Honduras sprawls across Central America, stretching from the Caribbean Sea on the north coast to the Pacific Ocean on the southwest. Its neighbors are GUATEMALA (northwest), EL SALVADOR (west), and NICARAGUA (southeast). With an area of more than 43,000 square miles, Honduras is Central America's second-largest nation, after Nicaragua.

See map in Central America (vol. I).

The landscape of Honduras is shaped by mountain ranges—not especially tall, but very rugged—that carve the country's interior into highland valleys that have always been the centers of settlement. The country's easternmost coast is part of the Mosquito Coast, a low-lying coastal plain that also covers the eastern part of neighboring Nicaragua. A similar lowland area in northern Honduras is known as the North Coast. Despite much timber harvesting, Honduras still has large forested areas that include tropical hardwoods in the coastal plains and pines in the central and western highlands. The country's two seasons are defined by rainfall. *Verano,* the dry season, lasts from January to May. The rest of the year is *invierno,* the wet season.

Early and Colonial History.

Before the arrival of Europeans, Honduras was home to various Indian groups. Among them were the Maya, who lived in territory that stretched from southern Mexico and the Yucatán to present-day Nicaragua. Today the ruins of the Maya city of Copán in Honduras are one of the most impressive sites of this Mesoamerican* culture.

The European exploration of Honduras began in 1502, when Christopher Columbus explored the northern coast during his fourth and last voyage, claiming the land for Spain. During the early 1500s, conquistadors* brought Central America under Spanish control. In Honduras, they established coastal settlements, such as Puerto Caballos, before moving inland to conquer and settle the interior. The Spanish sought to convert the Indians to Christianity and also to squeeze labor and tribute* from them. Soon, however, diseases, newly introduced by the Europeans, swept across Central America in devastating epidemics, killing perhaps 80 or 90 percent of the Native American population.

Throughout the colonial* period, the land that is now Honduras was part of Spain's Kingdom of Guatemala, which also included present-day Guatemala, El Salvador, Belize, Nicaragua, and Costa Rica. In the eyes of Spain, the Kingdom of Guatemala was only part of the larger colony called the Viceroyalty* of Mexico, and the colonists in Central America owed loyalty and paid tribute to Mexico as well as to Spain. But the real center of the Central American universe in colonial times was the city of Santiago, in present-day Guatemala, the capital of the kingdom. From here Spanish and Creole* officials and elite landowners imposed political, economic, cultural, and social unity on Central America for 300 years.

The province of Honduras was a remote and isolated area within the Kingdom of Guatemala until the 1700s. At that time, Spain introduced new policies called the Bourbon Reforms to change the way its colonies were administered, and one result of these reforms was growing interest in the economic development of isolated regions. Hondurans began to mine silver, and a flourishing ranching community emerged to drive large herds of cattle to markets in El Salvador and Guatemala.

During the late 1700s and early 1800s, two trends appeared in Honduras and the rest of Central America. First, provinces that had once been dominated by Guatemala began to develop their own identities

* **Mesoamerican** referring to Mesoamerica, a culture region that includes central and southern Mexico, Guatemala, Belize, El Salvador, and parts of Honduras, Nicaragua, and Costa Rica; an inhabitant of Mesoamerica

* **conquistador** Spanish explorer and conqueror

* **tribute** payment made to a dominant power

* **colonial** period between the European conquest and independence, generally from the early 1500s to the early 1800s

* **viceroyalty** region governed by a viceroy, a royally appointed official

* **Creole** person of European ancestry born in the Americas

and to become economically and politically important in their own right. Second, strong differences of opinion appeared among the colonial elite regarding such matters as the role of the church, economic development, and the question of independence from Spain. Few Central Americans of the early 1800s, however, pictured independence for the individual provinces of the Kingdom of Guatemala.

When Mexico declared its independence from Spain in 1821, a council of leading colonial citizens from the Kingdom of Guatemala agreed to become part of the newly created Mexican empire. But two years later an elected assembly declared the region's independence from Mexico and formed the United Provinces of Central America. Two Hondurans—José Cecilio del Valle and Francisco Morazán—were elected to the presidency of the United Provinces. But this loose confederation of states did not last long. By the early 1840s, it had broken up because of rivalries among the provinces and between liberals* and conservatives*. The civil wars and widespread strife of this period created regional hostilities and resentments that would affect Central America for many years beyond the brief lifetime of the United Provinces.

Since Independence. Honduras, along with Nicaragua and Costa Rica, declared itself independent of the United Provinces in 1838. In many ways, the country was ill-prepared to become a republic*. Honduras had fewer than 150,000 inhabitants, many of them living in small villages tucked away in isolated mountain valleys. Cattlemen on the eastern and southern plains had little in common with the mahogany* loggers of the northern coast or with the Indian and mestizo* peasant farmers of the interior. Treacherous mule paths winding over mountains and through rivers were the only link between these different parts of the country. In addition, there was considerable rivalry between Comayagua, the run-down old provincial capital, and TEGUCIGALPA, a new mining and commercial town that eventually became the nation's capital.

The conservatives came to power in Honduras after independence and remained in control of the country until 1875. Struggles with liberal leaders degenerated into personal feuds between rival caudillos* and their private armies. For years, Honduras was in a turmoil of civil unrest and banditry. During this time, Great Britain and the United States frequently interfered in Honduran affairs. For example, British ships fired on north coast ports to force loan repayments. In addition, an enormous debt that Honduras acquired when it borrowed money from London banks to build a short stretch of railway crippled the nation's economy for nearly 100 years.

In the late 1800s, Justo Rufino Barrios, the liberal president of Guatemala, arranged the overthrow of the conservatives in Honduras, enabling the liberals to come to power. They promoted modernization through road building and the installation of a telegraph system, and they encouraged rapid economic progress. In the 1880s, a brief silver boom spurred highway construction and the growth of small industries. Much of this progress was undone, however, during a bloody civil

° **liberal** person who supports greater participation in government for individuals; one who is not bound by political and social traditions

° **conservative** one who is opposed to sudden change, especially in existing political and social institutions

° **republic** government in which citizens elect officials to represent them and govern according to law

° **mahogany** hardwood that is used to make cabinets and fine furniture

° **mestizo** person of mixed European and Indian ancestry

° **caudillo** authoritarian leader or dictator, often from the military

213

Honduras

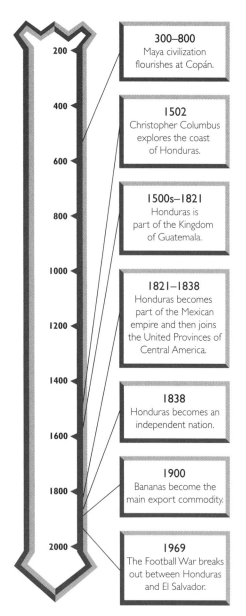

300–800
Maya civilization flourishes at Copán.

1502
Christopher Columbus explores the coast of Honduras.

1500s–1821
Honduras is part of the Kingdom of Guatemala.

1821–1838
Honduras becomes part of the Mexican empire and then joins the United Provinces of Central America.

1838
Honduras becomes an independent nation.

1900
Bananas become the main export commodity.

1969
The Football War breaks out between Honduras and El Salvador.

° **depression** period of little economic activity during which many people become unemployed

° **junta** small group of people who run a government, usually after seizing power by force

war between liberal and conservative groups in the late 1800s that ended with a liberal victory.

Throughout the 1800s, the Honduran elites had been poorer than the ruling classes in other Central American countries. The peasants of Honduras, however, existed comfortably by growing food for their families and selling small amounts of wood, tobacco, hides, and indigo. Plantation labor became more common in the early 1900s, when new developments, such as refrigerated cargo ships and the control of tropical fevers, enabled foreign and Honduran investors to establish a thriving BANANA INDUSTRY. By 1930, firms such as the UNITED FRUIT COMPANY had made Honduras the world's top exporter of bananas.

The rise of the banana industry came at a cost to Honduran democracy. Because the banana companies needed favorable decisions from the government on such matters as land grants for plantations, labor laws, and permission to build railroads, they increasingly meddled in Honduran affairs, supporting politicians who granted them favors.

The 1920s were a time of severe political upheaval in Honduras, with 17 uprisings during one four-year period alone. The United States sent gunships and marines to suppress a civil war in 1923. Then banana plant diseases ravaged the banana plantations, and the worldwide economic depression* of the 1930s brought a sharp drop in employment and earnings in Honduras. Although the government of Tiburcio Carías Andino was a dictatorship, it managed to keep order during this terrible time. In 1954, agents of the U.S. Central Intelligence Agency (CIA) in Honduras launched a secret military operation against the government of Guatemala, drawing Honduras into regional conflict.

A military junta* seized control of the Honduran government in 1957 and, except for a few short-lived periods of democratic rule, remained in power until 1978. During the 1960s, Honduras blamed its difficult economic difficulties on the more than 300,000 Salvadorans who had poured into the country to escape the civil war. Tension between El Salvador and Honduras erupted into the Football War of 1969—so called because rising tensions first erupted into violence during a World Cup football (soccer) game between the two countries during that year. The Honduran air force performed well and the Organization of American States (OAS) managed to halt the war before Salvadoran troops launched a major invasion into Honduras. In 1978, General Policarpo Paz García took control of the government and slowly returned it to civilian politicians. A peaceful, democratic election in 1985 made liberal José Azcona president.

The 1980s saw economic troubles and the buildup of United States forces in Honduras, sent there to combat antigovernment rebels in Nicaragua, El Salvador, and Guatemala. Many of these rebels, especially those from Nicaragua, operated from bases in Honduras. In 1990, however, political changes in Nicaragua and other Central America countries paved the way for the rebels and refugees to return to their home countries, although in 1997 there were still many refugees in Honduras, either living in United Nations camps near the borders or scattered throughout the countryside. Hondurans elected Carlos Roberto Reina of the Liberal Party president in 1994.

An American in Honduras

Ephraim George Squier was the official representative of the United States in Central America for one year, 1849. During that year, the busy diplomat shifted the balance of foreign influence in the region from Great Britain to the United States. The passage of thousands of gold-seeking "forty-niners" around South America on their way to California convinced Squier of the need to build an interoceanic railway across Honduras, but he was unable to make a success of this project. Nevertheless, he became the leading authority on the region. He is known today for his books on Central America.

° **infrastructure** basic framework of a society and its economy, which includes roads, bridges, port facilities, airports, and other public works

Modern Honduras. In the late 1990s, the population of Honduras numbered about 5.5 million people, with most of the population concentrated in the central and western valleys and along the North Coast. Two-thirds of the people live in rural communities. The remainder live in towns and cities, of which the largest are Tegucigalpa, San Pedro Sula, La Ceiba, and Choluteca. About 93 percent of Hondurans are of mixed Spanish and Indian ancestry and speak Spanish. Another 5 percent are Indians. The rest of the population consists of various smaller ethnic groups, including the Garifuna, or Black Caribs, English-speaking descendants of Africans who came to Honduras from Caribbean islands.

Bananas are still one of the country's leading exports, along with coffee. Other export products include sugarcane, cattle, tobacco, and seafoods. The timber industry has become economically important, and like other tropical nations, Honduras is wrestling with the difficulties of balancing timber harvesting and forest conservation. Tourism is another growing industry; two big attractions are the Maya ruins at Copán and the superb scuba diving around the Islas de la Bahia (Bay Islands) off the northern coast. Industries include the manufacture or processing of soft drinks, beer, cooking oil, rum, cement, cleaning products, and cloth.

Honduras has always been closely involved with the other parts of Central America, and in the 1990s, Hondurans were working to promote regional cooperation through such projects as shared ports, highways and railways, and electrical systems. However, in 1998, after hurricane Mitch hit the region, Honduras was devastated. The hurricane left more than 10,000 dead and more than 30,000 missing or injured, and caused enormous losses to the Honduran economy. More than 800,000 homes were also destroyed in this hurricane, and many consider Mitch to be the country's worst disaster. Honduras lost most of its infrastructure*, crops, and industries. Many countries, including France, the United States, and Japan, as well as the World Bank have offered billions of dollars in aid. Some countries have even canceled the debts that Hondurans owed to their governments. Even so, it will take more than 15 years for Hondurans to rebuild the nation and its economy. (*See also* **Central America, United Provinces of.**)

Houssay, Bernardo A.

1887–1971
Argentine medical scientist

° **physiology** branch of biology that studies living bodies and how they function

*B*ernardo Houssay was the first Latin American to receive a Nobel Prize for contributions to science. During his long career in physiology*, Houssay was greatly admired by the medical and scientific world, but he sometimes clashed with the political leaders of Argentina.

Born in BUENOS AIRES, Houssay studied medicine at the University of Buenos Aires, where he began teaching medicine in 1910. In 1933, he helped found the Asociación Argentina para el Progreso de las Ciencias (Argentine Association for Progress in the Sciences), which attracted and disbursed funds for scientific research in Argentina. Although he was one of many intellectuals who lost their positions under

Argentina's military government in the 1940s, Houssay pursued his scientific endeavors by working for private employers. He became known internationally for his writings on nutrition, diabetes, and medical education. In 1947, Houssay shared the Nobel Prize for physiology or medicine for his research on the role of the pituitary gland in carbohydrate metabolism. Houssay served as the president of Argentina's National Council for Scientific and Technical Research and remained active in his profession until his death in 1971.

Huari

° **archaeologist** scientist who studies past human cultures, usually by excavating ruins

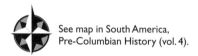

See map in South America, Pre-Columbian History (vol. 4).

° **imperial** relating to an emperor or empire

Pilgrimage to Pachacamac

As early as A.D. 540, Indians in the Andes region of South America worshiped Pachacamac, a god whose name meant "creator of the earth." His temple, near present-day Lima, was one of the most sacred places of the Huari empire. Pilgrims came from distant places to visit the shrine, which contained an image of Pachacamac. To appear before the idol, a worshiper spent a year in preparations that included fasts and rituals. The Inca adopted Pachacamac and his priesthood into their religion and enlarged his temple. However, in 1533, Spanish conqueror Hernando Pizarro visited the shrine and knocked down the sacred idol in front of several stunned Indians.

*T*he name Huari (or Wari) applies to the civilization that once flourished in PERU and also to the large city that served as its capital. Archaeologists* believe the Huari people developed the tradition of empire building that was later taken over by the better-known INCA.

The city of Huari and the Huari empire existed between about A.D. 650 and 1000. Located in the eastern portion of Peru's Ayacucho Valley, the city appears to have been built with highly organized urban planning methods. Archaeological examinations of the city's ruins show that the Huari buildings consisted of rooms of standardized sizes and shapes, arranged in orderly patterns. A square structure with a central courtyard or patio, surrounded by narrow two- or three-story balconies or hallways, was a common style of construction in the capital city. The architecture in smaller Huari towns was similar to that in the capital, leading archaeologists to believe that a central decision-making body might have planned all Huari towns, even if local builders completed the actual construction.

Huari architecture and pottery found at archaeological sites suggest the extent of the Huari civilization. Their power and influence reach out to distant territories north, south, and west of the central Peruvian valley. Archaeological evidence also suggests that the Huari brought other groups under their control through the use of military force and religious conversion. Images on pottery show that the Huari spread their religion throughout the empire, as did the Inca within their own empire in the Andes.

The Inca appear to have inherited several other features of Huari civilization. The Huari did not have a written language, but they used colored knotted strings called QUIPUS for record keeping. They also built roads connecting the capital to outlying districts. Centuries later, the Inca used quipus for information storage and built the imperial* highway system based on Huari roads.

Early European colonists and historians overlooked the Huari civilization because it was overshadowed by the TIWANAKU empire in Bolivia and the Inca empire in Peru. They failed to recognize the importance of the Huari ruins as they focused their attention on better-known ruins such as those at the Bolivian city of Tiwanaku. Modern studies, however, have given the Huari their rightful place in South American history as the oldest known empire in the region. (*See also* **Cultures, Pre-Columbian.**)

Huerta, Victoriano

1845–1916
Mexican general and president

° **conservative** inclined to maintain existing political and social views, conditions, and institutions

See color plate 8, vol. 4.

° **totalitarian** referring to a government that exercises complete control over individuals, often by force

Born in the state of Jalisco to a soldier and an Indian woman, Victoriano Huerta rose to become a powerful general who seized control of the Mexican government in 1913. Most historians regard him as one of the darkest forces of the MEXICAN REVOLUTION, a brutal tyrant who hoped to return Mexico to dictatorship. At least one historian, however, claims that Huerta was an improvement over some other conservative* leaders, especially in his policies concerning land reform, labor, and foreign relations.

Huerta graduated from the National Military College in 1876 and rose through the army ranks to become a general in 1912. He fought rebellious MAYA in the Yucatán peninsula and led federal troops against the forces of rebel leaders such as Emiliano ZAPATA during the revolution. In 1913, during a revolt in Mexico City, President Francisco Madero placed Huerta in command of all federal forces. However, Huerta betrayed Madero by making a deal with the rebels. He agreed to join forces with them in exchange for the presidency. He then forced Madero and his vice president to resign and probably issued the order under which they were shot to death.

Huerta's rule was harsh. Supported only by the Catholic Church and the extreme conservatives, Huerta closed the national congress, killed his opponents, militarized the nation, and rigged an election to ensure his presidency. His brutal and totalitarian* rule undermined his support and provoked his opponents. In April 1914, United States president Woodrow Wilson moved against Huerta by sending troops to occupy the port of Veracruz, thus reducing Huerta's income and his ability to import arms. In July 1914, with the armies of his enemies closing in on Mexico City, Huerta fled Mexico. A year later, United States marshals arrested him in New Mexico as he tried to sneak back into Mexico to attempt to regain power. Huerta remained in prison in Texas until his death.

Huichols

° **shaman** priest who uses magic or spiritual powers to heal the sick

° **hallucinogen** drug or substance that causes illusions, usually of something that is not present or real

The Huichols are a Mexican Indian group concentrated in Jalisco and Nayarit in the northwestern part of Mexico. They are the largest Indian group in that country to have preserved their ancient religion intact, without significant Catholic influence.

The Huichols, whose language and customs resemble those of other northwestern Mexican Indians, call themselves Wixarika or Wixarite. About half of all Huichols live in five traditional settlements in the rugged Sierra Madre Occidental, Mexico's western mountain range. They live in scattered homesteads, each occupied by an extended family. These homesteads often have their own *xiriki,* or "god-house," while larger temples are found in the ceremonial and governmental centers. Until recently, the Huichols did not occupy these centers except during festivals and rituals. They worship the gods of fire, deer, and the sun and the goddess of earth and creation among many others. Shamans* serve as priests and conduct ceremonies of worship either for the whole community or for a single family. Huichol rituals involve the use of the sacred peyote cactus, a hallucinogenic* substance.

217

For centuries, the Huichols have produced sacred art, including colorful woolen yarn images of mythological subjects and events. Recently, they have begun to make these items for sale as folk art. Some Huichols now live outside their traditional settlements and in or near cities such as Tepic, Guadalajara, Durango, Zacatecas, and Mexico City. Recognizable by their distinctive native costume, the Huichols continue to maintain ties to their homeland and religion.

Humaitá

° **siege** prolonged effort by armed troops to force the surrender of a town or fort by surrounding it and cutting it off from aid

Humaitá is a strategic point on the east bank of South America's Paraguay River. The massive fort at Humaitá defended PARAGUAY from Brazilian and Argentine forces during the WAR OF THE TRIPLE ALLIANCE and was the site of a long and bloody siege* in the 1860s.

During the late colonial era, the Spanish had established a guard post near Humaitá to discourage smuggling on the Paraguay River. In the 1850s, when Brazilian traffic on the river increased, the Paraguayans engaged British military engineers and built a large stone fort at Humaitá. When allied Brazilian and Argentine armies attempted to invade the Paraguayan capital of Asunción in 1867, the 380-cannon fortress held them off. A series of fierce battles outside the fort left as many as 100,000 men dead. Meanwhile, attacks from enemy vessels in the river made it impossible for Paraguay to supply the fort with fresh troops or supplies. After 13 months, the last starving defenders evacuated the fort, opening the way for the allied armies to march toward Asunción. Today Humaitá lies in ruins, but parts of it—especially the small church at its center—have been restored as a national monument.

Human Rights

° **totalitarian** referring to a government that exercises complete control over individuals, often by force

° **pre-Columbian** before the arrival of Christopher Columbus and other Europeans in the Americas in the 1490s

Human rights violations in Latin America became a major issue during the second half of the 1900s for two reasons. First, both the number and severity of violations were on the increase, especially in nations under totalitarian* military rule. Second, Latin American and international human rights organizations formed to protest and end these violations. Although human rights violations became more visible, they were not new. Human rights abuses dated from pre-Columbian* times, but only during the colonial period did protests rise against them.

According to the American Convention of Human Rights, everyone is entitled to certain basic rights, including the right to life, physical integrity (freedom from torture), due process (freedom from being arrested, tried, or punished unlawfully), and freedom of thought, conscience, and religion. Other groups classify human rights as civil rights (including freedom of speech, freedom of the press, and freedom from unlawful harassment), political rights (voting, organizing labor unions, holding meetings and assemblies, and being free to join any political party), and socioeconomic rights (access to jobs, housing, clean water, education, and medical care). Although people sometimes disagree on the order of importance of these rights or the degree to which the state should guarantee them, they all concur that governments should protect the human rights of all citizens equally.

Human Rights Abuses.　　Although it is difficult to date exactly when violations of human rights began in Latin America, it is known that during the colonial era, the exploitation of Native Americans, and later of African slaves, was widespread. In the beginning, the Europeans who colonized the Americas felt obligated to evangelize* the Indians and teach them how to work in order to assimilate them into the new colonial society. They believed these peoples were inferior. A notable exception in the early colonial period was Dominican friar* Bartolomé de LAS CASAS, who insisted that the Indians were human beings and that Europeans should respect their rights. Modern human rights activists* point to Las Casas as an inspiration for their work.

Despite the efforts of Las Casas and other learned Europeans, exploitation* and abuses continued throughout the colonial period. Early human rights violations were drastic and direct: slaughter, land theft, enslavement. Later, when the parent countries extended the rule of law to their colonies, colonial society became more structured. Obvious abuses gave way to more subtle, indirect violations, including unequal application of laws. Thus, human rights abuses became institutionalized in Latin America, that is, built into the social and economic structures and reflected in such institutions as the military and the legal system.

Beginning in the late 1800s, immigration, education, urbanization, and the expansion of suffrage* brought greater civil and political rights to ordinary citizens. However, socioeconomic rights did not spread as far or as fast. Nevertheless, no more than half a century later, the rise of dictatorial or military regimes* threatened the growth of civil and political rights in Latin America.

Dictatorial rule in NICARAGUA and PARAGUAY, military governments in EL SALVADOR and GUATEMALA, and guerrilla* warfare, drug trafficking, and lawless police and armed forces in HAITI, COLOMBIA, PERU, and MEXICO abused human rights. Some of the worst human rights violations were reported in BRAZIL, CHILE, ARGENTINA, and URUGUAY, where the military regimes attempted a complete restructuring of government and society. Massive violations resulted from their use of force, CENSORSHIP of the press, suppression of the congress, and repression of student groups, labor unions, and political parties. The police and the military arrested critics and protestors, calling them enemies of the state, often torturing or executing them without trials. Some of these victims became known as Los Desaparecidos ("the disappeared"), their whereabouts and fates remaining forever unknown to their families.

Similar disappearances occurred in El Salvador and Guatemala, where the state used terror to eliminate opposition and to prevent fragile democracies from gaining a foothold. Police and military death squads kidnapped or assassinated revolutionaries*, politicians, religious and labor leaders, and human rights advocates. Serious violations in Peru and Mexico resulted from those countries' long traditions that

* **evangelize** to preach Christian beliefs; to convert to Christianity

* **friar** member of a religious brotherhood

* **activist** one who takes action to promote a cause

* **exploitation** relationship in which one side benefits at the other's expense

* **suffrage** the right to vote

* **regime** prevailing political system or rule

* **guerrilla** referring to a group that uses surprise raids to obstruct or harass an enemy or overthrow a government

See color plate 15, vol. 4.

* **revolutionary** person engaged in a war to bring about change

Years of widespread human rights violations in Latin America have not gone unnoticed or unprotested. In Argentina, the Mothers of the Disappeared, shown here, gathered once a week outside the presidential palace in Buenos Aires, demanding an account of what happened to their missing children.

permit the military to operate outside the jurisdiction of the law. In Mexico, for example, an earthquake in 1985 revealed the graves of disappeared citizens located directly under the police headquarters. CUBA, which has had a one-party political system since Fidel CASTRO's revolution in 1959, has its own set of human rights problems. Although socioeconomic rights broadened under Castro's rule, especially in the early years, political and civil rights—such as freedom of speech and religion—remain restricted.

Human Rights Activism.   Years of widespread human rights violations in Latin America have not gone unnoticed or unprotested. Activists have joined to form hundreds of local, national, and international groups to document, publicize, protest, and end these violations. Organizations such as Amnesty International and Human Rights Watch are part of a global strategy to defend human rights. Other groups, such as the Washington Office on Latin America (WOLA) and the Inter-American Commission of Human Rights—a division of the ORGANIZATION OF AMERICAN STATES (OAS)—are concerned specifically with human rights violations in Latin America.

Some of the most effective activists have been the victims themselves and, in many instances, the families of victims. In Argentina, the Mothers of the Disappeared gather once a week to silently circle the plaza in front of the presidential palace, holding up pictures of their missing children. Similar groups in other countries have formed a regional network called the Federación Latinoamericana de Asociaciones de Familiares de Detenidos-Desaparecidos (Latin American Federation of Associations of Relatives of the Detained-Disappeared), or FEDEFAM. In Brazil, human rights groups have begun to focus on the problems of specific groups, such as women, native Brazilians, and street children. Many Latin American activists have gained international recognition for their efforts, including Adolfo PÉREZ ESQUIVEL of Argentina and Rigoberta MENCHÚ TUM of Guatemala, each of whom received a Nobel Peace Prize.

As a result of the work of human rights activists, many Latin American countries have set up truth commissions to establish responsibility for the violations in recent decades. The goal of these commissions is to lift the veil of secrecy that allows these violations to occur. Although the struggle against human rights abuses in Latin America continues, activists have won some important victories, and their achievements serve as models for human rights workers throughout the world. (*See also* **Asylum; Counterinsurgency; Dictatorships, Military.**)

Humboldt, Alexander von

1769–1859
German scientific explorer
of the Americas

° **Enlightenment** intellectual movement of the 1700s that emphasized reason, progress, and modernity

---

° **Creole** person of European ancestry born in the Americas

Alexander von Humboldt was the most famous scientist among the many Europeans who toured Spanish America near the end of the colonial period. As a keen observer of society and a gifted writer, he provided descriptions of the Americas and their inhabitants that are treasured and have remained popular.

Born into a wealthy family, Humboldt was educated at several German universities. He developed a love for foreign travel and an interest in the sciences, especially botany. In 1792, he began working for the Department of Mines, but after his mother's death in 1796, he devoted himself to his interests. In 1799, with permission from the Spanish monarchy, Humboldt embarked on a long voyage of exploration in Spain's South American territories.

Humboldt and his companion, French botanist Aimé Bonpland, spent five years traveling through Venezuela, Colombia, Ecuador, Peru, Cuba, and Mexico. During this time, Humboldt observed plant and animal life, landscapes, climate, resources, and the political, economic, and social conditions of the inhabitants. He mingled with the educated elite in the cities and gained access to numerous government documents. Through his associations with the elite, Humboldt also spread the scientific ideals of the Enlightenment*. During his expeditions, Humboldt discovered a cold ocean current flowing north along the west coasts of Chile and Peru. The current was later named the Humboldt Current in his honor.

On his return to Europe, Humboldt published a detailed account of his journey in 34 volumes as well as other scientific works and political commentaries. His observations offered new insights about the continent and inspired many scientists to travel and work in the Americas. His works also had political implications—his descriptions of Mexico's wealth and progress convinced Creoles* that they could survive independently of Spain.

Hurricanes

See map in Caribbean Antilles (vol. 1).

* **colonial** period between the European conquest and independence, generally from the early 1500s to the early 1800s

* **meteorology** science that deals with the study of the atmosphere, especially weather patterns and weather forecasts

Where Did the Word Hurricane Come From?

Modern scholars cannot agree on the origin of the word *hurricane*. Native Americans, of course, were very familiar with hurricanes before the Spanish arrived, and it is possible that the Spanish borrowed one of their words to describe these terrible storms. Some experts think that *hurricane* is a Mayan word, while others believe that it came from the language of the Taino people of the Caribbean. The Taino used a curved, legged symbol for hurricanes. Perhaps they knew that the storms traveled in rotating circles—something European scientists did not realize until the 1800s.

*C*hristopher Columbus, who explored parts of the Caribbean Sea during the late summer and fall of 1492, was fortunate that he did not run into hurricanes—the destructive storms that sweep through that region at that time of year. Soon afterward, however, a storm struck the Spanish settlement on HISPANIOLA and destroyed two ships. The damage was most likely caused by a hurricane and probably was the first time Europeans had experienced such storms.

A hurricane is a tropical cyclone—a circular windstorm with winds greater than 73 miles per hour. (Some have had wind speeds of 175 miles per hour or more.) Hurricanes usually include heavy rainfall, but the tsunamis, or tidal waves, that follow in coastal regions cause the greater damage. Most hurricanes originate in the Caribbean Sea or in the eastern Atlantic Ocean. Although they can strike along the coast of Central America, it is the Caribbean islands, the Gulf coast of Mexico, and the eastern United States that tend to be hardest hit. Hurricanes, which can form anytime of the year, usually occur between June and November, with the most dangerous storms striking in August and September. This period is commonly referred to as the "hurricane season."

Hurricanes have always been a threat to lives, property, and commerce in these areas. A Spanish governor of Puerto Rico in the mid-1700s claimed that the local people measured time by the arrival and departure of governors and fleets, the visits of bishops—and hurricanes. In the colonial* era, the Spanish timed the sailing of their treasure-filled vessels to Spain to avoid the hurricane season. However, late departures and early storms wrecked many a vessel. Ships full of silver sank during storms in 1622, 1624, and 1630, causing financial crises in Spain.

Hurricanes also destroyed colonial settlements in Santo Domingo (in present-day Dominican Republic) in 1508 and again the following year. In 1768, a storm struck Havana, Cuba, killing more than 1,000 people and destroying thousands of homes. The "Great Hurricane" of 1780 killed more than 13,000 people on the islands of Martinique and Barbados and smashed British, French, and Spanish fleets in the region. Hurricanes, which can also inflict agricultural losses by damaging crops, almost halved Cuba's sugar production in the 1840s. In recent years, hurricanes have brought other kinds of economic damage. Winds and waves have wrecked hotels and other tourist facilities. Looting often occurs in the disorder and confusion that follows such storms, resulting in further economic losses.

Technological advances in meteorology* and communications now enable scientists to predict, track, and prepare for hurricanes better than ever before. However, as populations in the coastal areas of hurricane-prone countries continue to rise, hurricane damage is increasing. Among the most destructive hurricanes of the late 1900s were Gilbert, which struck Jamaica in 1988; Hugo, which caused $200 million in damages in Puerto Rico in 1989 and battered the Virgin Islands; and Lili, which ripped through Central America and the Caribbean in 1996, killing at least ten people and driving thousands from their homes in Nicaragua, Honduras, Costa Rica, Cuba, and the Bahamas. In 1997, Pauline, a rare Pacific hurricane, struck the resort town of Acapulco on Mexico's west coast, killing more than 200 people. Most of them were

This photograph shows people rescuing chickens in the aftermath of Hurricane Mitch. The storm ripped through Nicaragua in October 1998.

poor people who lived in flimsy houses on steep mountain slopes and were washed out to sea. In 1998, Mitch ravaged the Central American nations of Honduras, Nicaragua, El Salvador, and Guatemala. The hurricane killed more than 10,000 people, left over one million people homeless, and devastated the countries' economies. Termed the worst disaster of the century, Mitch also destroyed more than 800,000 homes in the region. The World Bank and several countries—including France, the United States, Cuba, and Japan—sent billions of dollars as relief aid to these nations to help them rebuild their homes and economy. Throughout Latin America, it is the poor who suffer the most from hurricane damage because they live in the most unprotected regions.

Ibarbourou, Juana de

1892–1979
Uruguayan poet and writer

One of Uruguay's most acclaimed poets, Juana Fernández Morales was born in Melo, Uruguay. She married Captain Lucas Ibarbourou in 1914 and moved to the capital city of Montevideo. There Juana de Ibarbourou published several of her poems. Her poetry was so well received that the prestigious Argentine magazine *Caras y Caretas* devoted an entire issue to Ibarbourou and her work.

Ibarbourou's fame rose as she continued to write and publish her poems. *El cántaro fresco* (Fresh Pitcher) and *Raíz salvaje* (Wild Root) dealt with the themes of love and the pleasures of living. In *La rosa de los vientos* (Compass), she experimented with language, and *Loores de Nuestra Señora* (Praise to Our Lady) contained poems with religious themes. After her mother's death, Ibarbourou became ill and was depressed for years. She continued to write poetry that reflected her mood—*Romances del destino* (Tales of Destiny) and *Oro y tormenta* (Gold and Storm). In 1957, Ibarbourou was honored at a special session of the United Nations Educational, Scientific, and Cultural Organization (UNESCO). Although she enjoyed fame and a comfortable life, by the time of her death, Ibarbourou was poor and largely forgotten.

Iguaçú Falls

° **cataract** steep waterfall

° **hydroelectric** referring to electricity harnessed from waterpower

One of the most spectacular sights in Latin America is Iguaçú Falls on the Iguaçú River in southern South America, between Brazil and Argentina. The Iguaçú Falls are much more than a single waterfall. The falls are a series of cataracts* that cascade over a steep drop in the river's bed. Along this 2.5-mile-wide, horseshoe-shaped wall of rock between the two banks of the river are 275 waterfalls, including the world's fifth-highest waterfall. This majestic display has become a major tourist attraction.

Not far from the falls, the Iguaçú River flows into the Paraná River, which marks a stretch of the border between Brazil and Paraguay. In a project begun in 1973, the two countries built the enormous Itaipú dam and hydroelectric* plant on the Paraná. The Itaipú project has brought great changes to the Iguaçú Falls region, which now boasts of a population of more than 250,000 who live near the mouth of the Iguaçú River where it flows into the Paraná. (*See also* **Energy and Energy Resources.**)

The Iguaçú Falls are a series of steep drops along the Iguaçú River, including the fifth-highest waterfall in the world. A major tourist attraction, the falls also are a source of hydroelectricity for Brazil and Paraguay.

Immigration and Emigration

*E*migration occurs when people leave the countries of their birth to live and work elsewhere. When they take up residence in a new country, they are called immigrants. Everyone who lives in the Americas today is either an immigrant or is descended from immigrants who arrived in the Americas about 11,000 years ago. The mix of ethnic and cultural groups that today makes up Latin America is the result of years of emigration from many countries.

In colonial* times, Latin America was a destination for emigrants, both forced and voluntary. Even when the colonies became independent nations, immigration continued to swell. The movement of people, either in search of better economic opportunities or to escape war or other troubles, has created patterns of emigration and immigration in Latin America. Also, in the late 1900s, the emigration of Latin Americans has become a greatly debated political issue, especially in the United States.

To Latin America

During the colonial period, more than a million people emigrated from Spain to Spanish America, and a similar number went from Portugal to Brazil. The largest transfer of people, however, involved the 12 million or so Africans brought forcibly to Latin America and the Caribbean during the 350 years of the SLAVE TRADE. Although these enslaved Africans were not voluntary immigrants, they and their descendants became a vital part of the population of the Americas.

Spanish Emigrants. Following Columbus's discovery of the New World, the Spanish monarchy established rigorous rules for migration to prevent heretics*, Jews, and foreigners from reaching the colonies and influencing their Indian subjects. Nevertheless, using bribery and taking advantage of loopholes in the system, many non-Spaniards migrated to Spanish America.

Between 1492 and 1600, records show that about 300,000 people migrated from Spain to America. The migrants were mostly young male artisans*, who were leaving behind an increasingly lagging economy. A large number of *peninsulares* (Spanish-born Latin Americans) also emigrated during this period, mostly motivated by economic opportunities in the New World. In the 1600s, as Spain continued to decline, immigration to Latin America increased rapidly, attracting industrious northern Spaniards. During that century, about 450,000 people migrated from Spain, including men and women in their childbearing years, who were leaving to avoid plagues, economic depressions*, and other problems that were prevalent in Spain. In the 1700s, the influx of *peninsulares*, especially those who later married into local Creole* families, increased further. Basques and northern Spaniards continued to immigrate to Spanish America, particularly to Mexico City.

Portuguese Emigrants. Unlike the Spanish monarchy, the Portuguese monarchy was very lenient regarding migration to Latin America. Portugal, which did not begin systematic migration to BRAZIL until

° **colonial** period between the European conquest and independence, generally from the early 1500s to the early 1800s

Mennonites in Paraguay

The most successful colonists in Paraguay were the German-speaking Mennonites who came from Canada and Russia in the 1920s. Members of a religion founded in the Netherlands in the 1540s, Mennonites were attracted to Paraguay because the government gave them land and exempted them from military service. They established three colonies in the Chaco region and created successful agricultural and dairy complexes. To this day, the Paraguayan Mennonites proudly retain their traditional lifestyle, language, and faith, including educating their children in their own religious schools.

° **heretic** person who disagrees with established church doctrine

° **artisan** skilled crafts worker

° **depression** period of little economic activity during which many people become unemployed

° **Creole** person of European ancestry born in the Americas

225

Immigration and Emigration

° **non-Iberian** native or inhabitant of a country other than Spain or Portugal

° **indigenous** referring to the original inhabitants of a region

The majority of people emigrating from Latin America go to the United States. This graph shows the ten most common national origins of migrants arriving in the United States during 1996. As shown, Mexico accounts for more migration over the United States border than any other country in the world.

1534, admitted anyone who professed to be Catholic. However, many Jews, Dutchmen, and non-Iberians* also migrated to Brazil during this time. Records show that up to the late 1600s, about 2,400 Portuguese migrated overseas each year, and a small percentage of them went to Brazil.

During the 1700s, the Portuguese monarchy focused on transferring people from its Atlantic island possessions to Brazil. Those transferred included several hard-working farmers from the small islands of Madeira and the Azores. Colonial administrators, who held a low opinion of the indigenous* population in Spanish America, believed that these islanders would set an example and bring prosperity and civilization to Brazil. Moreover, at the time, Portugal was especially eager for these people to settle in the southern part of Brazil to prevent the Spanish from moving into that region. In 1747, Portugal ordered the massive resettlement of Azorian colonists.

By 1749, more than 1,900 people had moved to the new settlements, and more arrived in the years that followed. When Spain and Portugal reassessed their colonial borders in Latin America, Portugal pointed to its new Azorian settlements as evidence that it had effectively occupied the land. After Brazil's independence in 1822, Azorians continued to leave their crowded islands for Latin America, although

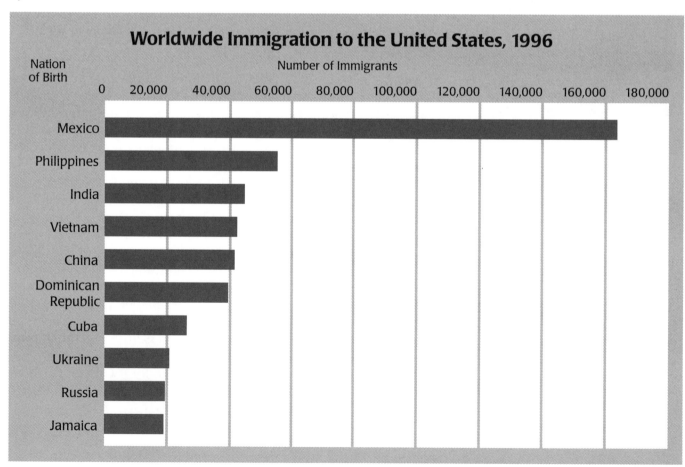

Worldwide Immigration to the United States, 1996

Nation of Birth — Number of Immigrants

Source: Statistical Abstract of the United States, 1997.

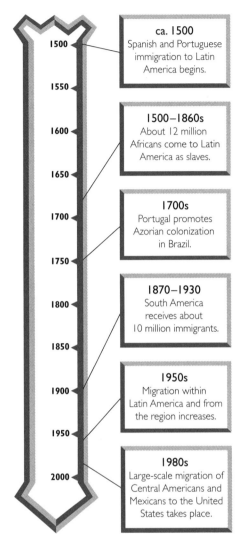

ca. 1500
Spanish and Portuguese immigration to Latin America begins.

1500–1860s
About 12 million Africans come to Latin America as slaves.

1700s
Portugal promotes Azorian colonization in Brazil.

1870–1930
South America receives about 10 million immigrants.

1950s
Migration within Latin America and from the region increases.

1980s
Large-scale migration of Central Americans and Mexicans to the United States takes place.

° **asylum** safe place to stay to escape danger or violence in homeland

their destinations now included British Guiana in South America, and Jamaica, Trinidad, and Bermuda in the Caribbean.

Postindependence Immigration. After independence, immigration to Latin American nations continued, especially from Europe, the Middle East, Asia, and North America. The bulk of this immigration occurred between 1870 and 1930, when more than 10 million people migrated to Argentina, Uruguay, Brazil, and to a lesser extent, Chile. These immigrants, pushed out of their homelands by the pressures of population growth, urbanization, and industrialization, were pulled to Latin America by the prospects of new and abundant land and economic opportunities, especially for farmers.

Many leaders and thinkers considered these European immigrants a positive influence for the modernization and growth of Latin America. Governments and social organizations sponsored immigrant settlers, often offering to pay for their passage to Latin America. During this time, Argentina and Uruguay received 3.4 million and 640,000 immigrants respectively, mostly from Italy and Spain. Brazil received 3.3 million immigrants, mostly Italian, Portuguese, and Spanish laborers to replace slave labor on the coffee plantations. Also in the early 1900s, more than 100,000 Japanese migrated to Brazil, forming the basis for a large Japanese-Brazilian population.

Some ethnic groups that migrated from Germany and Italy settled in southeastern Brazil, often in rural farming communities. These immigrants retained their language and cultural identity because of their isolation from mainstream Brazilian society. Similar patterns were visible in Paraguay, where nearly all immigrants settled in separate rural communities consisting of members of a specific ethnic group, religion, or philosophy. Paraguay received immigrants from Germany, Italy, France, Sweden, and Australia. Latin America also received immigrants from Syria, Eastern Europe, and Lebanon. Although some immigrants have returned to their homelands, most have stayed, adding to the multi-ethnicity of the region.

Within and from Latin America

Prompted either by civil unrest or by the desire to seek new economic opportunities, migration between Latin American countries increased during the mid-1900s. Thousands fled from El Salvador to Honduras to escape the violent Salvadoran civil war. Haitians, Cubans, and others sought political asylum* in the United States, Canada, and elsewhere. Most emigrants, however, leave home for economic reasons.

Immigration to the United States. The majority of Latin Americans who migrate to the United States are urban residents from fairly successful families. The sole exception is Mexico, whose migrants are usually from rural backgrounds. Unlike earlier waves of immigrants to the United States whose goal was to blend in with mainstream society, modern immigrants remain more emotionally, socially, and

227

economically tied to their homelands. Many travel to Latin America frequently and send money to their families there.

Immigration to the United States is governed by laws—but not all immigrants enter the country legally. Thousands bypass the laws and enter by sea or on foot across the United States border. In the mid-1990s, the U.S. Immigration and Naturalization Service (INS) estimated that there were more than 3 million illegal immigrants (sometimes called undocumented immigrants) in the country. Nearly half of them were from Mexico, El Salvador, and Guatemala—the Latin American countries closest to the United States. Significant numbers were also from Haiti, Nicaragua, and Colombia. Like legal immigrants from Latin America, many of these undocumented people cluster in California, Florida, and Texas—states where voters have begun debating such issues as the rights of illegal immigrants and policies for controlling undocumented immigration. (*See also* **Asians in Latin America; Asylum; Population and Population Growth; Race and Ethnicity; United States–Mexico Border.**)

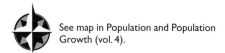

See map in Population and Population Growth (vol. 4).

Index

Index

Moche, 3:139–40 *(illus.)*
Nasca and Nasca lines, 3:154–55
Olmec, 3:173–74
Quetzalcoatl in, 4:26
South American art, 1:71–72
Artigas, José Gervasio, **1:72–73**, 3:176, 4:168–69
Aruba, 2:83
Arzú Irigoyen, Alvaro, 2:184
Ashkenazim Jews, 3:30
Asia
    banking crisis in (1997), 1:100
    diseases from, 2:67
    Portugal's last outpost in, 4:10
Asians in Latin America, **1:73–75**, 2:227, 3:26, 4:32
Asiento, **1:75–76**
Astronomy, **1:76–77** *(illus.)*, 1:149–50, 191, 2:23
Asturias, Miguel Ángel, **1:77–78**, 3:64
Asunción, 1:49, 50, **1:78–79** *(illus.)*
Asunción, Treaty of (1991), 3:104
Asylum, **1:79–81**, 3:52, 85–86
Atacama Desert, 4:197–98
Atahualpa, **1:81**, 3:4, 6, 209–10, 225
Athaide, Manoel da Costa, 1:66
Atlases, 3:82. *See also* Maps and mapmaking
Audiencia, 1:18, **1:81–83** *(map),* 1:125, 4:187
    of Caracas, 4:181
    of Charcas, 1:115
    evolution of, 1:81–82
    of Guatemala, 2:180
    high court of, 2:39
    laws and legal systems and, 3:51
    organization and function of, 1:82–83
    in Peru, 3:210
    of Quito, 2:93, 4:28
    of Santa Fe de Bogotá, 2:9
    of Santo Domingo, 4:76–77
Audiencia de los Confines, 2:180
Augustine, Saint, 2:109
Augustinians, 4:45
Austin, Stephen F., 4:131, 132
Authoritarian rule, roots of, 2:63. *See also* Dictatorships, military
Automobile industry, **1:83–85** *(illus.),* 3:15, 23
Avalos Corrientes, battle of (1820), 1:73
Avería, 4:123
Aviation, **1:85–86**, 4:77–78
Ávila, Pedro Arias de, **1:86–87**, 1:93, 2:114–15, 3:189
Aviz dynasty, 4:12–13
Axayacatl (ruler), 1:90
Ayacucho, battle of (1824), 1:112, 4:203
Ayala, Eusebio, 1:185, 186
Ayerza, Francisco, 3:220
Ayllus, 1:87
Aylwin Azócar, Patricio, 1:201
Aymara, 1:22, **1:87–88**, 1:114, 4:154
Aymara language, 3:47
Azcona, José, 2:214
Azevedo, Artur, 4:135–36
Aztecs, **1:88–91** *(illus.),* 2:51
    ancient highways of, 2:208
    art of, 1:70
    astronomy of, 1:76
    cacao seeds in religion of, 1:147
    calendars of, 1:149–50
    chinampas, 1:91
    conquistadors and, 2:20

Cortés' conquest of, 1:90, 2:20, 26, 3:76–77
    culture and civilization of, 1:90–91
    divinities of, 2:69–70
    expansion of empire, 1:89–90
    hallucinogen use by, 2:77
    history of, 1:88–90
    irrigation and water control system of, 3:23
    literature of, 3:59
    Malinche and conquest of, 3:76–77
    Moctezuma II, ruler of, 3:140–41
    in Postclassic period, 3:107
    religion of, 4:42
    smallpox among, 2:66
    Tenochtitlán, capital of, 4:128–29
    Toltecs and, 4:142
Azul (Darío), 2:57, 3:63

B

Báez, Buenaventura, 2:73–74
Bahamas, 1:138, 3:223
Bahia, **1:91–92**, 1:129
    architecture of, 1:46
    missionary activity in, 3:133
    Sabinada Revolt in, 4:59–60
    Salvador, capital of, 4:63–64
Baja California, **1:91**
Baker, Lorenzo Dow, 4:158
Balaguer, Joaquín, 2:76
Balboa, Vasco Núñez de, 1:87, **1:92–93**, 1:161, 2:114, 3:119, 183
Balboa (unit of currency), 2:6
Balladares, Ernesto Pérez, 3:186
Ball game, pre-Columbian, 1:44, **1:93–94**, 1:191, 3:95, 4:113
Balmaceda Fernández, José Manuel, **1:94**, 1:198
Banana industry, **1:94–96**, 2:30, 96, 135, 148, 214
Banco de Avío, 1:98
Banco de Buenos Aires, 1:98
Banco do Brasil, 1:98
Bandeirantes, 1:130
Bandeiras, **1:96–97**, 2:116–17, 3:127, 129, 4:78
Banderilleros, 1:144
Banditry, **1:97–98**, 4:57
Banking, **1:98–100**, 1:173
Bank of London and South America (Buenos Aires), 1:47
Banzer Suárez, Hugo, 1:119
Baptista, João Gomes, 1:18
Baptista Firueiredo, João, 1:135
Barbados, 1:138
Barbuda, 1:138
Baroque style architecture, 1:45
Barrio Alto in Santiago, 4:75
Barrios, 1:210
Barrios, Gerardo, **1:100**, 1:166, 2:104
Barrios, Justo Rufino, **1:101**, 2:182
Barrios de Chamorro, Violeta, **1:101**, 3:166, 178, 4:211
Barrundia, José Francisco, **1:102**
Barrundia, Juan, 2:181
Barú (volcano), 3:186
Basadre, Jorge, 3:156
Baseball, 1:170, 4:114 *(illus.)*
Bases (Alberdi), 1:15
Basoalto, Neftalí Eliecer Ricardo Reyes. *See* Neruda, Pablo
Bastidas, Rodrigo de, 2:9

Batista y Zaldívar, Fulgencio, **1:102–3**, 2:44–45, 189
    Castro and overthrow of, 1:169, 170, 2:49
Batlle y Ordóñez, José, **1:103–4** *(illus.),* 4:168, 171–72
Batouala (Maran), 3:157–58
Bautista de Anza, Juan, 3:161
Bay of Pigs Invasion, **1:104**, 1:170, 184, 2:46, 49
Beans, 2:134
Beef, 2:135, 3:97–98
Bejareque, 1:44
Belalcázar, Sebastián de, 1:150, 2:8, 9, 92, 115, 186
Belaúnde Terry, Fernando, 4:179
Belize, **1:104–6**, 1:107
Bello, Andrés, **1:106–7**, 3:61
Belmopan, 1:106, **1:107**
Belo Horizonte, 3:128
Beltrán, Manuela, 2:17
Bemberg, Maria Luisa, 1:206
Benedictines, 4:45
Beringia, 3:10
Berlanga, Thomás de, 2:151
Berni, Antonio, 1:68
Berro, Bernardo, 4:170
Betancourt, Rómulo, **1:107–8**, 2:75, 4:185
Beverages, 2:134–35
Bider, Haydée Tamara Bunke, 4:210
Big Stick Policy, 4:161
Bimetallic system of coinage, 2:6
Bingham, Hiram, 1:41, 3:72, 73
Biodiversity, preservation of, 2:111
Birds, 1:34–35
Birthrate, 4:210–11
Bishop, Maurice, 2:174
Bishops, 1:173–74
Blackbeard (Edward Teach), 3:224
Black Caribs (Garifuna), 1:162
Black consciousness, rise of, 4:33
Black Legend, **1:108–9** *(illus.),* 3:60
Black nationalist movement in Haiti, 2:84
Blacks. *See* Africans in Latin America
Blaize, Herbert, 2:174
Blanco Party, 4:170
Blanes, Juan Manuel, 1:67
Bogotá, Santa Fe de, 1:48, **1:110–11**, 2:8, 17, 4:193 *(illus.)*
    Audiencia of, 2:9
Boleadoras, 2:158
Bolívar, Simón, **1:111–13** *(illus.),* 3:184
    anticlericalism and, 1:35
    at Boyacá, battle of, 1:126
    Gran Colombia facilitated by, 2:173
    independence of Bolivia and, 1:117
    Peruvian independence and, 3:212
    Republic of Colombia established by, 2:11
    San Martín and, 4:68
    Santander and, 4:74
    Venezuelan independence struggle and, 4:182
    wars of independence and, 4:202, 203
Bolívar (unit of currency), 2:6
Bolivia, **1:113–20** *(illus.)*
    armed forces in, 1:62
    Aymara in, 1:88
    boundary disputes of, 1:123–24, 198
    Chaco War and, 1:119, 185–86 *(map),* 3:197
    claims to Chaco, 1:123
    colonial period in, 1:115–16

Index

Index

Index

Index

Index

Influenza, 2:66
Informal economy, 4:116
Inquietud del rosal, La (Storni), 4:115
Inquilinos, 1:194
Inquisition, Holy Office of the, **3:17–18** *(illus.)*
    Black Legend and, 1:109
    Cartagena as center for, 1:167
    Jewish settlers escaping, 3:30
    Protestants and, 4:17
Insects and spiders, 1:34
"Institutional" military governments, 1:62
Intendancy system, 1:125, **3:19**
    American Revolution and, 1:28
    cabildo under, 1:146
    Charles III and, 1:187
    in Chile, 1:195
    Intendancy of Venezuela, 4:181
    in Mexico, Gálvez and, 2:153
    Viceroyalty of Río de la Plata, 4:49–50
Inter-American Commission of Human Rights, 2:220
Inter-American Development Bank, 3:21, 22
Inter-American Foundation (IAF), 3:21–22
Inter-American relations, **3:19–22**
    in Central America, 1:180, 181
    current issues in, 3:21–22
    Good Neighbor Policy, 2:172
    origins of Inter-American System, 3:20–21
    postwar issues in, 3:20–21
    Rio Treaty and, 4:50
    United Nations and, 4:159
Inter-American Treaty of Reciprocal Assistance. *See* Rio Treaty (1947)
Intermarriage, 1:4, 211, 2:162, 3:194
Internal asylum, 1:79
Internal Provinces. *See* Provincias Internas
Internal trade, 4:147
International Border Commission, 1:124
International Conferences of American States, 3:20–21, 175, 192
International Military Education and Training Program, 1:62
"International" music, 3:150
Inti (unit of currency), 2:7
Intraregional trade, 4:147
Investment bonds, 2:139. *See also* Foreign investment
Iquique, port of, 4:198, 199
Irala, Domingo de, 1:49
Iron and steel industry, **3:22–23**
Irrigation, uses of, 1:10, **3:23–25**, 3:139, 4:102, 143
Isabel, Princess, 1:133, **3:25**, 3:203, 4:95
Isabella I of Castile, 2:14, 4:105, 109
Islam, **3:25–26**
Issei, 1:75
Isthmus of Panama, road across, 2:209
Itaipú dam and hydroelectric plant, 2:108, 224, 3:193, 198
Iturbide, Agustín de, 2:181, **3:26–27**
    Mexican War of Independence and, 3:113, 119, 4:203, 204
    Santa Anna and, 4:72
Itzás, 3:96
Itzcoatl (ruler), 1:89

J

Jades, Olmec, 3:173–74
Jagan, Cheddi, 2:193
Jaguar, **3:27**

Jai alai, 4:114
Jamaica, 1:137, 139, 2:85, **3:27–29**, 3:147
Japanese in Latin America, 1:74–75, 2:227
Jaramillo, Juan, 3:77
Jefe político, **3:29–30**
Jefferson, Thomas, 2:43
Jesuits, 1:173, 2:98, 4:44–45
    Anchieta, 1:30
    in Argentina, 1:50
    in Asunción, 1:78
    in Brazil, 1:130
    in California, 1:152
    cattle ranching among, 3:97
    Comunero Revolt vs., 2:17
    education and, 1:172
    expulsion by Charles III, 1:187
    missionary efforts, 3:133–34, 135, 4:190
    music education and, 3:148–49
    Pombaline reforms and, 4:2
Jewels. *See* Gems and gemstones
Jewish Colonization Association (JCA), 3:31
Jews in Latin America, 2:81, **3:30–31** *(illus.),* 3:126
João I of Portugal, 4:12
João II of Portugal, 2:14, 4:10, 12–13
João III of Portugal, 1:156, 4:13
João IV of Portugal, 1:17, 4:13
João V of Portugal, 4:13
João VI of Portugal, 1:131, 2:154, **3:31–32**, 4:13, 206
John I, king of Portugal, 2:206
John Paul II, Pope, 1:176, 2:42, 45, 4:62, 176
Johnson, Lyndon, 1:21
Jones Act (1917), 2:137, 4:24
Jorge Blanco, Salvador, 2:76
José I of Portugal, 4:13
Journalism, **3:32–34**
    censorship of, 1:177–78
Journeymen, 2:191
Juan Diego, 2:175–76
Juana Inés de la Cruz, Sor, **3:34–35**, 3:60, 4:135, 136
Juárez, Benito, 2:138, **3:35–36** *(illus.)*
    Díaz and, 2:61
    education reforms under, 2:98
    Maximilian and, 3:92
    presidency, 3:120
    Reform Laws of, 1:36
    Rurales founded by, 4:57
Juárez, Luis, 1:64
Juárez Law, 3:120
Juderías, Julián, 1:108
Judges on *audiencia,* 1:82–83
Judicial systems. *See* Laws and legal systems
Junín, battle of (1824), 1:111, 112
Junta, 1:111, **3:36**
Junta de Mayo, 4:168
Jury Tribunals, 3:52
Justice. *See* Crime and punishment, colonial; Laws and legal systems
Justo, José Agustín, 1:54–55, 4:58

K

Kahlo, Frida, **3:36–37**, 3:157, 4:52
Kardec, Allan, 4:112
Keith, Minor Cooper, 2:30, 4:158
Kennedy, John F., 1:20, 2:125, 3:175, 4:163
    Bay of Pigs Invasion and, 1:104
    CIA and, 1:184
    counterinsurgency policy, 2:32–34
    Cuban missile crisis and, 2:47–48

Khrushchev, Nikita, 2:47–48
K'iche', **3:37**, 3:96
Kidd, William, 3:223
Kino, Eusebio Francisco, 1:52, 59, 2:115, **3:37–38**, 3:84, 4:68–69
Kinship, 2:118–19
Kirchhoff, Paul, 3:104, 105
Korner, Emil, 1:62
Kotosh, **3:38**
Kubitschek de Oliveira, Juscelino, 1:127, 134, **3:38–39**
Kukulcan. *See* Quetzalcoatl
Kuna, 2:36, **3:39–40**
Kundt, Hans, 1:62, 186
Kurakas (chiefs), 1:87

L

La Angostura, battle of. *See* Buena Vista, battle of (1847)
Labor and labor movements, **3:41–44**
    anarchism and, 1:29–30
    in Argentina, 1:51, 3:207
    bracero program, 1:126 *(illus.)*
    changes in class structure and, 1:212
    changing trends in, 3:43
    Chicanos and, 1:191
    in Colombia, 2:13
    descamisados in Argentina, 2:59–60
    domestic labor, 2:71–72
    in El Salvador, 2:105
    emergence of labor organizations, 3:42–43
    in Grenada, 2:173–74
    growth of, 3:43
    maquiladoras system and, 3:84–85
    in Peru, 3:213
    railroads and, 4:36
    street vendors and, 4:115–16
    in Venezuela, 4:184
    yanaconas, 4:213–14
Labor courts, 3:52
Lacalle, Luis Alberto, 4:173
Lacandon forest, 4:37
Lafayette, Marquis de, 1:27
La Florida. *See* Florida
La Guyane. *See* French Guiana
Lake Pitiantutua, battle of (1932), 1:185
La Mesilla, Treaty of (1854), 1:61
Land, ownership of, 1:13, **3:44–45**. *See also* Agrarian reform
    colonial families and, 2:118
    economic development and, 2:90
    haciendas and, 2:195–96 *(illus.)*
    latifundia, 3:49–50
    of pampas, 3:183
Land Law of 1850 (Brazil), 3:45
Languages, **3:46–48**
    Andalusian, 2:20
    European, 3:47–48
    Inca, 3:5
    indigenous, 3:46–47
    Mayan, 3:94, 96
    missionaries' efforts to learn Indian, 3:135
    of Peru, 3:215
    Tupi, 4:155
    Zapotec, 4:217
La Paz, 1:115, **3:40–41**, 4:154
La Plata, appointment of archbishop to, 1:116
La Raza Unida, 1:191

Index

Index

Ocean currents. *See* Currents, ocean
Ocean fishing rights, 2:126
O'Donojú, Juan, 3:113, 119
O'Gorman, Juan, 4:164
O'Higgins, Bernardo, **3:172–73**, 4:203
  Carrera vs., 1:165
  Chilean independence movement and, 1:195, 196
  San Martín and, 4:67
Oidores, 1:82
Oil. *See* Petroleum industry
Oil crisis of 1973, debt crisis and, 2:138
Ojeda, Alonso de, 2:8, 83, 4:180, 186
Olid, Cristóbal de, 2:27
Olmecs, 2:50, 3:11, **3:173–74**
  archaeological study of, 1:40
  art of, 1:69–70
  La Venta, 3:41
  in Maya territory, 3:94–95
  as Preclassic society, 3:106
  religions of, 4:41–42
Olmedo, Bartolomé de, 3:134
Onas. *See* Selk'nams
Oñate, Juan de, 2:115, 3:160–61, **3:174**
Onganía, Juan Carlos, 1:56, 2:25
Onís y Gonzáles, Luis de, 1:1
Opera, 3:149
Opium, 2:78
Oreamuno, Ricardo Jiménez, 2:29
Orellana, Francisco de, 2:116 *(map)*, 186, **3:174**
Organization of American States, 2:75, 3:20, **3:175–76**, 3:192
  current issues for, 3:21
  Pan-American Conference of 1948 and, 3:191
  Unit for the Promotion of Democracy, 3:21
Organization of Central American States (ODECA), 1:181
Organization of Petroleum Exporting Countries (OPEC), 4:185
Oribe, Manuel, 2:186, **3:176**, 4:170
Oriente region in Ecuador, 2:91, 94
Orinoco River, 2:165
Orio, Baltasar de Echave, 1:64
Orixás, **3:176–77.** *See also* Candomblé
Orozco, José Clemente, 1:67
Orozco, Pascual, 3:73, 111
Ortega Saavedra, Daniel, 3:166, **3:177–78** *(illus.)*, 4:69, 70
Ortelius, Abraham, 3:82
Ortiz de Domínguez, Josefa, **3:178–79**
Oruro Revolt (1739), 1:117
Ospina Pérez, Mariano, 4:192
Otomanguean language family, 4:217
Ouro Prêto, 3:128
Outlaw bandits, 1:97
Oviedo, Lino, 3:198
Oviedo y Valdés, Gonzalo Fernández, 3:225

P

Pachacamac (god), 3:56
  temple to, 2:216
Pachacuti, 3:4, **3:179**
Pachacuti, Juan Santacruz, 3:60
Pacheco, María Luisa, 1:68
Pacific Northwest, **3:179–80**
Padrón real, 3:81
Páez, José Antonio, 1:112, **3:180–81**, 4:182, 183

Painting. *See* Art, colonial to modern; Art, pre-Columbian
Palenque, **3:181**
Palés Matos, Luis, **3:181**
Palma, Arturo Alessandri, 1:199
Palmares, **3:182**, 4:90
Palo, 4:41
Pampa de Nasca, 3:155
Pampas, 1:49, **3:183**
  Araucanian expansion into, 1:37, 38
  cattle ranching in, 3:97–98
  climate of, 1:216
  gauchos of, 2:158
  Indians driven from, 1:52
Panama, **3:183–87**
  Ávila, governor of, 1:86–87
  canal politics and independence, 3:184–85
  cultural geography of, 3:186–87
  history of, 3:183–86
  modern, 3:186–87
  Noriega's regime, 3:185–86
  Panama City, capital of, 3:189–90
  Pan-American Conference at, 3:190
  as part of Colombia, 3:184
  under Spanish control, 3:183
  Torrijos Herrera, revolutionary leader in, 4:144
  Watermelon Riot in, 4:205
Panama Canal, 3:164, **3:187–89** *(illus.)*, 4:160, 218
  Bryan-Chamorro Treaty and, 1:140
  canal operations, 3:188–89
  Canal Zone, 2:205, 3:186, 189
  economic development of Panama and, 3:184–85
  El Niño's effect on, 2:102
  growth of Cali with opening of, 1:151
  Hay-Bunau-Varilla Treaty and, 2:205
  modern imperialism and, 3:3
  Torrijos-Carter Treaty and, 4:144
  trade and commerce through, 4:148 *(illus.)*
  yellow fever and, 2:66
Panama City, 1:87, 3:186, **3:189–90**
Pan American Airways, 1:86
Pan-American Conferences, 3:20, **3:190–91**, 3:192
  Inter-American relations and, 3:19–22
  Monroe Doctrine and, 3:143
  Organization of American States and, 3:175–76
  photography and, 3:221
Pan-American Highway, 2:209 *(illus.)*, 210, 4:68, 75, 126
Pan-Americanism, **3:191–92**
Pan-American Union (PAU), 3:20, 175, 192
Pantanal, **3:192–93**
Pantheon of Heroes (Asunción), 1:78 *(illus.)*
Paracas culture, art of, 1:71
Paraguay, **3:193–99** *(map)*
  architecture of, 1:46
  Asunción, capital of, 1:78–79
  Chaco War between Bolivia and, 1:119, 185–86 *(map)*, 3:197
  claims to Chaco, 1:123
  clothing in, 2:2
  colonial period in, 3:194–95
  under the Colorados, 3:198–99
  Comunero Revolt in, 2:17
  economy of, 3:195, 197, 199
  Guaranís of, 2:179–80

immigration to, 2:227
independence of, 3:195–96
Japanese immigrants in, 1:75
land and resources of, 3:193
Mennonites in, 2:225
people of, 3:199
War of the Triple Alliance and, 3:196, 4:200–202
Paraguay: Image of Your Desolate Country (painting), 1:67
Paraguay River, 2:165, 218, 3:193
Páramo, 1:218
Paraná, Argentina, 1:53
Paraná Indians, 1:56
Paraná River, 2:108, 165, 3:193
Pardon, colonial, 2:40
Pardos. See Mulattos
Paricutin volcano, 4:195 *(illus.)*
Paris, Treaty of (1898), 4:111
Partisan press, 1:178
Pasteur, Louis, 4:81
Pastry War (1838), 2:146, 3:119
Patagonia, 1:49, **3:200**
Patent, 3:223
Patria potestad, 2:161
Patriarchal family, 2:118
Patria vieja, 1:195
Payaguá, 2:179
Payró, Roberto, 3:62
Paz, Ireneo, 3:200
Paz, Octavio, 3:64, **3:200–201**
Paz Estenssoro, Víctor, 1:119–20, 121, **3:201**
Paz García, Policarpo, 2:214
Peace activist, 3:205
Peasant uprisings, 3:43
Pedro I of Brazil, 1:31, 131, 3:31, **3:201–2**, 4:13, 206
Pedro II of Brazil, 1:131–32, 3:57, **3:202–3** *(illus.)*, 4:13
Pelé, **3:203–4** *(illus.)*
Pelée, Mount, 2:147, 4:195
Pellagra, 3:76
PEMEX, 1:158, 3:218
Peñaranda, Enrique, 1:186
Peninsulares, 1:179, 195, 211, 2:225
  on *audiencia*, 1:83
  in colonial Mexico, 3:117, 118
  tension between Creoles and, 2:37
  wars of independence and, 4:202
Penitentes, **3:204–5**
Penn, William, 4:18
Pensacola, battle of (1781), 1:28
Pentecostal groups, 4:18
Peons, 1:11, 12, 2:58
Peralta Barnueva y Rocha, Pedro de, 2:110
Percussion instruments, 3:153
Pereyra, Gabriel, 4:170
Pérez, Carlos Andrés, 4:185
Pérez de Cuéllar, Javier, 4:159
Pérez Esquivel, Adolfo, 3:205
Pérez Jiménez, Marcos, 4:185
Pernambucan Revolution (1817), 3:206
Pernambuco, 1:129, 156, **3:206**
  Dutch attacks on, 2:81–82
  missionary activity in, 3:133
  Recife, capital of, 4:38–39
Pernambuco Company, 4:150
Perón, Juan Domingo, 1:177, **3:206–7**
  Borges and opposition to, 1:122
  Córdoba and overthrow of, 2:25
  descamisados, supporters of, 2:59–60
  Dirty War and, 2:65

Index

craft work reflecting blend of Christian and, 2:36
cult of Chavin, 1:188
divinities of, 2:68–70
drugs as part of, 2:77
Inca, 3:5
messianic movements, 3:108–9
pre-Columbian calendars and, 1:150
spiritism and, 4:112–13
syncretism and, 4:122–23
Tzendal Rebellion and, 4:155–56
Religious festivals, 2:124–25
Religious groups. *See* Catholic Church; Islam; Jews in Latin America; Protestantism; Religions, African–Latin American; Religions, Indian
Religious orders, **4:43–46.** *See also* Dominicans (Dominican order); Franciscans; Jesuits
of Catholic Church, 1:172
in Códoba, 2:24–25
education and, 2:98
missions and missionaries of, 3:132–36
universities run by, 4:164
Remittances, 4:20
Rendón, Francisco, 1:28
Reptiles, 1:33–34
República Mayor, 4:218
Research
medical, 3:101, 4:81
nutrition, 3:171
scientific, 4:80–81
technological, 4:125
Reservoir-canal system, 3:23
Retablos and ex-votos, 1:65, **4:46**
Reyna Barrios, José, 2:113
Rezanov, Nikolai, 1:153
Rice, 2:135
Rice industry, **4:46–47**
Riché, Jean-Baptiste, 4:99
Ricketts, Juan Landázuri, 1:175
Rigaud, André, 2:202
Riggs, Francis, 1:16
Rights
human. *See* Human rights
of slaves, 4:93
Ring of Fire, 2:166
Rio de Janeiro, **4:47–48** *(illus.)*
Carnival in, 1:163
gold rush in, 2:169
Pan-American Conference at, 3:191
samba schools of, 3:150
Río de la Plata, 1:49, 51, **4:48–49**
confederation of, 1:72
gauchos of, 2:157–58
Treaty of Madrid and boundary of, 3:73–74
United Provinces of, 4:51
Viceroyalty of, 3:195, 216, **4:49–50,** 4:168–69, 187–88
Rio Grande, 2:176, **4:50,** 4:162–63
Rio Grande do Sul, 2:120
Rio Protocol (1942), 2:96
Rio Treaty (1947), 3:20, 175, 191, 192, 4:50
Ritual kinship *(compadrazgo)*, 2:119
Rivadavia, Bernardino, 1:52, **4:51**
Rivera, Diego, 1:67, 3:157, **4:51–52** *(illus.)*
Kahlo, wife of, 3:36–37
Rivera, Fructuoso, 2:120, 186–87, 3:176, 4:170
Rivers and river valleys, 2:165
Roa Bastos, Augusto, 3:64, **4:52–53**
Roads. *See* Highways and roads

Robusta coffee beans, 2:4
Roca, Julio Argentino, **4:53**
Rocafuerte, Vicente, 2:95
Roca-Runciman Pact (1933), 1:55
Rockefeller Foundation, 4:81
Rock salt, 4:63
Rodents, 1:33
Rodeo, 4:114
Rodó, José Enrique, 3:63
Rodón, Pancho, 1:68
Rodríguez, Andrés, 3:198, 4:117
Rodríguez, Hortalez and Company, 1:27
Rodríguez, Martin, 1:52
Rodríguez, Melitono, 3:220
Rodríguez de Toro, María Teresa, 1:111
Rodríguez Zeledón, José, 2:30
Rogers, Woodes, 3:224
Rojas Pául, Pablo, 2:195
Roldós Aguilera, Jaime, 2:96
Roman Catholic Church. *See* Catholic Church
Romanticism, 3:61–62
Romero, Oscar Arnulfo, 1:176, 2:57, 106, **4:54–55** *(illus.),* 4:68
Rondon, Cândido Mariano da Silva, 2:115
Roosevelt, Franklin D., 2:172, 3:190, 4:71, 98 *(illus.),* 145, 161
Roosevelt, Theodore, 2:70, 3:143, 4:55, 160
Roosevelt Corollary, 2:70, 74, 3:143, **4:55,** 4:160–61
Rosa de Lima, Santa, 4:55, 56 *(illus.)*
Rosas, Juan Manuel de, 1:15, 2:186, 187, **4:55–56,** 4:79, 135
national unity and, 1:52
Oribe and, 3:176
Urquiza's campaign vs., 4:166
Rousseau, Jean Jacques, 2:109
Royal patronage, clergy and, 1:172, 173, 174
Royal Protomedicato, 3:100
Rubber industry, 1:25, 118–19, 3:78, **4:56–57**
Rubens, Peter Paul, 1:65
Ruíz de Alarcón, Juan, 4:135
Rumba, 3:151
Rurales, 2:39, 3:120, **4:57**
Rural labor unions, 3:43–44
Rural society, 1:214
Russians in Pacific Northwest, 3:179, 180
Ryswick, Treaty of (1697), 2:197

S

Saavedra, Juan de, 4:175
Saavedra Lamas, Carlos, **4:58**
Saba, 2:83
Sábato, Ernesto, **4:59**
Sabinada Revolt, 4:59–60, 63
Sabino Álvares da Rocha Vieira, Francisco, 4:59
Sacasa, Juan Bautista, 3:165, 4:71, 97
Sacasa, Roberto, 4:217
Sacred music, 3:148–49
Sacrifice, human, 2:69, 4:42
Sacsahuaman, 1:41, 2:55, 3:4
Sá e Benavides, Salvador Correia de, **4:58**
Sáenz Peña Law (1912), 4:119
Sahagún, Bernardino de, 2:78, 3:80, 4:127
Sainete criollo (Creole farce), 4:136
Saint, first American, 4:55, 56 *(illus.)*
St. Augustine, **4:60–61** *(illus.)*
St. Barthélemy (St. Barts Gustavia), 2:147
St. Christopher (St. Kitts), 1:138, 139, 2:147

St. Croix, 4:194
St. Domingue, 2:72, 146, 147, 197–98. *See also* Haiti
St. Eustatius, 2:83
St. John, 4:194
St. Kitts. *See* St. Christopher (St. Kitts)
St. Lucia, 1:139
St. Martin, 2:83
Saints' days, 2:125
St. Thomas, 4:194
St. Vincent, 1:139
Sajama, Mt., 1:113
Salamanca, Daniel, 1:185, 186
Salesians, 4:45–46
Sales taxes, 4:123
Salgado, Sebastião, 3:220 *(illus.),* 221, **4:61–62**
Salinas de Gortari, Carlos, 1:100, 2:111, 3:122, 169, **4:62**
Salitreros, 3:168
Salsa (dance), 3:151
Salsa (sauce), 2:134
Salt trade, **4:63**
Salvador, 4:59, **4:63–64,** 4:99
Samaniego, Manuel de, 1:65
Samba, 3:150, 151
San Agustín, **4:64**
San Antonio de Valero mission, 1:15
San Blas Islands, **3:39–40**
San Carlos Borromeo mission, 4:84
San Carlos Canal, 3:173
Sánchez, Miguel, 2:176
Sánchez Cerro, Luis, 2:205–6
San Diego de Alcalá mission, 1:152
Sandinistas, 1:7 *(illus.),* 182, **4:69–70** *(illus.)*
Barrios de Chamorro and, 1:101
communism and, 2:16
contras vs., 2:22–23
control of Nicaragua, 3:166
Mosquito Indians and, 3:147–48
opposition to Somozas, 3:165–66
Ortega Saavedra, leader of, 3:177–78
Sandino as inspiration for, 4:71–72
Soviet relations with, 4:104
Sandino, Augusto César, 3:165, 4:69, **4:71–72,** 4:97
San Francisco Xavier, University of, 1:116
Sanguinetti, Julio María, **4:72,** 4:173
San Ildefonso, Treaty of (1777), 1:123, 3:74, 4:49, **4:64–65**
Sanín, Noemi, 2:9
San Jacinto, battle of (1836), **4:65,** 4:132
San José, Costa Rica, 2:28–29, **4:65–66**
San Juan, Puerto Rico, 4:22, 23, **4:66**
San Luis Obispo de Tolosa, mission of, 3:134 *(illus.)*
San Martín, José Francisco de, 1:165, 196, **4:66–68** *(illus.)*
Bolívar and, 1:112
independence struggle and, 3:212, 4:203
O'Higgins and, 3:173
San Román, Miguel de, 1:169
San Salvador, 2:14, **4:68**
San Sebastiá de Urabá, 2:8
Sansei, 1:75
Santa Anna, Antonio López de, **4:72–73**
at Alamo, battle of the, 1:14, 15
at Buena Vista, battle of, 1:142
Mexican-American War and, 3:114, 115
presidency of, 3:119, 120
at San Jacinto, battle of, 4:65
Texas Revolution and, 4:131–32

Index

Index

Index